THE MYSTIC OF TUNJA

FRONTISPIECE Anonymous portrait of Francisca Josefa de la Concepción, painted after her death. Inscribed on the painting itself is a 450-word story of her life written by her nephew, José Manuel de Castillo y Santamaría, in 1813. Photo reproduced by Jorge González with permission from the Collection of the Biblioteca Luis Angel Arango of the Banco de la República, Bogotá.

· THE · MYSTIC · OF · TUNJA

·

THE WRITINGS
OF MADRE CASTILLO
1671–1742

Kathryn Joy McKnight

UNIVERSITY OF MASSACHUSETTS PRESS
Amherst

Copyright © 1997 by
Kathryn Joy McKnight
All rights reserved
Printed in the United States of America
LC 96-40881
ISBN 1-55849-074-4
Designed by Milenda Nan Ok Lee
Set in Adobe Garamond and Bernhard Modern Engraved
Printed and bound by Braun-Brumfield, Inc.
Library of Congress Cataloging-in-Publication Data

McKnight, Kathryn Joy, 1961–
The mystic of Tunja : the writings of Madre Castillo, 1671–1742 /
Kathryn Joy McKnight.
        p.   cm.
Includes bibliographical references and index.
ISBN 1-55849-074-4 (alk. paper)
    1. Castillo, Francisca Josefa de la Concepción de, 1671–1742—
Criticism and interpretation.   2. Nuns' writings, Colombian—
History and criticism.   I. Title.
PQ8179.C369Z77   1997
861—dc21   96-40881
                                                                             CIP

British Library Cataloguing in Publication data are available.

For my parents

Martha and Ted McKnight

CONTENTS

List of Illustrations		xi
Acknowledgments		xiii
List of Abbreviations		xv
Editorial Method		xvii
I	Interested Readings	I
	Madre Castillo's Texts in Spanish American Literary Criticism	7
	Contemporary Readings	12
PART I	A THEORETICAL FRAMEWORK	
II	The Genre of the *Vida Espiritual*	17
	Subject, Agent, Heretic	20
	Autobiography and Subjecthood	24
	The *Vida Espiritual*	29
	Male Writing: Unambiguous Assurance	54
PART II	CONTEXTS	
III	Religious Women's Writing in Spain and Spanish America	63
IV	Female Monasticism: A Life Unbecoming?	73
	The Middle Ages: A History of Female Autonomy	74
	The Counter-Reformation: Palimpsests	77
	El Convento Real de Santa Clara desta ciudad de Tunja	79

v   Madre Castillo in the Institution:
An Ascension to Power 101

A Vow of Poverty 107
Convent Offices 111
A Family Base 112
Confessors 115
Elections and Administration 117

PART III   THE TEXTS

VI   *Su vida:* Spiritual Trials and Worldly Troubles . . . 129

The Old Child, The Conscience-Ridden Child . . . 132
A Spiritual Struggle in the Convent 135
The Cares of the World 141

VII   *Su vida:* Holy Archetypes 149

The Hermit 151
The Mystic 152
Mary Magdalene: Sinful Flesh, Redemptive Flesh . . 156
The Martyr 161
A Question of Agency 163

VIII   The *Afectos espirituales:*
Mysticism of the Incarnate Word 167

The Word Made Flesh 172
Knowledge in the Ritual of the Psalms 177
Opening the Doors of the Hermeneutic Halls 182
Madre Castillo and Sixteenth-Century Mysticism . . 189
The Gendering of Figures of Authority 193
Voice and Subjectivity:
Between the *Vida* and the *Cuaderno* 195

IX   The *Cuaderno de Enciso:*
A Theology of Humiliation and
Its Mystic Rewards 199

A Treatise for the Soul 201
Personal Prose and a Rhetoric of Theological Oratory . . 205

Humiliation as the Path to Resurrection   210
A Mystic Sepulcher   215
Conclusions   219

Notes   223
Works Cited   253
Index   269

ILLUSTRATIONS

Photographs

Frontispiece   Portrait of Francisca Josefa de la Concepción, painted
after her death   ii

1. Main plaza and surrounding hills, Tunja, Department of Boyacá   80
2. Front wall and entry to the Convento Real de Santa Clara   81
3. Upper choir and grille, Convento Real de Santa Clara   86
4. Original wall decorations in the upper choir, Convento Real de
    Santa Clara   87
5. Cell attributed to the use of Francisca Josefa de la Concepción,
    Convento Real de Santa Clara   108
6. Monstrance commissioned by the nuns of the Convento Real de
    Santa Clara in 1737   110
7. Presbytery of the Church of Santa Clara, Tunja   123
8. First page of *Su vida* by Madre Castillo   130
9. View of the church nave and altar from the upper choir,
    Convento Real de Santa Clara   153
10. Mystic poem (*Afecto* 46) from Madre Castillo's manuscript   175
11. Front pages of Madre Castillo's *Breviarium Romanum*   178

Tables

1. Number of choir nuns in the Convento Real de Santa Clara,
    Tunja, 1610–1730   90
2. Offices held by Francisca Josefa de la Concepción,
    Convento Real de Santa Clara, Tunja   106
3. Archival records of Madre Francisca Josefa de la Concepción's
    activities as abbess of the Convento Real de Santa Clara, Tunja   120
4. Abbesses of the Convento Real de Santa Clara, Tunja,
    1689–1742   124

ACKNOWLEDGMENTS

I owe the beginnings of this book to my friend Gladys White, who pointed me in the direction of Madre Castillo as I searched for early autobiographical narratives by women in a class offered by Anthony Zahareas at Stanford. I will always be grateful to Mary Pratt, whose inspiring scholarship and teaching, and whose enthusiastic support of my work at Stanford and beyond, have motivated and challenged me in shaping this project. My work has also benefited from generous and insightful readings by Stacey Schlau, Kate Myers, Hans Gumbrecht, Adrienne Martin, Dennis Perri, Jaime Concha, Emilie Bergmann, Jill Kuhnheim, Theda Herz, and Margarita Pillado-Miller, and from stimulating intellectual exchanges with the wonderful group of fellows at the Stanford Humanities Center in 1991–92. Nina Scott stands in a class of her own for the friendship and energy she has shown in reading my work and encouraging and mentoring me during this process.

I wish to express special appreciation to the many Colombians who responded with openness to the project and offered invaluable help. Archbishop Augusto Trujillo and Antonio Galvis aided me in establishing contact with the nuns of the present-day convent of Santa Clara. The nuns responded with great trust and generosity in allowing me to handle and read invaluable manuscripts from their archives. I thank the directors and staff of the Archivo General de la Nación, the Biblioteca Nacional, the Biblioteca Luis Angel Arango, and the Museo de Santa Clara in Bogotá, and the Archivo Regional de Boyacá in Tunja, for patient and expert help as I consulted manuscripts and rare books in their collections and for making photocopies of several important documents. Agustín Lombana and Consuelo Valdivieso of the Comisión para Intercambio Educativo opened doors for my research. Montserrat Ordóñez, Paulina Encinales de Sanjinés, Carolina Alzate, Ann Farnsworth-Alvear, and Betty Osorio provided companionship during my research stays, challenged me intellectually, and have continued to help through the blessings of e-mail. The project would not have survived without you. A very special thanks is due Jorge González, who agreed at the drop of a hat to grace the book with his photographic talents.

My research received essential grant support from the Institute of International Education (Fulbright) and the Colombian government, in addition to the Stanford Humanities Center dissertation prize given by Theodore H. and Frances K. Geballe and, from Grinnell College, two summer research grants and a full year of support in the form of a Harris Faculty Fellowship, given by Jack and Lucile Harris. Particular thanks are due Charlie Duke at Grinnell for his help in funding my trip to Colombia in 1994 to consult the colonial archives of the Tunja convent. I would also like to thank the University of Tulsa for its support during my year of writing, in the form of interlibrary loan services and a computer account. The expertise of Elizabeth Johns and Pam Wilkinson has been invaluable in the preparation of this book.

My profound thanks go to all of my family, friends, and colleagues who have supported and encouraged me over the past seven years. Most of all, I am deeply grateful to my partner, Lynn Mostoller, who has met every new turn of this project with unending patience, understanding, and encouragement.

ABBREVIATIONS

AE   *Afectos espirituales,* by Francisca Josefa de la Concepción de Castillo. Vol. 2 of the *Obras completas,* ed. Darío Achury Valenzuela. Bogotá: Banco de la República, 1968.

AGI   Archivo General de Indias

AHNB Archivo Histórico Nacional de Bogotá

AHT   Archivo Histórico de Tunja

ARB   Archivo Regional de Boyacá, Tunja

CC   *Cuaderno de cuentas del Real Convento de Santa Clara,* 1718, 1732, by Francisca Josefa de la Concepción de Castillo. MS 74. Manuscritos. Biblioteca Luis Angel Arango, Bogotá.

CE   *Cuaderno de Enciso,* 1694?–1728? by Francisca Josefa de la Concepción de Castillo. MS 73. Manuscritos. Biblioteca Luis Angel Arango, Bogotá.

EA   *Elecciones de abadesas, tomas de hábito y otros documentos importantes, desde el año de 1584 hasta el de 1687 . . . Legajo 1º.* Archivo Colonial. Convento Real de Santa Clara, Tunja.

LC   *Libro de capítulo y de las rentas quel monasterio de S[eñor]a Sancta Clara la R[ea]l tiene y posesiones y scripturas.* [Title on spine: *Rentas y profesiones y hábitos años 1584 a 1884.*] Archivo Colonial. Convento Real de Santa Clara, Tunja.

LV   *Libro de visita del convento de Monjas de Sancta Clara la Real de la Ciudad de Tunja y donde se asientan los bienes y cosas de sacristía e yglesia del que comiença desde [. . .] de junio de mil y seis y veinte años.* [Title on spine: *Visitas canónicas años 1620 a 1822.*] Archivo Colonial. Convento Real de Santa Clara, Tunja.

NEB   The New English Bible. Translated under the supervision of the Joint Committee on the New Translation of the Bible. New York: Cambridge University Press, 1970.

SV   *Su vida* by Francisca Josefa de la Concepción de Castillo. Vol. 1 of the *Obras completas,* ed. Darío Achury Valenzuela. Bogotá: Banco de la República, 1968. I also refer to *Su vida* in the text simply as Madre Castillo's *Vida,* as the possessive *su* often causes redundancy in the prose.

EDITORIAL METHOD

Tunja ['tün-hä]   Founded in 1539 by Gonzalo Suárez Rendón, Tunja today is a city of about 150,000 inhabitants. It lies in the mountains, nine thousand feet above sea level, a little over a hundred miles northeast of Bogotá.

Madre Castillo   The writer who is the object of my study was born Francisca Josefa de Castillo y Guevara Niño y Rojas. She took the name Francisca Josefa de la Concepción on entering religious life. When she was elected abbess, she would have been called Madre Francisca, or Madre Francisca Josefa de la Concepción. In literary histories, she is best known as Madre Castillo. I will refer to her as Francisca when speaking of her as a child, Sor Francisca and Madre Francisca when emphasizing her roles as nun and abbess, and otherwise as Madre Castillo when I speak of her as writer.

God   Although my own conception of God is a different one, I refer to God as "he" throughout this text, in consonance with the beliefs of Madre Castillo.

Translations   All translations are mine unless otherwise noted.

Transcriptions   In transcribing archival documents and Madre Castillo's manuscripts, I have respected the original expression, with the following exceptions: I have added punctuation to aid the reader. I have imposed modern usage of accent marks, tildes, and capitalization, maintaining capitalized personal titles according to usage of the time. I have completed abbreviated words, indicating additions in italics (P^e = P*adre*). Where variations in spelling produce common pronunciation of the words, I have left words unchanged (quadra). Where variations appear to be spelling errors, I have added letters in italics and have placed parentheses around extra letters (arebantaron = ar*r*eb(a)*e*ntaron). For the sake of consistency, I have modernized the spelling of proper names from archival sources in my own text and in English translations, but in Spanish language quotations, I have respected the originals with their variations in orthography. When transcribing quotes from the *Obras completas de la Madre Francisca Josefa de la Concepción de Castillo* (1968), I have set off speech with guillemets (« ») to regularize the text.

THE MYSTIC OF TUNJA

I

INTERESTED READINGS

My Father, today on the day of the Nativity of Our Lady, I begin in her name to do what your paternity requires of me and to think about and consider before the Lord all the years of my life in the bitterness of my soul, as I find all of them ill-spent, and thus I am terrified of making an account of them.

—MADRE CASTILLO, *Su vida* (Her life) [1]

A T THE BEGINNING of the eighteenth century, in the Convento Real de Santa Clara in Tunja, Nuevo Reino de Granada, Francisca Josefa de la Concepción took up her pen and opened her life story with these words. They are words of pain that convey a sense of heavy burden, an unwelcome task. Compelled by obedience, Sor Francisca reflects on a life unworthy of written affirmation. In the pages that follow, this ill-spent life takes shape through a language of self-censure, one that presents a prideful and scandalous sinner and a soul constantly tormented by the Devil. Sor Francisca is weak and unequal to the tasks she is called upon to exercise in the convent. She claims an evil and arrogant nature and wonders how anyone could tolerate such a poor, miserable, worthless woman if it were not for her confessor, in whose hands God has placed her. But there are times when her outlook changes. At these moments, the act of writing that has so troubled her takes on a different aspect, and she sees herself as an instrument in the hands of God. Then, the direct recounting of her actions gives witness to the emergence of a spiritual being whose soul traverses the way of perfection and enters into union with God.

It is in this way that two very different protagonists share the autobiographical "I" of Madre Castillo's *Vida:* a weak and sinful woman, tangled inextricably in the cares of the world, and a contemplative nun blessed by God's favor. The twentieth-century critic perceives a third figure, that of the self-reflective narrator who holds sufficient distance from each protagonist to judge the first and celebrate the second. From this contemporary view, it would seem that a reading of the autobiographical text as "confession" or "truth" could only become bogged down in a mire of confusion while subjectivities of mystic and worldly being, saint and sinner, pained and jubilant narrator execute a complicated dance. Yet the history of criticism that has addressed Madre Castillo's writings draws heavily on transparent readings of her text as truth and understands only isolated elements as rhetorical constructs.

Transparent readings are only possible if one ignores the resonance that the conflicted self-portraits of Madre Castillo's texts find in the long and rich tradition of Hispanic nuns' writings, which have become the subject of a growing field of feminist criticism. The only colonial woman writer apart from Sor Juana Inés de la Cruz to be consistently anthologized, Madre Castillo has remained relatively ignored outside of Colombia, and when she has been studied, she has generally been seen, like Saint Teresa of Avila (Spain, 1515–82) and Sor Juana Inés de la Cruz (Mexico, 1648–95), as a singular woman.[2] But as early as 1903, Manuel Serrano y Sanz showed in his *Apuntes para una biblioteca de escritoras españolas* (Notes for a library of Spanish women writers) that literally hundreds of women wrote between the fifteenth and eighteenth centuries in Spain, Portugal, and Spanish America, a great majority of them nuns. Only in the 1980s and 1990s has the proliferation of historical and literary studies on Hispanic nuns left the readings of Saint Teresa and Sor Juana as isolated figures clearly wanting. The same tensions that surround authority and authorship in Madre Castillo's texts appear repeatedly in the large body of autobiographical works that make up a significant portion of Hispanic nuns' writing before the mid-eighteenth century. Reading Madre Castillo within this context permits the identification of formulas and stories shared by many women's writings. The texts construct their subjects within similar social contexts and reveal a community of mutual readership among nun writers that spans centuries and oceans. I seek to return Madre Castillo's texts to this feminine milieu by examining her writing strategies as a case study, showing her to be both representative and unique.

Madre Castillo's reading and self-representational writing are deeply affected by her historical context, in which an unequal exercise of power derives from her society's conceptions of gender, civil status, race, class, and lineage. For her, the primary determining contexts are those of the Spanish Counter-Reformation and the Spanish colonial realities that privilege European blood, bureaucratic connections, religious profession, and spiritual excellence while they limit female authorship and agency. Madre Castillo is affirmed as the white daughter of a Spanish bureaucrat and a *criolla* lady of honorable family, but she is suspected and marginalized as a woman exercising authority and authorship within a male-dominated Church. The conflict between affirmation and suspicion also finds expression in her *Vida* when she counterposes the historical memory of strong women in the Church to the discourses and practices of her own times. On one hand, Counter-Reformation ideology and practice trouble her task as writer by throwing suspicion on any suggestion of female authority; the Inquisitorial state saw all women, being daughters of Eve, as easily deceived and drawn into heretical beliefs. On the other hand, an empowering hagiographical tradition bolstered by the authority available to women in colonial convents allowed some to write themselves into a holy legacy with their own pens.

In the present study, I set aside the transparent and isolating readings of Madre Castillo's critical tradition and examine the ways in which her texts "construct" her as a *subject* in the persons of protagonist, narrator, and writer, recognizing both the feminine literary tradition in which she wrote and her lived experience in colonial Spanish America. I identify a range of conflicting discursive practices that come together in Madre Castillo's texts, examining their historical trajectories and the use Madre Castillo makes of them. I study the relationship between the discursive practices in her texts and the exercise of power in her society. I propose a reading of the meanings that emerge in her texts from the contradictions that she pulls together. In these emergent meanings, I see Madre Castillo's *agency.*

Two terms need to be defined in this treatment: my choice of the word *subject* and my interest in *agency.* In speaking of Madre Castillo as a *subject,* I seek to avoid the concept of the liberal autonomous individual inherited from the Enlightenment. Instead, I use the term in its opposed meanings of being subjected to something and being the active subject who determines one's self and actions. Madre Castillo the writer is both a product of the ideologies and practices of her time and an agent who interprets herself within and against them. I am using a post-structuralist concept of the self as articulated by Felicity Nussbaum in her book *The Autobiographical Subject* (1989), in which she addresses the implications of such a subject to the study of autobiography. She proposes that the subject or "self" of autobiography is "an effect of ideology and a mediation of its conflicts" (xxi). Such mediation by the subject implies not only a politics of writing but also a politics of reading.[3] With one critical lens, then, I examine the self-portrait or autobiographical subject of Madre Castillo's texts as a space in which contradictory ideologies as well as subject positions and social practices are brought into confrontation. With another, I study a writer who must first read or perceive these contradictory ideologies and subject positions in order to incorporate them into her texts. I will presume, and at times explicitly study, Madre Castillo's role as a reader of the discourses and practices available to her, and specifically of a long feminine tradition of self-representation. This reading allows me to delineate the building blocks of her texts, to deconstruct or make evident those forces in conflict within them, and to see her self-portrait as her response to the conflicts she experienced while trying to live simultaneously as woman, nun, abbess, and writer. I also examine the ways in which the different genres Madre Castillo engaged allowed or exacted of her different degrees of freedom, submission, and conflict in her self-expression.

In concert with much of feminist criticism, I seek to break up master narratives such as literary canons and histories that have silenced women's actions and to find in these actions an *agency* of resistance and creativity. At the same time, my feminism faces the dilemma posed by post-structuralist conceptions of the subject that "kill" authors and make agency highly suspect (see Barthes 1975a; Foucault 1977). Felicity Nussbaum, Paul Smith, and Sidonie Smith, among others, have responded to this dilemma by proposing alternative ways to understand agency that work with, rather than against, a post-structuralist subject. Nussbaum proposes that, "[t]he interstices between . . . [hegemonic ideologies] may encourage imagined alternatives to the status quo as ideologies vie for dominance in the determinative order of intelligibility within textual practices. It is here, in the contradictions within the materials of culture, that we may locate the oppositional subject necessary for a materialist feminist politics" (1989, 36). Nussbaum's definition allows me to perceive an agency of authorship and authority in the slippage between the discourses and practices that are juxtaposed within Madre Castillo's texts. Such slippage might be likened to the grinding against one another of the mismatched blocks of various social ideologies and practices, such as that between the hagiography of Saint Teresa that honors her as Doctor of Mystic Theology and the simultaneous Counter-Reformation suspicion of all feminine authority. From these slippages emerges the possibility of seeing in Madre Castillo's subject an agent of subtle resistance.[4]

This book opens with my proposal of a theoretical framework for the study of both the genre of spiritual autobiography—the *Vida espiritual*—and its autobiographical subject (Part i). I begin with the importance of agency and the subject to the genre of spiritual autobiography (chapter 2), explaining my working definitions of these concepts. These definitions draw from a Foucauldian approach to the subject with its treatment of power and knowledge, and from recent feminist scholarship on nuns' writings and women's autobiography. The theoretical questions are firmly embedded in a discussion of the Counter-Reformation in Spain and Spanish America, and of both Spanish and Spanish American nun writers, with particular emphasis on Saint Teresa. As many scholars have noted, it was the publication of Saint Teresa's *Libro de la vida (The Life of the Holy Mother Teresa of Jesus)* that inspired generations of nuns to develop their spiritual and mystic lives and authorized many of them in their task of self-writing. With a theoretical base set, I propose a detailed framework to define the *vida espiritual* as a subgenre of autobiographical writing.

In Part 2, I give greater specificity to the various contexts within which Madre Castillo wrote and which provided the discourses and practices that she reworked in her texts. Chapter 3 presents the literary tradition of Hispanic religious women of the fifteenth to the eighteenth centuries as well as the recent scholarship that has illuminated their works. Chapter 4 studies female monasticism, beginning with a brief review of the autonomy of cloistered women in European history from the Middle Ages to the Counter-Reformation and the changes in the representation of feminine religious authority and intellectual pursuits over this period. These changes progressively limited the autonomy of female institutions and representation, though the memory of past strengths survived to empower the writings of Counter-Reformation nuns. I set my discussion of the Convento Real de Santa Clara within this history, focusing on the concerns most important to but often half-hidden between the lines of Madre Castillo's *Vida*. Some information on the history of the Tunja convent can be found in Colombian historiography, but I have gathered much of the detail from research in the regional archives of the department of Boyacá and the archives of the present-day Monasterio de Santa Clara in Tunja.

After discussing the institutional setting for Madre Castillo's life, I piece together a fragmentary biographical narrative that shows a Sor Francisca different from the portrait in Madre Castillo's *Vida* (chapter 5). Again, my work is based on archival material, though I use a careful reading of the *Vida* at some points in the biography. Here, the nun-writer's life is set within a monastic ambiance of feminine power and autonomy related to the more secular aspects of monastic existence, those of the day-to-day political and economic operations necessary to support the community. Madre Castillo's construction of a spiritual subjectivity that is weak and worthless, and the violent tensions she expresses between devotion and sin, must be read against her rise to power in the convent and in contrast to the language of such documents as those she signed during three terms as abbess.

Part 3 undertakes the textual analysis of Madre Castillo's writings, *Su vida,* the *Afectos espirituales* (Spiritual affects), and the *Cuaderno de Enciso* (The Enciso notebook). My analysis of Madre Castillo's *Vida* pursues two avenues. In chapter 6, I examine the spiritual autobiography against the biography developed through archival materials, using the secular representation of Madre Castillo to explain silences and tensions in her own text, and to propose a reading of contestatory agency in the *Vida*. In chapter 7, I read the *Vida* within its more patent tradition of "autohagiography," a term that has been used by critics to refer to the relationship between the self-writing of religious women and the saints' lives and devotional biographies that they read. Both avenues of study bring out the contradictions between self-affirmation and negation, secular and sacred realms, imitation and creativity, and between all of these and the expectations held of consecrated virgins, contradictions that create great discord in Madre Castillo's self-portrait.

The texts that constitute Madre Castillo's other major work, the *Afectos espirituales,* show a very different writer and protagonist from those of the *Vida* and form the material for my study in chapter 8. The *Afectos* consist of approximately two hundred short spiritual pieces whose composition spans more than thirty-five years. My reading discerns a writer's voice that, while still occasionally fearful, gathers extraordinary autonomy and authority to develop a method of interpreting the Scriptures. In so doing, this authorial voice creates feminine space within male terrain by veiling itself in the particularly, though not exclusively, feminine monastic practices of the Divine Office and the pursuit of mystic spirituality.

Finally, in chapter 9, I turn to a work, or more precisely a reworking, that has received almost no critical attention: a segment of the manuscript that has been called the *Cuaderno de Enciso,* named for the brother-in-law who gave the blank notebook or *cuaderno* to Madre Castillo. I am interested in those pages that Madre Castillo has dedicated to a revision and reframing of several of the texts from the *Afectos espirituales.* The changes she has made in rewriting the pieces and the content of the new texts that she provides in this notebook suggest a greater sense of public voice and authorial intent than has been generally attributed to her. These pages provide a well-developed spiritual treatise or guidebook for the soul. While there is no concrete evidence that Madre Castillo wrote with the intention of teaching others, the *Cuaderno de Enciso* invites such a reading.

Throughout this study, one of my primary concerns is the relationship between power and knowledge, or power and discourse. Before entering fully into the study of Madre Castillo's own life and works, there are two other moments of the power/discourse relationship that need to be addressed. One is the history of literary criticism that has developed around Madre Castillo's work; the other is the contemporary feminist approaches with which I align my reading. Post-structuralist critical and theoretical developments have brought to the fore both the need for critical self-awareness and the ultimate impossibility for the critic to step outside of her- or himself in order to gain such awareness. If I assume that Madre Castillo's act of writing implied an engagement with ideology on her part, then I must recognize that my own act of reading, as well as the readings I contest and complement, are also shaped by ideologies and practices of which I am aware of only a few. No reading of the past is objective or can be extricated from a simultaneous reading of the present. What I see and what I silence, whether intentionally or not, is shaped by my critical project. The knowledge produced by this project is related to my own positioning within a social exercise of power. The readings that I and others carry out remain stable (seem "true") only insofar as their ideological projects stay hidden. In order to admit the same provisional character of my own criticism as that which I attribute to critics who have preceded me, and to open up my work to dialogue, I choose to identify at least those "interests" that I believe give form and direction to my text.

As a feminist reader-critic, I seek to uncover spaces and forces of resistance in the history of literary production, places where writers who were in some way marginalized contested those master narratives that represented them in ways most convenient to the dominant social forces. I am interested in a criticism that itself interrupts a master narrative of literary history that has silenced the interruptions of marginalized voices. Thus, my imperative in this Foucauldian archaeology of knowledge leads me to deconstruct the critical tools of the readings that I contest and to present my own reading as process rather than conclusion, through discussion of my own critical tools. "Interested Readings" begins to address these problems.

Madre Castillo's Texts in
Spanish American Literary Criticism

Since the first publication of Madre Castillo's *Vida* in 1817 and of the *Afectos espirituales* in 1843, criticism has followed four main lines. The first is seen in the limitation of early references to a treatment of *vida y obrismo*, the consideration of the author's biography and a listing of works as constituting literary criticism. The second and third tendencies appear in the first studies that really engage with the content of Madre Castillo's writings. These initial studies establish the primary focal points of subsequent criticism: a philological approach to literary style that separates the text from the historical experience of the author, and a reverent glorification of the *national mystic,* supported by the study of literary style. Most recently, a fourth interest has arisen, that of psychoanalytic readings of Madre Castillo's life by means of her works.

After Madre Castillo's death in 1742, her manuscripts remained in the possession of the Convento Real de Santa Clara in Tunja until, in 1813, they were given to a nephew, Antonio María de Castillo y Alarcón, for publication.[5] In 1817, after obtaining official church approval, Castillo y Alarcón had the *Vida* published by T. H. Palmer in Philadelphia. The *Afectos* were printed for the first time in 1843 in partial form as the *Sentimientos espirituales de la venerable Madre Francisca Josefa de la Concepción de Castillo . . . ;* a more complete edition appeared on the bicentenary of her death in 1942. The latest imprint of her complete works is Darío Achury Valenzuela's 1968 critical edition, which he contends is a more faithful treatment of the manuscripts than past editions (cci). Achury Valenzuela offers a book-length introduction with this edition, providing valuable historical and critical research.

The first existent commentaries on Madre Castillo's texts are those of Francisco Domínguez Urregolabeitia and an unnamed ecclesiastical censor, both instrumental in the initial publication (Castillo 1968, 1: 217–26). Following traditional ecclesiastical and literary formula, Domínguez writes a "Brief information on the homeland and parents."[6] The piece combines historical and genealogical notes and a synthesis of the *Vida*. The ecclesiastical censor judges the writings to be authentic and filled with virtue and wisdom by means of the illumination of the Holy Spirit.

Early references to Madre Castillo's work in literary histories are limited to observations of her biblical erudition, the virtuous nature of her prose, the anomaly of a woman writer in her times, the autodidactic character of her knowledge, and her emulation of Saint Teresa (Marroquín 1929, 73).[7] The first serious treatment of the *Vida* came about in 1890, when Rafael María Carrasquilla marked his installation into the Colombian Academia de la Lengua with a speech on the works of the Colombian nun writer. Both Carrasquilla and his respondent, José Manuel Marroquín, mold their readings of Madre Castillo into their greater cultural-political projects, which ring with millenarian optimism. Carrasquilla decries the agitation of Colombia's past sixty years, a time of great liberal-conservative conflict that followed independence. He laments the breaking of literary relations with Spain and the (destructive) policies of recent (liberal) governments, which included attacks on the Church and, of special import to the question of Madre Castillo, the decloistering of religious orders in 1863 (1935, 136–37).

For Carrasquilla, Spain provides a cultural yardstick against which Madre Castillo's great value to Colombia can be measured as the author of the only colonial writings "worthy of unblemished comparison with the works of the Golden Age of Peninsular letters" (1935, 106). Carrasquilla's words express a nostalgia for the early Spanish Golden Age, whose values he wishes to reinstate. He holds up this era against the Gongorism that runs rampant in the period when Madre Castillo wrote, a time that the "progressives of Spain taught us to call servitude, darkness and retrogression" (106). "Our mystic author" (119), he declares, is a true mystic, participating in the loftiest literature created by the human mind (109). Carrasquilla sees, in his own induction into the Academia as a man of the cloth, a sign of a return to the true values that will extricate Colombia from its woes, and he marks this hope by molding a great spiritual icon from Colombia's past.

While early commentators note Madre Castillo's gender as a surprising fact, and while they most often compare her to the great female mystic Saint Teresa, they ignore the impact of gender on her writing. Rather, they treat her as an oddity, as a male in female clothing. Before revealing the identity of his subject, and employing the masculine article *el,* Carrasquilla speaks of Madre Castillo as "the most eminent of our colonial authors" (1935, 105),[8] as before him, others used the epithet of "virile woman" to refer to Saint Teresa (Weber 1990, 18). When he does reveal her identity, Carrasquilla's prior assertion leads him into the awkward statement that, "the [male] author of whom I am speaking was a woman" (106).[9] Carrasquilla uttered these words at the close of a century that had already witnessed such gender confusion with the eruption of women writers in significant numbers onto the literary scene of the Spanish-speaking world. Gender would not provide Carrasquilla or his contemporaries with a key to the interpretation of Colombia's mystic.

In responding to Carrasquilla's speech, Marroquín reiterates the latter's glorification of Spain and his preference for the early Golden Age over the Baroque. His reading resolves the apparent anachronism of Madre Castillo's clear prose, written during the time of the *Barroco de Indias,* by crediting her with great intellectual autonomy, that vision of the subject inherited from the Enlightenment. For Marroquín, Madre Castillo transcended the style of her times by designing a curriculum of divine inspiration and private scriptural studies for herself. Despite his assertion of her purposeful study, he does not believe that she saw herself as an author. His assumption—one that continues to frame contemporary criticism—while not entirely inaccurate, impedes a fruitful reading of the impact that an awareness of her possible contemporary audiences has on her words.

Interest in the colonial author increased notably in Colombia in 1942 with the bicentenary of her death. Darío Achury Valenzuela's contributions to this scholarship, appearing first in the late 1950s and rooted in the critical concerns of his day, remain unparalleled for their extension and thoroughness.[10] His edition of the *Obras completas* includes the *Vida,* the *Afectos,* the texts in the *Cuaderno de Enciso* that can be identified as original pieces, and the known epistolary exchanges between Madre Castillo and her confessors, as well as a letter written to her niece, abbess of the convent, from Diego de Moya, Madre Castillo's confessor, regarding the publication of his funeral sermon.

In his introduction, Achury Valenzuela characterizes his own work as preliminary. Rather than undertaking a thorough critical examination of Madre Castillo's writings, Achury Valenzuela proposes to bring together the resources necessary to that end (1968, cxlvii). He sets historical and biographical contexts, treating seventeenth-century Tunja, Madre Castillo's genealogy, and her life (as taken from her own writings), and he provides valuable biographical information on her confessors. Other sections offer information on the history of her manuscripts and discuss the biblical sources available to Madre Castillo, concluding that she probably used both the Latin Vulgate and the Roman Breviary. Achury Valenzuela carries out some textual analysis, beginning by setting a Colombian literary context for her writings, though treating only male authors. In separate chapters, he undertakes comparisons between the writings and ideas of Madre Castillo, Erasmus, Saint Teresa, and Juana Inés de la Cruz, focusing on questions of style and content. The picture that emerges bolsters the earlier efforts of Carrasquilla and Marroquín to hold up Madre Castillo as Colombia's mystic treasure, but even more it emphasizes her great value as a writer. While Achury Valenzuela treats both text and context, there are important questions that he does not or cannot ask, including questions concerning power, knowledge, and gender. He draws a number of connections between historical context and text, but in understanding Madre Castillo's works, he privileges a dehistoricized view of literary influences and of her interpersonal relationships.

The treatment of Madre Castillo as mystic launched by Carrasquilla, while less developed in Achury Valenzuela, becomes an underlying assumption of most twentieth-century criticism.[11] Today, her figure still wields cultural force as a mystic in the Colombian department of Boyacá. I have met representatives from a small group of contemplatives in Tunja for whom Madre Castillo provides deep inspiration, and a number of Boyacense women who, similarly inspired, write poetry on mystic themes.[12] A focus on mysticism also structures the 1968 work of Spanish scholar and nun María Teresa Morales Borrero: *La Madre Castillo: Su espiritualidad y su estilo.*

Morales Borrero positions her criticism within the tradition of veneration and religious discourse, studying Madre Castillo's life and environment, the spiritual doctrine contained in her works, and the value of the literary style of "la gran mística colombiana" (1968, 8). Again, the nun writer is treated as an autonomous creator of meaning and style whose lived reality can be read in a truthful text. To a greater extent than Achury Valenzuela, Morales Borrero brings into her discussion the importance of Madre Castillo as reader and identifies a feminine hagiographic tradition on which the colonial writer draws (49 ff.). She also names a series of ascetic and mystic influences: Augustinian, Franciscan, Ignatian, Carmelite, and Carthusian readings. She assumes that the ways in which these "influences" affect the writer are evident, and both they and the process of writing appear divorced from historical context and material practices. Using the language of early modern spirituality and its understanding of the three stages of spiritual life—purgative, illuminative, and unitive—Morales Borrero develops what she calls a psychological angle of her study. This estimation of Madre Castillo according to sixteenth-century canonical models reinforces the ideological purpose that operates in Carrasquilla's and Marroquín's studies: the texts are valued as Colombian contributions to world literature in their transcendence of the local and the specific and in their perceived attainment of literature's "highest expression" in mysticism. The texts' potential to interrupt or transform these models is silenced.

The history of criticism on Madre Castillo can be scanned in the bibliography of the reference book on Colombian women writers, *¿Y LAS MUJERES?* *Ensayos sobre literatura colombiana* (Jaramillo, Robledo, and Rodríguez-Arenas 1991, 342–49). Of the more than one hundred pieces cited, the majority appear to follow the critical trends that have been discussed.[13] It is Madre Castillo's women critics, belonging themselves to female communities of different kinds, who promote the importance of a feminine literary tradition as context for understanding her works.[14] Morales Borrero compiles a rich bibliography of European and Spanish American nun writers but omits an examination of Madre Castillo's interaction with that tradition, using the litany instead as a background to mark her uniqueness. A different strategy is seen in a piece of convent scholarship that was written in the 1940s and 1950s but only published in 1993; this is *Flor de santidad: La Madre Castillo* (Flower of holiness: Mother Castillo). The biographical manuscript was written by the late María Antonia del Niño Dios, who lived in the present-day Monasterio de Santa Clara la Real in Tunja.

In her introduction, Sor María Antonia relates that after completing several articles for "El ensayo," organ of the Academia de Escoto in 1944, she was asked by the Coristado Franciscano (the Franciscan Choir or Choir School) of the Convento de la Porciúncula in Bogotá to write Madre Castillo's full biography. The value of the resulting work lies in its extensive research into the colonial archives of the convent. In many cases Sor María Antonia transcribes lengthy portions of acts of profession, dowry commitments, convent elections, and canonical visits. The biography provides rich insight into the cultural life of the Tunja convent, returning Madre Castillo's writings to their rightful ambiance of convent governance, economic activities, and festive celebrations. Sor María Antonia shows nuns in their own community as capable administrators, servants of God, mutual collaborators, and musicians.

Perhaps most tellingly, Sor María Antonia shows the convent in a positive light, depicting supportive relationships between Madre Castillo and her sister nuns. Her monastic portrait contrasts starkly with the vicious and tumultuous atmosphere that Achury Valenzuela's reading emphasizes. The apparent contradictions between Sor María Antonia's assertion of harmony and Madre Castillo's visions of conflict are reconciled by the biographer in her belief that God leads each individual toward holiness through a process of torment, and that Madre Castillo's monastic sisters were blameless in their participation in her purification (1993, 48). The fact that an oral tradition surrounding Madre Castillo's life continues in the twentieth-century convent is evident at several points in Sor María Antonia's narrative—for example, in a reference to the collective memory of an unsuccessful attempt in the early 1900s to recuperate an icon that the young Francisca Josefa had brought with her to the convent (35). In citing this monastic biography, I propose that issues surrounding the interpretation of Madre Castillo's life and writings continue to play a vital role in the contemporary convent's status and interests.

CONTEMPORARY READINGS

In the 1980s an interest in psychoanalytic approaches to the texts began to appear in the study of Madre Castillo. Rocío Vélez de Piedrahita's chapter in the *Manual de literatura colombiana* (1988) combines psychoanalytic elements with those of an orthodox discussion of mystic process in an examination of Madre Castillo's personality. In a different use of psychoanalytic exploration, Angela Inés Robledo finds gender specificity and a feminine revindication of the weak within the mystic texts and mystic experience. Her work on Madre Castillo suggests that the discursive plurality employed by the author within a misogynic society is a psychological mechanism of self-affirmation. In her 1989 article, Robledo uses Freud's proposal that radical religious life leads to obsessive personality bordering on the paranoid—*Moses and Monotheism*—to bolster a reading of Madre Castillo's personality as alienated or split. In her 1991 study, she sees Madre Castillo's use of religious paraphernalia as a beneficial mask for psychic disturbances. Here, the culminating experience of mysticism is a liberating point of reunion with the split self.

Recent feminist scholarship offers new approaches to the study of Hispanic nuns. Much of this work owes a great debt to the pioneering archival investigations of Josefina Muriel that date from the 1940s and to those of Asunción Lavrín beginning in the 1960s, which led to the latter's valuable analyses of the social, political, and economic importance of feminine convents to colonial life. Literary and historical studies soon began to focus in earnest on gender and its impact on the writings of nuns. Since the publication of Electa Arenal and Stacey Schlau's *Untold Sisters* in 1989, the field has blossomed.

Untold Sisters is a rich resource that identifies many important Hispanic nun writers and employs a feminist methodology concerned with the relationship of power and knowledge—a study of the ways in which "power impinged on being/body/tongue" (1989b, 411). With an interdisciplinary methodology, Arenal and Schlau build the historical, ideological, and discursive contexts in which these women of the fifteenth through the eighteenth centuries wrote. They relate routines of daily life, Church economics and politics, confessor/ nun relationships, and female community to the types of texts written, the language used, and the strategies that created expressive freedom and subtle subversion. In short, Arenal and Schlau identify a wide range of elements present in the situations in which nuns wrote and to which they responded, treating above all issues of gender, race, and social hierarchy. They also show effectively both the great diversity of nuns' writings and the firm community of mutual readership that surrounded this writing, providing mutual support in frequently controversial circumstances. Such community is best illustrated in chapters on the Teresian legacy, whose trans-Atlantic passage is evident in the authors' discussion of Peruvian texts. Arenal and Schlau end their work with a recognition of its inconclusive nature; their book unearths much while it calls on others to continue their work. The studies of writing women that both preceded and followed their work provide the material for chapter 3, below.

An increasing number of single-author studies are gradually piecing together a clearer picture of that tension identified by Schlau and Arenal between the nun writers' uses of obligatory formulas and their success at breaking through them to create self-expressive and often subtly subversive texts. This critical work that brings out the sameness and differences between the texts makes both comprehensible and exciting works that have hitherto proved daunting because of their religiously charged language and their frequently confusing repetition. My own project joins in the wider critical intent to interrupt a homogenizing literary and cultural history that has silenced women's voices and has left us with an impression of meek and quiet foremothers for Hispanic women. I seek to bring out the struggles and triumphs of the self-representation of a single colonial writer, to open up her legacy to new readings of her strong-voiced quest.

PART

I

A THEORETICAL FRAMEWORK

• II •

THE GENRE OF THE
VIDA ESPIRITUAL

The autobiographical genre was little cultivated in Spain during centuries gone by, as we cannot include in its consideration the numerous spiritual lives that our female religious wrote, wherein external facts are left forgotten or mentioned only in passing; a rare exception among them is that of Saint Teresa, in whose privileged spirit were united both contemplation and action.

—MANUEL SERRANO Y SANZ, *Memorias y autobiografías*[1]

As has been so often repeated, it [Saint Teresa's *Libro de la vida*] is not an autobiography in the strict sense, neither is it the detached story of life, as it lacks any temporal and spatial elements. With rare exceptions, it contains no dates or names. The principal characters lack individualization, being referred to generically, and with depersonalizing appellations. In its formal appearance, it is, more than anything else, a didactic treatise based on the practice of mental prayer.

—DÁMASO CHICHARRO, introduction to the
Libro de la vida by Saint Teresa of Avila[2]

HUNDREDS of nuns and religious women wrote between the fifteenth and eighteenth centuries in Spain and Spanish America. A clearer picture of their writing—their concerns, their strategies, their struggle for self-expression while jostled by competing forces—is now emerging from a forgotten past, as more scholars focus their efforts on locating and understanding these texts. More than a dozen book-length works and a number of articles on Spanish and Spanish American nuns have appeared since 1989 alone, when Arenal and Schlau's *Untold Sisters* was published. These works study the writings of the nuns and religious women who wrote poetry and plays, letters, convent histories, biographies of saints and of their sister nuns, instructions for novices, sermons, scriptural commentaries, theological critiques, and, above all, autobiographical narratives of the mystically infused spiritual paths that so many of them followed.

Why, then, does Serrano y Sanz exclude feminine self-writing from autobiography, and why does Chicharro refuse to define Saint Teresa's *Libro de la vida* within the genre? These two critics expose the inadequate critical attention given to the *vida espiritual,* a genre widely practiced in Spain and Spanish America between the sixteenth and eighteenth centuries.[3] Since Chicharro wrote his introduction in 1979, theoretical interest in autobiographical writing has thrived, spurred on by post-structuralist conceptions of human subjectivity and agency. But when the field made strides in defining autobiographical writings, as scholars left behind a vision of autobiography as truth, and as the historical author disappeared behind the discourses that shaped *his* text, critical theory continued to omit the particularities of women's self-representation in its consideration. As Sidonie Smith protested (1987, 7), "where in the maze of proliferating definitions and theories, in the articulation of teleologies and epistemologies, in the tension between poetics and historiography, in the placement and displacement of the 'self' is there any consideration of woman's *bios,* woman's *autë,* woman's *graphia,* or woman's hermeneutics?" Recently, a number of feminist theorists and critics, both within and outside of Hispanic scholarship, have contributed to a new understanding of feminine self-writing.[4] Their work has brought out a number of characteristics widely shared in the autobiographical processes and texts of Spanish and Spanish American religious women writers, but it has left aside the task of defining the *vida espiritual* as a genre. I believe that such a definition is needed in order to better understand the many *vidas* that religious women have written, and to understand how these *vidas* differ from other types of spiritual autobiographical writing, especially in their engagement with subjectivity and authority.

The *vida espiritual* emerged out of the relationships between confessors and the women whose spiritual lives they directed. The genre bears a strong resemblance to the exercise in which people who were accused of heresy wrote out their general confessions for the Inquisitorial judges (Gómez-Moriana 1984, 84). In fact, at least one autobiographical text, that of Magdalena de la Cruz, was probably burned by the Inquisition before Saint Teresa of Avila even began to write her *Libro de la vida.* This abbess of the Order of Poor Clares was a renowned visionary from whom the Inquisition extracted a confession of lifelong falsification in 1546 (Imirizaldu 1977, 53–62). The relationship between Church, confessor, and autobiographer fostered the first modern narrative explorations of the human psyche and facilitated the development of a discourse on mystic practice. The writing was regarded as a spiritual rather than literary exercise and was not destined for direct publication. While Saint Teresa's *Libro* was published barely three years after her death, only a very few *vidas* since met similar luck. Many *vida* manuscripts, however, provided ample material for the numerous biographies that did reach the presses, written about these women by male clergy. Significant numbers of the priestly biographies incorporated extensive quotes from their subjects' own texts; thus, in fact, many women's writings did reach a wide readership.

A study of the *vida espiritual* demands a specific engagement with the emergence in early modern Europe of the phenomenon of human sub-jecthood: the human capacity and responsibility for naming and determining oneself. The *vida espiritual* confronted this subjecthood when the writer's purpose became primarily that of naming and explaining her or his inner experiences or psyche, both of which were of compelling interest to the Church and state, and were beyond their reach except through the subject's own words. Jeremy Tambling speaks of the role played by the confessional act in constituting the subject. "Those addressed by a confessional discourse are 'interpellated' (hailed, singled out by name), and are subjected, i.e. made to define themselves in a discourse given to them, and in which they must name and misname themselves; and secondly, made to think of themselves as autonomous subjects, responsible for their acts" (1990, 2).[5] That this genre appeared within the ideology and institutions of the Counter-Reformation marks its production with specific political objectives and philosophical con-ceptions. Through their *vidas*, women writers sought ways both to conform to Counter-Reformation ideology and to express often subversive creativity within the contradictions of their times. The tension created when the Church recognized human subjectivity but needed to compel that subjectivity to obedience led to the flourishing of the autobiographical genre.

Female subjectivity was perceived by the Church as more threatening than its male counterpart. Therefore, female self-writing, especially the spiritual autobiography of those women who claimed to bypass male ecclesiastical authority to engage in direct mystic communion with God, became even more necessary and was clearly marked with the feminine subjectivity of the writer and the gender-infused web of power relations within which she wrote. Each *vida espiritual* presented the Church with a potential threat that was also a potential tool with which to burnish its own glory. The writing might identify a dangerous heretic or provide the Church with a new saint or venerable role model with which to combat the Protestant menace. Each *vida* writer played the same high-stakes gamble that Saint Teresa had played before her, but each could also draw on the growing tradition of orthodox models, so frequently infused with creativity, self-affirmation, and subversion. A few men also wrote *vidas espirituales,* and a comparison of their self-representation and literary development of authority to that of the women illuminates the strategies with which women responded to the constraints placed upon them.

Let me undertake this definition of the *vida espiritual,* then, by drawing on the work of feminist scholars and on the broader field of critical theory on autobiography and the subject.[6] In the following pages, I examine the impact that Counter-Reformation ideology had on self-representation. I lay out the theoretical understanding of human subjectivity that allows me to read the *vidas* within this Counter-Reformation context. From this context and this theoretical approach, I develop a framework for studying the *vida espiritual.* Textual examples from Madre Castillo's contemporaries and foremothers help to build a framework, as I mesh theory with close readings. Saint Teresa's *Libro de la vida* plays a fundamental role, as her book opened the floodgates for a myriad of religious women to express themselves in writing. Finally, I close the chapter with a comparison between the impact of male and female gender on self-writing in the autobiographical *vida.*

SUBJECT, AGENT, HERETIC

Saint Teresa's *Libro* has been noted as unique among autobiographical writings of its time for its exploration of interiority—that is, of the human psyche (Pope 1974, 71; Gumbrecht, forthcoming). In fact, this focus definitively marks the tradition of feminine *vidas* that would follow, bringing with it a strong ambivalence concerning the writer's authority to give meaning to her inner experiences. This anxious ambivalence embodies the conflict between the relatively new recognition of subjecthood and human agency and the effort by forces of religious orthodoxy to reassert control over these aspects of human behavior.

The emergence of subjecthood coincided with the crumbling of medieval Christian certainty. Hans Ulrich Gumbrecht addresses the changes in the following manner: "[O]ne basic feature of medieval culture was the belief that, through the event of divine Creation, each object of experience (including the human body) had its specific cosmological place and its inherent meaning(s), furthermore, it was expected that such meanings would remain hidden from human understanding unless they were disclosed through divine Revelation" (forthcoming). In other words, meaning was preestablished and remained independent of human agency. This certainty began to break down when early modern Europeans found God to be no longer immanent in the world. They began to believe that appearances, rather than providing clues to true meaning, were actually deceptions and that truth resided within the individual. Marking the late fifteenth and early sixteenth centuries as symptomatic of this shift, Gumbrecht explains that, "the emergence of subjecthood brought forth two new and divergent modalities in the experience of signification. On the one side, it produced the growing conviction that irrefutable evidence could only be encountered in a self-reflexive movement towards the *inner spheres of the human psyche* . . . on the other side, the rise of subjecthood was accompanied by the feeling that the outside world, as constituted in human acts of signification, was '*but a theatre.*' "

One manifestation of the inward turn that arose within Catholicism was the search for the experience of God not in objects and images but in contemplation. The sixteenth-century mystics embarked on an impossible journey to bridge the chasm that had opened between human existence and the Divine (Certeau 1982). They spoke of life in "this world" as an exile and articulated the impossibility of reversing history in order to reunite the soul with God. The desired union would absorb the self into the divine Other and eliminate the uncertainty brought into the world by the separation from God inherent in the concept of human subjecthood. For the mystics, only death could end the spiritual exile, and yet the mystic journey could provide glimpses of the return home in fleeting moments of ecstasy.

The loss of certainty that ensued from locating the source of knowledge within the subject, within individual experience, coincided with a series of major events that destabilized a previously steadfast worldview. The monopoly that the Church had held in influencing thought and exercising power, through its theocentric explanation of the world, met progressive challenges in a secularizing society. The breakdown of a static feudal order, the consolidation and strengthening of secular knowledge and institutions—particularly the growing force of mercantilism, which built on scientific developments in cartography and astronomy—and the encounter with a "New World" all contributed to a growing struggle for authority over knowledge between sacred and secular realms. The belief that human beings could affect history through their own agency was displacing the concept of predetermination. Writing on the history of autobiography, Georges Gusdorf places the concern for autobiographical expression at this moment of historical upheaval. His description of "most of [the rest of] human history" (1980, 29), while exhibiting a broad generalization, holds value for explaining the significance of the subsequent philosophical shift. Outside of this age of human agency, "[c]ommunity life unfolds like a great drama, with its climactic moments originally fixed by the gods being repeated from age to age. Each man thus appears as the possessor of a rôle, already performed by the ancestors and to be performed again by descendants. The number of rôles is limited, and this is expressed by a limited number of names. New born children receive the names of the deceased whose rôles, in a sense, they perform again, and so the community maintains a continuous self-identity in spite of the constant renewal of individuals who constitute it" (30).[7] Gusdorf marks the sixteenth century as the point of emergence of a historical consciousness fundamental to a modern concern with the autobiographical act, and identifies the Copernican revolution as the major precipitating factor in the philosophical shift (31). In the sixteenth century the Church was reeling with the threats posed to its authority by these philosophical changes. Catholic Spain, in particular, suffered challenges from both without and within; not only did the emergence of the subject heighten the perceived danger of heresy but the very territorial integrity of the empire was being destroyed by its losses to the growing Protestant world.

The Spanish Counter-Reformation Church, allied with the state—embodied in Felipe II (1556–98)—responded to this challenge to its hegemony with a powerful ideological counterattack. It intensified the work of the Inquisitional tribunals; it carried out a full-fledged campaign of Catholic education through catechism and confession, and it infused a secularizing society with the spiritualized values of the *desengaño*. The ideology of the *desengaño* or disillusionment sought to convince the populace through Baroque art and spectacle that truth was to be found not in appearances but beneath them, not in this life but in the hereafter. According to George Mariscal, "the idea of the individual made its appearance in writing [in the seventeenth century] surrounded by a host of rival and inhospitable discourses. Almost everything in the culture worked against its further elaboration: relations of production and the institutions of aristocratic life blocked its formulation, and where it did appear, it was labeled as heretical, subversive, or mad" (1991, 94).

Those who experimented with subjectivity and human agency and resisted ideological control were punished. The Christian humanists of Alcalá, the Erasmians, and the *alumbrados,* having flourished under the sympathetic gaze of Carlos V and Cardinal Cisneros, fell to persecution in the 1530s.[8] By the end of the century, mystic discourse, itself a paradox in which subjecthood is both asserted and transcended, would find a deradicalized institutional form in the spiritual exercises of Saint Ignatius of Loyola. In the 1600s, the literary optimism of Cervantes and Lope de Vega would give way to the pessimistic dogmatism of Quevedo and Calderón.[9] The human subject as agent and creator of his or her own reality (*Don Quijote*) ceded in the picaresque to the condemnation of social climbing by a predestined protagonist (*El buscón*), and life became but a dream (*La vida es sueño*). The genre of the *vida espiritual* seems to follow a parallel development toward closure in which many later examples leave behind Saint Teresa's freer experimentation and seek instead to write themselves into the rigid formulas of orthodoxy, maintaining some ground for subversive, though often subtle, challenges to the totalizing force of Counter-Reformation ideology.

The shift of the locus of knowing into the interiority created by subjecthood confronted the Church with a loosening of its control over the production of knowledge. By holding out the clear threat of labeling as heresy or demonic deception that knowledge that was substantiated through experience, dominant discourses marked subjecthood as a space of inherent danger. "The heretic will be known, not by the faith, but by the *freedom of conscience* that he or she preaches *and because by making him or herself singular,* he or she sows *cizaña* instead of wheat" (Covarrubias [1611] 1979, s.v. *singu-*

lar).[10] If appearances no longer displayed the clear meanings of their substance and the human body now masked each subject from another with an opaque shield, Church and state sought ways to ensure submission. These powers would institutionalize a control based on suspicion, and exercise it through the gathering of knowledge of that subject's interiority by drawing out its inner truth. For religious women, such control included permanent vows of enclosure and the use of the confessional box and *vidas* to gain their acquiescence. Paradoxically, these last modes of control also provided a venue for religious women to develop and explore a complex and conflictive concept of the self, albeit a self very differently codified from those more familiar to us in the twentieth century—that is, the autonomous Cartesian individual and the nineteenth-century romantic subject.

The work of Anthony J. Cascardi on subjectivity in the Counter-Reformation proposes a very helpful explanation for understanding the paradox of the *vida espiritual*. Rather than discuss the lasting effect of the Counter-Reformation ideology in terms of a direct institutional control over the hearts and minds of faithful Spanish subjects, Cascardi sees the state as "producing subjects who would not wish to escape its control" (1992, 244). The difference lies in an external control that represses human subjecthood and agency versus a mode of persuasion that compels subjects to develop self-control. While both methods may result in a similar acquiescence, the latter explanation takes into consideration both the "crisis of subject formation" apparent in early modern Spain as well as the existence within written expressions of human agency—in *vidas espirituales,* for example—of a certain degree of "resistance to control" (237, 239).

The "crisis of subject formation" to which Cascardi refers is that of the emergence of a modern subject from a medieval world.

> On one level, the crisis of subjectivity in early modern Spain can be described as the product of a conflict between two distinct value systems, each with its own psychology and each with modes of recognition proper to it. On the one hand a hierarchical society, in which actions were evaluated according to a series of naturalistic principles, and in which social functions and roles were sedimented into near-static patterns, was confronted with modes of thinking, feeling, acting, and evaluating based on the premises of a psychologizing "individualism," in which the social order was dominated by what Weber described as "rationalized" structures, and in which the dominant cultural ethos was that of autoregulation or *self*-control. . . . [S]ocial conditions in early modern Spain generated a new class of individuals who could be imagined and had to be addressed as subject-selves; . . . Counter-Reformation ideology counted on the existence of subjects who would be responsive to relatively "modern" methods of psychological persuasion and

control. . . . And yet the cumulative effect of this psychology was to close off the resources of subjectivity, in effect reinforcing the ideological essentialism of the Counter-Reformation by creating in subjects a willingness for subjection to the principles of a "higher" rule. . . . it is thus only through an internalization of authority that the "modern" subject could represent itself as autonomous and free. (1992, 237–38)

While the neo-Scholastic philosophy of the Counter-Reformation ideology resisted the concepts of subjecthood and human agency, Church and state faced a crisis that had already brought to the fore the possibility of conceiving such agency. The cat was out of the bag, leading the Counter-Reformation to seek, rather, to elicit a self-control built on the neo-Scholastic concept of the faculties of the human soul: memory, understanding, and will. Thus the lesson of much Baroque art, in the service of the Counter-Reformation, was to pose the necessity of the successful integration of these three faculties. These same three faculties appear throughout the explanations of mystic experiences in autobiographical writings, as the nuns seek to subordinate the will in order to become absorbed by the Divine.

Autobiography and Subjecthood

The subject of the Counter-Reformation is a subject in conflict. It is a subject aware of the possibility of human agency but constantly faced with the persuasive arms of a Church and state that demand of it a submissive self-control. It is a subject interested in its own inner life and compelled to verbalize this interiority for the institutions that would control it. It is a subject that glimpses the possibilities of individualism without realizing them fully, due to the constant threat of Inquisitional sanction. When this subject, these men, and especially these women, represent themselves in writing, what is their relationship to the text that they write? What characterizes the texts that result from their acts of self-writing? How does gender affect their self-writing? How can one frame the study of their *vidas espirituales?* What help can the critical theory of autobiography lend to defining this historically and culturally specific genre?

Contemporary theorists recognize the difficulties in defining autobiography as a discrete genre. James Olney talks about the "dissolving of generic boundaries" that leads him to see much of literature, and even literary criticism, as autobiographical (1980, 3–5). "Autobiography," Olney says, "is not so much a mode of literature as literature is a mode of autobiography." Paul Jay and Paul de Man talk about autobiographical discourse as "self-reflexive" texts or "self-presentation" in the text, while Georges May proposes the idea of a fan or spectrum of autobiographical possibilities (Jay 1984; de Man 1984; May 1979, quoted in Bell and Yalom 1990, 3). Rather than identify definitive characteristics of a genre, much of contemporary theory seeks to describe the relationship between the author, the autobiographical subject of the text, and that hard-to-define "out there" in which the text appears: historical moment, linguistic and ideological context, social relations of power. These are the relationships on which I also seek to throw more light on a corpus of autobiographical writing, which I will argue, can be thought of as a discrete subgenre.

Sidonie Smith reviews the history of autobiographical theory from its early belief in the transparent truth of autobiography to a vision of the autobiographical subject as an autonomous individual who creates the self of the text. Georges Gusdorf's seminal essay "Conditions and Limits of Autobiography" is representative of this second theoretical stage. For Gusdorf, autobiography is a work of personal justification of a life lived at a point distant from the moment of writing (1980, 39). The autobiographer confers meaning on that past self and past events through his or her present understanding (42). "Every autobiography is a work of art and at the same time a work of enlightenment; it does not show us the individual seen from outside in his visible actions but the person in his inner privacy, not as he was, not as he is, but as he believes and wishes himself to be and to have been" (45). This explanation of the relation of writer and textual self would seem ideal for describing the strategy exercised by a nun living during the Counter-Reformation who faces the demand to verbalize her inner life in the suspicion-laden milieu of an Inquisitional society. Yet the forefront of critical theory has now left behind this transparent vision of human agency. "[A] third generation of critics, the structuralists and poststructuralists, has challenged the notion of referentiality and undermined comfortable assumptions about an informing 'I.' These theorists suggest that the *autos,* shattered by the influence of the unconscious and structured by linguistic configurations beyond any single mind, may be nothing more, and certainly nothing less, than a convention of time and space where symbolic systems, existing as infinite yet always structured possibility, speak themselves in the utterance of a *parole*" (S. Smith 1987, 5). The text becomes a *dialogical space,* a space in which discourses interact to create meanings that are seemingly independent of the author.[11] Any sense of human agency disappears.

If human agency slips away, at least two possibilities for women are lost. First is the idea that a woman writer might exercise some degree of control in creating new knowledge about herself to contest those representations of her womanhood that she inherits. This loss leads to the second and broader one, in which women have no agency to effect any social change in female roles within the gender-based web of power relations. All of this implies not that change is impossible but rather that human beings cannot intentionally, autonomously, create the new knowledge necessary for the instigation of such change. Change becomes entirely contingent, dependent on an impersonal and chance coalescence of events.

The scenario proves deeply disturbing to those of us who, as feminists, wish to unearth female agency in a tradition of women's writing, who desire social change, and who perceive ourselves as capable of human agency. Such concerns have motivated a number of critical theorists to seek an explanation of human agency consonant with a post-structuralist understanding of subjectivity. These scholars include Felicity Nussbaum (1989), whose work on the autobiographical subject informed my discussions of subject and agent in chapter 1, and Paul Smith, whose *Discerning the Subject* (1988) informs my current discussion of the self-representation of autobiography.

Paul Smith's explanation of the location of human agency coincides with that of Nussbaum's in his rejection of both the entirely free-willed autonomous human self of the Enlightenment and the post-structuralist self that is entirely subjected by discourse, that is, whose consciousness is no more than a space and a time in which numerous contemporary discourses coincide. For Smith,

> Resistance does take place, but it takes place only within a social context which has already construed subject-positions for the human agent. The place of that resistance has, then, to be glimpsed somewhere in the interstices of the subject-positions which are offered in any social formation. More precisely, resistance must be regarded as the by-product of contradictions in and among subject-positions. The subject/individual can be discerned but not by the supposition of some quasi-mystical will-to-resistance. What I propose, then, is that resistance is best understood as a specific twist in the dialectic between individuation and ideological interpellation. (1988, 25)

When the subject positions that a person is called to occupy contradict each other in some way, that person must engage in negotiation among those positions. A contemporary example can be found among feminists of color, whose identities or subject positions as women, called into solidarity with what are frequently white-dominated women's movements, often conflict with their solidarity with communities of color, whose needs white women's movements often ignore. Writers like Cherríe Moraga, Gloria Anzaldúa, and bell hooks must negotiate between the subject positions they are called to occupy on the basis of race and those to which they are called by their gender. It is in this process of negotiation between subject positions that " 'choice' or conscious calculation" is possible according to Smith (40). But who or what is it that chooses?

In a text that moves back and forth among Hegel, Adorno, Lacan, Barthes, and Kristeva, Smith reviews the approaches to the subject worked out by various strands of Marxism, post-Marxism, post-structuralism, psychoanalysis, and feminism. He identifies in each weaknesses relevant to his need to postulate human agency, and takes from each ideas with which to build an explanation of such agency. Smith draws particularly on Lacan's definition of the unconscious as a space of interface between the subject or self and the Other that is all language—all culture, all discourses. As the human self seeks to define itself, or "suture" itself off from that all-encompassing Other in order to conceive of itself as a whole and separate unity, it engages in this space of the unconscious interface. It is through this engagement that language and culture mold or subject the human self, but it is also in this process of subjection that resistance or negotiation among subject positions is possible in "a new and paradoxical subjectivity where the symbolic's hold is not total" (P. Smith 1988, 109).[12]

Moving toward his conclusion, Smith takes up Hegel's idea of negativity and uses it to refer to that process of mediation between the self and the Other that enables the subject to separate itself out (1988, 122).

> I have suggested that the "subject" is continually called upon to take on the marks of multifarious subject-positions but that it is nonetheless incapable of colligating these positions without contradiction (even by means of accepting the interpellation into the position of whole and coherent "self," the ideology of unity). This contradiction, or whole set of contradictions, and the negativity which underpins them and produces them are what releases the "subject" from perfect self-identity, homogeneity, and fixity. And yet the "subject" cannot subsist in radical heterogeneity. . . . Whereas Laclau and Mouffe talk about overdetermination as a principle of colligation among subject-positions, I would say rather more simply that what binds subject-positions together is precisely their difference. That is, the contradictions between them are a product of the negativity which enjoins the "subject" to construct, recognize, and exploit difference. It is negativity which also and simultaneously produces the human agent. (150)

It is this conception of human agency that allows me to posit the resistance offered by the nun writers of the fifteenth through the eighteenth centuries to the Counter-Reformation forces that saturated social discourses and practices with demands for submission. This understanding of human agency can explain how a nun such as Madre Castillo could write herself into an orthodox representation and at the same time open a space for her creativity and power within officially male territory.

Let me now develop the concept of agency in its relationship to the act of autobiographical writing. Sidonie Smith criticizes autobiographical theory for accepting the conflation of "male" and "human" forged in Western discourse, and for missing the significance of gender to autobiography by reading women's self-representation through male models (1987, 9). If the scientific and philosophical changes of the late Middle Ages ushered in a new *man* built from the idea of individuality or subjecthood, women's relationship to the new developments was not the same (S. Smith 1987, 22–26). The contradictions that nun writers in this new era experienced in trying to mold themselves into the various subject positions they occupied resulted from changes that had been wrought in both the ideology and cultural practices of gender between the Middle Ages and their own Counter-Reformation age. As the most prominent of these contradictions relate to authority and authorship, I turn to a discussion of the impact of gender on genre, of femaleness on the authority of autobiography.

While early modern *man's* subjecthood derived from intellectual freedom, woman was still conceived of as the daughter of Eve, and as such her intellect was chained. Christianity recognized an equality of the souls, but in this world women were cleaved to sinful flesh. Aquinas's conception of woman as misbegotten or imperfect man denied her "the possibility of achieving full intellectual, ethical, and moral stature" (S. Smith 1987, 27–28). Her imperfection was proven in her deception by the serpent. Her first participation in public discourse—with the serpent—resulted in her expulsion and that of Adam from paradise (29). It was for this "original" association with the weakness of the flesh that the authority of women was suspect, and that Saint Paul denied women public word or public authority in the Church. During the late Middle Ages, and even more strongly during the Counter-Reformation, the force of these ideological conceptions of womanhood had been brought to defend the ever-more-oppressive limitations placed on women's authority. Thus, when women dared to claim the authority of self-description in writing a *vida espiritual,* they had to respond to the fictions of femaleness that had been created about them (19). A woman's "very choice to interpret her life and to reveal her experience in public signals her transgression of cultural expectations. Her very voice in its enunciations remains haunted and haunting; for the language she appropriates has been the instrument of her repression" (43). Women autobiographers did draw on the stories written by and about those powerful women who preceded them—women such as Hildegard of Bingen, Saint Catherine of Siena, and Saint Teresa of Avila—but, as Smith points out, "those foremothers are powerful precisely because their life stories have been blessed and sanctified by male authorities, so that the autobiographer's authority derives, not from the foremother, but from the fathers who permit her her powerful script" (55).

These *scripts* that nun writers read, lived, and rewrote in their construction of autobiographical selves are those discourses that define the *subject positions* located by Lacan in the Other of language. They are the subject positions to which the Counter-Reformation called these women, but they are also the powerful models offered to them in stories of their foremothers. They are the scripts of the ideal nun, the holy virginal vessel of God's work, and the deceived and deceiving daughter of Eve, but they are also the scripts of the powerful abbess and scholar of the Middle Ages, the politically influential mystic, and the religious reformer. The act of writing the self into holy models has led such feminist scholars as Kate Greenspan, Kathleen A. Myers, Electa Arenal, and Stacey Schlau to refer to *vida* writing as autohagiography.[13] But while each nun wrote herself into these models, she did not write herself entirely out of any agency to represent herself with individuality. Avrom Fleishman notes the apparent paradox in this literary act, this agency, in which "such 'idealized' and 'ideologized' literary figures become 'the instruments with which autobiographers make themselves unique, by creative reenactment, revision, and reversal' " (1983, 49). I hear an uncanny echo of the medieval in this post-structuralist vision of subjectivity, as the emphasis is placed on fitting oneself into scripts. The resonance makes this vein of critical theory particularly compelling in reading the *vidas,* which hover in tension between the medieval demand to fit the self into a role in a static society and the early modern possibility of conceiving oneself as historical agent and source of knowledge. The crucial difference, of course, lies in the post-structuralist identification of a multiplicity of conflicting subject positions, while the medieval world believed in stability and the Counter-Reformation ideology struggled to restore it.

THE *VIDA ESPIRITUAL*

Women's writing has often been marginalized from canons by codes of aesthetics that have devalued the personal. Domna Stanton ponders that the term *autobiographical* itself takes on different values when applied to men and women, positive for Augustine, Rousseau, and Goethe—connoting self-conscious crafting and aestheticism—negative for women's texts, indicating a "spontaneous" and "natural" style (1984, 6). The comments of Chicharro and Serrano y Sanz dismiss women's *vida* narratives because they lack that "essential" autobiographical structure that situates them in the material world of historical time and personages. Yet, as the work of Alison Weber, Kathleen A. Myers, Jennifer Lee Eich, and others shows, the autobiographical narratives of Spanish and Spanish American religious women were not spontaneous and natural but carefully built out of complex narrative structures. The writers elaborated strategies of self-representation and applied sophisticated rhetorical skills in order to establish the authority of their narratives and of themselves as religious women and writers. If they did not always structure their stories through historical time, they did build them on the cyclical time of the religious calendar. If specific names were often replaced by generic titles—

"the abbess," "my confessor"—a host of heavenly characters populated the narratives with their very specific names: "my divine spouse Christ," "my father Saint Francis." These women writers worked out their narratives within the highly structured tradition of hagiography, and they ordered their representation of self according to categories of religious experience.[14]

That the act of confession structured the *vida* narrative is not surprising given its context of production and the recognition by nun writers of Saint Augustine's *Confessions* as a model or founding act of spiritual autobiography. James D. Fernández articulates a communicative scheme for religious autobiography that works with the idea of confessional narrative and provides an organizing base from which to examine both the context of production and the structure of religious women's *vidas* (1992). Fernández identifies four elements of the communicative scheme of religious autobiography: "(1) an old, unredeemed self; (2) a new, converted and writing self; (3) a community of human readers; and (4) God, an ultimate, ideal reader. The space of autobiography is constituted by the distance—the play—between these four pieces" (29). Ideally, in the conversion narrative, the writing self, in accordance with the will of God, reflects on her or his former self for the benefit of the human readership (30). In reality, as Fernández reads in Saint Teresa's *Libro,* the human readership that is embodied in confessors and Inquisition "brandishes the material power" of God—acts, that is, as God's institutional representation on earth—and in doing so questions whether the new self who narrates is different from the old self who sinned.

The nuns' readers exercised this suspicion in frighteningly material terms in that particularly Spanish context of the *vidas* production and popularity. A life of inner spirituality had flourished in the early sixteenth century, promoted as much by the Church itself in Cardinal Cisneros and the theologians at Alcalá de Henares as by the more marginal *alumbrados* (illuminists), whose members included many women, even in leadership positions. Despite the popularity of reformist ideas implicit in their actions, these groups found themselves on three dangerously unsteady legs: first, the affirmation of subjecthood through interiority threatened the Church as it withdrew authority and placed it within the individual; second, the members of these groups included a high number of *conversos* (Christians of Jewish ancestry); and third, to the ecclesiastical hierarchy the tenets of these groups sounded suspiciously like Lutheranism. The *alumbrados* "erred" in their increasing anticlericalism and in their attacks on religious formalities. The "sins" of the scholars of Alcalá included their association with the *alumbrados,* the promotion of Erasmian ideas, and the translation of the Holy Scriptures into vernacular, thereby making the sacred texts available to the untrained and uninitiated. By the 1530s these groups were suffering intense persecution from the Inquisition (Bataillón 1950, 2: chap. 9). Herself an advocate of mental prayer and a woman who claimed to receive divine visions, Teresa of Avila would need to distance herself from these suspect spiritual practices; she would need to prove that neither the sinful self of her narrative, nor her present writing self, could be associated with the heresies that infused her spiritual context. At the same time, the very heresies that threatened the power monopoly of the Church, and thus put *vida* writing at the service of religious women, also made the production of mystic saints and holy women, who had large popular followings, a very useful tool in the hands of the Church. The act of writing a *vida* represented, to Saint Teresa and later writers, both a required response to the suspicious vigilance that constrained them and a space in which to weave such a defense that might allow them to become popular and sanctified heroines.

Fernández's communicational scheme for the confessional autobiography, his emphasis on the suspicion that surrounded its writing, and the historical context of the Counter-Reformation provide a starting point for elaborating the many complicated narrative strategies of the *vida* genre. Fernández's assertion that the writing self examines the past sinful self in accordance with God's will for the benefit of the human readership plays itself out in the *vidas* of Hispanic religious women, as does their awareness that their human readers will doubt their separation as writers from the prior sinfulness of their protagonists. In fact, the repentant female writers of the *vidas* often cannot bring themselves to the prideful affirmation of a clear separation from their old and sinful being. The self-denigration demanded by the ideology of humility, a discourse in harmony with the Counter-Reformation's persuasive tactics to compel subjects to submission, does not satisfy the writer's desires for self-expression, but it must be engaged. The confrontation between personal desire and social demand plays itself out in a complex alternation between self-affirmation and self-denigration in the writers' examination of the sinful self.

Ideologies and practices of gender complicate self-representation in their denial of authority to women. This denial inflects itself into women's narratives in their need to defend both their act of writing and their authority to interpret themselves in their texts. As the majority of these women are mystics, and as mysticism falls under closer scrutiny, especially when exercised by a woman, the defense of the mystic self constitutes a concern with authority that structures narrative. *Vida* writers develop many shared narrative strategies, some perhaps consciously and others borrowed less consciously from social scripts, as they express a gendered authority and a bedeviled anxiety.

If contact with "this world" is dangerous for the soul of any Christian, the absolute extraction from the world demanded of consecrated virgins makes worldliness doubly fraught with difficulties. Consequently, women writers spiritualize their stories, giving them a slippery quality in which the incidents related lack concreteness in the naming of actions and actors and thereby they recognize the perils of the world.

Autobiographical *vidas* and their biographical counterparts form an inter-woven tradition as their shared history structures meaning in both. Building their narratives around these challenges and traditions, women exercised their agency to name themselves and their own experience of the spiritual and material worlds, examining their sinful selves, gendering their authority in the face of bedeviled anxiety, recognizing the perils of this world, and continuing their voracious practice as readers and reweavers of *vida* scripts.

One last characteristic of the *vida* distinguishes this genre from another type of autobiographical narration that many of these same women wrote, which I will refer to as a spiritual "journal" for lack of a uniform word used in the writings themselves. I am speaking of the role played in the *vida* narrative by the mandate to present an entire life, at least up to the writer's present. Both *vida* and "journal" share many of the four types of strategies outlined above, but the mandate of the *vida* places a different onus on the task. Here are the ways in which several women and one editor describe the *vida* imperative:

> I begin . . . to do what your paternity demands of me and to think about and consider before the Lord *all the years of my life.* (Castillo *SV,* chap. 1, 3, emphasis mine) [15]
>
> [H]aving written *the entire history of my life,* from my childhood until I left for this foundation from this city of Oaxaca. . . . My Lord and God, it is not the least of your mercies that which you now grant me and have granted me in admitting this my confession, giving *an account of my whole life.* (María de San José 1993, 81, 85) [16]
>
> In the name of the Most Holy Trinity . . . in whose name, and for whose love I obey this command . . . *revealing the course* and distribution of the time *of my life.* (Lorravaquio Muñoz, n.d., 2r) [17]
>
> Her confessors commanded her to write *her life* and *the special favors that she continuously received* from Our Lord Jesus Christ. (Lorravaquio Muñoz, n.d., 1r) [18]

The Lorravaquio manuscript contains a twenty-four-page *vida* (her *life*) and a series of journal-like spiritual episodes (*the special favors that she continuously received*), as well as a section describing her daily schedule. The three parts are clearly demarcated, showing their conception as separate texts and separate tasks.

This distinction can also be seen in other writers who describe such jour-nals:

> Some of the mercies that God gave Doña María Vela, whose life is the one written here, ordered by Father Salzedo . . . who . . . commanded that *every day she give him an account in writing of what she did and what passed through*

her soul, which is what follows [referring to a text separate from the *vida*]. (Vela y Cueto 1961, 125) [19]

[Father Francisco de Herrera] commanded me *many times to write and show him the sentiments* [affects] that Our Lord gave me. (Castillo *SV,* chap. 11, 34) [20]

I ordered her *to give me in writing an account of the interior sentiments* of *her spirit.* (Nava 1994, 45) [21]

While both types of writing are autobiographical, the totalizing force of the command to write a "life" places in the hands of the writer the responsibility both to judge herself and to convey a sense of a whole person and a whole life to her reader. The *vidas* in the bibliography of this book all begin with a birth or childhood of some sort. The obligation to judge the self constrains the *vida* writer more fully with the discourses that condemn the weakness of the feminine and that suspect feminine authority. The totality of a life also requires a different relationship between the spiritual and the secular. The stories must take the protagonist from birth to her or his present spiritual state, and the road includes a necessary treatment of "this world." Spiritual journals, while they might delve into earthly circumstances, are free to soar in mystic realms with little or no anchor in the everyday. Both the imperative to judge and the necessity to deal with the everyday help to explain the sharp difference in tone between many *vidas* and journals, and especially between Madre Castillo's *Vida* and her *Afectos espirituales.*

EXAMINING THE SINFUL SELF

The practice of confession during the Counter-Reformation directed the faithful to follow Isaiah's example: "I will consider before you, Lord, in my memory all the years of my life" (Granada [1570] 1925, 216a). [22] The opening words of Madre Castillo's *Vida* echo almost exactly this phrase, adding to it the bitterness of humble remorse of a life ill lived (see p. 1, above). The portrayal of a vile and unworthy self directed to the confessor in obedience to his order to write appears almost universally in the Hispanic female *vida espiritual.*

Yo, la peor del mundo.[23]

The first ten chapters of Saint Teresa's *Libro* reveal the overriding theme of the weak nun whose salvation has been wrought through the undeserved mercies of God. Reiterating this conforming subjectivity, her emulators will display a rich vocabulary of self-denigration. Favorite names that the Colombian Carmelite María de Jesús (d. after 1767) applies to herself included *beast, bully, culprit of all sins, vile, horse, the most wicked that exists, animal,* and *perverse creature.*[24]

Even the bold Juana Inés de la Cruz engages in a rhetoric of self-denigrating humility in her autobiographical "Respuesta a Sor Filotea": "Sor Juana's *yo* [I] is not her *yo* but many *yos*. One cannot fail to be puzzled by the wildly discrepant postures which her *yo* affects. Throughout the *Respuesta*, the auto-biographical *yo* swings from outright insubordination, self-glorification and exaltation to utter subjugation, humility and self-denigration" (Merrim 1987, 115). But self-denigration serves an enabling function. For Sor Juana, the extremes in her self-presentation allow her to defend her intellectual life by showing herself as possessed by the spirit of knowledge (Merrim 1987, 116). The Spanish peasant Isabel de Jesús turns her unworthiness into self-defense through the paradox of Christ's teaching that the last shall be first (Arenal 1983, 153). Nuns commonly remind their readers that the fact they are chosen for a special life of mysticism, prophecy, and teaching does not reveal any personal qualities but rather shows the immense glory of a God who can accomplish great works through an empty and unworthy vessel.

Self-Affirmation.

When religious women writers portray themselves in a favorable light, they respond to a personal desire for self-affirmation, possibly to a wish to reject Counter-Reformation misogyny, but also clearly to the demands of the *vida* task to defend the self in front of the confessor or the Inquisition. As Alison Weber shows, "to prove worthiness and humility at the same time implies the logical contradiction of the double bind, since humility is tainted by self-regard. As the religious writers of the times acknowledged, humility is a silent virtue, incompatible with self-defense. . . . This is Teresa's dilemma—to elaborate a rhetoric that can give a voice to a silent virtue" (1990, 46, 48). The results for both Saint Teresa and later religious women writers are paradoxical texts of interwoven and conflicting messages.

Saint Teresa develops a rhetoric of humility from strands that Weber identifies as affected modesty, a rhetoric of concession, alternative narratives, *captatio benevolentia*, and false humility. While the topic of humility was well established within a male tradition of writing, its place in men's texts was frequently limited to the prologue, while for women writers affected modesty took center stage (Weber 1990, 50). In a "rhetoric of concession," Saint Teresa concedes her guilt and innocence simultaneously, in a complicated doubling back of the text upon itself (51). Her speech acts have confessional force but a defensive effect (56, 64). She also "continually reshapes [the writer-reader relationship] in ways that subvert hierarchy and allow her greater flexibility of expression, mixing deference with equality." She redefines humility, stating that true humility is "the right to accept God's love," in other words, his elevating mercies. To refuse this blessing is a false humility (75). Finally, Weber identifies in *Camino de perfección* (The way of perfection) a rhetorical irony that Saint Teresa employs to split her audience into nun-readers and others, by using an in-group language and creating a subversive message accessible only to the nuns (86). While not often as brilliant as that of Saint Teresa or Juana Inés de la Cruz, much of the rhetoric religious women writers develop to escape retribution while contesting Counter-Reformation representations of themselves may also be read as ironic or multilayered.

Carefully constructed rhetoric provided one avenue for subversive self-expression while the manipulation and juxtaposition of social scripts provided another. My own experience of the *vidas* began with a naive reading of Madre Castillo's text as an intentionally convoluted representation of a life written by an autonomous individual. A subsequent dive into the plethora of autobiographical and biographical *vidas* left me gasping for air, unable to distinguish one from another on account of their seemingly infinite repetitions of the same stories and the same religious tropes. Madre Castillo's *Vida* was no longer so transparent. A third stage has brought me to see more clearly the differences in the various *vidas* in terms of what Sidonie Smith calls a self-interpretation that "emerges rhetorically from the autobiographer's engagement with the fictive stories of selfhood" (1987, 47).[25]

The most basic script, to which the confessional character of the *vida* belongs, is that of the master narrative of creation and redemption, and so sin and salvation center many *vidas*. Two central subscripts are those of illness and of visionary lives. Writers experience lengthy periods of bodily suffering with clear spiritual consequence. They develop mystic lives that seek union with the Divine but more often manifest prophecy, knowledge, and the affirmation of the mystic's actions in the world or convent. Both illness and visions reveal the redemptive force of God in his lowly vessel, his scribe, instrument, and human voice. The visions through which these messages are communicated come alive with the vivid images (or scripts) of Baroque art, from the divine to the horrendous. Illness, visions, and redemption more often than not carry messages for a concrete historical situation, involving the visionaries in politics both inside and outside of the convent. The feminine authority in the visionary representations of a powerful Virgin Mary, female saints, and foremothers conveys these messages that support the mystic writer's actions. If the nun writer authorizes her text by writing it into orthodox and affirming scripts, she must also face the question of her own authority head on.

GENDERED AUTHORITY AND BEDEVILED ANXIETY

Despite the long tradition of religious women authoring their own representations, both writing and self-interpretation demanded a degree of authority that was suspect when exercised by women. That the autobiographical *vida* was so frequently explored by women, and apparently very little by men, speaks to the exclusion of women from the realms of intellect and authority, which caused them anxiety even when entering the more feminine-marked relationship to knowledge given through experience, especially mystic experience. Male religious authors wrote sermons, biblical commentaries, theological and doctrinal treatises. Though some women dared to enter these discursive realms too, they often had to resort to complicated rhetorical strategies in order to veil their daring.

Male realms of intellectual activity demanded not only basic literacy, which nuns often possessed as well, but also a knowledge of scholastic theology and the Scriptures that was accessible only to those who knew Latin. The education of young men included Latin grammar, rhetoric, philosophy, and theology as a matter of course. But Latin was the language of religious power, used in part to prevent the uninitiated—which included all women—from manipulating theological truths. According to Fray Pedro de Soto, "the widespread reading of the Holy Scriptures is an inexhaustible source of heresies" (Bataillon 1950, 2: 142).[26] Although translations of the Bible were available, thanks to the intellectuals of Spain's early sixteenth century, by midcentury they began to appear on the index of prohibited books (Bataillon 1950, 1: 54). In some religious communities, however, Latin was taught to the novices not only so that they might read the Divine Office properly, but apparently also so that they might understand it, as practice in the Convento Real de Santa Clara in Tunja suggests (*LV* 41r). One might also understand the comprehension of Latin by nuns who spent hours every day reading aloud from the Psalms during their duties of praying the canonical hours. When religious women did acquire this basic tool of theology, they stood on ambiguous ground. Writing nuns who used Latin in their texts attributed their knowledge of the language not to study but rather to the intervention of the Holy Spirit. Studied knowledge was not a woman's realm; infused or mystic knowledge was.

Women's possibilities for intellectual pursuits during the early sixteenth century had encountered an official voice of limited support. Juan Luis Vives encouraged the education of girls in "letters" accompanied by a careful control over the books that they read ([1524] 1944, chap. 4, 18). These books were to include the Scriptures and the works of the Christian Fathers and of the philosophers, or, for those women who did not read Latin, books of morality or saints' lives that had been translated into Spanish (chap. 5, 33–34). Vives provided numerous historical examples of women who were both wise and virtuous, naming pagans (Sappho and Cassandra) and Christian women— Thecla, Catherine of Alexandria, Catherine of Siena, and Hildegard of Bingen (chap. 4, 19–22). Although his examples included both writers and teachers, Vives argued that women should not teach:

The Apostle Saint Paul, select vessel, giving form to the Church at Corinth says: "Let women be quiet in the church, as it is not permitted for them to talk, but rather to be subject according to the commandment of divine law, and if they wish to know something, let them ask it at home of their husbands." Elsewhere, the same Apostle writes to Timothy, his disciple, in this manner: ". . . Therefore, as long as woman is naturally a sick animal, and her judgment is not entirely sure, and she can be easily deceived, as our mother Eve demonstrated, who for very little allowed herself to be made foolish and to be persuaded by the Devil: for all of these reasons and others that remain unsaid, it is not right that she teach." (chap. 4, 26–27)[27]

Sixty years later, Fray Luis de León propounded a greater restriction of women's intellect than Vives had. Fray Luis contended that nature did not make good and honest women for the study of the sciences or difficult matters, "but for a single simple and domestic occupation, thus nature limited their understanding, and consequently, reduced their words and their reason" ([1583] 1987, chap. 15, 154).[28] The education of girls and women, limited to the home, the convent, and the home-based institution of the *Amigas*,[29] comprehended domestic tasks and the skills necessary for women to read devotional texts such as saints' lives. They should not, however, be taught to write, said the eighteenth-century Franciscan Antonio Arbiol y Diez (1714, 490). Arbiol also opposed the general concession of authority to women that was so closely linked to the power of the pen. For Arbiol and others this exclusion from authority marked even the feminine arena of mysticism: "Women, especially, should not be permitted to become Doctors of Mysticism, but rather they should learn to be silent, and to allow themselves to be governed, with prompt, humble and quiet obedience on the way of perfection" (317).[30] Ironically, he counts Saint Teresa among the "holy mystic doctors" (1724, 395). Those women who wrote were kept under constant scrutiny, and their writing, especially when dealing with mystic experiences, had to pass a more careful test than that put to men: "because of their sex, women are, generally, in these matters more easily deceived; and more apt to deceive, and consequently, their revelations and visions contain a special suspicion, that must be carefully excluded, by undertaking with them a more exacting examination" (Ximenes Samaniego 1670, 155).[31] Thus, while convents offered women possibilities for education and time to read, excused them from the duties of wife and mother, and even required them to read and write by virtue of the needs of the Divine Office and the convent record keeping, the Counter-Reformation ideology strove to limit and control these activities. It is also clear that nuns' writings far exceeded these limitations as they are spelled out in the statements of Fray Luis de León and Fray Antonio Arbiol, and often confronted their misogynist ideology directly—as when, in her "Respuesta a Sor Filotea," Juana Inés de la Cruz wrote her eloquent defense of her right as a woman to exercise her God-given intellect, and even to critique the sermon of a Jesuit priest.

Counter-Reformation ideology suggested the possibility of female error in several forms during the *vida*-writing process: firstly, a woman might willfully contradict Church doctrine or mislead others in her interpretation of inner experiences; secondly, as a daughter of the weak and easily deceived Eve, she might fall to the Devil's wiles and unwittingly produce lies or heresy; thirdly, her own lack of understanding of theological and biblical matters and the complex and delicate matter of mystic experience might lead her astray in her interpretation of her life and experience. With such a battery of challenges to their authority, women writers developed a broad and common repertoire of strategies with which to defend their act of writing and the authority of their words.

Virile Virginity.

Holy virgins could pull some clout in the question of authority that nonvirginal women could not because of their different relationship to the weakness of the flesh. Rather than posing clear binary oppositions, gender definitions of the sixteenth to eighteenth centuries and the areas of activities that they circumscribed provided a mix of both separate and overlapping spheres. Woman did not embody a clear Other but rather an imperfect version of man; she was, according to Aquinas, a defective human being (*Summa theologica* I, 92, 1, ad 1, quoted in McLaughlin 1974, 217). While Saint Augustine recognized the equivalency of man and woman as rational spirits, in her bodily nature woman stood for "the subjection of body to spirit in nature and that debasing carnality that draws the male mind down from its heavenly heights" (Ruether 1974, 158). Saint Augustine fixed woman's association with the body in her creation out of the flesh of man, and in her primary and unique purpose of procreation (*De Grat. Chap. et de Pecc. Orig.* II, 40; *De Genesi ad lit.* 9.5, quoted in Ruether 1974, 156). Aquinas affirmed that man possessed stronger rational faculties, while the inferior female body had a detrimental effect on woman's soul (*Summa theologica* I, 92, 1 quoted in McLaughlin 1974, 218). The explanation of woman as imperfect man rather than as absolute Other allowed certain "transgressions" into masculine realms—such as authority and authorship—to be seen as masculinization. Thus exceptional women were often favorably compared to men or called "virile." Fray Luis de León, for example, gives the title of *mujer de valor* or *mujer varonil* to the perfect wife ([1583] 1987, chap. 1, 86). "Leander of Seville speaks of virginity as freeing woman from the sexual oppression and male domination of the curse of Eve" (Ruether 1974,

159). Nevertheless, it was also clear that a nun could not fully conquer the "woman underneath" until death, and so her potential virility remained constantly threatened by her weakness. It was in death alone that her body could prove her final triumph, giving as a sign its continued incorrupt state upon later exhumation. In the meantime, the nun writer strove to prove her chastity in order to bolster her interpretive authority.[32]

Amanuensis of God.

The gendered discourses and practices of writing did not present a monolithic exclusion of women, but they did preclude the category of the female *author.* Male writers could be and were referred to as the *authors* of their texts while female religious writers were not.[33] The term *autor* differed importantly from that of *escritor,* which was used to refer to women. J. Corominas (1954) gives for the word *autor* the definitions of *creator* and *historic source* while Covarrubias ([1611] 1979) states that "commonly it is understood to mean the inventor of something." Covarrubias adds that *autoridad* refers to "the written reason that we allege as the basis for some purpose, and the very firmest is that which is taken from the Holy Scriptures, the Councils, the traditions of the holy doctors, and in proportion from others who have written and write."[34] The ultimate Author is God himself. In contrast, an *escritor* is "he who writes; at times it signifies the author of some written works, and at others the copier, whom we call the writer of books."[35] While *escritor* referred to the mechanical act, *autor* implied creative responsibility for the knowledge contained in a text. Being made more exactly in the image of God, men had access to the more empowering title.

The genres available to male religious authors offered a very different kind of knowledge than that imparted in the *vida* and demanded a different means of authorization. Authority in theological or doctrinal treatises, sermons, and even biographical *vidas* was built on scholarly study for which the authors merited admiration. "The slender pen of the very Reverend Father Alonso de Andrade, of the Company of Jesus . . . with so many and such erudite books has merited the applause which the world worthily gives him" (Andrade 1651, "Censura del R.P.M.F. Francisco Boyl").[36] Joseph del Castillo y Bolívar's text "breathes wisdom, exhales genius and ingenuity, and radiates braveries of art and scholarship, as, exhausting the artifice of all its cares, the rhetoric of its tropes, and all sacred and natural erudition of its concepts, it leaves only the admiration with something to do" (1733, 5).[37] Thus in the male clerical model, writing was the instrument by which knowledge built on scholarship established the authority and skill of the writer. Knowledge in the mostly feminine genres of spiritual self-exploration was mediated in ways that portray a dilution of the authority of the writer and of the agency of the self: either mystic discourse made of the writer a passive conduit of knowledge from the ultimate Authority, or the flesh-bound female in her greater weakness to the Devil obfuscated truth, thus requiring the submission of a raw text to the verification of the external authority of the clergy.

Examples of this displacement of authority and praise are abundant. The illumination of difficult scriptural points by the Spanish Franciscan Juana de la Cruz (1481–1534), a nun whose famed preaching predated the Council of Trent, was attributed by her post-Tridentine biographer to the communications of angels (Daça 1614, 71). María de Jesús de Agreda, whose *Mystica ciudad de Dios* (Mystical city of God) underwent multiple editions in the years following her death, was called not an author but a "prodigious writer" by the Bishop of Tarazona (Agreda 1670, 3: 19; pages follow Agreda's text). After submitting Agreda's texts to the five-point examination developed by Cardinal Torquemada, the bishop found them to be sound, containing scholastic, mystic, and expositive theology. But as Joseph Ximenes Samaniego clarifies, her history of the Virgin Mary was not "gathered from the writings of the Catholic saints, fathers and doctors, with human study, not imagined in the retreat of contemplation with devout affection alone, but as received by divine revelation in these latter times, the subject [Agreda] being an illiterate woman, to whom [the story] was communicated, and who was the instrument of its writing" (1670, 37).[38] For her part, Agreda assures the reader that she writes not as a teacher but as a disciple. An instrument of the queen of the heavens, she transmits what she is commanded, "since by occupation, women must be silent in the Holy Church and listen to the teachers" (1681, 3: 6).[39]

Being denied the process by which male scholars authorized their knowledge was not all bad. The search for alternative forms of authorization led to a partial freeing of knowledge. Without the necessary trappings of scholarly tools, Agreda, and with her hundreds of religious women, sought a mystic access to knowledge and authority. In this way, Agreda could discover through mystic paths many previously "unrevealed" moments of Mary's biography, filling in large gaps left by the scriptural narration and offering to a wide female readership a Virgin Mary almost equal in stature to her son.

The thought that religious women writers were not authors was matched by a conception of *vida* writing as a personal rather than public activity. The apparent privacy of the act of writing, however, is belied by the fact that so many of the *vidas* formed the basis for the biographical works written about their subjects by their spiritual directors in the Church's interest to foment the faith through purified models of sanctity. The very words of the women authors were read not only by confessors and other male clerics, and potentially by officials of the Inquisition, but often by a wide public. Innumerable quotes and, in some cases, hundreds of pages of original autobiographical text were incorporated into biographies and published, often with little editing on the part of the biographer. The possibility of such publicity made the act of writing even more ticklish.

Obedience, Martyrdom, and Celestial Endorsement.

The most widely shared trope in religious women's *vidas* that responds to the problem of writing is the characterization of the act as entirely motivated by obedience. *Vidas* frequently begin by directing themselves to "my father" or "your paternity" and by acknowledging the text as being produced under duress. The writer herself finds the task entirely contrary to her vile nature and lack of ability. Writing is often portrayed as a martyrdom, made more painful by the constant fear of deceit by the Devil. María de San José (Mexico, 1656–1719) writes: "It seemed to me, that at the hour of my death nothing should so torment me and cause me anguish as these writings" (Arenal and Schlau 1989b, 350, translation by Amanda Powell).[40] Many writers ask their confessors to allow them to burn the record of their words. Through these negative portrayals of the act, the authors distance their will from writing and write themselves into the misogynist discourse on women, and by so doing imbue their words with orthodoxy. The relationship between the writer and her confessor regarding the text lays the responsibility for the text on the appropriate shoulders of a man while it keeps the pen in the hand of the woman. Not all representations of writing are negative, however, as writing becomes a vehicle of healing and leads to the divine affirmation of the writer through her visionary life. Again María de San José: "At this point I heard a voice . . . which was that of his Majesty . . . and he explained thus: 'See how I aid you and fail you not; write it down, for everything comes from me, and nothing from you; if it were not so, think whether, left to yourself, you could have taken one single step or done what you have done'" (Muriel 1982, 397).[41]

Fray Antonio Arbiol y Diez dedicates an entire chapter of his biography of Jacinta de Atondo (1645–1716), a Poor Clare of Zaragoza, Spain, to her proclaimed repugnance to writing, a theme he notes as being the most frequent in her letters to him (1716, 119). He quotes her repeated expression of the fear that she suffers a deceived understanding of herself and that, in this light, it is only the force of obligation that overcomes her resistance. She asks her confessor to release her from the task of writing and to return her papers in order that she may burn them, for she is tormented by the thought that someday someone will discover her deceit. She expresses great concern that the papers not be made public, a concern that Arbiol violates—perhaps not unanticipated by Sor Jacinta—in his extensive quoting within his male and posthumous authority to judge her as virtuous and undeceived.

Pedro Calvo de la Riba (1752) writes a similar tale of the Dominican whom he served as confessor, María Gertrudis Theresa de Santa Inés (1668–1730) of the convent of Santa Inés in Santa Fe, Nuevo Reino de Granada. Calvo's representation of Sor María's struggle with writing imbues this act with a healing potential, albeit a cure by fire. As she had been consistently unable to speak her sins, a previous confessor ordered her to write a general confession. According to Calvo, the Devil tried to interfere, but Sor María was able to produce nine quires, some 225 sheets, covered with her small handwriting. The former confessor's superior ordered that the written confession be burned and that Sor María be made to confess orally, an event that Calvo portrays as sacrificial. When Calvo orders Sor María to repeat the written confession, his justification rests on the case that writing caused Sor María the greatest torment of her martyrdom.[42] This time the confession is accepted, and her pen becomes an instrument of a healing self-affirmation, as she writes Christ's instruction to her that she not doubt him in his manifestations in her inner life. Sor María circumvents the confessor to affirm her self through direct communication with Christ, after which she is once again able to confess orally.

The maneuvering is complicated, and while the first confessor appears to repress Sor María's self-expression and autonomy through the written word and Padre Calvo encourages it, both can be seen as acting out of orthodox motivation. The result is that Padre Calvo and Sor María align the act of writing with martyrdom, thus distancing Sor María from any desire for self-affirmation. The act of writing becomes part of the necessary purification of the soul by fire that leads a Christian toward God. I do not wish to make this all seem a textual game. Authorial anxiety is not merely a disembodied ploy; while Sor María's story of fear serves to elevate her, it is a story motivated by the material practices of the Inquisition, by the possibility of a real punishment.

The triangle of confessor-writer-Devil that forges the writing about writing in many *vidas* works in Madre Castillo's texts to authorize her pen by displacing authority from herself. Madre Castillo shows herself to be a constantly changing interpreter of her inner life, shifting from positions of confusion and submission to self-affirmation and back again. The only constant is the link between her writing and her obedience, mentioned five of the ten times that the *Vida* explicitly refers to the act of writing. The martyrdom she suffers in her fear of confusion by the Devil alternates with her portrayal of the compelling force of the writing itself, the consolation she feels when rereading her texts, and the celestial go-aheads that she receives.

Twice, Madre Castillo writes of her desire to burn her papers, once out of fear that they might be read by other nuns (*SV,* chap. 32, 122), and once out of a belief that the Devil has been deceiving her during her entire life (*SV,* chap. 42, 162). It is important to see that in both cases, her desire to burn the papers lies in the past and not within her present emotional state. Both moments of confusion elicit consolation from a higher authority, leading her as writer in the present to dispel her doubts. In the first case, her confessor, and in the second, God himself, pronounces the papers to be communications from God. Madre Castillo realizes that it was the Devil who had tempted her to burn her papers, causing her to believe that what she had written was based on a deluded understanding of her life. His power to confuse her was grounded in her sinful human nature, not in any willful collusion on her part.

Her present confidence concerning prior writings is based on an intellectual vision in which God gives her the very clear understanding that nothing she has written is of her own composition or has been spoken to her by the Devil (*SV,* chap. 42, 164). Her autobiographical *Afectos* also treat self-consciously the task of writing to a similar end of constructing her authority. In *Afecto* 90, having seen herself in perdition and filled with anxiety and tribulation because of having written "a few sentiments that have passed through my soul," she asks the rector of the Jesuit school to allow her to burn the papers (*AE* 207).[43] He responds by ordering her to pray to God for illumination. The result is a vision in which, "I saw that from the fingers of my right hand was dripping a richness, like precious and resplendent pearls, and like gold; but it was of a manner that ran as a liquid, like a balm, without losing its brilliance. . . . and I understood: that what was written in the papers, was not born of myself, nor of the evil spirit, but of God, and of his light, that by his incomprehensible judgment he has made me write it" (*AE* 207–8).[44] Her act of writing in the *vida,* however, still causes her occasional admissions of insecurity: "I do not know if I am correct in saying" (*SV* 129), or "[t]hese and other similar things I write, my father, because your paternity commands me to, and in order to give you more clearly a recounting of everything, not because I am firm in anything other than that which our holy faith teaches us, nor that I have more determination than to be at the judgment and order of my confessors and prelates, that I have always known to be the sure way" (86).[45]

Not all of the difficulty resides in her authority as subject to name experiences. In at least one instance of the *Vida* she depicts as unreliable the very act of transcribing divine communications: "All the steps and paths of my life were also brought to my memory, not as they can be written down here, but rather as God could manifest them to my soul, without risk of fears or doubts, without the forgetfulness of memory, or the confusion of the understanding. . . . But this would be better explained by some words that I understood at that time, or that I wrote (not because they were expressed as words, but rather a light that impressed itself on my soul, and convinced it, having received Our Lord in the Sacrament)" (*SV* 130).[46] Here God is again the ultimate Author/ Authority who locates within Madre Castillo a vision of truth that transcends the possibilities of doubt and confusion. Yet the ineffable quality of mystic encounter leaves doubt in the mediation of words. Madre Castillo's disclaimer mitigates her responsibility as writer-instrument for any error detected or interpreted by the confessor's gaze. The speech act carries the force of confession or concession of error, but its effect is defense and self-affirming.

Giving the Devil His Due.

The ubiquitous Devil and his entourage of lesser demons served the Counter-Reformation well. In naming as demonic interference those acts of human agency that moved the will to disobedience and away from self-control, the Counter-Reformation found a useful tool of persuasion with which to make visible and memorable the same will that was the invisible object of its persuasion (Cascardi 1992, 242). It followed that what was born of demonic intervention should be eradicated; and so, for example, Magdalena de la Cruz, once celebrated for her visions and ecstasies, received a sentence of perpetual silence and life imprisonment from the Inquisition in 1546, when convicted of deceiving the public into believing that the visitations she received from the Devil were actually visions of Christ (Weber 1992, 173).

The Devil gave *vida*-writing women constant hell, but often that hellish encounter was also a part of the nuns' defense. When a *vida* writer shows herself to be engaged with the Devil in an antagonistic relationship, she incorporates orthodoxy into her text. On one hand, she recognizes the threat posed to the salvation of any soul by the Devil and his primary tools of pride and lust, and on the other she fits her self-portrait into that of a weak woman facing temptation. Her encounter with the Devil can show either a sinful former self, from which the writer distances her present self, or a strength born of virtue in her present triumphs.

Alison Weber calls Saint Teresa's Devil "often more of a nuisance than a seducer," as he presents a limited and vincible threat (1992, 176). In Saint Teresa's contemplative practice, the Devil is not able to make her doubt God, in whom the favors she receives originate. In reference to several clergy members who judge that her visions are induced by the Devil, she professes that she fears those who fear the Devil more than she fears the Devil himself. Only the former can do her real harm by leading her trusting and obedient self astray, while from the Devil she will always be ultimately protected by God (1970, *Libro de la vida*, chap. 23, 148; chap. 25, 158). In *Camino de perfección*, she advises nuns not to let their fear of the Devil keep them from mental prayer (Weber 1992, 178). Unwilling to accept the confessors' verdict on her visions, she engages in her famous negotiation to find a sympathetic spiritual director and, while not attacking any specific cleric, develops a discourse regarding the guidelines for choosing appropriate spiritual direction.

Saint Teresa does experience the Devil as capable of interfering with the soul's progress in mental prayer, and provides methods of discernment and compliance that can serve as a defense against his influence. She enumerates the readable signs that are left by experiences induced by the Devil—dryness of the soul, disquiet and temptations and sufferings of uncertain precedence —and she warns against trusting in oneself to such a degree as to fall into deception (1970, chap. 25, 154). In order to prevent this, one must develop the controls of Christian doctrine: virtues (primary among which is humility), mortification, and detachment from the world (chap. 19, 125). Saint Teresa gives her spiritual daughters the tools to take on and defeat the Devil themselves and thus to maintain control over their spiritual lives and to keep their texts safe.

As Fernando Cervantes notes, the suffering by women at the hands of the Devil was considered an essential part of their spiritual progress and salvation (1994, 105–7). The Devil forged pure souls in his crucible of martyrdom. The biographer of the Mexican Sebastiana Joseph de la Santísima Trinidad affirms that, "[v]ery few saints placed in the high altar of glory have been untouched by the hand of the Devil. For, given that this cursed craftsman has always shown a great skill in cutting, edging and polishing, God has seen fit to grant him a general license to refine, polish and adorn with his hand all those who, in his wise providence, he has destined to fill the eternal niches that are found in heaven's immense reredos" (Valdés 1765, 285). The idea that God would permit the Devil to persecute souls for their own good allows many writers to explain the obstacles placed in the way of their actions in this world without committing the sin of pride by naming others as evil. In recounting her efforts to found San José, the first Discalced Carmelite convent, Saint Teresa projects the Devil onto the hindrance of her work by others (1970, *Libro de la vida*, chap. 33, 200). She yields briefly to temptation as the Devil engages her in a spiritual battle in which she doubts the goodness of the foundation, a doubt evoked, of course, by the fierce political battles that she faces in her work. Coming to her senses, she realizes that the Devil has made her forget the authorization and encouragement she received directly from God (chap. 36, 217–18). Curiously, in the *Libro de las fundaciones* (Book of the foundations), written at the end of her life and some twenty years after the *Libro de la vida*, the Devil plays a notably lesser role in her struggle to found the many convents of her reformed order. As her own authority within the power structure of the Church has become more firmly established, her need to defend a strong agency through such means as the deployment of the Devil decreases. Many other nuns, including Madre Castillo, understand the Devil to move behind the persecution they face from their peers and superiors in undertaking their spiritual goals.

There is one last aspect to the Devil that is too compelling to omit, though I have not as yet found a fully satisfying explanation for it; this is his racial typing. At times in Spanish texts, and frequently in Spanish American *vidas*, the Devil appears as a man described in specific racial terms. When he is a racial Other, the racial appearance is often accompanied by the qualification that he is ugly. In three of his visits to Madre Castillo, the Devil appears as an Indian, a mulatto, and a black man (*SV*, chap. 38, 147; chap. 39, 150, 151). The centrality of race as a category regulating social practices in Spanish America gives at least a hint of American identity to these texts, but what is their specific significance? The reference may simply designate the embodiment par excellence of the irrational Other that threatens to loose the control of the will. Or perhaps the frequently sexual suggestiveness of the visitations by racial Others remits to the great fear of miscegenation. The fearfulness of the encounter increases for the subject, and the drama of the visit increases for the readership if what is at stake is the honor of a white woman threatened by—an admittedly phantasmagoric—seductive racial Other. By deploying the incarnation of such great fear in her society, and showing her triumph over its evil, Madre Castillo strengthens her own portrayal as vanquishing evil.

Confessors as Authorizing Characters.

Michel Foucault (1978) opened the door to a reexamination of the confessor-confessant relationship, which had previously been perceived as a one-way power dynamic. Certainly, the Counter-Reformation sought control over its flock, and particularly over potentially wayward female mystics, through the obligation of the confessional and the practice of matching every spiritual seeker with an ordained (that is, male) spiritual director. As Foucault demonstrated, however, the power relationship was not one of control and repression but of negotiation, in which both sides benefited and together produced rather than suppressed discourses on controversial topics.

Confessors could often pose irritating obstacles to *vida* writers, but when the match was a good one, both sides benefited tremendously.

> Far from occupying positions of unqualified control, male confessors were strongly attracted to the idea of directing spiritually advanced women and, in turn, became deeply influenced by them, identified with them, and even became dependent upon them. The experience of dealing with and writing about extraordinary women aided clerics in formulating and articulating their own sense of identity. And the position of spiritual director provided priests with an acceptable channel for discussing controversial, even dangerous, theological topics. The most common vehicle for exploring these religious and personal issues was the biography of a female penitent by a male confessor, a classic genre of baroque spirituality that insured a place in posterity for both subject and biographer. (Bilinkoff 1993, 84)

Bilinkoff goes on to discuss how the relationship with the women they guided affirmed the role of the confessors as they wrote their subjects into exemplarity. This portraiture, which took several forms including sermons and biographies, also provided the confessor with an arena in which to discuss controversial matters, often rendering questionable women acceptable in the eyes of the ecclesiastical establishment (1993, 95). Darcy Donahue notes that in writing biographies, confessors also gave themselves a space for characterizing their role in the life of the exemplary nun and thereby elevating their own stature (1989, 233).

The respect and, even more, the loyal friendship of a confessor and other male clergy could help a nun to authorize her writing both within and outside of her text. If, as Bilinkoff writes, a confessor took the controversial actions and words of a religious woman and forged of them a favorable model, then the nun's words might be protected either while she wrote or for posterity after her death. If the visions of a mystic fell under suspicion, the good word of a confessor concerning the woman's life helped her cause. Once it had been established that the knowledge contained in a visionary's text did not contradict existing scholarship and Scriptures, its acceptance depended on the compliance of the writer's extratextual life to orthodoxy. The method of examination developed by Torquemada involved the identification of five signs in the visions being tested: "The first, that the visions are ruled by the knowledge of erudite reason and of the Masters experienced in the spirit. *The second, by the effect that they have on the soul of the one who receives this fervor.* The third, by the material that they contain and its truth. The fourth, if they are conformed with the Holy Scriptures or are opposed to them. *The fifth, on the part of the person, if she is of approved life, and known virtue*" (Agreda 1670, 3: 20–22; pages following Agreda's text).[47] Authorization of the knowledge contained in the text is negotiated within the writer's body and behavior and in practices that are embedded in the politics that surround her; and it depends on the good favor of the male clergy who judge her.

The confessor-writer relationship enters the texts themselves in ways that both limit and, by means of authorization, liberate. Most *vidas* are permeated with references to the confessor as addressee, references that indicate an attitude of humility and a relationship of dependence in which the destiny and content of the text demand the confessor's approval and, at times, receive his correction. Such references submit the texts to a patriarchal discourse (Myers 1992, 41), although that discourse is frequently undermined by subversive narrative threads of meaning. The effect of this deployment of the confessor as reader and judge within the text moves the text toward authorization.

If Saint Teresa's confessors command her to enter the treacherous territory of self-naming, she imposes on them a corresponding responsibility. "I am describing my own experiences, as I have been commanded to do; if he to whom I send this does not approve of it, he will tear it up, and he will know what is wrong with it better than I" (Teresa of Jesus 1949, 1: chap. 10, 60).[48] Saint Teresa claims to knock judgment back into her confessors' court by posing herself as incapable of true discernment, thus making them ultimately responsible for those texts that escape destruction. She posits her own lack of authority to write when she states that she is prevented from lengthy exposition of the mercies given her by the command she has received (1970, *Libro de la vida*, Prólogo, 53). Saint Teresa's repeated statements of submission to confessorial authority, and her reminders that her first readers should destroy unacceptable texts, are elaborated in greater detail in the first part of the *Libro de la vida*, tending toward brief formulaic punctuation of the later text. Parallel to these submissive statements, she develops a strongly optimistic voice of personal authority. While she dedicates two chapters (30 and 31) to a period when she experienced a great deal of confusion and temptation from the Devil, speaking in the present the author's voice does not doubt her own salvation. Thus her deployment of confessors in her text authorizes the text through them while not preventing her from developing a strong voice of her own.

Celestial Fans and Feminine Authority.

Madre Castillo's visions have shown how divine authority backs up the questionable meeting of woman and quill in the production of knowledge. Visions permeate the *vidas* of religious women and often take them over, important in their own right as signs of the writers' spiritual path but often also key in affirming the goodness of the subjects' actions in this world. Many of the *vida* writers of the centuries following Saint Teresa's death took up some form of her zealous energy to reform and engaged in a radical form of religiosity. Righteous attempts at reforming their convents and long hours spent in ecstatic visions brought many of these writers under the close gaze not only of their confessors but also of their sister nuns, causing them a great deal of grief in accusations, judgments, punishments, and taunts. Over and again, these women received divine confirmation for their goals and actions, as well as a celestial retreat from their painfully less-than-perfect convent worlds.

Beyond clear confirmation of specific actions, female holy figures often played a crucial role in establishing models of feminine authority that justified the actions of women religious writers, evidencing a memory of a time when feminine power and intellect were not as tightly restricted. Some of the creations of feminine authority most prominently studied in recent scholarship occur not in *vidas*, where primary focus is on the self, but in sermons and treatises. The powerful Virgin Mary of Agreda's *Mystica ciudad de Dios*, a book well circulated among convent communities, was the source of the redemptive knowledge she communicated to Sor María. She stood as the first among the apostles, key to spreading the Word as she took it upon herself to instruct them to write the Gospels. Mexico's María Anna Agueda de San Ignacio envisions an active and authorizing Mary, characterized by spiritual and intellectual dynamism, while she herself carries out the unfemininely active role of writing theological treatises.[49] Women autobiographers also evoked their human foremothers for validation. Best known is Juana Inés de la Cruz's "Respuesta a Sor Filotea," a secular autobiography rather than a *vida espiritual*, which places her own writing and intellectual activity within a tremendous female genealogy encompassing biblical leaders, pagan scholars of the Classical period, and medieval nuns and intellectuals of the Counter-Reformation (1957, 4: 460–62). Mexico's María de San José incorporates passages from the autobiography of her order's founder, Mariana de San Joseph, into her own, "to justify her own inclusion of what might have been considered controversial material" (Myers 1993b, 26). Colombia's María de Jesús patterns elements of her life after that of María de Jesús de Agreda (Germán María del Perpetuo Socorro and Martínez Delgado 1947, 246), while Madre Castillo emulates both the suffering of Saint Mary Magdalene of Pazzis and the reformism of Saint Teresa. Writing themselves into scripts of feminine authority that had already received the Church's blessing helped these women to authorize their own stories. None of my affirmations of intertextuality are meant to suggest less authenticity or sincerity on the part of the writers. If these women consciously imitated their foremothers, and if they carefully crafted their own stories to fit those that had gone before them, they did so in a world that struggled with and against the nascent individualism of the Renaissance, a world in which they understood and earnestly lived their lives as parts of this greater and often predestined whole.

RECOGNIZING THE PERILS OF THE WORLD

A final difficulty that characterizes *vida* writing by women involves the tension between their lives in this world and their avowed removal from it. Saint Teresa's *Libro de la vida* opened the floodgates for self-writing by Spanish and Spanish American nuns, but the model of her own actions—breaking out of the containment of the cloister and negotiating her terms of obedience—differed from the absolute containment and obedience she prescribed for her followers. Through constant involvement in *this world*—the realms outside of the convent in which the wills of human individuals, politics, and power must be negotiated in order to obtain her goals—Saint Teresa constructed the possibility for an enclosure that would extricate her followers from such dealings. Saint Teresa's *Libro de la vida* begins with the story of a sinner saved by God through prayer, subsequently distracted by the pleasures of the world, tempted into repeated falls, and eventually brought back into a relationship of grace and mystic union. In the worldly obstacles she faces while seeking to found the first reformed convent, Saint Teresa sees both the Devil's work and her spiritual triumphs by God's hand: "The Lord now showed me what a signal blessing it is to suffer trials and persecutions [wrought by the Devil] for His sake, for so great was the growth in my soul of love for God and of many other graces that I was astounded, and this made me incapable of ceasing to desire trials. . . . It was now that I began to experience the increasingly strong impulses of the love of God which I have described, and also deeper raptures, although I was silent on this subject and never spoke to anyone of what I had gained" (Teresa of Jesus 1949, 1: chap. 33, 225).[50] Time and again, it is Saint Teresa's proximity to sin that produces the fruits of spiritual good. The place of *this world* in her narration of her self is a place of distraction and danger for her soul, but it also becomes the necessary location of her activities in order to achieve the enclosure of her own body. This enclosure liberates her soul for contemplative union with God and encloses and similarly incorporates into the salvation story those nuns who would follow her. Her activities in the worldliness of economic and political maneuverings, with God's help, bring to fruition the holy seed of an idea conceived of while she lived in the worldliness of the unenclosed convent of the Encarnación.

Saint Teresa's spiritual daughters have no worldly outside in which to immerse themselves if they desire to emulate the deeply redemptive side of her life mission. In the cloistered world of Spanish American nuns' writings, then, the worldliness, like that of Saint Teresa's Convento de la Encarnación, often comes from within. Often religious women writers see their communities as lax in their religious observance. The sinful *murmuración* that divides communities becomes emblematic of the struggle of the righteous against the surrounding evil world. While the word *murmuración* can be translated as "gossip," in religious discourse it conveys a much stronger message. Covarrubias calls it "conversation born of envy, that tries to stain and darken the life and virtue of others" ([1611] 1979, s.v. *murmuración*).[51] He cites from Saint Bernard's Sermon I *De triplici custodia,* that "the cursing and murmuring tongue is the Devil's paintbrush and is similar to the serpent."[52] For Madre Castillo, in particular, the worldliness of the convent becomes her seed for cultivating spiritual fruits, and the *murmuración* against her becomes her cross. The worldliness on the outside of the convent walls, however, does not offer a space of redemption for Madre Castillo as it did for Saint Teresa, but rather proves disruptive of her textualization as a holy subject.

VIDAS AND BIOGRAPHIES: INTERWOVEN TRADITIONS

The years following the publication of Saint Teresa's *Libro de la vida,* in 1588, witnessed a burgeoning of the *vida espiritual.* Serrano y Sanz ([1903], 1975) has located some seventy references to *vidas,* although many more may have been lost. Saint Teresa's *Libro de la vida* gave religious women authors the example of a text published despite the writer's stated desire that at least some portions be kept secret. Nuns knew that their *vidas* might meet the public eye. The fact that only a handful of subsequent *vidas* have been published as written does not imply that the nuns understood their task to be entirely between themselves and their confessors, as I have already suggested. Priestly biographers incorporated extensive quotes, even lengthy sections or entire *vidas,* within their biographies, a genre that also flourished during the Counter-Reformation (Bilinkoff 1993, 83). These biographies formed part of the nuns' daily devotional reading; religious women writers—especially after the seventeenth century—were aware of the possibility that, were their lives to reach favored status, their own words, their own stories of themselves might be read by a wide public.

The interweaving of autobiographical and biographical traditions affected the form of the *vida* as the genre became increasingly structured by Catholic doctrine. While the prologues of the exemplary biographies state clearly that saint-making belongs to Rome, and that the text is not to be understood to proclaim sainthood, the structuring of the *vidas* follows the demands of the beatification process. The construction of the holy subject in this process sheds light on its use in both biographical and autobiographical *vidas.* Pope Urban VIII (1623–44) established official procedures for canonization in the early seventeenth century and forbade public cult of any person not yet beatified or canonized by the Church (*Encyclopaedia Britannica: Micropaedia,* s.v. Canonization). With the exception of martyrs, all candidates had to satisfy three general requirements: doctrinal purity, heroic virtue, and miraculous intercession after death (Weinstein and Bell 1982, 141). Heroic virtue consisted of the three theological virtues of faith, hope, and charity and the four cardinal virtues of prudence, temperance, justice, and fortitude. Doctrinal purity separated saint from heretic. Heroic virtue winnowed out the practitioners of magic. Miracles performed by intercession indicated that the saint sat already in the heavenly court.

Weinstein and Bell mark the beatification process of Teresa of Avila as precedent setting in the detail of the examination of her heroic virtue (1982, 142). Her beatification occurred in 1614 and her canonization in 1622. In comparing the declarations toward beatification taken from witnesses in her case with those following the death of the Discalced Carmelite Francisca María del Niño Jesús a century later, I perceive a growing complexity in the construction of the holy subject. The documents are the "Declaración en el proceso de beatificación de la Madre Teresa de Jesús: 1595" (Declaration in the process of beatification of Mother Teresa of Jesus: 1595) (Ana de San Bartolomé 1981–85, 1: 27–40); the "Deposición de la Hermana Teresa de Jesús, sobrina de la santa en el proceso de Avila (1596)" (Deposition of Sister Teresa of Jesus, the saint's niece, in the process of Avila [1596]) (Teresa de Jesús 1915, 2: 303–3); and the "Interrogatorio de preguntas a cuyo tenor se han de examinar los testigos que declararen en la Información de la Madre Francisca María del Niño Jesús" (Questionnaire regarding whose content must be examined the witnesses who declare in the Information on Mother Francisca María del Niño Jesús) (Márquez 1709).

The comparison is made problematic by the fact that the last document is an actual *interrogatorio* or questionnaire, while the first two contain only the responses of witnesses. To facilitate the examination, I have pieced together the gist of the questions that guided the first two documents through a comparison of the responses. A second problem lies in the lack of explicit confirmation that the *Interrogatorio* from 1709 is part of a beatification process, although the twentieth-century Carmelite chronicler Fray Alfredo del S. C. de Jesús believes this was its purpose (Germán María del Perpetuo Socorro and Martínez Delgado 1947, 260). The questions' tenor as well as the document's framing within canon law supports his assertion that it was drawn up by the *procurador general y abogado por la Real Audiencia* (attorney general and lawyer of the high court); the citation to the witnesses was called by the *promotor fiscal* (a type of ecclesiastical prosecutor, perhaps an *advocatus diaboli*); and the questionnaire was administered by the *canónigo doctoral y juez delegado en esta causa,* or the cathedral's advisor in canon law delegated as judge of the case, as requested by the archbishop whose responsibility it was to initiate an investigation of virtues in the process of canonization. A third caution lies in the danger of reaching the conclusion of historical evolution from examining only three samples from either end of a period being discussed. However, the codification and centralization of the canonization process following the death of Teresa of Avila, and the burgeoning of both hagiographical and autobiographical practices that take as their objects non-canonized subjects, support the hypothesis of a progressive construction of the holy subject over this time. Comparing the Teresian questionnaire with that of Madre Castillo's contemporary might also help to explain some of the differences between Madre Castillo's self-writing and that of her model.

The first two questions in the Teresian process are quoted directly in Teresa de Jesús's answers: (1) "if [the witness] knew Madre Teresa of Jesus, and her parents, and where she was a native of, and who her godparents were, and where she was baptized," and (2) "if [the witness] knows whether Madre Teresa of Jesus was a woman of great spirit and much prayer and that through prayer she obtained great experience of Our Lord God" (1915, 2: 303).[53] The third question asks about Madre Teresa's actions as founder and their motivation. The fourth concerns her exercise of the virtues of faith, hope, charity, humility, patience, poverty, and penitence. The fifth inquires of the tribulations she endured while founding new convents. The sixth pursues information about her final illness and death. The seventh refers to the incorrupt state of her body nine months after burial and to the fact that this was not a result of embalming. The eighth solicits comments on the miraculous attributes of Madre Teresa's body and clothing after her death. The ninth concerns the miracles worked by Madre Teresa in life, and the tenth asks about miracles worked by her relics and through intercession following her death.

In the process concerning Madre Francisca María del Niño Jesús the questions have multiplied to forty-seven sections, within each of which three to nine questions have been fashioned out of the specificities of Madre Francisca's life. As in the first two documents, these questions take the closed form of "Whether the witness knows *that . . .*" rather than that of an open-ended search for information. The responses themselves are lengthy, the entire process occupying over three hundred folios, most of them covered front and back. The first two sets of questions ascertain the background of the witness and the sources of her knowledge of the candidate. Four sets of questions focus on the candidate's family and her life prior to taking the habit. Examination of her virtues has expanded to nineteen sets of questions, one dedicated to each of the theological and cardinal virtues. This section also treats as virtues her strict obedience to the rules and vows of the order. Three sets of questions deal with her asceticism and suffering. Six inquire into various aspects of her devotions and into the supernatural gifts she received while in their exercise. A dozen delve deeply into her last illness and death, the public's response, the spread of her fame, and the extent to which she worked posthumous miracles.

In addition to the verification of doctrinal purity, heroic virtue, and miraculous intercession, special interest is placed on identifying signs of a mystic life, which builds a portrait of suffering and establishes the popular recognition of Madre Francisca's holiness. Madre Francisca's *Interrogatorio* conveys a sense of urgency absent in the Teresian document, as it seeks to plot every space of her life under a doctrinal grid and exhaust all of its possible categories and manifestations. This concern with charting the holy subject through catechism-like categories is reflected in contemporary biographical *vidas*. The chapter headings of five biographies written between 1651 and 1752 read like a summary of the *Interrogatorio,* sharing its concern for mapping out the holy subject and containing it within discourse (Andrade 1651; Arbiol y Díez 1714; Obregón 1724; Oviedo 1752; and Solano n.d.). The chapter-by-chapter organization that subsumes the subject into both the doctrine of the catechism and the manual on mystic theology marks the power of a biographer to judge the life of the holy person. This is not the organization of an autobiographer, who must avoid any hint of self-canonizing. Its elements, however, structure content and meaning as the *vida* writer is interpellated by the biographical tradition and responds to it.

MALE WRITING: UNAMBIGUOUS ASSURANCE

The anxiety expressed by religious women in their *vidas* cannot be extricated from the context of writing about the self, producing knowledge through naming their inner experiences in a society that suspects women's authority to do so. When their male contemporaries take up the same genre, do they share their sisters' anxiety about writing and self-representation? I have been able to locate only three *vidas espirituales* and three spiritual journals authored by religious men.[54] Because the texts are so few, I will discuss both *vidas* and journals, although my interest is in *vida* writing. Both provide examples of autobiographical styles of representation. However, the *vidas* are more important to the examination of gender within the subgenre. The texts include *A Pilgrim's Journey: The Autobiography of Saint Ignatius of Loyola* ([1552] 1985); his *Spiritual Journal* ([1544–45] 1958); the *Sentimientos y avisos espirituales* (Spiritual affects and declarations) and the *Meditaciones* of Father Luis de la Puente (1554–1624); the *Vida interior* (Inner life) of Juan de Palafox y Mendoza (1600–1659); and the *Vida interior* of Fray Joseph de San Benito (1654–1723). The existence and character of these texts suggest a number of hypotheses concerning the relationship of gender to genre, all of which indicate that maleness and femaleness do not divide the *vida* genre neatly in two, but that they do affect its form in discernibly different ways.

The context in which this confessional and spiritual genre is produced lends itself to values more frequently associated with the feminine, though not exclusive to women—for example, humility, submission, and an emotive relationship with the Divine. In this case it appears that the genre of the work rather than the gender of the author determines the norms of self-representation. However, while the *vida espiritual* was exercised by both men and women, the vast majority of its authors were women. Randolph Pope's analysis of the autobiographies of early modern Spain provides one explanation for this feminizing of the genre: the options of self-portrayal for religious men were much broader than for women, as they could and did show themselves unproblematically to be historical agents within a worldly realm of economic and political maneuverings. Some did not even make excuses for highly self-congratulatory narratives. Thus, if both men and women could be called to write themselves into the constraints of the *vida* genre, men had more options for self-expression, while women's limited choices led them more frequently into the types of self-representation required by the *vida*.

My initial study of these male texts also indicates that the genre did not lead to entirely similar expressions of subjectivity between male and female protagonists but rather produced a definite, though complexly gendered, difference. For the purpose of comparison, I recall here the primary characteristics of the *vida* genre as exercised by women religious writers:

- an alternating denigration and elevation of the self as either vile or divinely blessed, in response to the genre's demand on the author to judge herself and her life and the contrary desire for self-expression,
- the writing of the self into authorized hagiographical scripts, including those of mysticism, spiritually significant illness, and the lives of officially sanctioned foremothers,
- a self-conscious treatment of writing as anxiety producing, and as an act of obedience and martyrdom,
- repeated divine affirmation of the task of writing and of the subject's actions,
- the centrality of the Devil in establishing the authority to write and to name spiritual experiences,
- the key role of the confessor in authorizing the text,
- the elaboration of feminine figures of authority,
- and the frequently troublesome character of living in "this world."

Of the six male texts, the writings of Saint Ignatius of Loyola are the least difficult to distinguish from female self-representation. Unpublished until 1892, *The Spiritual Journal* ([1544–45] 1958) transcribes Saint Ignatius's personal experiences in practicing his own spiritual exercises (Ignatius of Loyola 1958). Recorded systematically by the days of the week, these journal entries narrate a spiritual and often mystic journey in which Saint Ignatius seeks to identify and embrace God's will. Tears become the most salient sign of Saint Ignatius's encounter with that divine will:

Tuesday [February 19th].—Last night I went to bed with the thought of examining what I would do in celebrating Mass or how. On awaking in the morning and beginning my examination of conscience and prayer, with a great and abundant flood of tears, I felt much devotion with many intellectual lights and spiritual remembrances of the Most Holy Trinity, which quieted me and delighted me immensely, even to producing a pressure in my chest, because of the intense love I felt for the Most Holy Trinity. This gave me confidence, and I determined to say the Mass of the Most Holy Trinity, to see what I should do later. I had had the same feelings while vesting, with lights from the Trinity. I got up and made a short meditation not without tears, and later much devotion and spiritual confidence to say successively six or more Masses of the Most Holy Trinity. (Ignatius of Loyola [1544–45] 1958, 12–13)

The author indicates no confessorial relationship as the context of writing, little internal conflict, much tranquility, self-affirmation, expression of an emotional spirituality, and an abundance of confidence in the interpretation of God's movements of his soul. Periods of spiritual doubt or aridity are brief and quickly overcome, and the "tempter" makes few appearances. The purpose of the text is primarily to identify God's will rather than to explore the emotional experience of God in and of itself.

Saint Ignatius's *Autobiography* expresses similar self-confidence. Dictated to a scribe at the request of colleagues—not in obedience to a confessor—the text is written in the third person, thus distancing the historical Ignatius of Loyola from the act of self-representation. Saint Ignatius yielded to the request, believing it his duty to show how God had guided him from his conversion to the present. The result is a text that is unproblematic in its exemplary character. The tale weaves together strands of historic agency with threads of spiritual experiences, as it relates Saint Ignatius's actions leading up to and including the founding of the Jesuit order. Expression of inner anxiety is relegated to the past as the text builds a heroic and saintly pilgrim of God.

Father Luis de la Puente's *Sentimientos y avisos espirituales* and *Meditaciones* on themes from the Ignatian exercises similarly chronicle his spiritual experiences, producing a mystically received knowledge of doctrinal content and taking on the apostolic privilege without fear or confusion.[55] Both texts appear clearly structured for teaching purposes and were given to Madre Castillo expressly with the intention of aiding her in her spiritual journey. The *Sentimientos,* while describing personal experiences of spirituality, are ordered thematically on topics such as obedience; humility; self-knowledge; God's providence, presence, and omnipotence; suffering; the Eucharist; mortification; and abnegation. De la Puente has given many of the sections Latin titles that express these concepts. One section is titled "Exercise to rise by degrees to the height of contemplation"; another is "Spiritual advice taken from prayer and meditation." The *Meditaciones* are even more explicitly paradigmatic, as De la Puente takes the Ignatian exercises and explores their application, alternating between the use of an impersonal subject and a first-person example. For instance, in the "Exercise for experiencing confusion and contrition for sins," he begins with the impersonal instruction, "[The] *first point:* rides on the consideration of the Immensity and infinite Wisdom of God, with his great purity. Imagining that Our Lord God is a substance of immense grandeur," and passes to the more personal application, referring to himself as example: "And to imagine myself, like a worm or mite, within this Divine Immensity, so full of eyes, and that within it, and in his sight, I committed all my past sins, and I commit the current ones, and with them, provoking him to anger, repugnance and vomit" (Puente [1671], 1958, 336).[56] His topics are common to women's autobiographical writing. Much of his prose in the *Sentimientos* is ardently expressive of his emotional encounter with the Divine, and at times it is self-deprecating, describing feelings of doubt and self-worthlessness. His narrative voice, however, emits confidence, and the act of writing remains neither explicitly examined nor framed as an act of obedience.

The case of Palafox y Mendoza is more complex and breaks down more than that of de la Puente the absolute clarity of gender distinction in the *vida* genre. A powerful though controversial figure, Palafox y Mendoza received a position on the Council of Indies at the age of twenty-six.[57] He later brought a fervent reformism to his duties as bishop of Puebla and to a brief stint as Viceroy of Mexico. His ardent activities on behalf of the Crown and the diocese, attempting to force the Jesuits to pay tithes on their immense wealth, embroiled him in a deep conflict that lasted from 1641 to 1649. The struggle involved his temporary excommunication and secret refuge, but eventually he received the support of Felipe IV and Pope Innocent X (Simmons 1966, 402).

Despite his great power, Palafox y Mendoza produces some of the most self-deprecating language of the three male *vidas,* calling himself "this poor worm, dirt, dust, nothing, prostrate with full heart, powers, faculties, and feelings" (1772, 10).[58] He introduces laments throughout his text with the words, "this sinner weeps."[59] The illnesses he suffers link his subjectivity to that of many female *vida* writers. He is ridiculed for his radical religiosity (chap. 5, par. 2, 68) and persecuted by the Devil (chap. 17, par. 10, 78), and he desires to suffer the passion of Christ (par. 11), all characteristics shared by most female *vida* writers. His description of his sermonizing—a male prerogative—takes on a feminine touch when he becomes a vessel of God's authorship and preaches without preparation (chap. 7, par. 8, 252). He describes highly emotional moments charged with physical sensation—"his love has grown to such an extent that sometimes, if his inner affects do not erupt through his eyes, it seems to him that they will explode his breast; and until he sheds tears, and with this he unleashes his heart, the soul suffers a great deal in these inner movements" (chap. 36, par. 2, 242).[60] But, as is evident in this description, much of the text is written in the third person, interspersed with apostrophic exclamations directed to God in the voice of a first-person "I."

In fact, the entire framing of the narrative differs from that of the feminine *vidas* and is clearly directed toward publication. Palafox omits his and others' names that would identify him as the author, though the published controversy that followed the appearance of his *Vida interior* belies this tactic. Both Palafox's anonymous attacker and his defender, Fray Juan de la Anunciación, recognize that his identity could not be so easily hidden (Anunciación 1698, 43, no. 8). Palafox's opponent, evidently intending to impede his beatification, attacks his supposed holiness in pointing out that Palafox wrote with his confessor's permission but not his mandate. In this way he accuses Palafox of writing to earn praise (Anunciación 1698, 12, no. 2; 31, no. 5). Palafox himself gives five reasons for writing the *Vida* that include a clear intention for both publication and exemplarity of the tale (1772, chap. 1, 15–16). His first motive is to glorify God and to move others with his example to love God. His second justification is that, "having consulted with his confessors, they judged it useful and important; as it would not be published while this poor sinner yet lived, nor afterwards, except maintaining ignorance of his name, and hiding as much as possible about the identity of the subject" (chap. 1, 15).[61] His third and fourth motives are personal and are the most like those of female *vida* writers, as they involve his need as a sinner to keep his sins constantly in his thoughts and to live between fear and hope. The fifth reason takes up the divine self-affirmation shared by women writers: God has instructed him to write his mercies and has threatened his anger if Palafox does not comply. Palafox exhibits no confusion about the task of writing in the text and accentuates its character as instructional model in the fifty-six pages of chapter 41 titled "Of the daily [routine], and the exercises in which he occupies himself twenty-four hours a day when he is not carrying out his official visits."[62]

Fray Joseph de San Benito's *Vida* expresses more humility about writing. His motivation for writing is the illumination that he has received through mystic experience (1746, 22). He explains that he began to record this knowledge for his own use, though when he was moved to write further about the occurrences, he experienced both repugnance and excitement at the thought. Eventually, he felt compelled by the knowledge that had been communicated to him to record the experiences more extensively. At this juncture other people advised him to write, but he feared deceit from the Devil, who tried to persuade him that what he had written was false, that it put him at grave risk, and that he should burn it. The voice of the author in the present expresses no doubt concerning the veracity of what he writes. From his vantage point it is clear that the Devil's intervention signified an attack on the truth that he had been faithfully reporting. In contrast to texts by religious women authors, Fray Joseph limits his references to the act of writing to two moments rather than allowing anxiety to permeate the text as a whole.

For Fray Joseph, the confessor functions peripherally to motivate the writing, the command to write being mentioned only at two points in the narrative, but neither the confessor nor others are brought in to authorize the text. The entire framing of the narrative diverges from that of its feminine counterparts. In a note that follows the main body of the text, Fray Joseph presents the circumstances under which he writes the *Vida*. Although he is "reprehended and persuaded that he should write the present treatise," a second request is necessary before he can overcome his repugnance to the task:

"Being, then, unmindful of this, I was commanded to write in the present year of 1706" (1746, 41).[63] Even the second order is not sufficient and he has to be persuaded by "appropriate reasons." Unlike the female authors, he directs the text not to his confessor but to an unnamed audience that includes "whoever at any time after my death reads this."[64] Obedience as the sole motive for writing is displaced, and in its stead stands the glorification of God and of Mary, the queen of heaven and earth (1). Finally, the text is framed by an introductory note in Latin in which it is directed to God as its originating will.[65]

This exploration of the *vida espiritual,* its theoretical considerations and their manifestations in the texts, has identified a number of defining elements. These elements are embedded in a historically specific and gendered context of power within which the genre emerged. Deployed by the Church in an attempt to coerce a radical religious subjectivity into submission, the genre allowed the development of the very subjectivity that posed a threat to Church authority, thus revealing conflict in the mere act of the writers to authorize their texts. This arena of conflict genders the *vida* when carried out by women. Its marks include a vacillation between confession and affirmation, a painful self-consciousness about the act of writing, a widely shared repertoire of feminine scripts and rhetorical strategies, an explicit struggle with the evils of the world, and an engagement with the contemporary construction of holiness through the biographical tradition. When men enter this discursive realm, their stories share only a few of the constraints manifested in the texts of their spiritual sisters. Overwhelmingly, male writers chose other genres that were either closed to women or much more dangerous for them to enter: those genres that depended on a scholastic argument rather than personal experience, a reasoned rather than an infused knowledge, authority rather than instrumentality. Yet, in spite of the daunting confines of gender, women's exercise of the *vida* genre could and did earn them posthumous fame and lives of power. The tightrope, when deftly walked, promised both salvation and inscription into popular memory. Meeting the challenge with creativity, devotion, and skill, these authors filled their texts with politically and personally effective prophecies and admirable actions and often took up, within their texts, that apostolic privilege Saint Paul sought to deny them as they wrote spiritual treatises and biblical commentaries into the stories of their lives.

PART

II

CONTEXTS

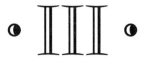

RELIGIOUS WOMEN'S WRITING
IN SPAIN AND SPANISH AMERICA

[The Lord] ordered, that by the very same hand of the tormented María be written the notice of her spiritual guidance: this being the greatest torture of her martyrdom; because it seemed to her that she feigned everything that she wrote, persuaded that the Lord would not speak through such a vile instrument and unworthy hand.

—PEDRO CALVO DE LA RIBA,
Historia de la singular vida de . . . Sor María Gertrudis Theresa de Santa Inés[1]

THE PAST FIFTEEN years have seen exciting work accomplished in unearthing manuscripts, revisiting published works, and shedding new light on the tradition and strategies of women's writing in Spain and Spanish America. A few recent critical works have offered an overview of the critical field or the corpus of nuns' writings, as do Electa Arenal and Stacey Schlau's *Untold Sisters* (1989) and Kathleen A. Myers's bibliographical essay in *Word from New Spain* (1993), but the body of scholarship in new areas is rapidly growing. In this brief chapter, I wish to review both primary and secondary texts, adding some works that have appeared since 1993 and showing women's writing as an historical tradition. My intentions are twofold. Most importantly, I am breaking Madre Castillo's isolation by returning her to the context in which she wrote and showing the history of a tradition that profoundly shaped her thought. I also hope to offer a representative—rather than exhaustive—view of the state of critical scholarship to any who might enter the field through this book.

Few women wrote in the European Middle Ages, during which reading and writing were privileged activities, and yet the era witnessed the emergence of a number of great female scholars and mystics. The best known of the early scholars are Hrotsvit of Gandersheim (c. 932–c. 1000), dramatist and poet, and Hildegard of Bingen (1098–1179), whose *Scivias* (1152) combines both scientific learning and spiritual insight. These women wrote in the time before the intellectual pursuits of women began to lose ground through the growth of the exclusively male university in the twelfth century. The late Middle Ages saw growing limitations on women's roles in the Church and a decline in the quality of intellectual preparation in the convents. Turning their search for knowledge from scholarly treatises to the "interior castle," a significant number of visionary women writers wrought profound effects on the religious and secular politics of their times, as well as on the future of their religious orders and women's self-representation.[2] Among these late-medieval women were Mechthild of Magdeburg (1207–82), Saint Gertrude the Great (1241–98), Saint Clare of Assisi (1196–1253), the Blessed Angela of Foligno (1248–1309), Saint Bridget of Sweden (c. 1303–73), Julian of Norwich (b. 1342), Saint Catherine of Siena (1347–80), Christine de Pizan (1364–c. 1429), and Margery Kempe (1373–1439). Much of their writings recount personal visions whose messages are spiritual and political. Saint Clare's *Testament* left instructions for her spiritual daughters in the monastic order that she founded. Christine de Pizan wrote texts centered on women's experience and concerns. Margery Kempe produced the first known autobiography in the English language.

The first Spanish texts thought to have been authored by women are found among the eleventh-century Mozarabic *jarchas,* verses of love appended to Hebrew and Arabic poems, but it was not until the fifteenth century that Spanish women writers began to leave a rich legacy (Deyermond 1978, 27–37; 1983, 27). From this period, the earliest text that has received much attention is the *Relación que deja escrita para sus descendientes Leonor de Córdoba* (Written account that Leonor de Córdoba left for her descendants).[3] In her brief testament, Leonor López de Córdoba (c. 1362–c. 1412) gives voice to a lament that her condition as a woman and her status as a member of a royal family bring her suffering. Thus, the impact of gender on lived experience marks Spanish female autobiographical tradition from its inception.

In the time between López de Córdoba's life and that of Saint Teresa of Avila, a number of religious women wrote, leaving evidence that Spanish convents, like their French, German, English, and Italian counterparts, provided centers of learning for women. Ronald Surtz (1995) begins to reconstruct the female literary context that set the stage for Saint Teresa. He examines the prayers, devotional works, and liturgical offices written by Constanza de Castilla (pre-1406–c. 1524), the treatise on the spiritual benefits of illness by Teresa de Cartagena (c. 1420–35 to >1460)—*Arboleda de los enfermos* (Grove of the ill)—and her subsequent defense of her right as a woman to literary expression —*Admiraçion operum Dey* (Awe of God's works), the sermons of Juana de la Cruz (1481–1534), and María de Santo Domingo's (c. 1486–c. 1524) *Libro de oración* (Book of prayer). Surtz's scholarship, and that of Mary Giles in the case of María de Santo Domingo (1990), explore the expression of women's experience by women writers, their battles against silencing forces, and the strategies with which they authorize their acts as women who enter proscribed terrains, such as those of scriptural exegesis, theological prose, preaching, and political advising.

The religious and political climate in sixteenth-century Avila, forged by women such as these as well as by men, helped bring Teresa of Avila to her own mysticism and reform activities. It was a climate infused with the impulse to reform religious institutions and to bring a more personalized religion into common practice. Saint Teresa's foundational role in the Carmelite reformation, and thus her importance to both the Spanish Counter-Reformation and to the hundreds of religious women who patterned their lives and *vidas* after hers, make it necessary to note her works in greater detail. Volumes have been written on the greatest and most influential of the women authors of early modern Spain, but two recent studies, one primarily historical, the other an interdisciplinary examination of her writings, are especially helpful for understanding the legacy she left her female intellectual followers. Jodi Bilinkoff's *The Avila of Saint Teresa* (1989) and Alison Weber's *Teresa of Avila and the Rhetoric of Femininity* (1990) address Saint Teresa's life and writing in their relationship to the complex web of power relations of Spain and Europe during the mid-sixteenth century, relations formed by ideologies of lineage, nobility, and gender and interwoven into specific economic, political, and religious events.

Bilinkoff focuses on the coalescence of two developments. The first is the conflict for power and status between a growing class of non-noble merchants, financiers, and professionals—including many *conversos* (1989, 53)—and the aristocratic class that retained political power on the basis of its nobility and purity of blood (15–52). The second consists of the religious reform movements fomented by leaders such as Cardinal Cisneros, Juan de Avila, Pedro de Alcántara, and the Jesuit order of Saint Ignatius of Loyola. While the climate of reform allowed Saint Teresa to formulate her goals, the rise of a new economic class offered her the necessary means. "Teresa de Ahumada was deeply affected by Avila's reform movements of the mid-sixteenth century. She attempted to adapt the features of apostolic service, religious autonomy, mental prayer, and asceticism, and the reception of direct religious experience, to a female, monastic, and contemplative context" (107). Religious autonomy for the female convent, which would allow the renewal of a long-absent egalitarian atmosphere as well as full development of the interior life of prayer, demanded economic independence from the aristocratic system of monastic patronage. Saint Teresa sought to eliminate the social hierarchies that were so sharply mirrored within the convent of her day, and that led convent communities to focus attention on the worldly questions of status and wealth. She also opposed the custom of noble patronage, which demanded much time and energy from the nuns to say vocal prayers and masses for their benefactors in return for economic support, thus distracting them from their inner spiritual lives. It was the growing prosperity of the heavily *converso* class that provided funding and independence for Saint Teresa's foundations of convents that reformed the order of Discalced Carmelites. Excluded definitively from the top levels of political power in the failure of the 1520 *comunero* revolt (70), this class sought alternative avenues to social status and power, one of which was the support of the reformed convents.

Within this context, Teresa of Avila's actions were highly charged with political and religious consequence. As she carved out a space of autonomy for women, she confronted and threatened the powerful Spanish nobility. When she developed a method of mental prayer, she took on the authority of the Church. Saint Teresa risked danger of association with the *alumbrados,* whose troubles stemmed from their emphasis on a personal spirituality, a visionary life, and independence from the clergy. Founding communities of Discalced Carmelites and training her female followers in a life of inner spirituality, Teresa of Avila carefully, but radically, rejected the misogynist control of the Counter-Reformation that denied women the authority of the written word and apostolic privilege. Her life and works boldly and repeatedly challenged the oft-cited Pauline dictum that women remain silent in the Church (1 Cor. 14:34).

Alison Weber also recognizes the importance of Teresa of Avila's political allies in accounting for her success in the high-stakes gamble that would transform her posthumously from object of the Inquisition in 1589 to saint in 1622 (1990, 3, 35), but she insists that this political explanation is only partial. Taken alone, it ignores the key role played by the rhetorical strength of Saint Teresa's writing in the defense of her life work and authorship (5). Weber examines each of the reformer's works, identifying the gender-marked rhetorical strategies that mold each book to the context of its writing, its audience, and its specific content. She discusses a complex rhetoric of humility in Saint Teresa's autobiographical *Libro de la vida.* She demonstrates how *Camino de perfección,* written for the nuns of the first Discalced Carmelite convent that Saint Teresa founded, utilizes the double register of irony; self-effacing for male readers, it effectively teaches the female in-group. In *Las moradas* (The interior castle), Saint Teresa tackles the dangerous task of providing a treatise on mental prayer, disguising her daring in a careful rhetoric of obfuscation that appears merely to be "women's chatter" (Weber 1990, 109). The *Libro de las fundaciones* reflects Saint Teresa's consolidation of alliances and authority, but it also reveals her ambivalence toward authority. "One of the central paradoxes of Teresa's life is that she fought so long and so persistently against hierarchical authority precisely in order to return her order to a much more authoritarian monastic rule" (Weber 1990, 123). Teresa of Avila enclosed her followers within tight walls and "made Spain safe for the Counter Reformation" (Arenal and Schlau, 1989b, 10), but she also gave her emulators a written record of how she constantly skirted danger and exceeded her own prescriptions.

Nuns of the Discalced Carmelite order carried on Saint Teresa's legacy with a passion. Ana de San Bartolomé (1549–1626) and María de San José (1548–1603) developed close relationships with the reformer during her lifetime and continued the active work of foundations in a climate of controversy, negotiating doggedly through and around the obstacles posed by a male ecclesiastical hierarchy. Their lives impacted the reform movement as they also suffered personal persecution. They dedicated their intellects to chronicling this history and to continuing their founder's passion for instructing and molding the order. The Discalced Carmelites María de San Alberto (1568–1640) and Cecilia del Nacimiento (1570–1646) were not convent founders, but rather showed the great intellectual legacy encouraged by Saint Teresa's life in her successors. These two sisters of the Sobrino Morillas family lived in the convent of La Concepción in Valladolid and continued in their writings the great humanistic culture to which their intellectual mother introduced them. Their deeply collaborative work includes scriptural translation, poetry, biography and autobiography, spiritual narrative, theater, theological treatise, letters, and family history. Arenal and Schlau explore the historical significance of the lives and writings of these immediate heirs of the saint of Avila and, each in her own way, defenders of the intellectual rights of women (1989b).

Nuns of the Augustinian Recollect convents, like the Discalced Carmelites, were intensely involved in lives of prayer, mysticism, and convent foundation. Founder Mariana de San Joseph (1578–1636) crafted spiritual guides for her followers and trod the same treacherous terrain that troubled both Saint Teresa and Saint John of the Cross when she wrote a commentary on the Song of Songs (Myers 1993b, 29). Isabel de Jesús (1586–1648), an illiterate shepherdess who professed as an Augustinian Recollect, dictated her autobiography to Inés del Santísimo Sacramento. Typical of *vidas,* her narrative mixes heavenly and earthly planes, but "demonstrates an originality and boldness rare even among women mystics" in an erotically charged union with a feminized Christ (Arenal and Schlau 1989b, 202–3). Her *Vida* proves that while the posterity granted by authorship was more accessible to the elite, women of various social classes attended the gathering of holy writers during these years. Her shepherding niece, Isabel de la Madre de Dios (1614–87), also entered the convent of the Augustinian Recollect and founded new communities in both Serradilla and Calzada de Oropesa. Madre Isabel's *Manifestaciones* provide a classic example of the divine affirmation received by mystics for works that further the glory of God on earth. Written between 1656 and 1665, her mystic experiences chronicle her journey to found the convent at Serradilla, the numerous obstacles she faced on her path, and God's repeated blessing and instructions regarding the foundation.

The *Vida* of the Cistercian nun Doña María Vela y Cueto (1561–1617) foreshadows the painful expressions of self that become particularly characteristic of the writings of many Spanish American nuns. Jodi Bilinkoff suggests that Doña María's problem was to have lived at the wrong time. By her time, the era of Saint Teresa with its positive—albeit careful—reception of women engaged in radical religiosity was giving way to greater antagonism (Bilinkoff 1989, 184–85). An aristocrat who took on the style of a humble *beata* (devout lay nun) in a Cistercian convent uninterested in Saint Teresa's austere rule, Doña María was considered a fraud by many during her lifetime. In her spiritual autobiography, she admits her own vileness but also emerges as a martyr of religious conflict, as she continually struggles for power and authority in her relationships with confessors and other superiors. Her return to a more medieval expression of religiosity, with its extremes of penitence and mortification in her imitation of the suffering Christ, will become common in Spanish America.[4]

Two more prominent writers bear mention before we leave the literary scene in Spanish convents; these are the Conceptionist María de Jesús de Agreda (1602–65) and the Discalced Trinitarian Marcela de San Félix (1605–87). Agreda's biography of Mary, *Mystica ciudad de Dios,* was published in numerous editions and translations, becoming embroiled in long controversies over its orthodoxy. This portrait of the mother of God, which attributes prominence and leadership to her actions both before and after Christ's death, was widely read by female monastic communities and offered many subsequent writers a justification for feminine authority.[5] Clark Colahan (1994) translates and studies a number of Agreda's lesser known but fascinating works including her *Face of the Earth and Map of the Spheres,* a report of her missionary travels to New Mexico by mystic bilocation, and *The Crucible of Trials* (a later prologue to *Face of the Earth*), in which she expresses a purifying anguish akin to that found in many nuns' *vidas.* Marcela de San Félix's literary interests diverge sharply from those of Agreda's. The daughter of the playwright Lope de Vega and Micaela Luján excels in theater and poetry, using humor to critique the patriarchal view of convents and nuns, and belying the "image of women as beatific angels," to parody her "father's pompous pretensions regarding lineage" and to ridicule national obsessions such as the hunting out of *conversos* and witches (Arenal and Schlau 1989b, 238, 240). Sor Marcela writes to entertain while she educates her audience.[6]

The Mexican historian Josefina Muriel pioneered the study of religious women's writing in Spanish America with her 1946 study of the convents of New Spain. Her more recent *Cultura femenina novohispana* (1982) provides a rich bibliography of Mexican nuns' writings. The *vidas* that Muriel describes include those of the Hieronymite María Magdalena Lorravaquio Muñoz (1576–1636), who spent most of her life suffering grave illnesses and experiencing mystic transports from her sickbed, the Conceptionist María de Jesús Tomelín (1574–1637), and the aristocratic Sebastiana de las Vírgenes Villanueva Cervantes Espinosa de los Monteros (1671–1737).[7] The scholarship of Kathleen Ann Ross, Electa Arenal and Stacey Schlau, Manuel Ramos Medina, Kathleen A. Myers, and Jennifer Lee Eich complement that of Muriel in constructing a full and vibrant picture of the variety of life experiences and social backgrounds of New Spain's literary nuns. These nuns took up their Spanish sisters' traditions of recording convent history through biographies and chronicles, and they included not only white *criollas* and Spaniards but also the Indian daughters of *caciques* (nobility).[8]

Three very prolific nuns wrote in the Viceroyalty of New Spain, the most famous being, of course, the Hieronymite Juana Inés de la Cruz (1648–95), whose poetic and dramatic genius was recognized and included in the literary canon long before feminist scholarship began to tease out its complexity. A defense of women's intellectual activity runs throughout Sor Juana's work, alongside a scathing though often cleverly occult criticism of the bars placed around women's minds.[9] Less well known than Sor Juana is the Augustinian María de San José, who spent three decades writing her life story in twelve volumes that comprise more than two thousand pages. The first volume of her *vida,* edited by Kathleen A. Myers, offers a fascinating glimpse into the everyday life and childhood of a Mexican girl (María de San José 1993).[10] Myers reads this *vida* as a "paradigm of the forging of a feminine Creole identity" with its "tensions and contradictions—between the ideal and the personal; rhetoric and colloquial language; authority and the individual; the body and spirit; orthodoxy and mysticism; the Spanish and Creole" (1993b, 54). Her proposition that the text anticipates the development of Creole identity prompts the related question of how we define any of these texts in terms of national identity: is there a corpus that can be called Spanish American convent literature? While Sor Juana's writing brings to the fore the cultural and racial particularities of a colonial Mexican rather than solely Spanish context, the *vidas* of other writing nuns are not always so forthright. All of the genres and models taken up by Spanish American religious women are inherited from Spain, while even Indian daughters of *caciques* demonstrate a strong cultural alienation in their internalization of Spanish ideologies (Arenal and Schlau 1989b, 357). Yet the works inject peninsular discourse with colloquialisms; they engage with the politics and economics particular to their colonial situations, and they frequently paint their devils with the racial typings specific to the colonial world. The implications of these possible elements of *criollismo* in the texts still require much study.

Finally, the Dominican Recollect María Anna Agueda de San Ignacio (1695–1756) did not follow the more common path of *vida* writing but dedicated herself intentionally to the realm of theology (so treacherous when manipulated by feminine hands), having received official permission to do such work (Eich 1992, 68). Jennifer Lee Eich attributes the freedom the Mexican nun assumes in usurping the apostolic privilege of teaching to her "demonstrated power as an intellectual and scholar of sacred texts and her adherence to traditional sacred rhetoric," but Eich also discusses a textual process that gives authority to her Marian ideology. The Mexican nun imbues her first two treatises with a daringly sermonic quality, by substantiating them with hagiographical, biblical, and scriptural sources (165) as well as by imitating in them the forms of authorization common in male discourse (76). While in her third treatise she gives the more acceptably feminine explanation of mysticism as the source of the knowledge contained therein, this mystic framing is boldly absent from the first two treatises. Throughout her texts, María Anna Agueda constructs an alternate and active model of femininity in her reading of Mary's role in conversion and salvation and in her own modeling of interpretive authority.

Leaving New Spain for the South, we find the unearthed texts to be few and far between. Arenal and Schlau have studied the Peruvian Antonia Lucía del Espíritu Santo (1646–1709), who boldly appropriated male roles when she named her new order with the female version of the titles of "apostles" and "Nazarenes" (1989b, 357). Madre Antonia Lucía also stirred up controversy in designing a habit that expressed not the feminine role of bride of Christ but an imitation of Christ's passion in its use of a purple tunic, a rope around the neck, and a crown of thorns (306). This founder plays the protagonist in the patchwork text compiled by the convent's historian, Josefa de la Providencia (seventeenth century), which incorporates a three-page report of a prophetic vision written by Madre Antonia Lucía (1793). The manuscripts of another writer from Lima have been brought recently into the scholarly light by Elia Armacanqui Ticpacti (1993), but a full study of the *Vida* and *Correspondencia espiritual y poesías* of María Manuela de Santa Ana (1695–1793) has yet to be published.

From Colombia, the only autobiographical writings by colonial nuns available in twentieth-century publications are Madre Castillo's *Su vida* (1968) and the narrations of the Poor Clare Jerónima del Espíritu Santo Nava i Saavedra (1669–1727) and the white-veiled Discalced Carmelite María de Jesús (ca. 1696–ca. 1767) (Nava 1994; María de Jesús 1947). The reported *vida* written by Madre Castillo's correspondent, the mystic Francisca María del Niño Jesús (1665–1708), and that of María Gertrudis Theresa de Santa Inés of the convent of Santa Inés in Santa Fe (Bogotá) (1668–1730) form the basis for eighteenth-century biographies but have not resurfaced in the twentieth century.[11]

Women in the Nuevo Reino de Granada also wrote founding documents for their convents. Doña Elvira de Padilla's constitutions for the Discalced Carmelite Convento de San José in Bogotá (1947, 140–51), and Magdalena de Jesús's constitutions for the Poor Clares of Pamplona (1722) show the active negotiation by women with the male ecclesiastical hierarchy over how life was to be lived within the convent walls.

Finally, a single published nun writer from Chile is recognized in recent scholarship: Ursula Suárez (1666–1749). Kathleen A. Myers gives a fascinating analysis of this text, which is highly unusual in its use of the picaresque (1993a; Suárez 1984). While before her Saint Teresa occasionally played the holy *pícara,* Sor Ursula's entire narrative is founded on an interweaving of the genres of the picaresque novel and the spiritual autobiography, delighting in a transgression that escapes the final pessimistic closure of the novel but ends all the same with the confessor's dismissal of the nun's word. With her juxtaposition of transgression and silencing, Sor Ursula emits a strong protest against the breaking of her spirit in the vise grip of the Church. While Sor Ursula closes this presentation of the literary world of the convents in Spain and colonial Spanish America, the present state of scholarship promises to burst it open again immediately. There are yet many texts to discover and a world of knowledge about women's intellectual life and writing to be found in convent and national archives and in private collections.[12]

· IV ·

FEMALE MONASTICISM
A LIFE UNBECOMING?

I found that the convent was going to ruin in full haste: in terms of its income, indebted to great amounts; the archive, with no paper; nor anywhere from which to obtain information of anything, because everything was the responsibility of the syndic and he said that he had nothing, and that if a load of firewood was to be bought, it would have to be by pawning a cloak or sword. There were many disputed cases and very distressing ones, and everything was so confusing, and in my view so off track, that I knew not what to do but to cry out to Our Lord and to the Mother of life and mercy, Most Holy Mary. I found myself ignorant of everything; not even the manner of speaking with laypeople did I know.

—Madre Castillo, *Su vida*[1]

MADRE CASTILLO builds her life story on that embattled Counter-Reformation terrain that comprehended the feminine and the religious. She is a subject produced on this ground of discourses and practices, beneath which the memories of a more powerful feminine possibility remain.[2] She is an author whose agency produces new subjectivities for herself out of these potentially treacherous, potentially triumphal elements. The discourses range from official Church doctrine that seeks to contain women, to powerful legal language associated with abbesses through the documents they signed, to formulas for writing the lives of saints and the mystic traditions of sixteenth-century Spain. The terrain becomes treacherous when Madre Castillo chooses to allow into her *Vida* the cultural practices that occupy her daily life and that contradict the dominant prescription for holy femininity, that is, to be without authority and "dead to the world."

In her texts, Madre Castillo juxtaposes the contradictory elements of experience lived in this world and Church discourses that would exise her from the world. To the postmodern eye, the resulting self-portrait turns on the axis of conflict. Her self-portrayal communicates the impossibility for her to live out in a unified self the demands made on her as woman, nun, abbess, and writer. A few of the sharpest conflicts can be explained by historical changes in the definition of the feminine, wherein accepted spheres of activity had become greatly diminished by Madre Castillo's time while the stories of hagiographical tradition kept alive a memory of greater possibilities. To appreciate the force of this collective memory, which must have awakened in her desires for greater agency than the Church explicitly allowed, it is helpful to survey feminine monastic history beginning in the Middle Ages. To understand the contradiction Madre Castillo felt between the model nun of hagiographic tradition and the concrete demands of convent life, it is necessary to examine the specific social situation of her own Convento Real de Santa Clara in Tunja.

With information and representations collected from Colombian historical and archival sources, I lay out those elements of convent life that structured the conflicts of Madre Castillo's self-portrayal in her *Vida*. Key materials include convent legal documents from the Archivo Regional de Boyacá, Madre Castillo's account books from two terms as abbess, records of professions, elections, and canonical visits from the archive of the present-day Monasterio de Santa Clara in Tunja, and *Flor de santidad*, the biography of Madre Castillo written in the 1940s by the late Poor Clare from Tunja, María Antonia del Niño Dios (1993). In this historiographical portrait of the convent and, in chapter 5, of Madre Castillo herself, I do not pretend to provide an empirical base against which to compare Madre Castillo's texts. All versions of the life of convent and writer, whether written by Madre Castillo, convent secretaries, colonial notaries, or myself as critic are likenesses and not truths. Nevertheless, each one is real and operates forcefully within a culture to define and to remember the institutions, individuals, beliefs, and practices it addresses.

THE MIDDLE AGES: A HISTORY OF FEMALE AUTONOMY

Convent life in the eighteenth-century Nuevo Reino de Granada retained a relatively small measure of the autonomy, political activity, and cultural, artistic, and intellectual life that female monasticism had enjoyed during its early European history. Biographies of female saints and model nuns written during the early modern period precluded the representation of the more autonomous and secular aspects of earlier convent life, yet memories survived. These memories remained in practices of female self-governance, though with reduced strength, and in occasional problematic palimpsests, stories of this more powerful past, keyholes through which eighteenth-century religious women writers glimpsed female paradigms that exceeded contemporary restrictions.

A century ago, Lina Eckenstein traced the imposition of limits on nuns' activities as they grew progressively throughout the history of the Church up to and including the time of the Reformation and Counter-Reformation. She begins *Woman under Monasticism* (1896) with the sixth century, when contact with Roman culture offered advantages to male nobles of the invading Anglo-

Saxons but created domestic difficulties for their female partners. These women began to choose the convents of Roman Catholic culture over marriage (45). Often double convents or communities of nuns and monks were ruled by powerful abbesses who ranked only below bishops in the Church hierarchy (87). These women, not limited by vows of enclosure, included famed scholars, strong political movers, and powerful feudal ladies. They were less encumbered by the expression of misogyny than their monastic descendants would be. Certainly the suspicion of the daughters of Eve explicit in the fifth-century writings of Saint Augustine had limited Catholic women; and yet, according to Penelope Johnson, this negativity was held back in great measure until the twelfth century, "when a hostile backlash slammed the door on female monastic equality" (1991, 5).

Women exercised powerful leadership in Anglo-Saxon monasticism of seventh- and eighth-century England; they studied scriptures, taught, administered double monasteries that housed men and women, and were not censured for these activities (Browne 1910, 32–39). According to Eckenstein, an abbess of a royal Saxon convent during the tenth and eleventh centuries acted with the power of a feudal lord. "[S]he issued the summons when war had been declared and sent her contingent of armed knights into the field; and she also issued the summons to attend in her courts, where judgment was given by her proctor (*vogt*). In short she had the duties and privileges of a baron who held his property of the king, and as such she was summoned to the Imperial Diet (*reichstag*)" (1896, 152). In France, the status of abbesses, equal to that of feudal lords, granted these women the homage and fealty of their tenants (Johnson 1991, 167). Their convents participated actively in the outer world, founding and running hospitals and almshouses (50). They played an integral role in the structure of the Church rather than the subordinate, auxiliary position they would later hold (62).

While scholarship was rare among women, it was not taboo as would later be the case. The tenth century witnessed the authorship of Hrotsvith of Gandersheim in Saxony, and during the eleventh, another nun at Gandersheim won fame for entering into successful disputation with learned men (Eckenstein 1896, 151). The twelfth century produced such prolific writers as Herrad of Hohenburg, Saint Hildegard of Bingen, and Saint Elisabeth of Schönau.[3] Most importantly, this activity found stature in prominent discourses; a woman author might be unusual, but she was not an aberration or a threat. In the eighth century, the male scholar Ealdhelm praised the women of Barking for their scholarly writings on the Prophets, the Gospels, the Catholic fathers, law, and the rules of grammarians (*De laudibus virginitatis*, quoted in Eckenstein 1896, 113). In the twelfth, the philosopher Abelard praised his lover, Héloïse, for her supreme knowledge, which included a command of Latin, and for her erudition and skills of logic (Abelard and Héloïse 1977, 24). Peter the Venerable, abbot of Cluny, wrote that Héloïse "devoted all her application to knowledge of letters," and told her, "you have surpassed all women in carrying out your purpose, and have gone further than almost every man" (Abelard and Héloïse 1977, 114). He called her a "woman wholly dedicated to philosophy in the true sense" (114).

Between the tenth and early twelfth centuries, the great boom in monastic foundations coincided with an acute decline in the power and intellectual possibilities for nuns (McLaughlin 1974, 243). Following the Norman conquest in 1066, the previously independent Anglo-Saxon abbesses came under the dominating control of male bishops (Robertson 1990, 170–71). Increasingly, male clergy expressed concern about the physical freedom of nuns and "loose women," and consequently an ever-stricter enclosure of women began (Eckenstein 1896, 193; McLaughlin 1974, 243). Concern grew with the increased homelessness caused by the breaking up of the feudal system. Groups of self-appointed nuns who led a popular reclusive life in thirteenth-century England found opposition to their autonomy in the Church hierarchy; controls were imposed on their lives through the restriction of their contact with society and with sacred objects of worship. Male ecclesiastics held up to them the contemplative model of Mary Magdalene to take the place of the worldly activity of her sister Martha.[4] Increased enclosure for women religious placed them in a relationship of total dependence on the male clergy, who represented them in their external business (Johnson 1991, 160), a consequence that would haunt female monasticism for centuries.

Historical changes from the twelfth to the sixteenth centuries brought a severe blow to nuns' economic and political power as demonstrated in the case of the abbess of Huelgas. In 1187 Alfonso VIII organized a Cistercian abbacy at Huelgas near Burgos as the powerful seat of governance for twelve northern Spanish monasteries (Eckenstein 1896, 191; Vañes 1990, 1–23). His invitation the following year to six women prelates along with six abbots to a general chapter at Burgos speaks of the power of women leaders. In 1210 the abbess of Las Huelgas even took upon herself sacerdotal functions (Eckenstein 1896, 191). But this female power was not to last. "In the year 1260 she refused to receive the abbot of Citeaux, whereupon she was excommunicated. After the year 1507 the abbess was no longer appointed for life, but for a term of three years only. Chapters continued to be held under her auspices at Burgos till the Council of Trent in 1545, which forbade women to leave their enclosures" (Helyot 1714, 5: 376). The power and autonomy exercised by nuns through their own control of provincial organization was cut off on the very eve of the expansion of female orders to the New World. Thus, the founding of female orders in Spanish America would involve much greater control by male clergy and would lack the degree of independent female networking that their European predecessors had enjoyed.

During the course of the late Middle Ages, the range of activities open to women was limited not only outside but also within convents. England was famed in the early fourteenth century for the production in its female monasteries of weavings, tapestries, embroidery, painting, and the writing, copying, and illuminating of manuscripts (Eckenstein 1896, 238). By the latter half of the century, however, the concept of religious life narrowed as these arts were taken over by town-based guilds and universities (354). In the late Middle Ages, Latin was still taught in nunneries so that nuns could follow Mass, but their knowledge and use of the language were decreasing (357). In France, in the twelfth century, universities attracted the brightest male religious; but lacking this educational option, women fell behind (Johnson 1991, 147). By the sixteenth century, written instruction in Latin became an area of official feminine exclusion. As women were shut out from certain forms of intellectual exercise during the late Middle Ages, Eckenstein argues, they sought expression in mystic literature (328). It is in this period that Carolyn Walker Bynum locates the development of a radical female religiosity built on a symbolic linkage of the female body to that of Christ (1987). The female body—which would be controlled or repressed to an ever greater extent within its mandated enclosure—became increasingly the expressive focus of the mysticism of these exceptional nuns and nun writers. As certain modes of expression were closed, women sought others, often maintaining their focus on the object of control.

THE COUNTER-REFORMATION: PALIMPSESTS

The most restrictive prescriptions yet for femininity, female monastic life, and literary and artistic representations of both were ushered in by the Protestant Reformation and the Catholic Counter-Reformation, the latter led by the decrees of the Council of Trent (1545–63). Protestants attacked the unmarried status, narrowing the feminine ideal to that of wife and mother (Eckenstein 1896, 432). The Council of Trent added perpetual enclosure to the nuns' vows of obedience, chastity, and poverty. Teresa of Avila traveled across Spain to found Discalced Carmelite convents, discovering ways to exceed in her own actions the Council's strictures in her provision of constitutions for her monastic daughters that opposed the very mobility she exercised. Her reformation of convent life sought to remove nuns from preoccupation with the temporal realm in order to free them for total dedication to their inner spiritual lives, through a mendicant or unendowed status like that established for the Franciscans in the thirteenth century by Saint Francis and Saint Clare. A lack of property was also to remove them from engagement with constant financial negotiations. What the community did own was to be held in common. Teresa of Avila also worked to remove worldly concerns from the convent atmosphere by creating a more egalitarian community—for example, eliminating the use of social titles within the convent in order to suppress the awareness of social differences that permeated and divided life in the convents of her day (Bilinkoff 1989, 127). The Discalced Carmelite community was limited to thirteen nuns; and though more nuns were later allowed, the size was always kept small in order to avoid divisive factions and politicking.

In Spanish America, the contemplative ideals promulgated by Saint Teresa became the model for many nuns; but her opposition to property could not be endorsed by convents, which were required by the Crown to guarantee their own subsistence through endowments. Spanish American nun writers describe lives spent both in silent contemplation and in voicing the prayers of the Divine Office required by the rule and by their obligations to donors. The tension between vocal and mental prayer is evident in the *vidas* of Saint Teresa's American followers, who seek their highest realization in silent contemplation but in so doing often bring upon themselves the criticism of their sisters for their radical religiosity.

While the Counter-Reformation excised, sanitized, and co-opted representations of historically powerful female autonomy and intellectual production, the memory of holy foremothers and the authority they wielded was not obliterated. Saints' lives reveal the historical process of rewriting that accompanied changing canonical values, often erasing older feminine autonomy and intellectuality in later retellings. They also show how pieces of that more powerful feminine past survive in palimpsests, despite changing ideologies. One such story is Pedro de Rivadeneira's retelling of the life of Saint Thecla in his *Flos sanctorum*. Rivadeneira attributes to heretics early versions of her life in which the saint preaches publicly and performs baptisms; these activities, he affirms, do not conform to the state of womanhood (1601, 357). On the other hand, "unwomanly" moments do slip by his purifying pen as he allows Mary Magdalene to preach publicly and to live thirty years alone in the desert (48–57), and as he recounts Catherine of Alexandria's victory over the wisest philosophers of the times in a disputation over the existence of God (610–17).

That these remnants of women's history found resonance with the search by nuns of the Counter-Reformation for feminine figures of authority is borne out in the writings of María de Jesús de Agreda and Juana Inés de la Cruz in the seventeenth century. In Sor María's *Mystica ciudad de Dios* (1670), woman is allowed to assert authority over man in Mary's teaching of Joseph. As her son's disciple, Mary becomes a mobile evangelist. She is primarily responsible for spreading the Good News when she calls on the apostles to take up the task of writing the Gospels. It is she who, through Sor María, now communicates her own story to a world woefully in need of spiritual renewal, and it is Sor María who actively takes up the pen to communicate the story of renewed salvation. Mexico's Sor Juana demonstrated her clear reading of a powerful feminine past by drawing forth a litany of scholarly foremothers in her eloquent defense of the education of women, the "Respuesta a Sor Filotea." Here Sor Juana parades before those in the Church who would silence women the wise female writers and political leaders of the Bible and ancient Rome, as well as powerful European noblewomen (1957, 4: 461–62). She understood the power of the stories of Saint Catherine of Egypt, Saint Gertrude the Great, and Saint Bridget of Sweden and the authority of those exceptional writers of more recent times: Saint Teresa and María de Jesús de Agreda (4: 467).[5]

The female saints who populate Madre Castillo's texts are not the powerful medieval baronesses and scholar-abbesses whose lives Eckenstein rereads, but they are models of feminine authority and thereby undergird Madre Castillo's own exercise of power. They are the nurturers and mystics of the twelfth through the sixteenth centuries: Saint Clare of Assisi (1193–1253), Saint Elisabeth of Hungary (1207–31), Saint Catherine of Siena (1347–80), Saint Teresa of Avila (1515–82), Saint Mary Magdalene of Pazzis (1566–1607), and Saint Rose of Lima (1586–1617). At least two of these women, Saint Catherine and Saint Teresa, resist confinement within the prevailing model of the Church of the Counter-Reformation. Stories about Catherine of Siena recounted her wide travels, her arbitration of feuds, and her exhortations to towns (Butler 1756–59, 125–29). Readers knew that she authored a book of conversations and engaged in personal conferences and correspondence with the Pope, advising him on the political battles of the schism. Madre Castillo must have found support for the political import of her visionary life in her understanding of Saint Catherine's model. Despite misogynist suspicion of women's authority, Saint Teresa became known as a *doctora mystica* (Arbiol y Diez 1724, 395). Madre Castillo's reading of her *Fundaciones* foreshadows in her own *Vida* her preoccupation with the politically charged activity of convent reform. Her use of mystic discourse shares with that of Saint Teresa a pedagogical character in a Church in which teaching by women was at best a questionable activity. If from the twelfth century to the Counter-Reformation the male hierarchy of the Church time and again reduced the sphere of activities allowed monastic women and attempted to eliminate the memory of the past, their efforts were never entirely successful. Nun writers such as Saint Teresa, María de Jesús de Agreda, Juana Inés de la Cruz, and Madre Castillo were able to read that memory and to draw authorization from it for their exceptional and sometimes transgressive activities.

El Convento Real de Santa Clara desta ciudad de Tunja[6]

The narratives of the ideal consecrated virgin available to Spanish American nuns may have been highly spiritualized, but the enclosure imposed on their lived experience proved permeable. From the pages of Madre Castillo's *Vida* emerges an insistent concern with the strong worldly forces that threaten her

FIGURE I. Main plaza and surrounding hills, Tunja, Department of Boyacá, Colombia, 1996. Photograph by Jorge González ©.

FIGURE 2. Front wall and entry of the Convento Real de Santa Clara, Tunja, 1996. Photograph by Jorge González ©.

salvation because she cannot remove herself from their demands if she is to fulfill her duties as nun and abbess. Three principal aspects of the perilously secular side of convent life addressed in the *Vida* are the laxity of convent rule (partially due to the great social diversity of the convent community), the politicking necessary to win election to the post of abbess, and the contamination with worldly concerns that endangers the soul of the nun who wins the election. These phenomena are the marrow of Spanish American convent historiography: the constant battles of the Church hierarchy against lax clerical and monastic communities, the active involvement of entire towns in the internal elections of their convents, and the economic management involved in sustaining convent life. These are the issues that guide my exposition of the colonial life of the Convento Real de Santa Clara in Tunja as I delineate the specific sources of conflict to which Madre Castillo responds in the *Vida,* whether because she perceives an invasion of worldly concerns into her spiritual life or experiences the gendered conflict of a woman who exercises worldly authority. To this end, my narrative examines the history of her convent's foundation and content of the order's rule, the ritual duties of the community and its involvement in cultural production, the community's social stratification, the demands of convent governance, the economic and political dealings in which nuns were involved on a daily basis, and the implications of the history of Santa Clara's population, economics, and relations with the ecclesiastical hierarchy.

FOUNDATIONS AND RULES

The relaxed observance of the rule in convent life, a complaint implied in much of the scandal recounted in Madre Castillo's narrative, relates to the circumstances of convent foundations in Spanish America. A comparison between the expansion of convent orders in Europe and their expansion overseas is instructive. In Spain and France, for instance, the female branch of the strictly observant Discalced Carmelites was able to maintain strong interconvent connections, which facilitated the order's control, through the founding of new convents by highly regarded members of established convents and through the extensive correspondence engaged in between nuns in distant convents.[7] In contrast, colonial historians emphasize that Spanish American convents responded not primarily to the desires of mother orders for expansion but rather to locally perceived social needs. The founding abbess was often not a nun from a mother convent but a widowed or childless donor. She was trained by male clergy or by the nuns of another order rather than through experience in an established female community (Pacheco 1971; Lavrín 1986). This was not always the case, however; and research on relationships between the nuns of sister convents, such as is exemplified in Madre Castillo's reported correspondence with a Carmelite abbess, could greatly enrich our understanding of female religious culture in colonial times.[8]

While a newly founded convent might lack the experience and guidance of nuns from an older house, lay founders could take great care to establish the appropriate rule themselves. Doña Elvira de Padilla, who founded the Discalced Carmelite convent of San José in Santa Fe in 1606, wrote the convent's constitution drawing on her devout and lifelong study of the works of Saint Teresa (Germán María del Perpetuo Socorro and Martínez 1947, 140). Madre Magdalena de Jesús, the widowed donor and founding mother of the Poor Clare convent in Pamplona, Nuevo Reino de Granada, also elaborated her convent's constitutions. The documents of both of these laywomen-turned-nuns demonstrate the second type of conflict that Madre Castillo found in the act of relating her monastic life, that of the negotiation of authority with male religious figures. Ultimately, male approval of the constitutions was necessary, but the ability to write their convent's own guidelines gave both of these women the power to negotiate certain rules for the life of their communities. Archbishop Arias de Ugarte provided constitutions for the Poor Clare convents of both Pamplona and Santa Fe sometime around 1630 (De Vances 1699, 4–5). Finding these insufficient, Madre Magdalena de Jesús rewrote the constitution in 1633. From her preface emerges the portrait of a female leader confident that she is better able than the distant male cleric to provide guidance for her nuns as she bases her revision on her own close observations (Magdalena de Jesús 1722, xiii). Madre Magdalena's nuns had found it difficult to "keep the Rules and Orders, that the Lord Archbishops of Santa Fe have made, removing some and imposing other temporary ones among the perpetual ones, whereupon they have caused confusion."[9] The history of the constitutions of the Discalced Carmelite convent in Santa Fe shows a similar process of negotiation between male and female religious, with less success by the female founder. In 1626 the cathedral canon Juan de Bonilla Navarro did give pontifical authorization to the constitutions written by Doña Elvira de Padilla, but he insisted on contradicting a number of her instructions.[10]

Though she professed in the Franciscan order of the Poor Clares, Madre Castillo held as her ideal of monastic rule the reformed Discalced Carmelite order and the constitutions provided by Saint Teresa. The strictly ascetic and prayer-centered Carmelite rule buttresses the absolute removal from the world of the model nun of the Counter-Reformation. The Convento Real de Santa Clara in Tunja, like most if not all early convents in Spanish America, could not follow the absolute poverty manifest in the Teresian and Franciscan ideals because of stipulations by the Crown that licenses be granted only to adequately endowed convents. Founded by a laywoman, the Convento Real de Santa Clara was the first monastery for nuns in the Nuevo Reino de Granada, receiving its earliest postulants only thirty-four years after the colonial town of Tunja itself came into being. In 1572 Doña Juana Macías de Figueroa and her husband, Captain Francisco Salguero, established Santa Clara with the donation of the *encomienda* of Mongua (Achury Valenzuela 1968, xxxi). Two hundred indigenous tributaries provided eight hundred pesos as yearly income to the *encomienda,* five hundred of which would go to the economic support of the nuns (Pacheco 1971, 353). Throughout its lifetime, the demands of administering the convent's economic base would pull the nuns away from their ideal retreat.

Saint Clare of Assisi had founded what would become the order of the Poor Clares in 1212, amid the fervent piety of the early thirteenth-century monastic reforms. The strict poverty and asceticism of her rule and its focus on spirituality anticipated Saint Teresa's renewal of reform in the sixteenth century. The guiding light of Saint Clare's monasticism was poverty, a theme that infuses both the original rule approved by Pope Innocent IV in 1253 and her own testament, which is appended to the rule (Merinero 1748, 21–25). A privilege given by Pope Innocent III in 1216 emphasizes the centrality of poverty to the order by mandating that the nuns cannot be constrained by any person—whether secular or ecclesiastical—to receive income (*rentas*) or to own property (27–28). Such impoverished orders usually survived on alms and by the labors of their own hands, selling embroidered work, for instance.

It is not this *Regla primera* or First Rule, however, but the second, "mitigated" rule (*Regla segunda*) given by Pope Urban IV in 1263 that the Convento Real de Santa Clara de la Ciudad de Tunja followed (*LV* 61r). Both rules are strongly ascetic in nature, but the second relaxes some of the severity of the first, particularly in the question of poverty. Both rules lay forth the central purpose of the nuns in their total dedication to the love and service of God through the praying of the Divine Office, and in their removal from the cares of the world through silence and frequent fasting. Both exhort the nuns to a communal unity based on virtuous character. But while the *Regla primera* revolves around the nuns' divestment of their property, this theme is absent from the *Regla segunda*, which makes only the briefest mention that property is to be held communally (Merinero 1748, chap. 8, 27–28). The general constitutions of 1639 reiterate the Urbanist prohibition of private property and the prescription that all properties be held by the community (Merinero 1748, chap. 5, 109–12). This document allows nuns to keep a small private sum of alms or family gifts and to spend the money with the permission of the abbess. Upon a nun's death, all articles that had been in her use during her lifetime were to be given to the community. The changed attitude toward property would allow the order to return to the accumulation of wealth that had been so fundamentally opposed by Clare of Assisi (Ancelet-Hustache 1929, 56).

Where the *Regla primera* centers on the divestment of property, the primary concern of the Urbanist rule is the construction of a tightly enclosing edifice that will control all movement between world and convent. The original rule prescribes vows of obedience, poverty, and chastity while the *Regla segunda* adds the fourth vow of enclosure. Fully eight of the twenty-six chapters of the *Regla segunda* pertain to the guarantee of enclosure for all except those religious who are present as servants and have made only three vows. The behavior of the serving sisters is to be regulated so that they will not bring into the convent news of the world nor harm the holy image of the convent outside through careless speech. The *Regla segunda* also relaxes the austerity of daily life by diminishing the severity of the fasting demanded of the nuns.[11] An additional relaxation is suggested in its reference to "serving sisters." The *Regla primera* names "serving sisters" who work outside of the convent, but the *Regla segunda* indicates the entrance of a class of serving women who do not make a vow of enclosure (Merinero 1748, chap. 2, 32), who wear white rather than black veils (chap. 4, 34), and whose presence anticipates the Tunja convent's seventeenth-century wealth of servants.

While the ascetic ideals contained in both rules of Saint Clare and in Saint Teresa's constitutions find resonance in the desires expressed by Madre Castillo for the Tunja convent, monastic life in Spanish America was renowned for its relaxation, which inspired periodic attempts at reform on the part of certain archbishops. Such relaxation was fostered by the distance of the convents to the mother order in Spain and by the fact that convents served a uniquely important social function in Spanish America. The *audiencia* (high court) in Santa Fe articulated this purpose in its response to the founding of Santa Clara, which it saw as "very Christian, very important and necessary to the city of Tunja and neighboring areas, due to the high number of maidens of poor parents without a dowry to be able to marry" (Pacheco 1971, 351).[12] The license granted by Pope Urban VIII in 1628 for the foundation of the Convento Real de Santa Clara in Santa Fe de Bogotá refers explicitly to the danger to the honor and honesty of poor, dowryless maidens, which peril could be avoided by the establishment of the convent (De Vances 1699, 19–20). In Spanish America the high sum required for marriage dowries prevented many families of the dominant class from marrying off all of their daughters, a difficulty heightened for many by the mining crisis of seventeenth-century Nuevo Reino de Granada.[13] The fear of miscegenation provided another motivation for enclosing colonial women in convents. Historian Susan Soeiro maintains that a Poor Clare convent in Brazil provided families of the "racially pure" elite a means by which to preserve the stratification of colonial society, avoiding "inconvenient" marriages by sending their daughters to the convent when a sufficient dowry was not at their disposal (1974, 67–84). Colonial convents answered the desires of a white elite to defend its status against the *mestizo* caste it so despised by avoiding the marriage of its daughters to men of racially "inferior" blood.[14] The flood of women who entered the convents despite feeling little dedication to an austere religious life could not be stayed, even by the Tridentine decrees that required a postulant's free will to profess to be ascertained before she made her final vows.

RITUAL, ART, AND INTELLECT

The charge of the Poor Clares was to serve God in daily adoration, a ritual task that led to a flourishing of various arts within colonial convents, including musical performance and devotional writing. Obligatory ritual created a context for nuns to develop artistic and intellectual pursuits that allowed self-expression. Black-veiled or choir nuns of the Poor Clares were to pray the Divine Office at the canonical hours, reading from the Breviary, which demanded the ability to read Latin if not necessarily to understand or write it.[15] On official feast days Mass was sung; thus the nuns valued musical skills. In 1620 the musical instruments of the Convento Real de Santa Clara included four violins, two harps, two *vihuelitas* (small guitars), two *sonajas* (tambourines), a zither, a clavichord, two *caracoles* (conch shells), and an organ. The choir library held antiphonaries, books of vespers, masses, motets, Magnificats, Salves, *villanescas,* and *chanzonetas* (*LV* 9r).[16] In 1647 the ecclesiastical visitor Señor Doctor Don Pedro Rodríguez de León insisted on the need for

FIGURE 3. The *coro alto,* or upper choir and grille, where the nuns gathered to pray the canonical hours. Convento Real de Santa Clara, Tunja, 1996. Photograph by Jorge González ©.

proper worship through music in his instruction that great care be taken to teach the novices to sing with daily lessons, and that the most skillful be singled out with praise (*LV* 86v). Madre Castillo participated actively in the musical life of the community. Having studied the organ during childhood, she continued her practice in the convent and was named during one year to the post of choirmistress. The frequent musical metaphors that permeate both the *Afectos* and the *Vida* find their source in her musicianship and the infusion of monastic ritual with music and give testimony to the creative potential of ritual in the nuns' lives.

The development of such intellectual and artistic pursuits as literature, music, theater, and painting in the nunneries of the Nuevo Reino de Granada has not been as well studied as that of Spain, Mexico, and Peru. Critical tradition has constructed Madre Castillo as an anomaly, a great intellectual surrounded by a less cultured community. Local Tunja lore asserts that her unique status lay at the heart of her persecution by the other nuns. The absence of a viceregal court in the Nuevo Reino de Granada before 1718 may have resulted in less stimulation of the arts, but Madre Castillo was certainly not alone.

Evidence of intellectual culture in the convents of the Nuevo Reino is

FIGURE 4. Portions of the original decorations that have been uncovered in the upper choir, Convento Real de Santa Clara, Tunja, 1996. Photograph by Jorge González ©.

scattered. The records I have found of a library in the Convento Real de Santa Clara, from the *Libro de visita* and the *Libro de capítulo,* show very few holdings. The list of books in the choir collection of Santa Clara in 1650, forty years before Sor Francisca's entrance, include, in addition to books of liturgical songs, the *Breviarium Romanum,* an *Abecedario espiritual* (Spiritual alphabet) by Francisco de Osuna, a book of the revelations of Saint Gertrude, a book titled *Vida christiana,* another about Saint Dominic and the Dominican order, the fourth and fifth parts of *Ley de Dios* (God's Law), and two copies of *Vitae Christi* (*LV* 94v).[17] The list does not reflect all of Madre Castillo's readings; she mentions works by Saint Ignatius of Loyola, Luis de la Puente, Saint Teresa of Avila, and Antonio de Molina, and she transcribed poetry by Juana Inés de la Cruz and Saint John of the Cross as well as a *vida* of María Magdalena de Pazzis. María Antonia del Niño Dios has also uncovered evidence of books in the private use of Sor Francisca, including a copy of Juan Eusebio Nieremberg's *Devoción y patrocinio de San Miguel príncipe de los ángeles* (Devotion and patronage of Saint Michael, prince of the angels) (1993, 279 n. 1).[18] The interest of other nuns in literary pursuits is suggested in the hosting of at least one poetry contest by the convent, on January 28, 1663, in celebration of the birth of the Spanish prince Carlos José (Achury Valenzuela 1968, xxv). Elsewhere in the Nuevo Reino, the Pamplona rule of Madre Magdalena de Jesús shows an awareness of the existence of convent theater when it stipulates that "in no case may the nuns dress up in the clothing of either men or secular women in order to perform, even among themselves, which is a very serious affair, very alien and unworthy of a nun, and dangerous" (Magdalena de Jesús 1722, chap. 12, par. 10).[19] María Gertrudis Theresa de Santa Inés, a nun in the convent of Santa Inés in Santa Fe, was famed for her beautiful voice and singing abilities, while the archbishop provided her community with musical instruments and a salaried instructor of music, plain chant, and polyphonic singing (Calvo 1752, 42).

While in New Spain convents played a central role in educating girls (Muriel 1946, 37), it is unclear how much emphasis the convents of the Nuevo Reino de Granada placed on this function. That young girls were present in the Convento Real de Santa Clara is evidenced in the convent's book of *Elecciones de abadesas, tomas de hábito y otros documentos importantes* (Elections of abbesses, conferring of the habit, and other important documents). This book, which records the licenses for profession and taking of the habit, documents at least thirteen cases of girls who entered the convent between the ages of three and eleven in the mid-seventeenth century.[20] For all but two of these girls there are records of later profession as choir or lay nuns and, in one case, as a *donada* (a servant, literally "donated one"), indicating that their convent childhood was meant to ready them for monastic life. I have found no indication that these children lived in the convent for primarily educational purposes, however, and no reference is made to the existence of a convent school.[21] In a number of cases, the girls had been given to the convent's care by their fathers after the death of their mothers. The presence of these children was a concern of the canonical visitors, who continually attempted to regulate their presence. The education that did occur in Santa Clara involved the novices, who could be as young as twelve. On a clear path toward profession, these girls were trained in singing, in domestic arts such as embroidery, and in reading, including the Latin they would need to pray the Divine Office. Doctor Don Francisco de Borja noted in his 1636 visit that the novices read well from a Latin book and gave a good explanation of what they had read, implying that they were taught not only to pronounce the words but also to understand their meaning (*LV* 41r). Meager as they are, these bits of information suggest that Madre Castillo did not write in a cultural void.

SOCIAL STRUCTURES

Serving social as well as religious functions, the female monastic communities of Spanish America mirrored the diversity of the outer world, a fact that proved troublesome for Madre Castillo in her express concern for strict religious observance. *Monjas de coro* (choir nuns), also called *monjas de velo negro* (black-veiled nuns), made up only a fraction of the women who lived in the convent. These nuns, of the convent elite, were obligated to carry out the convent's duty to pray the Divine Office. They ran the convent, holding the offices of power and responsibility. They were to bring with them a dowry of a thousand, fifteen hundred, or two thousand pesos.[22] *Monjas legas* (lay nuns), *legas de casa* (lay women of the house), or *monjas de velo blanco* (white-veiled nuns) entered the convent to serve the entire community with their labor, such as in food preparation or in the infirmary. Nuns of this category might enter because they felt a spiritual vocation but lacked the dowry required of choir nuns. Lay nuns brought a dowry of only three hundred pesos.[23] They were obliged to pray the Divine Office only when not occupied by their other duties (Merinero 1748, chap. 16, 144). These women often had not received the same education as the choir nuns, and provisions were made for those who could not read the Breviary to repeat the Lord's Prayer a specified number of times. A few *monjas legas de coro* (lay choir nuns) lived in the convent in the mid-1600s. These were women with special talents who desired to serve in the choir but who could only afford a five hundred–peso dowry. They were not included in the decision-making bodies or offices of the convent.[24] Several categories of servants are recorded in the *Libro de visita*. *Sirvientas del convento* (convent servants) and *donadas* served the entire community; the latter were obliged to bring small dowries to the convent, though canonical visitors complained that the convent often did not ask for the money (*LV* 63v, 136v). Choir nuns could also bring with them one or two women to serve them privately—*sirvientas de monjas* (nuns' servants), *indias* (Indians), *chinas* (maids), or *esclabas* (slaves) (*LV* 9r, 50r–52r, and 74v–78r). As the categories indicate, the social milieu included great racial diversity; the convent housed white *criolla* and Spanish women, *mestizas* descended from Spanish and Indian ancestry, and women of indigenous and African ancestry.[25] While Santa Clara's constitutions do not address race, and while constitutions of contemporary convents did allow for *mestizas* and free *mulatas* to take the black veil, such cases would have been unlikely.[26] Rather, the ruling choir nuns of Santa Clara were almost surely all daughters of Spanish or *criollo* parents.

The number of women living in the Convento Real de Santa Clara varied greatly between its founding in 1572 and Madre Castillo's lifetime, but it always exceeded the small community set by her monastic ideal of the Discalced Carmelites. Originally planned as a community of 24 black-veiled nuns (Paniagua Pérez 1993), the choir numbers had grown to 52 by 1610 and a high of 92 in 1644. The numbers dropped to a low of 19 in 1707, returning to 30 in 1730 (see Table 1). A clearer sense of the social atmosphere of the convent, however, demands examination of the total number of convent residents and not just the choir nuns. The records of the *Libro de visita* and other convent documents that I have consulted are incomplete but give some idea of the

Table 1
Number of choir nuns in the Convento Real de Santa Clara, Tunja, 1610–1730

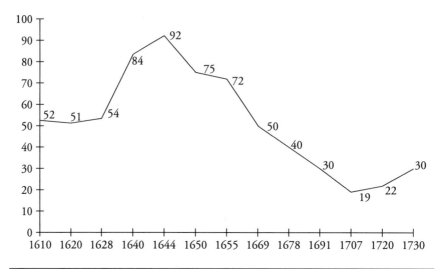

Data are from the *Libro de visita, Libro de capítulo, Elecciones de abadesas,* Archivo Histórico de Tunja, and *Cuaderno de cuentas* kept by Madre Francisca Josefa de la Concepción (Castillo 1718, 1732).

milieu. The canonical visit of 1620 lists 51 choir nuns, 4 novices, 4 lay nuns, 25 *donadas,* and 11 *indias* for a total of at least 95 women (*LV* 9r–10r). In 1638 the number had grown to 256: 88 choir nuns, 21 novices, 9 professed lay nuns, 3 lay novices, 17 *donadas,* and 118 women who served individual choir nuns (50r–52r). In the years prior to Madre Castillo's profession, then, the convent resembled the bustling milieu of the Convento de la Encarnación, which Saint Teresa had so eagerly left, more closely than it did the reformer's tiny Discalced community of San José. Tunja's *Libro de visita* does not record the total number of convent inhabitants during Madre Castillo's lifetime, though it had decreased significantly from its high mark; and yet the noisy surroundings of a convent full of children and servants still plagued her and drove her to express her longing for the Teresian ideal.

GOVERNANCE

The *Regla segunda* of the Poor Clares prescribes a governance infused with love, exemplarity, and service on the part of the abbess, and love and obedience in the actions of the nuns (Merinero 1748, chap. 22). Nonetheless, elections and governance riddle Madre Castillo's *Vida* with disputes. The web of governing relationships prescribed by the constitution and ecclesiastical visitors created many possibilities for conflict over decision-making power. A certain democracy among the choir nuns was demanded by the *Regla segunda* through the abbess's regular presentation of financial accounts to the chapter —all of the choir nuns—and her consultation of either the chapter or the council on decisions regarding the acceptance of postulants, the approval of dowries, any official convent correspondence, and significant financial dealings (Merinero 1748, chap. 3, 32, chap. 22, 50). In the Convento Real de Santa Clara, the council or *difinitorio* consisted of six to twelve senior nuns, including the deputy abbess or vicaress, several appointed *difinidoras* (council members), and the *madres de consejo* (mother advisers), who earned their position after serving as abbess. The fact that canonical visitors repeatedly instructed the abbesses to present financial accounts before the council and to make no decisions without the council's approval suggests that such democracy did not always function as well as intended (*LV* 63r, 70v, 142r, 155r, 167v, 172r, 167v). Financial consultations often involved not only the abbess and the *difinitorio* but also two male ecclesiastics: the convent's vicar, who served as a liaison with the ecclesiastical hierarchy, and the syndic or steward.[27] It was the latter's job to represent the convent in its external affairs, collecting income from its property investments, money and products from the indigenous tributaries, and the profits or products from the convent's haciendas. Important decisions demanded approval of this group and, in addition, a final license from the archbishop or his representative. As is evident in the history of the financial woes of the convent described below, these relationships, especially between convent and syndic, were riddled with tensions.

The abbess and vicaress were elected to three-year terms by secret ballot. The ritual was also attended by male representatives from the city's monastic orders and from the secular clergy, whose purpose was to oversee the process, but not to vote. After the elections were approved as canonical, which required a simple majority vote, the visitor general made public the results and handed over to the new abbess the seals and keys to the convent, informing her of her obligations. She was then carried in procession through the cloister while the nuns sang to her the *Te Deum Laudamus* and pledged to her their obedience (*LV* 139r). The abbess's first charge was to appoint the *difinidoras,* a mistress of novices, a choir vicaress, sacristans, portresses, parlor and grille chaperones, nurses, a secretary, an attendant to the revolving window, chaperones for outsiders who entered the convent (builders, doctors, and chaplains), the purveyor or keeper of the larder, and workers.[28] One of the primary internal duties of the abbess was to ensure that the rule and constitutions were followed, primarily through example and loving correction. Such correction called for weekly chapter meetings at which nuns were instructed in virtuous behavior and punished for their individual faults, an event that Madre Castillo found especially odious from both the receiving and the giving end (Merinero 1748, *Regla segunda,* chap. 22, 50).

That the election of an abbess could be fraught with conflict was demonstrated by an incident in 1683 in the Convento de la Concepción, also of Tunja (Conventos, AHNB, vol. 19: 24–26). The Conceptionist nuns repeatedly resisted the attempts of the local male clergy to force a resolution of their political conflict. They defied successive admonitions by the vicar and ecclesiastical judge to carry out a peaceful election worthy of a religious order. They cast ten separate ballots in a process that began at nine in the morning and remained undecided at midnight. Archbishop Sanz Lozano of Santa Fe finally imposed a resolution by naming a third nun to the post of president for a three-year term.

The vicar's report shows the struggle of the local clergy to impose a submissive subjectivity on the nuns through appeals to spiritualized values. Male authority over the process is emphasized in the clarification that the elections proceed only with due license given by the archbishop, whose importance is heightened by the length of his title. The assertion of male power becomes more obvious and ironic to the twentieth-century eye when juxtaposed against the recalcitrance of the female actors. The notary who reports the election attempts to mask in a spiritualized discourse a hotly contested and very worldly political process of the kind that often brought turmoil to entire cities. But the attempt at smooth representation in formulaic language breaks down when the nuns resist the admonitions to look only to the spiritual good. The report draws for the archbishop a picture of stern authority exercised by a tower of holy masculinity against the nuns' repeated refusal to adopt a passive feminine submission. The nuns of La Concepción have dared to disobey. Disobedience and conflict surround every mention of elections in Madre Castillo's narrative of her life in Santa Clara, the consequence of a colonial situation that threw her and her convent into violation of the ideals of the order.

CANONICAL VISITS

Perhaps the most anxiety-producing symptom of the secularization of monastic life for Madre Castillo is her convent's laxity in adhering to the rule. In Spanish America, the highest representatives of the Church hierarchy were engaged in a constant battle against the scandalous lives of clerics and monastic orders. It was not uncommon for priests openly to maintain relations with concubines, while the enclosure of nunneries was never complete (Juan and Ulloa 1918). José Manuel Groot's history of the Church in New Granada reads like a series of reform cycles, renewed attacks on excesses coinciding with each instatement of a new archbishop from Spain (1953, 1: 643; 2: 7–23, 43). In

1606, only thirty-six years after the founding of the first convent in New Granada, Archbishop Bartolomé Lobo Guerrero of Santa Fe directed stern mandates to abbesses to punish harshly the abuses that had been "introduced by the Devil," referring thus to profane "devotions" or amorous attentions lavished on nuns by men (Lobo Guerrero 1606, chap. 17, 18–19). Aside from their confessors, nuns' conversations with the outside world were to be limited to their relatives. The bars that divided the *locutorio* (parlor) into convent and outside world were to be constructed such that a hand could not fit through them and the veil that lined the inner side of the bars was not to be drawn open except when nuns talked with their parents and siblings. Other offenses that Lobo Guerrero noted include the nuns' contradiction of their vow of poverty and their imperative to dress modestly and without such luxuries as saffroned wimples, rings, or jewelry. These repeated cycles of reform show how convents provided a space where strong-willed women created their own version of religious life, constantly negotiating their ability to do so against the control of male hierarchies, and how internal conflict arose between the more observant and less observant nuns.

The *Libro de visita* of the Convento Real de Santa Clara chronicles a history of relations in which male clerics both opposed and supported the nuns, imposing Tridentine controls but also exercising advocacy on the nuns' behalf and even serving as mediators within the convent.[29] The canonical visitor always concerned himself with the holy image of the convent in a secular world. In formulaic language, the visitor explains the purpose of his visit in terms of remedying the ills of the community and aiding its members to strive for greater holiness in their obedience to the demands of the order. Despite the lengthy corrections that close each report, the visitor almost always begins his instructions to the nuns with extraordinary praise that alludes to their exemplarity in the republic through their faithful adherence to the rule.

Despite the nuns' perfection, the visitor wishes to encourage them to strive for even greater service to God. The details of his mandates are based on a visual inspection of the convent's physical structures and on the *secreta,* a private consultation with each member of the community, during which time the convent is closed to all communication with the outside world. The visitor's questions concern the proper keeping of the four vows; the correct fulfillment of the obligation to pray the Divine Office; the life of the community; obedience to the rule, constitutions, and the instructions of prior visitors; the care of the sick; and the existence of any improper behavior or problems in the convent (*LV* 7v, 122v). Nuns are asked to report on their own behavior and on that of others, under threat of severe penalty.

Throughout the history of the Convento Real de Santa Clara, the primary concerns of its visitors lay in two main areas: the spiritual quality of the communal life and the economic health of the convent. The first manifested itself in a variety of specific concerns. Visitors sought a balance between observance of a strict religious code of duties and behaviors and sufficient moderation so as to make life livable. Especially pertinent to an understanding of the radical religiosity exercised by Madre Castillo and its repercussions among her sister nuns is the repeated insistence by visitors that the fasts, mortifications, and penances carried out by the nuns not be so severe as to threaten their health or lives (*LV* 63v, 81r, 90r, 98r). The visitors instructed the abbess and her spiritual daughters in questions of respectful fulfillment of ritual duties as well as in the regulation of the nuns' intercourse with the world. Especially troublesome in this area were the presence of servants, children, and dogs in the convent and the entry of male clerics, doctors, and workers. The harmony among the choir nuns themselves, or lack thereof, and between the nuns and their abbess were discussed in a number of visits. Here the visitor mediated conflicts, at times backing the abbess and at times trying to moderate her stern rule.

The presence of children and servants in the convents caused the visitors constant consternation. One reason was the economic drain they occasioned despite stipulations that their support be provided for by either their families or the individual nuns who cared for them. Another was their disruption of the prescribed quiet of the monastic existence. Although servants would have helped care for these children, at least some of the burden of supervision and instruction fell to the nuns, thus causing them added distractions. In the seventeenth century, four ecclesiastical visitors tried to regulate the presence of young children in the convent. Their continued insistences give evidence to their failure to resolve the problem they perceived (*LV* 46v, 64r, 92r, 98v, 106r). Part of the difficulty lay in the differing opinions among the visitors themselves over whether girls under the age of twelve should be allowed in the convent.

Servants were of graver concern. They were essential to the convent's daily functioning, but because they included adults among their ranks, they could represent a real threat to the modesty of the convent's chaste world. Many of the visitors' instructions regarding servants attempted to reduce their numbers for the economic health of the convent, limiting each nun to one or two servants or denying any additional licenses for the entrance of servants, asserting that the convent had sufficient servants for its needs (*LV* 63r, 81v, 90v, 98r). Admonitions show that their "worldly" behavior was perceived by the visitors to have a negative effect on nuns' lives, to the point of causing conflict between them.[30] On various occasions, visitors attempted to prevent the servants from moving freely between the convent and the outside world, apparently with little success (155r, 163v). In an especially sharp invective in 1694, Archbishop Fray Ignacio de Urbina demanded that no nun could have more than two servants, and that every other secular person, even the very young who attended the nuns, must leave within thirty hours following notification (166r). The penalty for noncompliance was severe: excommunication of every black- and white-veiled nun in the convent. According to biographer María Antonia del Niño Dios, this was the injunction that precipitated the young Francisca Josefa de Castillo to profess rather than be forced to leave the convent, as she had already worn the habit for two years (1993, 49; cf. *SV* 33). Certainly, most of these servants did not choose vows of obedience, poverty, chastity, and enclosure, or a life of silence, and their subversion of such control is not surprising as they attempted to live out their own lives with such fulfillment as they could create.

The choir nuns' own behavior also slipped from the austerity demanded by their rule and constitutions. The details of their weaknesses as perceived by visitors help explain Madre Castillo's implicit campaign for greater observance and religiosity in her *Vida* and the animosity that she reports as resulting from her attempts. While most visitors couched their corrections in relatively gentle terms, Archbishop Urbina in 1694 found much to criticize and exercised little restraint in his invective. He reprehended the nuns for ignoring the community of their rule by not eating in the refectory and by their lax attendance at choir. He expressed great disconsolation in seeing how few nuns participated in the Friday procession for the redemption of the souls in purgatory. As with his expulsion of laypeople from the convent, he threatened severe punishment if these ills were not remedied (*LV* 167r). Other visitors noted immodest practices in the attendance at the convent door and at communion of nuns without the wimples that should have covered neck, forehead, and cheeks (142v, 175r), the indecorous use of the lower choir for needlework, chatting, and eating (143r), and the distraction with which the nuns prayed the Divine Office, trampling it and rushing through the holy ritual (175r). Even vanity and the opinions of peers had let a bad seed into the practice by which the nun appointed to sing Calends on Christmas, and the nun who arranged the yearly nativity scene, drew attention to themselves by investing such personal sums into their work in order that it might shine that they suffered economic hardship (128r, 135v, 142v, 177r).

A final threat to the nuns' extraction from worldly sin came in the form of male visitors entering behind the cloister walls. Of course many of these visitors were priests whose religious duties called them inside, but their presence was never entirely above suspicion so long as nuns and priests remained women and men underneath their self-control. Two methods were attempted to guarantee the probity of visits: the limitation of the number of male visitors and constant vigilance over those visitors once they were inside the convent. Any outsider was to proceed directly to his ministry without entering any cell or other part of the convent, and he was to be constantly accompanied by two appointed nuns (*LV* 106r). Even when hearing the confession of a very ill nun, the priest was to be watched from out of the range of earshot. These visitors were to leave immediately upon completing their office (142v). No priest was to say mass, give communion, or hear confession except in the case of grave need, with very ill or dying nuns, and then he was not to bring in extra wafers and wander from cell to cell with great indecency to distribute the consecrated Host, as had been the custom (143v).

The visitors' second major area of concern, that of the convent's economic health, reveals an almost constant struggle to respond to the basic needs of the nuns in food and clothing. The sources of difficulty lay with the general economic crisis of the times, but the abbess and the syndic shared the blame. Financial problems plagued the convent from early in its history and drew the nuns time and again out of their holy retreat into the concerns of the world. In 1620 Archbishop Arias de Ugarte set at fifty-one the limit of choir nuns that the convent could successfully support on dowry investments of a thousand pesos per nun; above this number, any entrant would be required to bring a dowry of fifteen hundred pesos (LV 15v, 22v). But exceptions were made for women entering at all levels: dowries were excused or lowered when the postulant had special musical talent or demonstrated special piety, having been brought up in the convent, or when the convent population had reached very low levels.[31] Canonical visitors repeatedly insisted that *donadas* not be allowed into the convent without a dowry because of the convent's financial need, a repetition that speaks of noncompliance (63v–64r, 71v, 136v, 144r). Even when the required dowry was promised, it was often given in the form of investments with shaky guarantees. In 1640 Archbishop Cristóbal de Torres demanded that no dowry be invested without the entire satisfaction of the abbess, the mothers of the council, and the vicar, and that firm guarantees be required (63r), implying that some abbesses had been granting special favors that increased the convent's financial difficulties.

A second cause of ruin can be found in the Council of Trent's imposition of the vow of enclosure, which led to the nuns' complete dependence on the male syndic for the management of their properties. While the nuns made decisions on investments, they depended on the syndic to represent them outside of the convent. In this relationship, the ecclesiastical visitors acted as advocates for the nuns, expressing their suspicion of the syndics who were notorious for deceiving the convents they served. Santa Clara's visitors implemented a number of reforms aimed at bringing the nuns and the vicar to exercise greater control over the syndic.

In 1678 Señor Licenciado Don Augustín del Sotomayor was sent with a special commission to the convent by the archbishop, whereupon he placed the blame for the convent's financial straits squarely on the shoulders of the syndics, though he faulted also the lack of care of the abbesses. He decried the domination of the nuns by the syndics, who had exercised more ownership of the nuns' income and properties than the nuns themselves, having done so through misinforming the nuns of their accounts. The monastery's loss of more than 252,000 pesos since its foundation was due, he charged, in great part to the freedom given the syndics and to their acts of omission. The abbesses, however, also shared the blame by following their affections in the appointments they made of syndics and by offering them the liberal salaries they requested (*LV* 158r). Sotomayor's first remedy was to deprive Don Nicolás de Arzo of his office of syndic and to transfer legal power to the vicar Don Antonio de Osa Guerbillano (158v). But he also made specific demands on the abbess to show greater accountability, giving the convent more control over whichever male representative was to collect the convent's income. Finally, the vicar was charged with attempting to recuperate those lands whose deeds had been lost. These measures did not cure the convent's woes. In 1682 and 1694 visitors repeated their laments of the scarcity experienced by the nuns and the grave prejudice to the religious state implied in the economic decline of the convent (163r, 165r). The *Libro de visita* does not contain similar reports on the financial situation for the first term that Madre Castillo served as abbess (1718–21), in which she recounts an economic crisis and its miraculous resolution, but the documents she signed as abbess show that difficulties continued in the collection of debts and in disputes with the syndic. In chapter 5, I examine the economics of this period further.

ECONOMICS AND POLITICS

Not only were Spanish American convents in general, and the Convento Real de Santa Clara in particular, permeated with the turbulence of secular society, but, to Madre Castillo's distress, enclosure could not prevent the involvement of nuns in political and economic activities that broke down the wall between convent and world. An incident in the early history of the Tunja convent demonstrates the measures taken by nuns to defend their own interests in actions that extended far beyond their walls. Rather than simply resist the ecclesiastical hierarchy, as the Conceptionists did in their elections, the Poor Clare community sought help from one side of the male Church against another in order to obtain what they desired for their convent. Between 1580 and 1585, the Poor Clares of Tunja rebelled against their Franciscan guardians, claiming that they had suffered scandalous and unjust offenses. "That in coming to our convent saying that they wished to visit us, and on our responding that the visit had to be carried out through the communion grille or in the parlor, they replied that it could not be done other than in the cloister. And because we defended the entrance against them, they came armed and broke down the doors and bolts and finally entered with a great uproar, saying ugly words to us and removing from me, said abbess, my veil and laying on their hands with very confrontational words" (Conventos, AHNB, 68: 299–300).[32] The nuns were victorious in bringing to their aid the secular clergy—those obedient to the archbishop rather than to a religious order—and the convent was transferred to the stewardship of the archdiocese.

Involvement in external politics on the part of the female convents did not always mean such negative strife. In 1655 the governing council of the Convento Real de Santa Clara in Tunja wrote one of several letters directed to the king by city institutions in support of the government of the *corregidor* (district governor and magistrate) Don Juan Bautista de Valdés. The letters unanimously requested a prolongation of his term of office (Audiencia de Santa Fe, AGI, 66). In 1668 the Poor Clare abbess Madre Paula de San Ignacio presented testimony in her convent's collaboration with the city's effort to involve the Council of Indies in resolving its perennial water shortage (Audiencia de Santa Fe, AGI, 66).

The most common involvement of the nuns in extramural affairs was demanded by their economic sustenance, as can be seen in the instructions given by Sotomayor in 1678, in his attempt to get the convent back on its feet. The convent's governing body, and particularly the abbess, were forced to gain experience in extensive matters of financial management as they administered the properties and loans whose income covered their daily expenses. By the seventeenth century, the entire region of the Nuevo Reino de Granada faced deep economic problems. Conquest and colonization had reduced the indigenous population of the Tunja region by 80 percent between 1551 and 1636 (Colmenares 1970, 69). Mining, which had supported an increasingly luxurious lifestyle for the Spanish and *criollo* elite, was plunged into a crisis with the destruction of its own worker pool, the exhaustion of mineral deposits, and its primitive production techniques (Colmenares 1982, 244). Convents, which had accumulated wealth and properties through dowries and donations, emerged as the primary banking institutions, providing the loans that undergirded the transition to an agricultural economy.

In Tunja's notary archives, Santa Clara and San Agustín are the convents most frequently represented in loan and mortgage transactions (Pino Alvarez 1989, 46). Banking could provide a steady income, but it also forced the nuns to invest great efforts in pursuing delinquent debtors and their heirs. According to Gladys Pino Alvarez, Santa Clara managed more money than any other convent in Tunja during the eighteenth century, three times as much as the second-place Augustinian friars (1989, 46).[33] Ninety-five percent of Santa Clara's income as recorded in the notary archives came from *censos*—roughly translated, these were mortgages or leases guaranteed on properties—from dowries paid through annuities, and from the auction of properties whose owners defaulted on payments.[34] The remaining 5 percent of the convent's income came from rental properties, donations, and *capellanías*—endowments for choir nuns to pray for the souls of their benefactors. The abbess, often accompanied by the *difinitorio* and aided by the vicar or syndic, represented the convent to the outside world in managing these economic affairs (Notaría 2, ARB, [1719], vol. 169: 10–11). As stipulated in the constitutions, the entire governing council of Santa Clara and occasionally the entire community witnessed transactions and signed documents in a number of major decisions concerning the approval of loans or sales or during extended land disputes.[35] If what historian Susan Soeiro reports in the case of the Brazilian convent of Santa Clara do Destêrro was also true for Tunja, relatives of the nuns secured loans more readily, and rules of collateral and guarantees were not rigorously enforced in these cases (1974, 85). Such circumstances thoroughly integrated external colonial politics with the actions of the nuns and would have made the question of which nuns reached the governing council of paramount economic importance to their families. This economic and political relationship would at least partially explain the town's interest in convent elections, and it would lend background to the accusations reported by Madre Castillo surrounding her own involvement in the internal power struggles of the convent.

The community of nuns and laywomen in the Convento Real de Santa Clara in Tunja during the seventeenth and eighteenth centuries lived with intensity the extremes of the monastic possibilities of its times. Restrained by the Counter-Reformation from an entirely free exercise of their artistic and intellectual talents, the choir nuns applied their energies to musical expression, extensive readings, and in at least one case to writing. The nuns' environment was filled with the rich and vibrant colors and the dynamic lines of Baroque religious art, aimed at moving the soul to tears and compelling the faithful to obedience. This physical setting inspired the images of visionary lives. Fulfilling a vital social function for the Nuevo Reino de Granada, the convent opened its doors to dozens, and at times hundreds, of women of all social classes and races. Steeped in their colonial atmosphere, most or all of these women were deeply religious, but some exercised their religion with an especially radical fervor. Others, in particular many of the laywomen who carried out the domestic labors of the convent, had not chosen the extreme asceticism of their radical sisters. The coexistence of the various groups and personal goals created tensions in the community. If strict regulations were devised to contain the nuns, the convent walls and parlor grilles proved exceedingly permeable to the political and economic concerns of the times, leading nuns to immerse themselves in the concerns of the world. They exercised a strong voice in the interests of their convent and their extended families of origin, though always depending on their male representatives to carry out their wishes in the world. This great mix of people, intentions, and activities inevitably led to conflicts and to a collective life less observant of the constitutions and rules of the order than some nuns and male clerics desired; but in the process, Santa Clara was home to a group of admirably strong women struggling to determine and guide their own lives.

MADRE CASTILLO IN THE INSTITUTION
AN ASCENSION TO POWER

María Antonia del Niño Dios watches me at the computer. I see on her silent face a sense of betrayal. I have read her biography of Madre Castillo and refuse to understand it. My writing of this holy woman's life replaces spiritual struggle and the glorification of God with social and economic determinisms. I ask Sor María Antonia to read on. I insist that an integrated study of not only spiritual but also political, social, and economic concerns, discursive traditions, and narrative strategies can provide enriching knowledge for the Church as well as for feminist scholars. She does not respond. Is there a common language?

I BEGIN with a daydream that expresses an ethical quandary that I feel very deeply as a feminist scholar. In chapter 4, I hung out the historical laundry of the Convento Real de Santa Clara. Certainly I am not the first to have described the less-than-perfect adherence to Tridentine reforms within Spanish American monasticism. Madre Castillo herself alludes to many of the situations I have treated, though she omits names and dates and reaches a different interpretation. In fact, most of the history I have narrated does not constitute new discovery regarding colonial monasticism but rather examines its manifestations within a specific historical space and time—before and within which Madre Castillo wrote her version of her life and that of her convent. For contemporary scholars, this information can provide an invaluable narrative, one which, in dialogue with Madre Castillo's own story, constructs a new understanding of her life and struggles as a female religious writer. My conversations with Colombian Catholics lead me to believe that some readers could also find this narrative troublingly secular and critical. And so I respond with a serious daydream that expresses both my awareness of these concerns and my firm belief that an archaeology of the convent's history can lead to greater appreciation and respect for Madre Castillo and for the life of her community.

To read Madre Castillo's life as an ascension to power imposes a framework that her own narrative contradicts. Against the portrait of political scheming painted by her accusers in the *Vida*, Madre Castillo claims for herself the subjectivity of a weak and ignorant woman. Months of research in Colombian national and regional archives, the examination of María Antonia del Niño Dios's biography, and consultation with three volumes from the colonial archive of the Convento Real de Santa Clara have brought Madre Castillo's life into sufficiently clear focus to construct a partial documentary biography. My reading of the archives does not prove a purposeful ascension to power through relationships with her confessors, accumulation of support from her important colonial family inside and outside of the convent, demonstrations of skill and intelligence, and calculated politicking. Yet each of these elements is strongly suggested by reading the documents pertaining to Madre Castillo's life against the more general background of colonial monasticism. At the very least, this documentary biography makes problematic an innocent reading of Madre Castillo's self-portrait. Moreover, it aids in a deconstruction of the edifice of her writings: that is to say, it brings to the fore those discourses and practices that shape her writings and the character of their interrelatedness. If my biography does not sketch an indisputable path from novice to abbess, it does ground the conflicts that surface in Madre Castillo's works within a record of the specific problems and conditions of her convent.

Madre Castillo was born into a family of the local governing elite on the feast day of Saint Bruno, October 6, 1671, and was baptized on the same day by the Jesuit priest Diego Solano.[1] Her father, Francisco Ventura de Castillo y Toledo, a jurist born and educated in Spain, had been sent by Felipe IV to Tunja to act as lieutenant to the *corregidor* (district governor and magistrate), Captain Juan Bautista de Valdés, from 1660 to 1668 (Rojas 1962, 397). He served as *alcalde ordinario* (city councilman and magistrate) for Tunja in 1685 and received commissions of high honor, including that of special ambassador to the presidents of the royal *audiencia* (high court) in Santa Fe (Restrepo and Rivas 1928, 231). Madre Castillo's mother, Doña María de Guevara Niño y Rojas, *tunjana* by birth, was the daughter of Don Diego de Guevara (also an *alcalde ordinario* of Tunja) and Doña María Niño y Rojas.[2] Madre Castillo's brother, Captain Pedro Antonio de Castillo y Guevara, *encomendero* of the town of Paipa (the recipient of grants of Indian labor and tribute) and commissary general of the Spanish cavalry and militias in Tunja, continued to uphold the family's social status and honor as *alcalde ordinario* of Tunja in 1703, 1716, and 1729, *alguacil mayor* (chief constable) in 1710, and general lieutenant to the *corregidor* in 1729 (Restrepo and Rivas 1928, 236). His six daughters would all profess in Santa Clara during their aunt's lifetime (*LC* 146r, 152r, 152v, 128r [pt. 2]). One of Madre Castillo's two sisters, Catalina Ludgarda de Castillo y Guevara, married Don Agustín José de Mesa Cortés, who was *juez de cobranzas reales* (justice of royal collections) in Mérida,

Spain, and later took up residence in Tunja in 1694 (Restrepo and Rivas 1928, 233). Widowed, Doña Catalina married Captain Lucas Camacho de Guzmán, *alcalde* of Tunja and *alférez real* (royal standard bearer, member of the town council) (189, 236). Her two daughters, Mariana de San Joseph from the first marriage and Margarita de la Cruz from the second, would also profess in their aunt's convent, in 1711 and 1720 (*LC* 144r, 149v). Madre Castillo's second sister, Juana Angela, married Governor José de Enciso y Cárdenas, *encomendero* of Tunja, and, once widowed, entered the Convento Real de Santa Clara, where she died as a novice on April 28, 1714 (Restrepo and Rivas 1928, 233; *LC* 144v). As a nun, Madre Castillo would have found the honorable status of her family and its economic and political power very helpful in her political battles; in her position as abbess, these connections aided in resolving the financial problems of her governance.

Besides the certificate of baptism and the *Vida,* which will be discussed in chapter 6, there is no documentation on the young Francisca's life before she entered the convent. When she decided to enter in 1689, destined to remain enclosed until her death in 1742, her choice may have been guided by a number of factors: her early immersion in the deep religious values of her family and society, a desire to reject the all-consuming tasks of marriage and the dangers of childbirth, the autonomy and opportunity for artistic development possible in the convent, and, finally, the fact that the convent offered women practically their only avenue for both spiritual and social prominence. The combination of family ties and proximity played a strong part in the young Francisca's choice of the Convento Real de Santa Clara. Family ties dated back to the convent's inception; Francisca was the great-great-granddaughter of the founder's sister, Doña Catalina de Sanabria, and thereby niece in the third degree to the founding mother, Juana de Jesús.[3] More recently, an aunt of Francisca's had professed.[4]

Madre Castillo does not mention consideration of Tunja's other female monastery, the Convento de la Concepción founded in 1599 under Franciscan rule (Achury Valenzuela 1968, viii). A third convent does figure strongly in her *Vida;* it is that of the Discalced Carmelites in Santa Fe, which stands as both the imagined ideal and the path not taken. Madre Castillo mentions in her *Vida* her correspondence with a Carmelite abbess who died in 1708. This is the year in which Madre Francisca María del Niño Jesús of the Carmelite convent died. This nun, whose fame of holiness spread widely after her death, is identified by María Antonia del Niño Dios as Madre Castillo's correspondent (1993, 119).[5] The Discalced Carmelite and the Poor Clare were related by marriage; Madre Castillo's sister-in-law, Doña Josefa de Caicedo y Salabarrieta, was Madre Francisca María's niece.[6] It is almost certain that the letters between the two fed Madre Castillo's desire to follow the rule of the

Discalced Carmelites, a desire she identifies in her *Vida* as having been born when she listened as a child to her mother read Saint Teresa's *Libro de las fundaciones* (*SV,* chap. 1, 5). It is to the Carmelite convent, according to Madre Castillo, that her brothers tried to move her in a moment of great tribulation (chap. 26, 96). She also claims to have intercepted key letters in order to prevent the move. It is interesting to note that two nephews, Don Juan Estevan de Castillo y Caicedo and Don Francisco de Castillo y Guevara, attempted unsuccessfully to found a Discalced Carmelite convent in Tunja ten years after their aunt's death (Conventos, AHNB, vol. 14: 742).

Francisca Josefa took the habit of novice on August 12, 1692, at the age of twenty-one after the *difinitorio* requested the necessary permission from the archbishop. The *difinitorio*'s letter of May 13, 1692, states that "all unanimous and in conformity, received her with great pleasure, attending to her virtue and exemplary life, whereby she will be a very useful and important nun."[7] This official representation, as we will see in chapter 6, contrasts starkly with the strife that Madre Castillo recalls as surrounding her presence in the convent from the moment of her entrance. The discrepancy between the embattled Sor Francisca of the *Vida* and the virtuous novice of the *difinitorio*'s letter most likely involves the context in which each text was produced. On one hand, the conflict portrayed by Madre Castillo herself responds to both her lived experience and her need to maintain humility as a writer, claiming a worthlessness that excites criticism. On the other, the *difinitorio* needed to preserve the convent's image of holiness in a secular world by giving an external audience a picture of a model nun supported by a tranquil community, and masking in the process any internal conflict. The separation between public and private information for the good of the convent was strictly enforced, as is clear in an incident that occurred in the Poor Clare convent in Cartagena in 1664. The community was thrown into an uproar when it was discovered that the abbess had allowed a book containing the proceedings of the elections to leave the convent (Conventos, AHNB, vol. 68: 463–79). One of the abbess's accusers testified that the book held "secrets of the convent wherein are expressed punishments, sentences that have been executed on different occasions" (472).[8] The penalty for violating the convent's secrecy was severe; the abbess was removed from office, and her voice in the following chapter of elections was revoked (479).

After two years as novice, and a total of five years in the convent, Sor Francisca professed under the pressure of Archbishop Ignacio de Urbina. During his visit to the convent in August 1694, Archbishop Urbina mandated that the majority of the servants, *donadas,* and girls in the convent be expelled. Sor Francisca, still a novice, would either have to profess or leave (*LV* 166r; María Antonia del Niño Dios 1993, 49; *SV,* chap. 11, 33).

On the fourth of September, 1694, Francisca Josefa de la Concepción made her profession as black-veiled nun, legitimate daughter of Don Francisco Ventura del Castillo and of Doña María de Guevara, with permission from the Most Illustrious and Reverend Master Don Fray Ignacio, Archbishop of this Nuevo Reino, having preceded it the necessary steps that the Holy Council of Trent demands. She professed in the hands of the Mother Vicaress Antonia de los Angeles, with permission of His Illustriousness, the Mother Abbess Paula de San Ignacio being ill, in presence of the community, with the attendance of our father vicar Doctor Don José Osorio Nieto de Paz, and so that it be made manifest, it was signed by: [signatures] Doctor Don José Osorio Nieto de Paz, Antonia de los Angeles, vicaress, María del Niño Jesús, secretary, Francisca Josefa de la Concepción. (Castillo [1694] 1942)⁹

This profession opened up for her the exercise of a series of convent offices that would eventually lead to three terms as abbess, the first of which she began at the age of forty-seven (Table 2).

Early in her monastic life, probably during the same year that she professed, Sor Francisca began to express her spirituality in short written pieces.¹⁰ She would continue to write these *papeles* (papers) at the command of Father Francisco de Herrera until at least 1728.¹¹ These papers would later be gathered and published under the title of *Sentimientos espirituales* (1843) and *Afectos espirituales* (1942). Madre Castillo's writing of her *Vida* resulted from her confessors' reading of her *papeles*. The exact year that she began the *Vida* is unclear; it was well underway by 1715 when, in writing chapter 41, she mentions that she has arrived at the age of forty-four (*SV,* chap. 41, 160). María Antonia del Niño Dios dates the initiation of the task to around 1713, attributing to Madre Castillo's confessor Padre Diego de Tapia the command that she record her experiences and concluding that the final chapter of the *Vida* was sent to this confessor in 1723 (1993, 276). The last datable event in the *Vida* is the death of Madre Paula de la Trinidad, recorded in the *Libro de cuentas* of the convent archives on March 15, 1723 (María Antonia del Niño Dios 1993, 269). Madre Castillo wrote both the *Vida* and the *Afectos* in installments that she submitted periodically to her confessors, as evidenced by the notes addressed to these spiritual directors, which frame sections of the texts, as well as by the confessors' occasional responses interspersed with her own texts.

In writing about Madre Castillo's institutional life, some attention to chronology is necessary in order to support the hypothesis of her rise to power. On the other hand, for the purpose of illuminating the lived context of some of the key conflicts in the *Vida* it is more useful to treat a number of themes independently of a strict chronology. The author's own text rejects a clear and

Table 2

Offices held by Francisca Josefa de la Concepción, Convento Real de Santa Clara, Tunja

Date appointed	Age	Office	Source[a]
1694	22	secretary[b]	
Jan. 19, 1695	23	assistant to the sacristan	55
1696		—no information—	
1697		—no information—	
Jan. 20, 1698	26	assistant to the sacristan/secretary	74
Jan. 20, 1699	27	assistant to the portress/secretary	80
1700		secretary	
Jan. 20, 1701	29	nurse	83
Jan. 20, 1702	30	mistress of novices/secretary	89
Jan. 20, 1703	31	parlor chaperone/secretary	98
Jan. 20, 1704	32	sacristan/secretary	103
Sept. 27, 1705	34	choir mistress	111
1706	35	nurse/secretary	115
July 20, 1707	36	mistress of novices/secretary	121
1708	37	grille chaperone	136
Oct. 13, 1709	38	organist	146
1710		—no information—	
Oct. 13, 1711	40	portress	154
Oct. 13, 1712	41	mistress of novices	171
1713		—no information—	
Oct. 13, 1714	43	portress	203
May 8, 1715		portress	211
1716		—no information—	
May 8, 1717	46	mistress of novices	228
May 8, 1718–1721	47	abbess	250[c]
April 2, 1723	52	mistress of novices	272
April 11, 1729–1732[d]	58	abbess	323[e]
April 14, 1738–1741	67	abbess	415[f]

[a] The information is based on convent documentation quoted in María Antonia del Niño Dios (1993) on the page numbers shown. The dates of her terms as abbess are confirmed by documentation from the Archivo Regional de Boyacá.

[b] Francisca Josefa de la Concepción's signature as secretary appears on documents from 1694, 1698 through 1700, 1702–3, and 1706–7 in the Archivo Regional de Boyacá and in the convent archives.

[c] See also the *Libro de capítulo* (147v–149v) and documents signed by Madre Francisca Josefa de la Concepción in the Archivo Regional de Boyacá.

[d] Date the election was confirmed by the archbishop.

[e] See also the *Libro de capítulo* (152v–153v) and documents signed by Madre Francisca Josefa de la Concepción in the Archivo Regional de Boyacá.

[f] See also the *Libro de capítulo* (128v–129r; these pages belong to a second section that starts over in its numbering) and documents signed by Madre Francisca Josefa de la Concepción in the Archivo Regional de Boyacá.

consistent provision of historical markers, constructing instead a time frame based on the repetitive character of the liturgical calendar, lengths of illnesses, offices held, and occasional references to her age. Under this cyclical sense of time, however, lies submerged a historical dateline that can be read in her changing official duties, in the movements of her confessors, and in the deaths of her convent superiors. The following narrative, then, is organized by both the passage of time and the themes relating to Madre Castillo's probable path to power; these include her economic situation, the offices she held, the entrance of family members into the convent, her relationship with her confessors, the elections for abbess in which she is implicated or participates, her growing power within the convent, and her administrative work as abbess.

A Vow of Poverty

The vow to divest oneself of personal property, so central to Saint Clare's and Saint Teresa's ideal retreat from the world, posed problems for any Spanish American nun who chose to write the story of her daily life. Madre Castillo depicts her life in the convent as fraught with economic difficulties, a portrayal that shows this child of Tunja's upper class to be poor. She has run away from a loving home to the convent fearing that she will sleep her first nights in a corridor for lack of a cell (*SV*, chap. 63, 19). Claiming economic hardship, she reports having eaten flowers at times, as she has no food (chap. 9, 25). A few years after taking vows, she receives from another nun the offer of the sale of a cell and box or narrow gallery that affords visual access to the church and thus spiritual sustenance for her soul. Without money to pay for the rooms, she must work off the debt (chap. 14, 45; chap. 16, 52). She tells that seven years after professing, she becomes the object of a vicar's community talk, in which he berates her for the poverty that has come to her household (chap. 21, 72). This picture of a nun who lives out her vow of poverty perforce is not entirely consistent with convent records or even with certain other comments made by the author herself. The reduction of five hundred pesos from the required two thousand that Sor Francisca received on her dowry speaks of economic need, yet most nuns at the time brought only one thousand pesos with them.[12] Madre Castillo also mentions two servants who have accompanied her from home (chap. 9, 25). Such information would indicate that the Castillo family represented above average wealth among the convent's elite. If her self-portrait does not always coincide with other sources, it does respond to a radical religious desire to imitate Christ and to follow the rule of the Poor Clares.

Late in life, Madre Castillo produced a substantial sum of personal wealth to donate to the convent's commissioning of a new monstrance.[13] The famous treasure, now considered national patrimony and kept in the Museo de Oro of the Banco de la República, was fashioned by Nicolás de Burgos out of gold,

FIGURE 5. Cell attributed to the use of Francisca Josefa de la Concepción, Convento Real de Santa Clara, Tunja, 1996. Photograph by Jorge González ©.

silver, and hundreds of precious gems. Inaugurated on August 12, 1737, the day of the convent's patron, Saint Clare, the treasure boasted 813 *castellanos* of fine gold and two ounces of silver, 657 emeralds, and 291 other precious stones— including diamonds, amethysts, pearls, and topazes—for a total cost of four thousand *patacones* (María Antonia del Niño Dios 1993, 389).[14] Madre Castillo's personal contribution included thirteen hundred pesos and "a rose of thirty-seven diamonds, one larger than the others . . . two more small roses of emeralds . . . one of fourteen stones and the other of nineteen, which in total make thirty-three emeralds" (392).[15] The jewelry holding the stones also contained gold worth fourteen pesos and five *reales.*

Madre Castillo refers in her *Vida* to accusations that she has hoarded such worldly possessions after the death of her sister (*SV,* chap. 37, 143; chap. 55, 214); suspicion and animosity regarding the possible hiding of wealth is not surprising under a rule that strictly limits possessions and prohibits inheritance from deceased family members. Madre Castillo's reporting of the accusations participates in her complex picture of herself as sinner, reformer, and scapegoat, as someone campaigning for austerity of life and, paradoxically, accused of violations of the vow of poverty. As in the criticisms by canonical visitors of the ostentation of the Calends singers, a large donation toward the commissioning of an object of worship central to the duties of the Poor Clares could be read as elevating the status or ensuring the memory of the donor. The disparate accounts of Madre Castillo's personal wealth pose contradictions that are not resolved by either her *Vida* or convent documentation. Perhaps the family fortune fluctuated, allowing her greater economic latitude toward the end of her life, or perhaps the discrepancies reflect the contradictory demands of the *Vida* and the archives, the first posing impoverishment as virtue, the second asking for a strict accounting of economic contracts regardless of the implications.[16]

A reading of Madre Castillo's donation should not remain limited to cold calculation. The order of the Poor Clares was dedicated from its inception to continuous vigilance over the host, as it was the power of Christ's consecrated body with which Saint Clare repelled the Saracens from Assisi. Both routine and belief revolved around this transubstantiated element, which often centered nuns' visions, providing a palpable symbol of the union of their bodies with the mystical body of Christ. Held by the new monstrance, the Host would radiate with gold and jewels that echoed the imagery of mystic visions, imagery that describes the Divine in terms of what was most beautiful and precious within worldly existence. Great status and comfort were felt by the cities that housed the consecrated virgins who cared for the Host, glorified God, and prayed prayers of intercession in return for small gifts or substantial endowments from the faithful. Great importance was placed on the object of their prayerful attention.

FIGURE 6. Monstrance commissioned by the nuns of the Convento Real de Santa Clara, Tunja, in 1737. Photo reproduced by Jorge González, with permission, from the Collection of the Biblioteca Luis Angel Arango of the Banco de la República, Bogotá.

Convent Offices

Soon after taking her vows, Sor Francisca was appointed by the abbess to share the duties of secretary with an older nun, a position she held intermittently during a number of her early monastic years (see Table 2). The secretary served as aide to the abbess. She was to "keep very faithfully the secret of things, what is said to her, what she writes, or knows through letters. She attends in chapters and elsewhere, including in business affairs, to all of which she must attest" (Magdalena de Jesús 1722, chap. 6, par. 3).[17] From the inception of her professed life, Sor Francisca was given a heavy responsibility and was privy to the delicate affairs of convent management. The charge appears to have been given to her unusually early. While, after examination of convent and regional archives, my data are still incomplete, the earliest I have found any nun in Santa Clara to exercise the office is seven years after her profession. Such an honor may well have been bestowed on Sor Francisca because of her intellectual capacity and the social stature of her family.

The various offices to which Sor Francisca was appointed play a key role in her development of the self as protagonist in the *Vida,* and they contribute to the constant vacillation in the text between the self as exemplar and its antithesis. In narrating her obedience or ineptitude at carrying out the tasks of her offices, Madre Castillo imbues her character with a changing symbolic worth. As sacristan or vestry nun, Sor Francisca prepared the objects and vestments used in worship, which allowed her physical contact with the most sacred adornments and receptacles of the convent. As portress, she regulated the passage of people, messages, and goods between the protected inner and threatening outer worlds. As *escucha* and *gradera* (parlor and grille chaperone), she undertook a similarly delicate vigilance during an age when amorous parlor advances were famed for threatening virginal virtues. As nurse, she played a very humble role of service, at one time carrying the office as a cross of punishment (María Antonia del Niño Dios 1993, 115). As will be seen in chapter 6, these symbolic values operate in the *Vida* to configure Sor Francisca in the contrary directions of inept sinner and guardian of strict monastic rule.

The offices of nurse, choir mistress, and mistress of novices required musicianship, the ability to provide spiritual guidance and teaching, and the qualities of nurturance and love (De Vances 1699, 157, 159, 164). They placed a high degree of responsibility in Sor Francisca's hands for the lives and performance of others. As choir mistress, she was to lead the Divine Office—the raison d'être of the convent—seeing that "the Office be sung, and the divine worship and prayer with much devotion; ensuring that it is said with the due pause, beginning all of the nuns together, and ending at the same time, so that there is uniformity and consonance, taking great care that the nuns help the choir in what is sung and prayed, and when anyone is careless, she should note this with charity" (157).[18] The importance of this office makes Sor Francisca's expulsion from it all the more sharply felt when, as she reports in the *Vida*, the abbess punishes her for her craziness and for giving her soul to the Devil, by taking away the choir keys and books and sending her to work in the infirmary (*SV*, chap. 25, 91).

Madre Castillo's recounting of her tenure in guiding the novitiate shows a more positive picture of her monastic self than the ineptitude she records in most other offices. According to María Antonia del Niño Dios's records, Sor Francisca was assigned five times to the office. This post more than any other shows evidence of her growing favor within the convent. The Franciscan *Constituciones generales* emphasize the importance of the position, saying that it must go to one of the most virtuous, prudent, and zealous nuns in the convent (Merinero 1748, chap. 10, 134). Although in the *Vida* Madre Castillo claims to have fallen from such estimation in the eyes of Abbess Antonia de la Trinidad (1705–7), her successor, Catalina de San Bernardo, tells her that "she want[s] to return the credit that ha[s] been taken away from [her] and to name [her] once more mistress of novices" (*SV*, chap. 27, 101).[19] In this role, Sor Francisca prepared future postulants in a capacity that would allow her to influence them with her own vision of religious life and to elaborate strong emotional ties with the young nuns. Her influence probably helped her toward the prelacy. Madre Castillo suggests the loyalty she has won from her novices when, under great attack from most of the convent, in 1706 she receives visits from two of her former pupils, who suffer scorn to see her (chap. 25, 91). The following year, she suggests her success as teacher when she affirms that some of the novices had been on the point of leaving the convent until she was appointed to guide them. She, of course, indicates that it was Christ who consoled them, not herself (chap. 27, 101). She also tells that a few of her ex-novices turned against her after the 1715 election, when she won half of the votes. On May 8, 1718, when Sor Francisca was elected abbess, as many as seven of the approximately twenty-four voting nuns would have been among the novices she directed.[20] If she was successful in winning their favor, then by 1727, a date during Madre Castillo's tenure on the council for which the names of the council members are available, she would have found herself surrounded by allies. As many as four of the seven other nuns on the council had been novices under her care and direction.[21]

A FAMILY BASE

The profession of a large number of family members within the same convent was a common occurrence in Spanish America and reconstructed for the nuns the social base around which their lives were articulated prior to their entrance. During the first 150 years of the history of Santa Clara in Tunja, well over half of the professed nuns had at least one sister in the convent, and it was not uncommon for three or four sisters to live together within the cloister. Although the Pamplona founder, Madre Magdalena de Jesús, and Doña Elvira de Padilla from the Carmelite convent of Santa Fe both legislated against family power by assigning an entire family a single vote within the convent, such precautions were stripped from the Carmelite constitutions, and they do not appear in the Spanish constitutions for the Franciscan order or in the Urbanist Rule of Saint Clare. It is not surprising, then, that Madre Castillo's *Vida* surrounds with controversy the entrance of each new relative into the convent.

Family-centered problems began for a different reason, though, when Sor Francisca's ill mother entered the convent in 1699 (María Antonia del Niño Dios 1993, 81). According to the *Vida,* prelates opposed the potential economic burden that Sor Francisca's mother would place on the convent by entering late in life. Ill and blind, she would take her daughter away from convent duties in her need for care (*SV,* chap. 14, 46). Fourteen years later, on September 24, 1713, Sor Francisca's widowed sister Juana Angela took the habit (*LC* 144v). According to the *Vida,* the request made by Sor Francisca's sister for license to enter the convent was initially denied, at which point the vicar meted out a harangue upon Sor Francisca (*SV,* chap. 33, 125). María Antonia del Niño Dios reports that when Doña Juana de Castillo y Guevara was allowed entrance, she brought with her a large dowry, jewelry, and slaves and renounced her inheritance in favor of the convent, all of this due to the additional expectations placed on her because of her advanced age (1993, 178). Doña Juana died on April 28, 1714, while still a novice; and, according to Sor María Antonia, her dowry and other possessions including jewelry and slaves were reclaimed by her brother Don Pedro Antonio del Castillo, since her death prior to profession meant that these did not belong to the convent (178 n. 2). The accusations that Madre Castillo relates that she has kept the belongings involve even convent outsiders, who go to the extreme of threatening excommunications (*SV,* chap. 37, 143). In these two cases, the conflict surrounds the appropriation of resources where collusion between family members may be perceived as an unfair benefit from and drain on the convent.

In 1706, Sor Francisca's second sister, Doña Catalina Lugarda, who had married Don Agustín de Mesa Cortés, proposed the entrance of her daughter, Mariana de Mesa Cortés y Castillo, as a choir nun. Convent secretary at the time, Sor Francisca penned the letter of petition from the *difinitorio* to the Vicar General for Doña Mariana's license to take the habit. The tone of special petition that the letter expresses suggests that a dispensation from full dowry is being requested at a time when the convent's numbers were very low.[22] Madre Castillo's comment at the time of her niece's death, that Sor Mariana had been given one of the places in the convent not endowed with active or passive voice in decisions, also indicates her special status, like that of the *monja lega de coro* (*SV,* chap. 45, 171). "[B]eing without inheritance or any right thereof from her parents, in great poverty, favoring her pious desires, Governor José de Enciso y Cárdenas, her uncle, offers one thousand pesos for her dowry. And being the above said Doña Mariana endowed by the heavens with one of the best voices that has been heard in this city, and having been examined before our Father Vicar, and finding her to be very necessary for the divine worship in the choir, which with the loss of the daughters of Don José Paredes Calderón, the one having died and the other having abandoned the habit, is found destitute of voices" (*Actas de elecciones de abadesas y de peticiones para las tomas de hábito y profesiones del Real Convento. Legajo especial*).[23]

While Mariana de San Joseph takes the habit on June 10, 1706 (*LC* 133r), welcomed with apparent joy into the convent, she soon becomes a player in her aunt's difficulties. This period in Madre Castillo's *Vida* is troubled with a "scandal" in which accusations are made about her to her confessor. She writes that her niece has violently disassociated herself from her aunt, returning only after the vicar has assured Sor Francisca that the troubles were caused by the passions of the accusing nuns and are not her own fault. These nuns have so much leverage in Santa Fe that the vicar is afraid to act on her behalf (*SV,* chap. 26, 97). The family division portrayed in the *Vida* defends Madre Castillo against accusations of power gathering, and it may also symbolize the depth of destruction inflicted by the community's attacks on a suffering Sor Francisca. Her niece professed on August 12, 1711 (*LC* 144r), but died only six years later. When the vicar requested of Sor Francisca the property of the deceased, she insisted that her niece was poor (*SV,* chap. 45, 171)—again a hint that she has broken her vow of poverty by harboring possessions, again a point at which family and allies lead to controversy in the convent.

A second niece professed as a black-veiled choir nun on January 19, 1718 (*LC* 146r), the first of the six daughters of Captain Pedro Antonio de Castillo and his wife, Doña Josefa Caicedo, to wear the habit of Santa Clara. María Antonia del Niño Dios identifies this niece as the child whom her aunt had raised in the convent from the age of five (1993, 247). Madre Castillo relates that the year before her niece's profession, the nuns "said that I wanted to rise up with the convent and take away the keys [be elected abbess], that I had stirred up the convent and divided it into bands, and that my *jarcia* [rigging, jumble, mess] (as they called my relatives) were destroying the convent by day and by night" (*SV,* chap. 44, 168).[24] She writes that votes in favor of her niece's profession are denied and that letters are written to the archbishop requesting that the license be refused (chap. 46, 175). The affront occurs at a key period in Sor Francisca's ascent to the head of the convent, one marked in the *Vida* by election-related visions of temptations. Nevertheless, Francisca del Niño Jesús did profess and, twenty years later on April 14, 1738, would win the election for vicaress to accompany her aunt in her final term as abbess (María Antonia del Niño Dios 1993, 414–15).

Doña Catalina Ludgarda's daughter by Captain Lucas Camacho de Guzmán took the veil as Margarita de la Cruz on April 27, 1720 (*LC* 149v). She would be joined by five more cousins—the remaining daughters of Captain Pedro Antonio de Castillo and Doña Josefa de Caicedo. María Gertrudis del Sacramento and Ana Josefa de la Trinidad professed on December 8, 1727 (152r). Antonia de Jesús, who had been raised in the convent from the age of two, professed on May 21, 1730 (152v).[25] Her last two sisters, Clara María de Jesús and Ignacia de San José, completed the convent family on September 24, 1737 (128r). Insufficient documentation has been uncovered to show the full extent of involvement of Madre Castillo's family within the convent's financial and political life. One can speculate on the type of connections that might have caused controversy before her election to office, and would have helped her when she faced financial crisis as the convent's abbess. The presence of the six daughters of Captain Pedro Antonio de Castillo may have provided important dowry moneys to bolster the convent's suffering investments. More important was Don Pedro's political and social clout in resolving questions of financial debt owed to the convent. As much as the entrance of new family members reported in the *Vida* is surrounded by controversy, Madre Castillo and her family proved successful at building a strong family presence within the convent. Madre Castillo's niece Francisca del Niño Jesús would carry on the family tradition within the convent, taking the office of abbess by 1746, shortly after her aunt's death (Achury Valenzuela 1968, xcvi). Achury Valenzuela sees a growing sense of security for Madre Castillo when he notes that during the years from her profession until about 1710, her various adversaries within the convent—especially abbesses, as well as certain nuns, syndics, and vicars who opposed her—began to die off, leaving her much freer of her earlier turmoils (lxxxii).

Confessors

If the numerical growth of Madre Castillo's clan within the convent helped to cement her exercise of internal power, and thus reinforced the family's economic and social status, her relationships with confessors strengthened her personal image and protection outside of the convent. Achury Valenzuela identifies ten Jesuits and two Franciscans who acted as Madre Castillo's spiritual directors, and he provides biographical information for these men.[26] Madre Castillo's correspondence with her confessors tells of relationships of mutual respect and of her support within a powerful male order. Nine letters addressed to Madre Castillo from five confessors, four named and one anonymous, have been preserved. The dated letters span the years from 1724 to

1735, but they contain references to an ongoing mutual correspondence. The admiring tone of the letters is set by the use of terms such as "my very esteemed Lady," "my Mother Francisca," "Your Reverence," and expressions of affection such as, "I have never forgotten you and I have a thousand desires to see you."[27] The confessor-nun relationship has been analyzed by Michel Foucault in the first volume of the *History of Sexuality* (1978), and its spiritual and material elements form an important axis of much recent scholarship on nuns' writings. These relationships played a central role in Madre Castillo's own writings. In a world both suspicious and admiring of mystic manifestations, the letters from Madre Castillo's confessors center on the tribulations she suffers and the reassurance she seeks in her radical experience of spirituality. Her confessors urge her to continue on her chosen contemplative path, and they reinforce the interpretation, which she offers in her *Vida* and *Afectos,* of her suffering as a purification by fire. While Madre Castillo often indicates concern in the *Vida* over her infamy outside of the convent, her confessors repeatedly express their belief that her isolation from the other nuns in the convent and the attacks that she is suffering result from God's special love for her soul, that God desires her constant suffering, and that this is a sign that she will be consoled in the afterlife.

Not only do her confessors' letters seek to bolster her inner spiritual confidence, they also indicate effective support in an antagonistic world. One reference in the *Vida* to the retraction of a threat made against Madre Castillo suggests that the loyalty of her confessors was instrumental in protecting her in important ways (*SV,* chap. 44, 169–70). A sale of land to the Jesuits during Madre Castillo's third term as abbess manifests her special relationship with the powerful order. In this decision, she abstained from the council vote because she was, as María Antonia del Niño Dios puts it, "very dear and known to the Society,"[28] and she did not want to be seen as acting out of passion (*Legajo Especial*). The letters between her and her Jesuit confessors hint at an ongoing collaborative discussion of economic and political events in which the confessors provide Madre Castillo with advice and information. Through these religious men she developed her own connections in Santa Fe in the figure of confessors who had moved on to posts in the city of the archdiocese, to which they might have close access and where they might intervene on her behalf.

The cryptic nature of the references in her correspondence with her confessors might indicate a precaution, despite "safe" messengers, to facilitate continued written exchange about delicate matters (Castillo 1968, 2: 540), or it could simply reflect a shorthand in situations that Madre Castillo knows well. In a letter written on October 20, 1724, from Santa Fe, Padre Diego de Tapia advises Madre Castillo not to worry about the failure of a certain doctor Montalvo to carry out a "diligencia" and requests that she state what a certain quantity of money was spent on (Castillo 1968, 2: 537). He also refers to the judicial sentencing of "Don Pedro," the denial of a request for a change of parish, and a doubt as to whether "esos señores" will appeal the decision. Padre Diego is responding to concerns Madre Castillo has raised regarding a member of the clergy. It is possible that the comments refer to Don Pedro Montalvo de Tobar, *vicario juez eclesiástico* (ecclesiastical judge) of Tunja and its convents between at least 1720 and 1722, and that they have to do with the conflicts between the community and its male representative.[29] The written exchange between Madre Castillo and Padre Diego de Tapia provides some idea of the ways in which she developed private relationships with specific confessors in order to work out her own political concerns and those of her convent.

That these relationships were perceived as problematic by the other nuns of Santa Clara is clear in Madre Castillo's report in the *Vida* that the blame for a *pleito* (dispute) between the convent and the Jesuit school is placed on her (*SV*, chap. 44, 167). María Antonia del Niño Dios maintains that the litigation concerned certain Haciendas de Gámeza on which the Jesuits had been paying a *censo* to the convent since at least 1696 (Archivo Colonial de la Parroquia Mayor de Santiago de Tunja, "Capellanías de los Rojas" [1696]; *Libro de cuentas* of the Abbesses Francisca de la Trinidad [1695–98] and Catalina de San Bernardo [1698–1704]).[30] The political significance of this economic dispute is not clear, but the positioning of the event in the *Vida* is key. It occurs alongside several other instances of blame that are laid on Sor Francisca for internal convent disturbances and punishments, all in the year preceding her first election as abbess. Together these build a convent case against her as power-hungry and proud. As it becomes clearer that *Sor* Francisca will soon become *Madre* Francisca—she claims to have received almost half of the votes in the 1715 elections—her opponents have greater reason to attack her connections to power.

ELECTIONS AND ADMINISTRATION

María Antonia del Niño Dios does not quote documents from the 1715 election for abbess, which, if still in existence, might confirm the growing support for Sor Francisca. Madre Castillo reports in the *Vida* that the entire city is in an uproar about the fact that she has received almost half of the votes. The nun who wins the office is very angry and tells a convent outsider that Sor Francisca wants to become abbess and that she is unfit for the office (*SV*, chap. 41, 158). Convent archives show that the same abbess, in 1717, held Sor Francisca in sufficient confidence to name her to a fourth term in the important position of mistress of novices, from which she would win her first election to the prelacy on May 8, 1718 (*Cuaderno de Cuentas*, quoted in María Antonia del Niño Dios 1993, 250, n. 1).

If her family's social and economic status, the entrance of relatives into the convent, and the influence that Sor Francisca wielded as mistress of novices did in fact aid her in configuring favorable power relations, then her first term as abbess (1718–21) presented a pivotal point in this balance. In 1720, Madre Castillo was the most recently professed member of the *difinitorio,* but the majority of choir nuns had professed later than Madre Francisca, and at least seven of those nuns spent part of their novitiate under her guidance.[31] Seven years later, in 1727, just before Madre Castillo's second term as abbess began, she ranked second only to the abbess, Lugarda de Santa María (see n. 20). Four of the nine newer members had experienced her tutelage as mistress of novices. In other words, the *Vida,* completed around 1724, was written during a period when her political trajectory was less secure but on its way to success. It is likely that the actual writing of the *Vida* functioned as a defense and a mechanism by which to build authority in communicating to her confessors her version of her monastic self.

Madre Castillo's first term as abbess occurred at a low point in the size of the convent, and she complains of a severe economic crisis that she faced in her tenure, a claim that is borne out in external sources. Keeping in mind the possibility of incomplete evidence, one reads in Pino Alvarez's study that the convent's income decreased from 25,281 pesos between the decade of 1700–1709 to 17,048 pesos for the period of 1720–29 (1989, Table 1); during the same time the community's needs grew with a 50 percent increase in the number of choir nuns (*LV* 173v; Castillo 1718, pt. 4, 27; 1732, pt. 3, 53).

Facing the crisis in the *Vida,* Madre Castillo adopts a mask of ignorance concerning economic affairs and fears that the convent will fail under her governance. She lays these affairs in God's hands and is rescued by his will through the help of a priest and her brother Captain Pedro Diego de Castillo (*SV,* chap. 47). The specific events that she narrates during these three years portray her as a weak victim of the community rather than as its strong leader. She is expelled from the common dormitory that she is charged to oversee; she is accused of mishandling convent affairs; she is told by persons outside of the convent to relieve of his duties the man who manages the convent's income; and, in a canonical visit, the archbishop removes from the refectory a large image of Christ because the other nuns complain that she has placed it there only to condemn them with it (chap. 48, 184). The post is a martyrdom from which she asks to be relieved during her first year in office, in order to avoid participating in those "very costly diversions" (185).

It is these worldly diversions to which I turn next in my representation of Madre Castillo as a convent CEO, actively involved in her community's economic affairs and positioned to take on the tough legal language of the times. Abbesses acted as both general managers and representatives of their communities, responsible to their sister nuns and to the male hierarchy. The account books they kept may best attest to these dynamics. Madre Castillo's records from her first two terms as abbess are preserved in the Biblioteca Luis Angel Arango in Bogotá. The section dedicated to the years 1718–21 is divided into three parts: one records the interest income paid by tenants, a second details weekly expenses for items of food and clothing as well as medical and pastoral services, and a third notes "extraordinary" expenses such as the purchase and fabrication of objects of worship and convent repair and construction. The set of records from 1729 to 1732 lacks information on convent income, while in contrast the weekly expenses are recorded in such detail as to suggest that little could have been forgotten. At the end of the abbess's term, the entire community of nuns witnessed a reading of the accounts for their approval. María Antonia del Niño Dios relates that at this time the abbess removed herself so that any nun who might wish to bring forward complaints against her would feel freer to do so (1993, 435).

The seventy-one documents representing Madre Castillo's economic dealings with the outside world that I have found in the Archivo Regional de Boyacá (Notaría 1–2) probably illustrate only a fraction of her activities as chief economic officer, many more such documents having been kept within the convent walls or by the convent's clients (Table 3). These documents do not include, for instance, the hundreds of tenant receipts that would correspond to Madre Castillo's governance. Such biannual transactions were signed by both the abbess and the *síndico* and would require of the abbess repeated visits to the parlor.[32] Madre Castillo was occupied in many more than the seventy-one economic transactions reported in the Archivo Regional de Boyacá, being pulled frequently away from the ideal state of ignorance of "this world" and prevented from dedicating herself fully to worship, writing, and mystic contemplation.

The language of the legal documents challenges strongly the unified subjectivity of the model nun. Using prescribed formulas, the papers do not shy away from representing the abbess as powerful and knowledgeable about economic affairs. The case against one Francisco López for allegedly occupying the lands purchased by another man from the convent is a typical one. The documents record a complex history of sale, attributing the voice of the history's narrator to Madre Castillo, as abbess. Her statements are direct and forceful:

Mother Francisca de la Concepción, in the cause that I am pursuing concerning the restitution that I have requested be made to my convent of the [city] blocks that it owns near the big fountain of this city, those which Francisco López occupies without just title, I say that although on my behalf he was advised of his default for not having responded or said anything regarding the notification that on my request was given him, and neverthe-

Table 3
Archival records of Madre Castillo's activities as abbess of the Convento Real de Santa Clara, Tunja

Year	Section	Volume	Folios[a]
1718	Notaría 1	176	225–26, 226–28, 261–65, 277–78, 300–302, 326–28, 348–52
1719	Notaría 2	169	10–11,* 30–35, 106, 149–50, 237–38
1720	Notaría 1	177	1–3, 16–20,* 29–30, 79–82, 120–24, 159, 186–88, 205–9, 248–53, 273–80*
1721	Notaría 2	170	52–57
1729	Notaría 2	172	48, 90–95, 100, 101–2, 102–5
1730	Notaría 1	180	51–57, 58–62, 71
1731	Notaría 2	173	107–11, 131–37
1732	Notaría 1	180	289–90
1738	Notaría 1	182	282–86, 315, 363–66, 437–38,* 448
1739	Notaría 2	183	20, 36–37, 70–71, 75–77, 115–17
1739–40	Notaría 2	180	248–52, 260–61, 275–77, 283–84, 289–95,* 295–96, 297–98
1740	Notaría 1	183	5–9, 17–18, 43–44, 89–93, 103–7, 107–9, 109–14, 114–15, 174–76, 177–80, 190–91
1719	AHT	148	Document no. 44
1720	AHT	149	59, 113
1729	AHT	156	336
1738	AHT	161	271–97
1739	AHT	172	238, 670–71
1740	AHT	174	Document no. 63
1741	AHT	175	31–85

[a] Documents marked with an asterisk report the participation of either the *difinitorio* or the full community in the decision made or in the signing of the document.

less he has not responded. Whereby I advise him of second default so that Your Mercy be served, as I implore, to consider the default advised and to order what I have requested in my first document being conformed to and by means of justice.

I request and implore Your Mercy to rule and order that which I have requested with justice, costs and the necessary, etc.

Francisca Josefa de la Concepción, Abadesa [September 24, 1738] (AHT, ARB, 1733, vol. 161: 295)[33]

Such language ascribed to the abbesses precise and authoritative demands, in which they did not hesitate to request that debtors be brought to jail or that their properties be auctioned off to satisfy convent debts. The weak and ignorant voice of Madre Castillo's self-characterization in the *Vida* stands in stark contrast to the authority that her figure wields during her business negotiations in the convent parlor.

The strong first-person language and the familiarity with legal process associated with the person of the abbess do not prove Madre Castillo's willful construction of this image of herself using this language. The uniformity of the language suggests that the documents were drawn up by the magistrate or a notary. But while the language may have been supplied by the male representatives of the convent, it was not foreign to the nuns who sometimes wrote or transcribed such legal language themselves. Among the documents in which Madre Castillo "speaks" in the first person, two of them appear to be in her hand (AHT, ARB, 1720, vol. 149: 86; 1729, vol. 156: 336). Others may have been drawn up by the convent secretary—as is true for such documents as letters to the archbishop concerning convent affairs. It is probable then that Sor Francisca processed and learned the language during her many years as secretary. Through this language, the powerful public subjectivity that she is called to take on as abbess enters her consciousness and opposes the image of the consecrated virgin that she believes she must show to the world, thus complicating her task of self-representation.

In the *Vida,* Madre Castillo responds to the economic crisis that focuses her preoccupations with a grand deus ex machina maneuver in which God saves the convent through the intervention of her male relatives. This plot and the mask of weakness it provides save her own nontemporal image. Recently elected, she laments the scene she faces of a convent "going to ruin in full haste." [34] Ignorant of the proper actions, she is told to replace the syndic, for which she enlists the help of an unnamed preacher. But before the preacher can move against him, the syndic dies. There is reference to the incident in Tunja's notarial archives. On February 4, 1719, the members of the *difinitorio* attest their unanimous agreement to nominate maestro Don Francisco José Caicedo y Aguilar to fill the position of "apoderado general," or convent attorney, left vacant by the death of Alférez José de la Verde y Castillo (Notaría 2, ARB, 1719, vol. 169: 10–11).

The lengthy disputes of which Madre Castillo despairs mirror the general economic crisis of the Nuevo Reino de Granada. The defaulting of debtors gravely affected the quality of convent life and enmeshed abbesses in prolonged antagonisms. One case involved the heirs of Francisco de Alvinogorta and his wife, Catalina de Guevara, who had signed a deed for 1,050 pesos in 1627 in favor of the convent (AHT, ARB, 1717, vol. 146: 315–466). The debt was left pending for two generations as the convent's representatives remained unable to exact payment. Madre Castillo became involved in the dispute in 1718, eighty-six years from its initiation. The two granddaughters of Catalina de Guevara, after four years of trying to argue their way out of the debt, lost their case and recognized a new *censo* on the lands of Tey and Santa Ana for the above amount. The deed was signed by Madre Castillo and the attorney de la Verde (Notaría 1, ARB, 1718, vol. 176: 300–302). The conflict appears related to the help Madre Castillo attributes to her brother. In 1720 the novice Juana de la Encarnación, cousin to Madre Castillo and Don Pedro, left 1,000 pesos to the convent, along with an additional 1,986 pesos that had been donated to her "on behalf of her cousin Pedro Diego de Castillo y Guevara owed by his grandfather to the heirs of Catalina de Guevara, our grand-mother" (Notaría 1, ARB, 1720, vol. 177: 248–53).[35] This appears to be the Juana de Garay who is named as one of Catalina de Guevara's granddaughters in the earlier lawsuit. These few indications of the personal involvement of Madre Castillo and her family in the financial intricacies of the convent underlie the enormous tensions she expresses in her *Vida* when trying to submerge this subjectivity of the world behind the model nun.

Having inherited her office fraught with severe challenges, Madre Castillo can affirm in the *Vida* that great changes have been wrought in both temporal and spiritual affairs. Everyone, even her enemies, recognizes that the convent has benefited greatly from the powerful hand of God during her prelacy (*SV,* chap. 49, 188). The convent's path from crisis to comfort is substantiated by her *Cuaderno de cuentas* (accounting book), which records the distribution of new habits in 1719 and the purchase of additional cloth the next year at Christmas for the black- and white-veiled nuns and the novices (*CC,* pt. 4, 48). The following year, over eight hundred *patacones* or *pesos* were spent on new adornments for the church, the convent, and the priest (48–49). Toward the end of Madre Castillo's first term, money did not seem scarce for the glorification of God through the decoration of the church and its minister.

Aside from a fifth assignment as mistress of novices in 1723, Madre Castillo's primary involvement in convent management during the years between her terms as abbess was as *madre del consejo,* or mother adviser on the council, where it is probable that she exercised substantial weight in convent decision making. Her second and third elections to the post of abbess demonstrate the strength of her support within the convent. On April 2, 1729, she received twenty-two of twenty-four votes, and on April 14, 1738, thirty of the commu-nity's thirty-one votes were cast in her favor (*Legajo especial, elecciones de abadesas, profesiones y tomas de hábito, desde el año de 1690, hasta el de mil setecientos cuarenta y dos (1742);* María Antonia del Niño Dios 1993, 415). Madre Castillo occupied the position of abbess for a total of nine years. This constitutes a longer exercise of the office than was claimed by any other nun during her convent lifetime (Table 4). Of the twenty-eight abbesses who served the convent between its foundation and Madre Castillo's death, only four others held office as long or longer than she. She remained a member of the inner council as either mother adviser or abbess for a total of twenty-four

FIGURE 7. Presbytery of the Church of Santa Clara, Tunja, 1996. Photograph by Jorge González ©. The colors that dominate the interior of the church are red and gold.

Table 4

Abbesses of the Convento Real de Santa Clara, Tunja, 1689–1742

Dates of office	Abbess	Source
June 28, 1689–1692	María de San Gabriel	75r
June 28, 1692–1694	Paula de San Ignacio †	75r
Sept. 26, 1694–1695	María de San José †	75r
Jan. 19, 1695–1698	Francisca de la Trinidad	75v
Jan. 20, 1698–1701	Catalina de San Bernardo	75v
Jan. 20, 1701–1704	Catalina de San Bernardo	75v
Jan. 20, 1704–1705	Francisca de San Joseph †	76r
Feb. 15, 1705	Francisca de la Trinidad †	76r
Sept. 27, 1705–1707	Antonia de la Trinidad †	76v
July 20, 1707–1708	Catalina de San Bernardo †	FdS 121
Oct. 13, 1708–1711	Isabel de Jesús María	77r
Oct. 28, 1711–1714	Paula de la Trinidad	77v
Oct. 13, 1714–April 1, 1715	Tomasa de San Antonio †	FdS 203
May 8, 1715–1718	Isabel de Jesús María	FdS 211
May 8, 1718–1721	*Francisca Josefa de la Concepción*	FdS 249–50
May 8, 1721–March 15, 1723	Paula de la Trinidad †	FdS 257
April 2, 1723–1726	Felipa de San Ignacio	FdS 272
April 2, 1726–1729	Lugarda de Santa María	FdS 322
April 2, 1729–1732	*Francisca Josefa de la Concepción*	FdS 322
April 2, 1732–1735	Josefa de San Andrés	FdS 328
1735–1738	Felipa de San Ignacio	FdS 363 n. 1
April 14, 1738–1741	*Francisca Josefa de la Concepción*	FdS 414
April 14, 1741–	Josefa de San Andrés	FdS 436

Compiled from the *Libro de capítulo* (folio numbers) and from documents cited in María Antonia del Niño Dios, *Flor de santidad (FdS)* (1993).

† Indicates those nuns who died in office.

years. If, as she tells in the *Vida,* Madre Castillo began her convent life marginalized and persecuted by the women in power, archival records paint a picture of fully consolidated power during the latter half of her life as a Poor Clare.

Madre Castillo died at the age of seventy after having lived for almost fifty-three years in the Convento Real de Santa Clara. The only record of her death to be found is in the account books of the abbess who took office in 1741. There Madre Castillo becomes an itemized expense: "And on February 23, 1742, the burial of Mother Francisca de la Concepción was carried out, and for the masses that were said for the body in state, novena, wax, torches and masses, and vigils of the day of the last honors, fifty-seven pesos were spent" ("Gastos extraordinarios," *Libro de cuentas de la R. M. Abadesa Josefa Gertrudis de San Andrés* [1741–44], 2v).[36]

Madre Castillo's life ended with an apparent lack of fanfare. No biography was written at the time, nor have I found any inquiry into her mystic life such as was carried out after the death of the Carmelite abbess Madre Francisca María del Niño Jesús in 1708 (Conventos, AHNB, vol. 66: 1–353). The Discalced Carmelite had gained early popularity within her convent and was elected prelate only five years following her profession (Germán María del Perpetuo Socorro and Martínez Delgado 1947, 234). Her enormous popular following after her death, evident in the lavish descriptions of her funeral rites, strike a sharp contrast with the more controversial reception given Madre Castillo during her life and the relative silence surrounding her death. The lengthy questionnaire and numerous responses given by sister nuns, priests, and secular acquaintances of the Carmelite speak to her virtues and supernatural experiences and, together with her own writings, lay the foundation for her future biography (Conventos, AHNB, vol. 66: 25). Why Madre Castillo, in contrast, lived only in oral tradition until the publication of *Su vida* in 1817 has not been explained, apart from a reference to the personal interests of one of her last confessors, Padre Diego de Moya, who preached her funeral sermon and then refused to undertake the biography until the sermon was published with the backing of the convent and Madre Castillo's niece (Castillo 1968, 2: 548–50), a step that was never taken. While the reformist zeal of both Madre Castillo and Madre Francisca María evoked heavy censure from their peers at one time or another, the coming together of personalities, struggles, and power worked much more in Madre Francisca María's favor. The controversy that surrounded Madre Castillo's life may have defeated attempts by supporters to create of her a venerable memory. Madre Castillo's good name, still mixed today in local lore with criticism of her revelation of monastic strife in Santa Clara, emerged seventy-five years after her death, not from a popular following or a priestly biography but from the legacy of her own pen.

P A R T

· III ·

THE TEXTS

SU VIDA

SPIRITUAL TRIALS AND
WORLDLY TROUBLES

Well, many times they have said, shouting, that since this demon entered this convent, it has been intolerable; that I am rebellious, a troublemaker, a sham; that I do not know who God is; that I even disinter the bones of the dead with my tongue; I used to consider and have considered this, although by God's mercy my conscience does not give me cause for remorse, but what do I know whether my self-esteem deceives me, having so much of it; it would be easier and more believable that I deceive myself, than that so many others should, as I see how well they serve God, etc.

For a long time, and I don't know whether I am recounting something very ordinary, as my body takes on sleep, my soul remains in prayer with more burning affects than is possible when awake, and with great peace. . . . In particular, one night, when I seemed to see him [Christ] naked and on the cross, kneeling, and that a very slight cloud was binding itself to him and rising up his body, and my soul, undoing herself in affects of her Lord, understood that she[1] was that little cloud, and it seems to me that I understood that Our Lord's showing these things to me in sleep, is the cause of my having continuous confusion and fears.

—Madre Castillo, *Su vida*[2]

MADRE CASTILLO'S self-portrayal weaves in and out of degradation and elevation, ascending to rapid heights of mystic blessing and doubling back in self-chastisement to create an infinitely complex tapestry of contradictions. The contradictions are rooted in the context in which she writes; the possibility for exploring subjectivity that the *vida* genre offered its authors collided with the repressive force of Counter-Reformation doctrine and its particular suspicion of women and of radical female religiosity. Expression and repression stage a violent clash in Madre Castillo's autobiographical text as she resists the unity of a submissive Counter-Reformation subjectivity.

Four narrative strategies frame my examination of Madre Castillo's *Vida* and of the autobiographical subject that it constructs. Firstly, the author

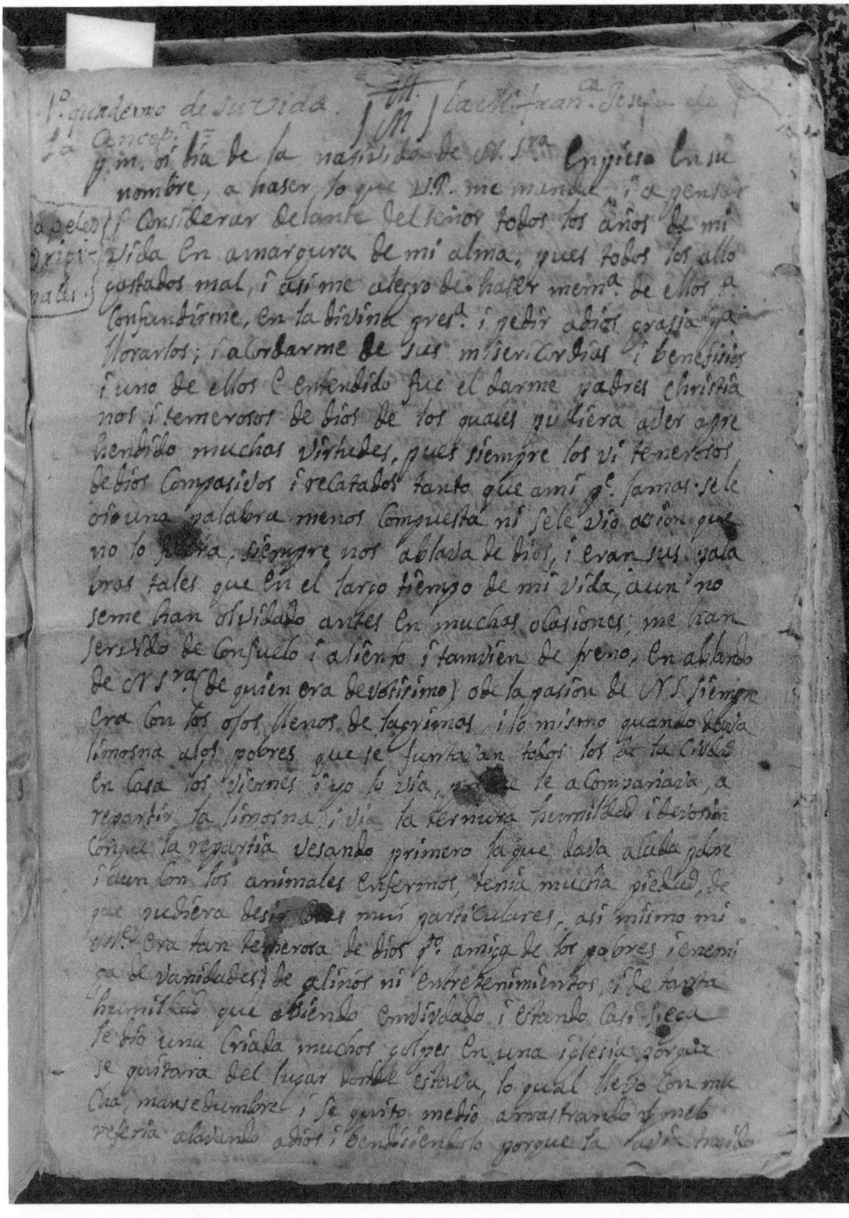

Figure 8. The first page of *Su vida* by Madre Castillo: "p.m. oi día de la natividad de N. Sra. . . ." Photograph by Jorge González ©. Reproduced with permission from the Manuscript Collection of the Biblioteca Luis Angel Arango of the Banco de la República, Bogotá.

recounts a childhood that prefigures the discrepancy between the ideal and the real that will frustrate her throughout her life; even before she attains the age of reason, her evil nature derails her from the saintly path she appears destined to take. Secondly, she encases everyday events in a spiritualized discourse, fitting over the physical, interpersonal, economic, and political the narrative of a painful spiritual journey. Thirdly, Madre Castillo seeks to conform her protagonist to the ideal removal from the world of the consecrated virgin, and yet the world erupts insistently into her narrative through a secular atmosphere and activities that are unbecoming to a model nun. Finally, the author fills the space of the self's subjectivity with holy archetypes in a narration that tries to prove its orthodoxy while seeking the immortality of both text and heaven, risking a pride that threatens both. The present chapter treats the first three narrative strategies while the fourth occupies chapter 7. The characteristics of the *Vida* that are outlined in chapter 2, page 55, continue to inform my analysis of Madre Castillo's writing throughout.

Our knowledge of the circumstances surrounding Madre Castillo's writing of her *Vida* is fragmentary at best. The words of obedience that she addresses to her confessors, their presence as explicit readers, and the framing of her task—"to do what your paternity demands of me and to think about and consider before the Lord all the years of my life"—situate the work within the *vida* tradition (*SV,* chap. 1, 3). This task differentiates the narrative from the more fragmented and journal-like autobiographical *Afectos* in which Padre Herrera commanded her *many times* to write for him the sentiments that God gave her (chap. 11, 34).

Madre Castillo wrote her *Vida* in segments that were reviewed by her confessors as she completed them, but the story weaves the narrative thread of that totalizing project of constructing and judging its subject, beginning at birth and ending in the present. Biographer María Antonia del Niño Dios calculates that the period of writing stretched from 1713 to 1724 (1993, 276, 281). By her own word, Madre Castillo was well into the autobiographical task when she turned forty-four in 1715, and she did not complete the *Vida* until after her first term as abbess, 1718–21. The manuscript's 106 folios are divided by the author into fifty-five chapters, which are maintained in the various editions of the work. The autograph is preserved in the collection of the Biblioteca Luis Angel Arango in Bogotá. A note by Madre Castillo's confessor Diego de Moya at the end of the manuscript certifies that it was written by her hand (*SV* 214). The story of the *Vida* follows a roughly chronological order. It begins with the birth of Francisca Josefa de Castillo and ends some three years after Madre Francisca Josefa de la Concepción's first term as abbess of the Convento Real de Santa Clara, when she is about fifty years old.

THE OLD CHILD, THE CONSCIENCE-RIDDEN CHILD

Madre Castillo's account of childhood shares with those of many contemporary religious women writers the very early signs of a special relationship to the Divine. Solitude and prayer, confusion, and the consciousness of sin replace children's games as the very young Francisca echoes those patterns in saints' lives that Weinstein and Bell designate as the "old child" and the "conscience-ridden child" (1982, 20–29). Every event that Madre Castillo narrates leads her protagonist toward the convent. Every episode carries a weighty spiritual interpretation, though much of the significance of this early life she understands only now, as an older narrator. The spiritual quest she paints is a picture of opportunities ignored. Time and again Francisca is taught how to live a righteous life, and just as often her weak nature fails her in the execution of the lessons. Despite her faults, God sends her repeated signs of her destiny in his service.

Near death as a tiny baby, Francisca is saved with a cure prescribed by an uncle. His act prefigures his role in the salvation of her soul when he later encourages her to become a nun (*SV,* chap. 1, 4). Barely able to talk, Francisca tells her mother that a family icon of the Baby Jesus has called her to him. Having just learned to walk, and far from entering the age of reason, she hides away to cry as if she could see all the sins into which she will later fall. Her parents provide a perfect example of Christian life in their humility and in their love for her and for the poor, but she can never live up to it (chap. 1, 3). She accepts a young playmate's childish proposal of future marriage when she is not yet seven and is overcome with torment for so doing. She is so distraught that she allows the Devil to tempt her to consider suicide (chap. 1, 4–5). Madre Castillo shows herself to have been a child burdened far beyond her years with the guilt of human sinfulness.

Rather than play with other children, Francisca seeks retreat. She arranges images of Jesus and Mary, desires to imitate the Discalced Carmelites as she listens to her mother read Saint Teresa's *Libro de las fundaciones,* and converses with two virtuous family slaves about Christian life. Though her pious play appears to move her along the path of her holy destiny, though she wears the habit of Saint Rose of Lima, and though she already suffers the frequent illnesses characteristic of her holy contemporaries, she also engages in the worldly joys of adorning herself with jewelry and reveling in the great love that she attracts. Again she balances between salvation and the fall. A stark warning of the evils toward which this worldly behavior impels the not yet nine-year-old Francisca arrives in the form of a dream, a sort of stigmatic experience in its physical manifestations. "I seemed to walk on a mezzanine made of bricks placed end to end, as if in the air, and with great danger, and looking down I saw a river of fire, black and horrible, and within it were moving as many serpents, toads and snakes as faces and arms of men who could be seen submerged in that well or river" (*SV,* chap. 1, 5).[3] Waking from the dream, Francisca finds her fingertips burned, as if the warning has shown her how close to the torments of hell she walks.

At the age of eight or nine, Francisca finds her first real occasion to sin when the "plague of souls" that are *comedias*—that is, secular fiction—enters her house (*SV,* chap. 2, 7). Having learned the alphabet from her mother, she teaches herself to read and devours the books, only to learn much later that, while such reading itself is not a sin, many souls would not have found themselves in hell but for such diversion. The mature narrator interprets the child's subsequent prolonged ailment as punishment for her pleasures. In this psychosomatic illness, Francisca experiences a horrible fear of sin that prevents her from eating or sleeping adequately. This results in her emaciation and, in turn, makes her the butt of other children's cruel jokes. It is at this time that Francisca has her first prophetic dream, in which she foresees the death of a very sinful person. The dream is another warning to live a good life, another warning from which she cannot benefit because of her vile nature.

When Francisca is twelve or thirteen years old, her family begins to spend more time in their house in Tunja and less on the rural hacienda. She studies music, a skill that will serve her well in both convent life and in her own writing. The move to Tunja facilitates greater contact with religious life, as her mother takes her to the Jesuits for confession (*SV,* chap. 2, 8). Francisca continues to live tightly enclosed—only relatives are allowed to visit—but enclosure does not keep her from the temptation of the flesh when a cousin professes such strong love for her that he wishes to go to Rome for dispensation to allow their marriage. She entertains his letters but is saved from sin when her father intervenes. She is shaken and begins to see in her cousin the shadow of death (chap. 3, 9).

At about fourteen, Francisca has a type of conversionary experience. She has already shown signs of a religious life and will continue to acknowledge her frequent sin long after this conversion. Nevertheless, her family members note a sudden change when she undergoes the sacrament of confirmation. Francisca has already given up reading *comedias* for the writings of Saint Ignatius, on the recommendation of her aunt who lives in the Convento Real de Santa Clara. She now sets aside the pretty dresses that she had been wearing. She begins to lead an ascetic life, praying for hours wherever she finds quiet: in the hen house, the fields, or a small cave that she has discovered. Punishing her body for its sins, Francisca mortifies herself with "various instruments" until her blood runs. These "instruments" probably included some type of whip or thong and barbed metal chains. Francisca also wears hair shirts and chains that become embedded in her flesh (*SV,* chap. 4, 11). As she enters fully into this radical practice of spirituality, she begins to hear the *murmuraciones*[4] that criticize her "holy pretenses," attacking her as a *santimoñera* or one who affects a false piety.

An intensification of Francisca's fears and torments accompanies her increased religiosity. While a book on prayer by Molina and the *Spiritual Exercises* of Saint Ignatius lead her to contemplation, the lonely inner place to which her prayer takes her offers horror rather than the consoling presence of God (*SV*, chap. 5, 13).[5] For four years, the Enemy—her preferred term for the Devil—causes her to believe that she is committing great sins. Dreaming of persecution, she finds refuge in the monstrance and understands that only in the Holy Sacrament will she be safe from her enemies. In an irony born of her vile nature, the space that allows constant proximity to the Host—that is, the convent—incites in her an intense dread. Though the thought horrifies her, Francisca explains her new piety to mocking relatives by stating that she wishes to become a nun. Madre Castillo's retelling of these deeply ambivalent emotions distances the good act of dedicating her life fully to God from her evil and weak nature, which abhors the thought. Word spreads, and her relatives all attempt to dissuade her from monastic life. Her parents express special distress and do everything in their power to provide her with a "convent" at home. Despite the war of emotions these efforts produce in her, her relatives ultimately fail (chap. 6, 15).

Madre Castillo provides several comments on her final decision to run away to the convent against her parents' wishes. On one hand, she sees in the act the damnable motive of pride: she is too haughty to submit her own will to that of another mortal in marriage (*SV*, chap. 6, 17). On the other, she sees goodly motivation: she desires to give herself entirely to Christ rather than to an earthly spouse. Reading—that practice of consuming and reworking others' stories that will center her entire life—plays a weighty role in her decision. When she reads that virgins—she means either martyrs or nuns—may follow Jesus, the divine lamb, as spouse, she knows that she would rather suffer martyrdom than give herself to anyone else. She is comforted in her turmoil to know that many saints whom she wishes to imitate fled their homes for the convent against their parents' will (16). But when she leaves the house alone, she does so "as one who tears out her bowels . . . with repugnance, as if to torture" (chap. 7, 19).[6] When her family receives word of her flight, parents and siblings alike cry; her father does not stay his tears for three days, and her mother becomes very ill (20).

A childhood that is not a childhood already separates Francisca from her peers and estranges her from her family, leading her into a struggle for solitude that marks her entire story. Her life is touched with both asceticism and visionary mercies. She expresses a deep desire to serve God but struggles constantly against her natural evil. This nature has not yet fully developed in her early years, but its root in pride has already appeared in her admission of vanity, her refusal to submit her will to that of another mortal, and the possibility that her piety reveals an affected self-righteousness. Francisca knows that true solitude, refuge in God alone, is her salvation, but her life is instead plagued by a painful isolation born of antagonism, an isolation that speaks not of God but of her imprisonment by the opinions of others.

A Spiritual Struggle in the Convent

A reader unfamiliar with *vida* writing might initially apply Dámaso Chicharro's criticism to this autobiography, stating that it is not structured by temporal and spatial elements, or say with Manuel Serrano y Sanz that external events are forgotten; but such a reading cannot withstand closer scrutiny.[7] If dates from the Gregorian calendar do not propel Madre Castillo's narrative, a calendar of Church and convent does. The feast days of Saint Bruno, Saint Ignatius, and the birth of Mary provide more meaningful notice of the passage of time for Madre Castillo than do the denominations of October 6, July 31, and September 8. This manner of marking time is shared by other *vida* writers. The significance of these days brings Madre Castillo to understand her experiences in light of the lives of their namesakes and molds her actions and visions. She is born on the day of the mystic Saint Bruno, founder of the contemplative Carthusians, which signals that her life ought to be guided by prayer and retreat from the world (*SV,* chap. 1, 4). She begins to write on the birthday of the Virgin Mary, thus invoking her holy mother's protection and consolation in facing a troubling task (3). Her visions, too, are shaped by the movement of the calendar; Holy Week, for example, inevitably brings a special sensitivity to Christ's torments.

While a calendar of feast days carries a cyclical rhythm, it does not eliminate a sense of historical time. The religious conception of time echoes the nun's withdrawal from the world within convent walls and rejects the historical calendar that dates every document of worldly negotiations in which she is involved. Still, it is relatively easy to match Madre Castillo's use of religious markers of time against her references to the offices she holds, the elections of abbesses and their deaths, and the lengths of her illnesses, to arrive at a chronology that carries her story through her entrance into the convent in 1689 to the present of her writing, sometime around 1724. The events that anchor her story in historical time were understood by her immediate readers. If her discourse is cloaked in a removal from worldly time, the detachment is not complete.

Madre Castillo's narrative also shares the thematic structuring of other female *vidas*. Kathleen A. Myers notes that María de San José subverts historical time by ordering her *vida* with the "categories of virtue and religious experience" (1993b, 20). In the tradition of Saint Augustine, the Mexican nun structures her conversion narrative on the "story of the fall, conversion, and struggle of the soul as it strives for perfection," revealing a tension between the ideals of the convent rule, the paradigm left by the order's founder, and her own lived experience (23). Likewise, Madre Castillo relates episodes of a spiritual journey, though any progress is intentionally difficult to discern. The journey is structured by experiences of suffering that instruct the soul. These experiences involve spiritual and physical travails, antagonistic encounters with nuns, servants, abbesses, and vicars. They revolve around religious practice and convent politics, relationships with confessors, the trials and consolations of convent duties, participation of family members in convent life and affairs, and an awareness of the status of the souls of others both inside and outside of the convent. These motifs return repeatedly throughout the *Vida*.

There is a pattern to the episodes of spiritual trial that carry Sor Francisca on her journey. Most contain an early visionary warning of the turmoil to come. The turmoil inevitably involves either her confrontation with internal temptations or her becoming the center of scandal, the object of the attacks of the entire convent community. Very often the suffering is brought to an end or mitigated by a second vision, this time of affirmation, a heavenly revindication or a comforting lesson spoken to Sor Francisca's soul, which rescues her temporarily from the depths of despair. Many of these messages heard by the soul are communicated through Latin Scriptures. Sometimes the celestial revindication is echoed in earthly relationships. If the affirmations elevate Sor Francisca as the blameless victim of her peers, superiors, and servants, Madre Castillo also carefully and consistently affirms the goodness of those through whom God allows the Devil to abuse her. She closes the episodes with the assertion that anyone else would have benefited immensely from the lessons learned but that a vile nature impedes her own improvement. Thus, Sor Francisca seems only to spin her wheels.

An episode that occurs during the first two years of Sor Francisca's life as a professed nun illustrates well the structure of her spiritual journey. Chapters 12 and 13 concern those temptations that cause spiritual turmoil and distance her from God. Specifically, she is afraid of the possible heresy of her own life of mental prayer and divine favors. (The words *favores* [favors] and *mercedes* [mercies] are commonly used in *vidas* to refer to these visions, ecstasies, suspensions, and other mystic experiences.) Sor Francisca's fears are spurred by stories of a *beato*, or lay religious man, who was burned for heresy after the Devil deceived him in his life of mental prayer. Even before Sor Francisca entered the convent, relatives had warned her that she could end up in such delusions. Her religious sisters reiterate the warnings.

Sor Francisca holds in great esteem a certain nun whose virtue has won her fame (*SV*, chap. 12, 38). This exemplary nun fears any suggestion of the supernatural with respect to prayer. She even refuses to read anything treating the subject. Sor Francisca, however, has already found joy in knowing that the soul can be united with God during this lifetime. Thus, she faces a deep conflict between the attitude of her role model, the dire warnings she receives, and her lived experience. Her attempts to conform place her soul, like a caged bird, in a prison of fear. The fear is aggravated by signs of her tendency toward evil and deceit in the attacks leveled at her by other nuns: "Well, many times they have said, shouting, that since this demon entered this convent, it has been intolerable; that I am rebellious, a troublemaker, a sham; that I do not know who God is; that I even disinter the bones of the dead with my tongue" (see epigraph, above).

Having shown her reader her spiritual dilemma and the profound distress with which it floods her soul, Madre Castillo sets about reaffirming her original desires over and above the fear imposed by the climate of suspicion that surrounds her. Before exercising any authority of interpretation over her life, she assures her reader of her submission to the authority of others. Fear of self has always led her to seek the security of a male spiritual guide, one who attends her inner experiences by reading her *papelitos*. This affirmation is timely, for her confessor, Father Francisco de Herrera, has recently refused to hear her confessions. The estrangement occurred after other nuns made un-named accusations about her to him, and she, too prideful to accept the criticism, insisted on making excuses. She now inserts a text much like one of her *papelitos* into the *Vida*. She introduces the *afecto-*like piece with a key for its interpretation: this knowledge that she has understood is a consolation from God instructing her to avoid interaction with other people. She is not to seek comfort from them for her troubles but should wait for God either to move her confessor to return to her or to send her another. She is not, how-ever, to understand this as a vindication of her disobedience (*SV,* chap. 12, 39).

As in the *Afectos,* the lyrical reflection that follows explores a highly sym-bolic parable in which Madre Castillo weaves seamlessly into her own voice passages from the Song of Songs and the Psalms. The opening phrase resounds with the mystic metaphors of Saint John of the Cross and Saint Teresa—"My beloved is mine, and I am his" ("Mi amado para mí, yo para El") (Song 2:16) —and it articulates the key to the entire text: Sor Francisca must listen only to God and seek comfort in him alone, ignoring the fears of mortal creatures. Madre Castillo writes with a pedagogical tone of the imprudence of the pelican, who builds a nest among the most heavily threshed fields, where nest and young are lost to the fires set by laborers. Her soul must rather be like the eagle, who nests on high rocks, or like the dove, who seeks a cavern in the fenced orchard. The pelican's field represents this world, the care and dealings with other people and the dangers of this intercourse, while the lofty crags and the protected cavern are secret and solitary places where the soul can be alone with God. Madre Castillo's triumphant affirmation of her life of prayer through God-given knowledge against the fear of heresy is confirmed on earth when Herrera, no longer angry, reads her visionary knowledge and finds in it no sign of the serpent but only of God. Still, he warns, chastising her earlier pride, she must not flee her confessor even though he might treat her harshly and wound her. Madre Castillo has redefined temptations to mean not the Devil's interference in prayer but the fear of mental prayer itself.

Though chapter 12 ends here, its theme continues in 13, where the practice of mental prayer is confounded by the sin of pride. At about the same time that Sor Francisca hears of the *beato* who was punished for his heresy, the nuns of her convent warn her of a priest who, though known for his virtue, has lost his mind. The popular explanation is that his pride has drawn evil spirits to torment him. The nuns also taunt Sor Francisca with accusations that she is just like the *seglara* (laywoman) who has recently fled the convent, having spent her time there telling everyone of her revelations from God. Both stories make Sor Francisca fear that she errs through deceit, hypocrisy, and *soberbia oculta* (hidden pride). Once more Madre Castillo recognizes that the ill lies not in Sor Francisca's spiritual practice but in the weeds sown by the Devil in the useless soil of her heart that choke out the good desires that God has placed there. With these metaphors, she sets her soul into a biblical parable (Mt 13:4–8). Divine affirmation of herself and her writing returns after she refuses, out of fear, to write down her supernatural experiences for Herrera. God shows her that the sentiments he has given her soul are written on his own heart with his own blood (*SV,* chap. 13, 44). A second confirmation is spoken softly to her soul in the words of the Scriptures: "Quis nos separabit?" (Rom 8:35) (Then what can separate us? [NEB]); and later, "Cur fles? et quare non comedis? et quam ob rem affligitur cor tuum? Numquid non ego melior tibi sum quam decem filii?" (1 Sm 1:8) (Why are you crying and eating nothing? Why is your heart so vexed? Am I not more to you than ten sons? [NEB]). Sor Francisca understands that these words, with which God calls her to him, tell her to ignore the ill-placed warnings of her earthly cohorts; they fill her soul with joy and love. Yet these mercies cannot bring her to complete faith in God, as her virtues are choked out by the weeds of mistrust and tepidness that the Devil has been able to sow in her heart because of her pride (*SV,* chap. 13, 44). Like Saint Teresa, who sought a new confessor when the first one judged her mysticism to be diabolical, Madre Castillo too sees a great danger in the fears that mortals have of mental prayer, fears that can lead one off the path to God. The "temptation" that troubles Sor Francisca in these chapters is the temptation to believe the fears of others rather than to trust in God.

Madre Castillo's double bind is a dangerous one: either she conforms her will in obedience to her superiors who criticize her spiritual life and thus distances herself from God, or she demonstrates her love of God by conforming to his will and accepting his supernatural favors and disobeys her superiors.

Either error implies a prideful defiance of authority, one earthly, one divine. This double bind is her crucible and cross, her purifying fire and imitation of Christ, which lead her soul to accept torment as both God given and the path to the Divine. This redemptive cross sometimes provides the symbolic images to the warning visions that prefigure the episodes: at one time, for example, Sor Francisca tries to help Christ, who is being whipped while tied to the column (*SV,* chap. 23, 79); at another, a Dominican archbishop and a layman anoint her upper back and shoulders in preparation for her to receive a cross large enough for two (chap. 52, 196).

The irony of the episodes—their simultaneous elevation and degradation of Sor Francisca as subject—like the irony explained by Alison Weber in Saint Teresa's "rhetoric of femininity," seems clear to this twentieth-century critic, and yet such double entendre may or may not have been a conscious rhetorical strategy by the eighteenth-century nun. Madre Castillo constructs a protagonist whose primary sin is that of pride, shown through others' accusations as well as in her own recounting of her actions. Her pride leads her to criticize and correct others. According to her monastic superiors, pride underlies her audacity to call on prominent clergy to confess her when other nuns have been unsuccessful. It leads her at times not to submit to every order. Sor Francisca suffers deep turmoil when others accuse her, and this turmoil reveals pride where she should rather imitate Christ's humility and revel in her punishment. The twentieth-century critic sees a brilliant and strong-willed woman who must formulate, and probably believe, an orthodox self-condemnation, but who can never entirely submit her will, insisting on expressing a belief in her vindication and her salvation.

A rhetoric of irony also lies within Madre Castillo's application of the Scriptures as a balm for her pain. The eighteenth-century Church warns her that the love of self will lead her to perdition. Her peers and superiors criticize her willfulness. These condemnations send her into an isolation in which her inner spirituality at times proves desolate, at others affirms her, but almost always leads her to the texts of the Divine Office, especially the Psalms. Herein she finds authoritative wisdom, consolation, and affirmation. Ironically, her very claim that the lessons she learns never bear the fruit of actions inscribes her humility in brilliant prose, interpreting Latin Scriptures that may be inaccessible to many of her monastic peers. She has learned Latin, she writes, as a divine mercy during her praying of the Hours, in an apprenticeship begun when she was a novice and that continues throughout the *Vida* (chap. 8, 23). Surely part of her explicit self-condemnation also arises from a recognition that, when she humbles herself in writing, her powerful biblical exegesis on humiliation expresses great singularity despite the fact that she attributes every word to God.

If in following the imperative of humility with brutal dedication, Madre

Castillo does not show her soul on a steady climb toward perfection, she does intimate spiritual development about midstory and again at the end of the *Vida*. In 1712, after many extended battles in the convent, Sor Francisca comes to a realization of the purpose of her martyrdom, and her fear and confusion are vanquished (*SV,* chap. 35, 133). The catalyst is a vision in which she sees an abundant field filled with beautiful trees, flowers, and fruits, which she understands to be the rewards born of humiliation. Her peace does not last, yet she is now better able to see as ovens of purification her antagonistic relationships, including the rigor of her confessors in their spiritual guidance. Writing about the years following her first term as abbess, Madre Castillo offers a second hint of progress in the most mystic of the visions of her *Vida,* that is, the vision that most expresses that highest point on the spiritual path, comprehended in the union of the soul with God. This vision is recounted, above, in the second of the epigraphs that open this chapter.

At the end of the *Vida,* Madre Castillo turns to the present and although still proclaiming herself as vile, is simultaneously able to offer the image of a good soul by uttering the great desires for God that she feels at present (*SV,* chap. 55, 209). Unlike the narration of past events in which she is called to judge herself, here, in promises for the future, she faces an open book and so can avoid self-condemnation. She relates a vision in which an apocalyptic discourse issues from the lips of Christ, as he seems to say to her:

> Poor little one, tossed by the tempest without any consolation, do not fear, you will not die. . . . More are for you than against you. The prideful dragon pulled down the third part of the stars; and the power of my omnipotent arm will triumph over him as if he were a poor, thin and weak straw. . . . Listen! encourage your heart, poor little woman, drown yourself in the sea of my mercies. Look, the dawn will come and the struggle and battle will end, and there will be an end to the darkness when Mary enters as the dawn, strong, soft, peaceful and merciful. (211)[8]

As Madre Castillo closes her *Vida* with a hope that speaks of triumphant salvation, albeit in patriarchal terms, she cannot avoid submission in a post-script to her confessor. Here she returns to the themes of obedience, fear of delusions, and renewed accusations in the convent—that she has applied to her own possessions a great quantity of silver and other things (214). In closing, she echoes her opening words: "I see all the time passed in my life so full of faults and so off track, that I lack eyes to cry, being as I am in this region and so far from living as a true daughter of my Father God."[9] Only the blood of Christ will suffice to cleanse her of her filth. Though Madre Castillo cannot bring herself to end in full triumph, she has allowed a defiant voice of self-expressive singularity to surface in her story.

THE CARES OF THE WORLD

Madre Castillo exalts a spiritual path that demands perfect disinterest toward the cares of "this world," and yet she herself is unable to follow it, plagued throughout the *Vida* by adversity, scandals, and politics. From the day she first runs away from home and enters Santa Clara, Sor Francisca's relationships with other nuns are primarily antagonistic. Those mutually supportive relationships she does relate she nurtures with novices and confessors and only very occasionally with other nuns. When, in 1701, five years after her profession, she begins to make friends and to receive visits in her cell, there erupts in the convent the "greatest war" she has yet suffered, as the friends of those nuns who visit her turn against them, causing great scandal and divisions in the community (*SV,* chap. 16). One convent group that Madre Castillo names over and again as her accusers is the servant class. No member of this group ever shows her compassion, which explains her avowed preference for those convents in which servants do not live and where few distractions would take her from her desired retreat.

Though she denies almost all specific accusations made against her, especially those that would suggest any attempt to seek power and high office, Madre Castillo cannot—or chooses not to—keep these incriminations out of her text. They focus on questions of obedience to vows and rules, her ability to carry out the offices assigned her, her embodiment of virtues or lack thereof, and her spiritual experiences—their sincerity and their divine or diabolical origin. Some charges echo the instructions left by ecclesiastical visitors, while others resonate with doctrinal discourses. Texts from her practice of reading appear in her self-examination; for example, during the episode in which friendship brings disaster, Sor Francisca reads in the choir from Saint Teresa's *Camino de perfección.* She chooses a passage on the danger of particular friendships and thus incurs even greater wrath when she is denounced as a hypocrite (*SV,* chap. 16, 53).[10]

In short, Madre Castillo's self-portrayal allows her to develop a tremendous narrative of doctrine-in-action to address the worldliness of convent life while maintaining great ambivalence about her own guilt or exemplarity. She creates ambivalence in that polyvalent rhetoric that denies specific sins, claims a sinful nature, and counterposes terrible acts on the part of other nuns to praises of their great virtue. One can solve the question of guilt as she does by seeing the convent turmoils as the fiery crucible in which her soul is purified by God through the Devil's torments, leaving her attackers blameless. Yet such a small lid does not fit tightly over such a tumultuous pot and allows other meanings to escape. The accusations leveled at Sor Francisca directly, and those she suggests in representing the actions of other nuns, do interest those clergymen who sought to reform convent life and who requested that *vidas* be written.

Sor Francisca is even alleged to have written to Santa Fe reports regarding convent affairs. The tumultuousness of her *Vida* conveys more than simply her own spiritual purification. She is also engaged in writing about that struggle between worldliness and spirituality that she cannot satisfactorily resolve in either her own life or that of the convent.

Pride is the quality, the sin, that most intimately links Sor Francisca to worldliness, and her pride implicates her in struggles for power within the convent. Thus the struggle between worldliness and spirituality centers on her relationship with power and with the powerful. Sor Francisca receives bitter humiliations at the hands of almost every abbess as well as from the vicars who generally take the abbesses' side. By leaving these superiors anonymous, in contrast to her naming of confessors, Madre Castillo might intend to give her discourse a degree of abstraction or to protect herself from further accusations of *murmuración;* on the other hand, her readers would have known who the abbesses were. If she does not name the abbesses, it is useful to identify them to appreciate the totality of the oppositional force that she sees lined up against her. Their identification also reveals an intimation in the *Vida* of a waning opposition and a totality of revindication for Sor Francisca, as each abbess dies and, before death, asks her forgiveness. One after the other—Paula de San Ignacio, who governed from 1692 until her death in 1694; Catalina de San Bernardo (1698–1704, 1707–8†); Antonia de la Trinidad (1705–7†); Isabel de Jesús María (1708–11, 1715–18); and Paula de la Trinidad (1711–14, 1721–23†)—each takes on Sor Francisca as a bane to the convent.[11] Only Francisca de San Joseph (1704–5†) stands out in Madre Castillo's special praise for the unity that her benevolent governance achieved among the nuns, while Francisca de la Trinidad (1695–98 and 1705†) seems to escape any negative mention. Nevertheless, each anonymous abbess, like each attacking nun, is called good and virtuous.

Sor Francisca falls into Madre Paula de San Ignacio's bad graces even before her profession, when her insistence on wearing a plain wimple implies criticism of the abbess's rule (*SV,* chap. 10, 29). In 1699 Madre Catalina de San Bernardo throws obstacles in the way of Sor Francisca's mother's entrance into the convent (chap. 16, 52) and three years later sears her with scathing chastisement, calling her crazy for her presumptuous request that Father Juan Martínez Rubio, the distinguished rector of the Jesuit school, confess her (chap. 21, 71). Sor Francisca incurs the wrath of the convent's vicar when, as secretary, she asks him for some papers that have been lost from the archives (72). In a third term as abbess, in 1707, Catalina de San Bernardo promises to restore Sor Francisca's good name, but when the vicar sends a notary to the convent with a document accusing Sor Francisca of teaching a laywoman to write, the abbess turns against her, reprehending her for lack of loyalty to the order (chap. 27, 101). Madre Antonia de la Trinidad says that the Devil has Sor

Francisca's soul (chap. 25, 88), promises to put her in stocks and whip her, and demotes her from choir vicaress to lay helper in the infirmary (91). Madre Paula de la Trinidad, who had cared lovingly for Sor Francisca during her illness, gives her the responsibility of portress in October 1711, but by Holy Week the next year this abbess too proves adversarial (chap. 31, 119). At about this time, the council mother Isabel de Jesús María denounces Sor Francisca's actions to the community, threatening vengeance by having Sor Francisca's confessor, Juan Romero, prohibited from visiting the convent (chap. 33, 126). Though she names Sor Francisca mistress of novices in 1717, abbess Isabel de Jesús María directs a full rage at her in blame for the disturbances that plague the convent (chap. 44, 168). In all of these troubles, Sor Francisca becomes the frequent object of public humiliation in chapter meetings. Her confessors express concern that her bad name is on every tongue in the city. In a society consumed by the importance of honor, hers is shattered.

Throughout her ordeals, Sor Francisca often finds solace in her relationships with her Jesuit confessors. During the periods when she is without a confessor, she feels lost in a dark night of loneliness. In the cases of Juan de Tovar and Juan Manuel Romero, Madre Castillo implies a certain triumph in stating that these priests had refused to confess other nuns in the convent but agreed to take her under their wing (*SV,* chap. 12, 37; chap. 32, 121). Her confessors often stand by her and protect her from the full wrath of the abbesses and vicars. Juan de Tovar aids in gaining entrance to the convent for her mother in the face of great opposition from the abbess and vicar (chap. 16, 51). Juan Martínez Rubio protects her in the conflict over the missing archive papers (chap. 21, 72). Romero quiets the unnamed priest who has written a letter threatening Sor Francisca with the Inquisition (chap. 44, 170). Sor Francisca seems to play these more authoritative male members of a very powerful order against the less powerful abbesses in political and moral battles. The confessors interpret her suffering as a God-given purification of her soul, they judge her experiences to be of God, and they console her both while in Tunja and in later correspondence. She, in turn, expresses great trust in their guidance, as in a vision in which she sees herself following Diego de Tapia up a steep and dangerous incline—she frightened, he calm—steadying herself when she falls by catching onto his cape (chap. 40, 153). Her relationships with confessors are not all comforting, however. She loses Francisco de Herrera's ear for a time after denying blame for convent disturbances (chap. 11, 35). An Augustinian friar refuses to confess her, finding her at great risk and with the Devil in her heart (chap. 31, 118). Even Romero treats her with harshness, believing the rigor of his guidance an appropriate cross for the honing of her soul.

If her portrayal of her relations with the abbesses enables Madre Castillo to own her pride with humility and to indict her disobedience, these relationships also provide the materials of a narrative that denies any desire for power.

Her narrative of negation takes both explicit and implicit forms. The charges that she is seeking power in the convent, and her denials, begin in about 1706, ten years after her profession, when other nuns allege that she wants to remove the abbess from office, an idea she calls nonsense, not knowing where they have conceived of it (*SV,* chap. 26, 95). In 1715 Isabel de Jesús María accuses Sor Francisca of desires for the prelacy, though she denies any such wish (chap. 41, 158). It is during this election, however, that she claims to have been named by almost half of the votes. The year before she will take the office—1717—Sor Francisca is denounced for stirring up the convent into bands and wanting to grab the keys of the convent, an implication that she is politicking in preparation for the next elections (chap. 44, 168).

The accusations are crystal clear, and so Madre Castillo mounts a second offensive to separate her protagonist from any suspicion of power mongering. She does this by portraying the office as a danger to the soul and, later, by expressing her own experience of it as an unwanted martyrdom. Before the election of Isabel de Jesús María in 1715, Sor Francisca is shown by the Devil a room filled with the faces of prior prelates who have been condemned by the diversions of the office (*SV,* chap. 41, 158). The vision calms her, presumably consoling her that she will not be elected. When she falls dangerously ill in 1717, she receives a vision of a holy court in which her illness is discussed. Some of the angelic figures think it better that she not live because if she does, she will become abbess in seven months, putting her soul at grave risk; some believe that God can keep her from becoming abbess if she lives, while still others express optimism that God might even keep her from guilt in the eventuality of her election (chap. 46, 175–76). Thus, she removes responsibility for her election from her own hands and prefigures the divine intervention that will later help her face its dangers.

When she relates her first term in office, Madre Castillo distances herself as carefully as she can from any hint of delight in power; in fact, she constructs a subjectivity of great ineptitude and ignorance.[12] Not knowing how to proceed, she asks advice of a senior nun, who shames her for doing so (*SV,* chap. 47, 180). She fears the future of the convent in her incompetent hands (181) and laments that she must constantly be involved in the disputes of laypeople. Her obligations as abbess chain her in cruel torment to the grille, where she must engage in intercourse with the world, listening to words of deceit and greed that draw her away from the eternal values of God (182). The challenge of punishing a nun with the necessary rigor makes her sweat blood as she shrinks from her authority (chap. 49, 188). After a year in office, she asks the rector to remove her from the position (chap. 48, 185). Despite Madre Castillo's professed helplessness, the convent thrives under her rule, to the extent that certain projects are accomplished that had not been possible during the entire history of the convent. They have been achieved, she affirms, by God's mercy alone, who acted through the instrument of her brother, Pedro Antonio de Castillo.

If the duties of abbess lead the soul to risk perdition in the exercise of power and in contact with the world, then the other abbesses who have exercised that power fall under critical light. Again, the message oscillates between condemnation and justification. Madre Castillo seems driven to vindicate herself, in earthly and heavenly scenarios, vis-à-vis those prelates who have tormented her. At the same time, both her earthly situation and the *vida* genre oblige her to affirm the goodness of every abbess whenever she might be seen as casting aspersions. Three of her greatest tormentors, Antonia de la Trinidad, Catalina de San Bernardo, and Isabel de Jesús María, come to Sor Francisca shortly before they die to ask her forgiveness for their treatment of her (*SV,* chap. 26, 96; chap. 27, 104; chap. 49, 189). These acts of humility might show the great virtue of these authority figures who punished her justly if they were not accompanied by lessons and visions that throw a shadow of doubt on the self-incriminating force of the representation. From Madre Antonia's plea for forgiveness Sor Francisca learns not to fear God's creatures but to trust in him: "Do not fear those who kill the body" (Mt 10:28 NEB), she hears; "[d]o not fear the words of men:[13] quia hodie extollitur, et cras non invenietur: quia conversus est in terram suam" (1 Mc 2:63) (today he shall be lifted up and tomorrow he shall not be found, because he is returned into his dust [Deutero-canonical Books of the Bible]) (chap. 26, 96). If the abstracted message emphasizes trust in God, the juxtaposition of the biblical passages to the abbess's actions implicates the latter in the earthly—and therefore insignificant—harm done to Sor Francisca. In a moment when Sor Francisca attempts to recover emotionally from a scathing attack in the convent chapter, she sees in the choir, "a river or piece of the sea, and the nuns who walked on its surface [were] like mosquitoes or worms on the water; and later some of them, in particular the mother abbess, giving a few turns, sank into that water and disappeared; and I was left terrified, and understood that the abbess would soon die" (chap. 27, 104).[14] Again, the message might be humble enough—all humanity passes, heaven alone is eternal—but her own wisdom in comprehending the message, juxtaposed against the insignificance of the abbess as worm, uplifts the writer in relation to her superior.

Even the good abbesses do not escape Madre Castillo's critical word. Having penned a mini exemplary *vida* after the death of María de San Gabriel, Madre Castillo follows it up with a vision of the former abbess before the heavenly court, where tremendous accusations are leveled against this model nun. At the end of the paragraph, Madre Castillo dangles the brief comment that the nun she is telling about was abbess at a time when (amorous) "devotions" were permitted (*SV,* chap. 20, 68). The sin of her permissive rule indicts the abbess. Similarly, Madre Francisca de San Joseph, whose governance Madre Castillo has credited with uniting the nuns, faces a lengthy stay in purgatory because she did not receive the absolution of the Bull of the Holy Crusade, which Madre Castillo relates to the vow of poverty (chap. 26, 98).[15] She does not condemn all individuals as sinful, however. In contrast to the punishments faced by these abbesses, her confessor, Father Juan Martínez, appears to her in the dying image of Saint Ignatius, which shows his great virtue (chap. 29, 114). She also recounts many visions of the salvation of her sister's soul—that sister whose entrance into the convent had caused a furor among the nuns and prelates alike—as she stands at the right hand of Christ and appears with Mary in heaven (chap. 38, 145–46). These contrasts suggest that the visionary criticism she levels at the abbesses serves a narrative effect of revindication of self.

All of the instances of conflict in which Madre Castillo implicates her younger self show the less-than-ideal atmosphere of religious life in Santa Clara, but some of these battles develop explicitly her desires for reform. Always ambivalent, she shows herself as both the instigator of reform and its opponent. Denying specific accusations, her admission of a constant battle with pride projects onto the conflicts over convent reform her hauteur and her disobedience. She begins her reform efforts as a novice when she insists on wearing a plain wimple, implicitly criticizing the governance of the current abbess in allowing vanity of dress (*SV*, chap. 10, 29). Sor Francisca's disillusionment with convent life during her first two years is so painful that she longs for the Carmelite habit. But in a vision she is challenged by a Franciscan to devote herself to Saint Francis's stigmatic wounds, and she understands that the habit does not make the saint (30–31). Madre Castillo observes that the quality of religious life improves after Archbishop Urbina's visit, with more silence and quiet individual prayer and fewer communications with the outer world (chap. 11, 34). Sor Francisca is partially vindicated, nine years after her initial rebelliousness, by an Augustinian missionary who facilitates the wearing of plain wimples throughout the convent (chap. 17, 59). When in 1708 a further renewal of religious life is brought about by Madre Catalina de San Bernardo and the new vicar, echoing the desires Sor Francisca has felt in her heart for communal prayer in the morning, common spiritual lessons, and a sharing of meals in the refectory, she is publicly chastised for resisting the changes (chap. 27, 103).

In many of the instances in which Sor Francisca expresses her desires for a stricter obedience to the rule, she does so by criticizing the actions of others. An episode in 1706, shortly following the entrance of her niece Mariana de Mesa Cortés into the convent, reveals the slipperiness of guilt as blame bounces from one subject to another, indicting all. Sor Francisca sees the Enemy—her name for the Devil—dressed in male religious garb, enter a neighboring cell (chap. 25, 89). Whether the condemnation is the grave implication of amorous relations between nun and priest, or a less harsh reference to the prohibition of unaccompanied male visitors, the violation of the rule and constitutions is clear. Her accusation unleashes tremendous forces against her as the nun in question takes up the same rule book and throws it at her, pointing out that Sor Francisca's niece should not be living in her cell. The outcome of the battle favors the neighbor and leaves Sor Francisca martyred. The servants, including her own, murmur against her and even shout her condemnation. She falls ill, and a maid tries to suffocate her during a faint. A younger niece—Pedro Castillo's daughter Francisca—is thrown out of the convent as Sor Francisca is accused of freely consuming the convent's rations, of doing what she pleases, and, in a tit-for-tat blow, of faking illness in order to keep the convent door open at all hours to allow the entrance of priests. Abbess Antonia de la Trinidad concludes that the Devil possesses Sor Francisca's soul (90). Her confessor tries futilely to douse the flames. Her siblings wish to move her to another convent, but she intervenes, as her move would dishonor the Poor Clares (chap. 25, 91; chap. 26, 96). She is demoted from choir vicaress to lay nurse, and the nun whom she has accused with the frocked Devil is entrusted with the delicate souls of the novices (chap. 25, 91).

Punished by earthly hands, Sor Francisca is lifted up by God. In a vision she sees a number of Dominican fathers, harps in hand, singing from the psalm: "Quemadmodum desiderat cervus ad fontes aquarum" (Ps 42:1) (As a hind longs for the running streams, / [so do I long for thee, O God] [NEB]). Surrounded by malicious boys who appear like common representations of the enemy, the Dominicans hold steadfast in their peaceful repose, singing:

> Come, pilgrim soul,
> on wings of love;
> wounded deer to rest
> in the bosom of your God.
> Come now to the currents,
> that are glory and life,
> of that river of delights
> in the city of God.
> (Chap. 25, 92)[16]

Are the nuns who accuse Sor Francisca guilty because of their diabolical possession? Or are they blameless inasmuch as God allows the Devil to refine Sor Francisca's soul in this hottest of torments so that she might be saved? With either reading, Sor Francisca's narrative stands as a condemnation of the worldliness into which weak humans in general and monastic communities in particular too frequently fall.

If Madre Castillo takes on the voice of orthodoxy in these condemnations of worldliness that are framed in patriarchal discourse, she also resists it. In fragmenting her subject, she consciously or unconsciously releases a critique of the incompatibility of the roles and discourses that define her. As a woman she is considered sinful and distanced from authority. As a nun she is to be chaste, poor, obedient, humble, and removed from the world. As a writer she is empowered to document and mold her protagonist and her authorial self. As an abbess she is required to exercise authority, to act in the world, and to involve herself in its economic and political power. These roles pit confidence against humility, temporality against spirituality, the embodiment of evil against virtuous virginity. The ideal discourse of the *vida* favors the model nun above the others, and yet Madre Castillo does not exclude the other positions she is made to and chooses to occupy. Against the unified subject of the humble model nun who inhabits the biographical *vidas,* Madre Castillo allows the fragmentation of her own subjectivity, her own experience of self, to show through. As the fragmentation of her subjectivity can be seen more and more as an expression of the incompatibility of her roles, her text becomes a critique of where the discursive and the material situate her in Counter-Reformation times.

It is key that Madre Castillo names as her first literary model not Saint Teresa's *Libro* but her *Fundaciones.* Saint Teresa's voice in the *Fundaciones* is confident and authoritative; she is not constrained to judge her own life but rather free to write the history of a reform movement as a nun who has successfully negotiated her right to work on either side of the convent walls. As I have noted, however, the legacy of Saint Teresa and the Council of Trent left spiritual daughters such as Madre Castillo excluded from the freedom she gave herself. Madre Castillo brings the *Fundaciones* into her *Vida* as a primary model to strengthen the possibilities of transcending the convent enclosure within the realms allowed her as abbess. She patterns her behaviors and desires after those of Saint Teresa, but shows the impossibility of working out a positive role in the world and in the position of leadership by marking these consistently with scandal and sin. The absolute enclosure of nuns in the post-Tridentine era denies her this possibility and so the portrayal of this denial emerges in the *Vida* in the lack of resolution left between sinfulness and redemption.

· VII ·

SU VIDA
HOLY ARCHETYPES

We must look to hagiography rather than autobiography as the genre to which medieval women's spiritual autobiography is most closely related. Women's "autohagiography" demands examination as a popular subgenre of medieval religious literature, with conventions, narrative strategies, and purposes distinct from those employed by autobiography.
—KATE GREENSPAN, "The Autohagiographical Tradition in Medieval Women's Devotional Writing"

MADRE CASTILLO, like many nun writers, finds comfort, affirmation, and salvation in her adoption into a holy family. While she proclaims her earthly family to be good and Christian, in contrast to her own sinfulness, her various relationships with its members nonetheless surround her spiritual and, later, her monastic life with conflict. Her holy family, in contrast, offers an escape to a wholly peaceful and loving environment. Her father, who dies before she has taken the habit, is replaced by God and her confessors, while Saint Francis plays godfather to her mystic profession (*SV,* chap. 24, 83). Mary, dressed like her own mother, presents her with a baby Jesus who has been born for her (chap. 9, 26). When the baby returns as a grown Christ, he makes claims on her as his bride that fill her with love (chap. 28, 109; chap. 35, 134; chap. 55, 211). Her holy family includes several saints, too. Clare of Assisi, founder of Sor Francisca's order, gives her a model of moral strength against the Devil (chap. 26, 97) and, during her prelacy, bolsters her spirit in a visionary visit in which she disciplines the nuns severely for having, in a sense, abandoned their abbess (chap. 48, 184). Teresa of Avila, Mary Magdalene, Catherine of Siena, and Mary Magdalene of Pazzis also play significant roles in her spiritual family. Madre Castillo does not develop the Virgin Mary as extensively as a model of feminine and active authority for her own actions as do the prolific Marian theologians María de Jesús de Agreda and María Anna Agueda de San Ignacio. The Virgin's importance lies more in her relationship with Sor Francisca as loving mother and intercessor on her behalf, though one can see a likeness to Mary, as the archetype of maternal-virginal redemption, in Sor Francisca's nurturance of the novices and in her own intercession on behalf of souls in danger. In fact, it is this role of archetype played by saintly predecessors that authorizes Madre Castillo's *Vida* even more than their intervention as family figures.

While female saints of earlier times included the archetypes of royal founder, scholar, and preacher, these were not life options for the early eighteenth-century *tunjana* and do not shape her autobiographical subject in the *Vida.* Nor did the Teresian possibility of founding a reformed order present itself to her. Four holy archetypes do profoundly shape the contours of Madre Castillo's *Vida:* those of hermit, mystic, martyr, and a merging of three archetypes—repentant sinner, scapegoat, and redeemer—into the single image of suffering flesh. Kate Greenspan's differentiation between autobiography and medieval "autohagiography" is pertinent to Counter-Reformation *vida* writing (see epigraph to this chapter and the related discussion in chapter 2). Madre Castillo's choices of archetypes by and large coincide with those most popular in Pedro de Rivadeneira's *Flos sanctorum* (1601), a likely source for much of her knowledge of the saints.[1] Beyond the various women of Jesus's family, the only archetypes offered in the second part of Rivadeneira's work are those of virgin, martyr, repentant sinner, and Mary Magdalene's unusual roles as hermit and preacher.[2]

The life of the solitary hermit was not an option for Madre Castillo, but the archetype permeates her text as a frustrated desire. She finds eremitic models in the lives of both Mary Magdalene, who wandered the desert for thirty years, and Saint Teresa, whose rule allowed a life of separation within the community, in rooms or separate structures called hermitages. The second archetypal script, that of the mystic, seems the most popular among female writers during the two centuries that followed Saint Teresa's beatification. It pervades the *vidas* I have consulted. It constitutes a prominent mode among the writers studied by Arenal and Schlau in *Untold Sisters* (1989b, 10). Despite its popularization by that doctor of mystic theology, Saint Teresa, the aspect of mysticism that constructs the holy subject in the *vidas* is not the Teresian inner path as much as it is the production of exterior signs of mysticism in both the body and texts of the mystic. These signs allow others to confirm or deny the mysticism and the sanctity of its subject. The set of archetypes that is my third concern embed themselves in feminine flesh, condemned as sinful by nature in Church doctrine and symbolized most often in Eve but also in Mary Magdalene's prostitution. This fleshy feminine becomes imbued with redemptive qualities by late medieval and Counter-Reformation mystics alike, as they invert the earlier symbolism through their radical religiosity. Finally, the image of martyrdom returns to the fore in popular veneration by the end of the Middle Ages. It dominates the ranks of the saints in the sixteenth and seventeenth centuries as Christianity again imposes itself across borders, and evangelists give their lives for the faith in heretical Europe and heathen America and Asia (Weinstein and Bell 1982, 161). Stopping short of sacrificial death, Madre Castillo inserts herself within this mold by sustaining the faith despite the severe suffering it causes her. She draws heavily on all of these archetypal scripts, countering the audacity of such self-affirmation with both the model of repentant sinner and the infusion of her text with Catholic doctrine. In so doing, she expresses the options and the constraints of the life of an exceptional consecrated virgin in the colonial society of the Nuevo Reino de Granada.

THE HERMIT

The first chapter of Madre Castillo's *Vida* is inscribed with many of the major themes of the subsequent narrative: her writing as an act of obedience, her wretchedness in the midst of the goodness of others, her prophetic moment of birth on the day of Saint Bruno, her desire to imitate Saint Teresa. But the privileged concluding sentence is reserved for her desire to live as a hermit rather than as a nun in community: "Sometimes I made processions of images or I imitated the professions and habits of the nuns, not because I had any inclination to take that state; as *I was solely inclined to live like the hermits in the deserts and caves of the countryside.*"[3] In fact, Madre Castillo reports that her family tries to dissuade her from entering the convent in favor of the quiet of the family home, telling her that some convents are filled with gossip and turbulence (*SV,* chap. 6, 15).

If the eremitic life was not a possibility for Madre Castillo, it is not surprising, given her spiritual ideals, that the distracting and distressing din she describes as convent life, together with her reading of figures like Saint Teresa and Mary Magdalene, would drive her to desire such contemplative isolation. The figure of Mary Magdalene had evolved in the Middle Ages to combine the prostitute who anointed Christ's feet with oil (Lk 7), Mary of Magdala, who arrived at the empty tomb (Lk 8 and 24), and Martha's sister, who sat absorbed in Christ's teachings rather than take care of the house and guests (Lk 11). The combination of sinful flesh with the prefiguring of a contemplative life becomes important for Madre Castillo's deployment of a symbolic redemptive flesh, which I discuss below; but for now what is important is Mary Magdalene's mysticism out in the desert. She is one of those few saints whose activities as preacher and converter of souls slipped by the purifying pen of Rivadeneira's seventeenth-century *Flos sanctorum.* His story of her relates an eremitic life in the desert, a life that combines contemplation with isolation and autonomy from human society and permits her to dedicate herself entirely to God. Her story provides one of the texts that allow nuns to desire the solitude that monastic enclosure denies them and to imagine this fruitful desert in great mystic detail. When the young Francisca reads Mary Magdalene's story, she is drawn to pray the Divine Office, just as the saint (while in the desert) was lifted by angels to heaven seven times a day in imitation of the canonical hours (*SV,* chap. 6, 16). But once Sor Francisca can exercise that Divine Office in the convent, she finds ritual prayer to be surrounded not by a desert but by a throng.

Inside the Convento Real de Santa Clara, Sor Francisca expresses doubts about taking permanent vows there, as the Carmelite life seems to offer a more eremitic possibility. Saint Teresa established her communities, Madre Castillo states, so that her nuns had only to enter the convent and die to all else, living for God, united with each other in love, unlike the reality she encounters in Santa Clara (*SV,* chap. 10, 30). Despite her decision to profess as a Franciscan, her desire for the Carmelite life continues. She corresponds with Madre Francisca María del Niño Jesús, and her siblings attempt to move her to the Carmelite convent (see chapter 5, p. 104, above). It is this contrast between the ideal and the immediate reality that she perceives that gives meaning to the persecution she suffers. She exercises agency to define herself by preventing her transferal to the Carmelite convent, and so translates her choice into a symbolic self-denial of the easy road of solitude. Instead she will live within the worldly ambiance of a relaxed rule in order to play a redemptive role therein.

The Mystic

The legacy of Saint Teresa and of the Counter-Reformation provoked a surge in the popularity of the mystic paradigm in the Spanish-speaking world. Arenal and Schlau point out that despite the obstacles presented by the institutional suspicion of heresy, the threat of the Inquisition, and censorship, for many nuns the "visionary and ecstatic path became a road to self-expression, power and prestige" (1989b, 10). Almost all of the religious women whose writings or biographies appear in the bibliography of the present book experienced frequent visions, adopted a mystic discourse, or were said to demonstrate those characteristics codified as the signs of the mystic subject, the most notable exception being Juana Inés de la Cruz. Books on meditation and mystic theology, such as Saint Ignatius of Loyola's *Ejercicios espirituales* (Spiritual exercises) (1548), Francisco de Osuna's *Tercer abecedario espiritual* (Third spiritual alphabet) (1527), Miguel Godínez's *Práctica de la theología mystica* (Practice of mystic theology) (1682), and Antonio Arbiol's *Desengaños mysticos* (Mystic dilucidation) (1724) aided the nun, with her confessor's guidance, along a safe and fruitful road of mental prayer.[4] These spiritual guidebooks outline both the steps of a practice and the discernment of exterior and interior signs of the hoped-for intervention in the soul by God.

FIGURE 9. View of the church nave and altar that the nuns would have had from the upper choir, Convento Real de Santa Clara, Tunja, 1996. Photograph by Jorge González ©.

The biographies that write of those who experienced the supernatural inner movements, however, even more than the guidebooks, provide the materials for the construction of the holy and mystic subject. Exemplary biographers look to the body of the mystic for the signs of this inner reception of divine knowledge and its effect. Some biographical *vidas* apply the adjective *mystica* to their subject or the expression *theología mística* to her practice. Most note as evidence of interior love or of communication with God resplendent faces, burning breasts, ecstatic absences from the body, or audible colloquies between the mystic and Christ, Mary, God, or the saints. The bodies of nuns and nun writers produce signs that can be read as defining the mystic subject.

Godínez defines several different forms of mystic absence that characterize the most visible aspect of the mystic moment. He discusses *rapto, éxtasis, pasmo,* and *suspensión* (1682, 4), while *vida* writers also use the word *arrobamiento.* The terms refer to states of rapture, ecstasy, wonder or shock, suspension of the senses, and trance. What is common to all is an extreme absorption of the soul that results in a dulling in the operation of the senses. The mystics are seen by others to be outside of themselves, as in this description by Padre Chinchilla of Madre Francisca María del Niño Jesús:

> Thus I certify having heard in said convent the continuation of her raptures and suspensions that occurred daily, and for many hours, whereby was manifested the very eminent degree of union to which she arrived, and sometimes these raptures lasted two or more days, as I found out had occurred three days before the Purification of Our Lady, in which she remained almost three days outside of herself. The nuns, judging this to be some illness, called the doctor. The servant of God Father Martín Niño of the Society of Jesus entered and recognized it to be a rapture and suspension; and consoling his daughters, ordered them to give her a substance, and when they did so, the servant of God [Madre Francisca] repeated: *Leave me alone, I am with my beloved.* (Conventos, AHNB, vol. 66: 262r)[5]

The state of trance, while visible to those around them, does not inhibit these nuns either from carrying out their obligations or from taking communion. This ability is evidence of the holy rather than heretical origin of the phenomenon. The nuns, then, must balance the freedom from religious control that they experience in mysticism with the obedience necessary to protect that freedom.

The signs produced in the body of the mystic form part of the text read by the convent community and by the directing confessor in their attempts to determine whether the inner experience is provoked by God or by the Devil. At one level, interpreting these signs ensures control over the flock. On another level, it can lead to the mining of a spiritual wealth. As Jean Franco puts it, the Church used these women to "replenish the store of edifying examples in the fight against heresy" (1989, 3). The signs of mysticism place the nun in the public gaze and often reward her with fame, as in the case of María de Jesús de Agreda: "The devotion of some, perhaps sharpened by curiosity, created such strong insistence on the founders that they allow them to see the miracle, that they won them over, such that finding the Servant of God in suspension after having taken communion, as was wont to occur, they would open the communion grille, so that they might see her through it. Doing this, the nuns removed the veil that she had over her face so that they might see her extraordinary beauty, and the laity had the experience of moving her with a breath from the outside" (Ximenes Samaniego 1688, 59).[6] With-drawn from the world by cloister and "mystic death," as these raptures are often called, Sor María transcended enclosure to become a spectacle in the eyes of the world.

In the tight relationship between *vida* writing as an autobiographical act and the biographical tradition, nun writers produce the signs of their mystic encounters not only in their bodies but also in their texts. Adopting the discourse of mysticism in her written communications with her confessors, Madre Castillo provides them with exterior signs of her inner practice. The most salient case in which her body exhibits the outward signs of an inner experience of God is her fourteen-year "affliction" of eventide faints, when she loses all bodily strength and sensations, and any memory of her actions, but carries out her duties as if unaffected (*SV,* chap. 22, 75–76). She understands these moments as a returning of the soul to God.

Many of the signs of the mystic subject that Madre Castillo produces, however, take a form in her texts that does not refer to her body, nor to the mystic process, but to its results. She substantiates her supernatural illumina-tions by submitting her writing for an examination of the orthodoxy of its content, to prove that the knowledge is God given. She demonstrates the gifts of prophecy by foreseeing in visions the deaths of several people. She experi-ences the discernment of souls—that is, she is given the knowledge of the status of their salvation through visions. All of these signs she submits to her confessors in the writing of her *Vida.* She even writes herself into a miraculous occurrence. During a near-fatal illness, she receives a vision of Saint Dominic as he intercedes on her behalf to Mary. Simultaneously in another room several nuns sing a Salve for her before a painting of Mary. The painted image of Saint Dominic who kneels before the Virgin begins to sweat (*SV,* chap. 46, 175). In these instances, the author presents her supernatural blessings not as dangerously inaccessible manifestations of subjecthood—as inexpressible experiences that could be either divine or diabolical—but rather as exterior signs that can be verified by others. These signs, as she recounts them, fulfill contemporary expectations of the mystic who is blessed with a virtuous life and union with God (Godínez 1682, 122). By writing the signs of mystic subjectivity into her *Vida,* Madre Castillo provides the materials for *others* to read her as a mystic subject.

MARY MAGDALENE: SINFUL FLESH, REDEMPTIVE FLESH

Two of Madre Castillo's favored foremothers, Saint Catherine of Siena and Saint Teresa, had suffered persecution for their involvement in battles over defining the Church and its mission. Her visionary evocation of Saint Catherine, in a field whose lilies represent the trials she suffers, echoes the grand politics of the saint on the much smaller scale of day-to-day interpersonal struggles over what is right religious practice (*SV,* chap. 16, 53). This vision comforts her amid the attacks she suffers for choosing to bear the cross of her mother's illness in the convent or, as her opponents see it, for the trouble she causes the convent by bringing in an extra mouth to feed and taking her own labors away from the common good. Madre Castillo writes Saint Teresa and her reformist ideals into her autohagiographical *Vida* on several occasions, not aspiring to monumental reform herself but bolstering her religiosity under fire, just as Saint Teresa was criticized and persisted before her. Though Madre Castillo sees the need for a wider church reform in the Nuevo Reino de Granada, she cannot exceed the bounds of the convent as Saint Teresa did to enact it, and therefore she focuses primarily on her own community.

Many *vida* writers in Spain and Spanish America reiterate this model of righteousness and persecution. These women appeared in different religious orders and throughout the Spanish empire. Perhaps the heightened containment of these Counter-Reformation women explains the intensity of their practices: elaborate and frequent visions, prophetic intercession for the souls of both the living and the dead, daily communion, ecstatic reveries, and spectacular punishment of their flesh. As the boundaries set by a patriarchal Church increased, so did the excesses of the spiritual expression of these strong women in those arenas that were still left open to them, though carefully guarded.

Doña María Vela y Cueto (Cistercian, Spain: 1561–1617) hears Christ lament that humanity has forgotten that he suffered for them, and so she suffers with him to renew the observance of the rule within her convent. The spectacle of her mortified flesh brings the image of Christ's Passion before the eyes of her community, which responds with ridicule and scandal. Madre María Magdalena Lorravaquio (Hieronymite, Mexico: 1576–1636) lived forty-four years ill in bed, according to the inscription on the 1650 manuscript copy of her *vida* and mystic favors. This extraordinary illness cannot be extricated from her mystic interpretation of its symptoms. During this almost lifelong illness and its mystic mercies, she prays for the salvation of others: a dying priest, the outcome of convent elections, the profession of a nun, and the prevention of harm from a comet that had appeared in Mexico. Juana Palacios Berruecos, who would profess as María de San José (Augustinian Recollect, Mexico: 1656–1719), exhibits beginning in childhood the radical religiosity of her trans-Atlantic writing community and the persecution that this religiosity brings upon her. Learning at an early age to fast, to mortify her flesh, and to withdraw herself from the world in mental prayer, she incurs great persecution from her own sister, who suspects perversion in her apparently pious behavior (Myers 1993b, 46). Later, in the convent, Sor María recognizes her first ecstasies as God-given mercies, but her mother superior considers them illnesses, treats them as such, and later punishes her, believing that she is possessed (Muriel 1982, 385–86). Like her writing sisters, Madre María understands these attacks to be the purification that will purge her soul of its guilt and imperfections (391).

Common to these nun's writings and those of many contemporaries are their visions, their ascetic lives, implicit or explicit critique of a nonascetic religious environment, and lengthy and painful illnesses in which the spiritual and physical cannot be separated. They also all share the ridicule brought upon them because of their radical religious practice. Peers and superiors find them crazy, possessed, or heretical, while they insinuate in their texts that these peers and superiors have forgotten Christ in their tepid practices. Their ill flesh, which suffers the interventions of God and the Devil and resists the medical treatments of the day—purges, plasters, and bloodletting—embodies a redemptive force. For some nuns, the explicit redemption touches only themselves; for others their sinful flesh, beaten into submission and elevated to an imitation of the suffering Christ, expresses a redemptive force that the writers project onto the ills of their surrounding worlds.

Such is the suffering of Sor Francisca. The construction of her body as sign permeates the *Vida* through terrible illnesses and their powerful spiritual interpretation. The illnesses begin very early when a brush with death in her infancy marks her closeness to God. Her return to the world of the living, however, begins a life-long yearning for the death that will take her back for eternity to her heavenly father and husband. At eight years old, in divine punishment for reading *comedias,* Francisca experiences a spiritual illness whose manifestations are both physical and psychological (*SV,* chap. 2, 7). From this time on, she will spend her life in and out of bed, close to death on a number of occasions, always struggling despite illness to fulfill her duties.

Soon after taking vows, Sor Francisca embarks on the fourteen-year affliction, discussed above, whose outer signs suggest supernatural inner movements. The illness defies both medical and spiritual cures. The primary symptom is a suspension of her senses every evening at sundown. "I only remember that when the sun began to set, I found myself like the little dog that seeks its master throughout the house and does not find him; this was what it seemed to me that my soul felt for its God, and for my soul, everything would begin to vanish" (*SV,* chap. 22, 75).[7] This interpretation of the condition highlights the goodness of her soul as it seeks separation from the world. That she understands the phenomenon in terms given by Francisco de Osuna —that the soul is resting on the Lord's breast—should make the experience emotionally positive, but instead her outward behavior serves to earn her taunts and punishments, imposing on her a fourteen-year trial. Her suffering symbolizes the purification by fire spoken of in the Bible and the purgation of the soul outlined by contemporary spiritual guidebooks. This psychosomatic condition expresses the anxiety of a nun striving for spiritual perfection and constantly harassed as the source of the convent's ills.

Twelve years after making her vows and ten before she would acquire the power of abbess, Madre Castillo reports the growth of a black tumor in her mouth (*SV,* chap. 28, 110). The appearance of the tumor culminates a chapter of accusations by the other nuns that she has sown discord in the convent. It is at this point that Isabel de Jesús María, a deservedly esteemed nun as the author describes her, confronts her in public humiliation, calling her a demon who pardons none (108). The mouth that hosts the evil tumor is the location of Sor Francisca's unpardoning tongue. Her tumor defies medical cures: even if the lip were removed, says the prior of the hospital order of San Juan de Dios, the visible emergence of the illness demonstrates that it has already taken root throughout the body. The tumor betrays the evil of the words formed in her mouth, an evil that is fixed deeply within her inner being.

The evils of *murmuración,* symbolized in her buccal tumor, permeate the *Vida,* causing Madre Castillo's own suffering and threatening to destroy the convent. Under the letter "M" in her *Cuaderno de Enciso,* she has copied a treatise against this social disease (Castillo 1968, 2: 527–28). If the cancer implicates her in the evil, this treatise suggests her innocent victimization. Those who suffer the *murmuración* of others, it states, include patient souls, people who exercise temperance in food and dress, the pious and the chaste. Although many other personages are called "good" in the *Vida,* it is Madre Castillo's actions that find reference in this description of ascetic virtue.

The buccal tumor bursts on the evening of Pentecost, May 29, 1709— also, Madre Castillo notes, the day of Saint Mary Magdalene of Pazzis (1566— 1607). When the tumor opens, more blood flows out of Madre Castillo's mouth than was thought that a body could hold. Some of the nuns tell her later that they had requested the extreme unction for her, she appeared so close to death (*SV,* chap. 30, 117). The outpouring of blood imitates the medical practice of bloodletting that was understood to cleanse the body of its impurities.

The episodes are rich in symbolism. A cancer of the mouth rooted deep within the body is juxtaposed to accusations of Sor Francisca's evil tongue. This tongue has infected the convent with division through its prideful *murmuración* about the faults of others, and yet Madre Castillo portrays herself as its victim. Timing is not coincidental. Saint Mary Magdalene of Pazzis is another of Sor Francisca's favored models, whose charitable attitudes she tries to apply to her own interaction with the novices in her care and to her outlook on her own suffering. The *vida* of the Florentine saint, copied by Madre Castillo's hand into a devotional book, witnesses her importance to the *tunjana* (*Devocionario* n.d.). Dwelling on the saint's sustained physical illnesses, this *vida* gives clearly spiritualized explanations of their effects, linking her suffering to that of Christ. Interestingly, Madre Castillo has underlined a statement that disassociates the saint from the sin of *murmuración*, the very sin that is symbolized in the tumor that bursts on the day of the saint's commemoration: "They never saw her angry or upset nor say an injurious word or murmur (gossip) against those who condemned her frequent communion" (94).[8] The story of Sor Francisca's tumor, while seeming to implicate her sins, inverts its own symbolic meanings. If she is a sinner and the cause of evil, she is also a suffering Job tormented by the Devil at God's consent. She is the scapegoat who suffers the evil of others and the mirror in which they might see their own sins. The day on which the tumor bursts is also marked by Pentecost, the advent of the Holy Spirit. The illness has drawn Sor Francisca near to death. As Christ returns to her in the Holy Spirit's Pentecostal visit, she moves closer to the afterlife. Suffering constant illness, Sor Francisca lives always at the threshold of death, a death for which she longs because it would overcome her exile in this world of sin and unite her soul at last with her celestial spouse.

Despite her constant denials of specific accusations of misdeeds, Sor Francisca becomes the object of gossip that floods the city. She has lost her honor. She has become, in some sense, a public woman, a Mary Magdalene. When Madre Castillo inverts the symbolism that points the finger at her own sins, and shows herself to be an innocent, Job-like victim, she names herself the convent scapegoat. She suggests, in a subtle narrative move, that the accusations leveled against her reveal the sins of the accusers. But are the others, themselves pawns of the Devil, not innocent? She says that it is the "Enemy" who spurs them all to anger and antagonism (*SV,* chap. 16, 53). Too many portraits of laxity pervade the *Vida* to clear the nuns of guilt. Sor Francisca's flesh is martyred by the ills of the larger social body: a convent in which nuns resist the simplicity of dress mandated in their constitutions, where priests enter nuns' cells alone, where the noise of scandal reigns rather than the peace of prayer, and where servants dance with glee at the very moment when an abbess who represents committed spirituality—Madre Castillo—retreats from her office at the end of her term.

A key vision in the *Vida* helps to unlock the redemptive force of Sor Francisca's suffering flesh and tormented soul:

> The whole city was involved in making penitence, restitutions, confessions, etc.; well, finding myself one afternoon in a small garden, and seeing an image of Our Lord Crucified, I felt weak, as if they were dislocating all of my bones, and it seemed to me that my soul was coming apart, and I understood the great torment caused to Our Lord when they nailed him [to the cross], the dislocation of his bones from their places, and it was one of the afflictions and pains that tormented him most; as much for the most intense pain that he felt in his body as for what it meant: which is the division and disunity of spiritual people, and especially those who are like the bones on which the entire harmony of the body is supported, that is, the preachers and prelates. (*SV,* chap. 17, 60)[9]

Face to face with the crucified Christ, Madre Castillo's body feels the pain of his dislocated joints, pulled apart by a fatal torture. Divisions in the Church of Tunja and of the Nuevo Reino de Granada and divisions in the Convento de Santa Clara cause the pain that is shared by the reflected bodies. Separately, Madre Castillo and Christ represent the Church and society as sinful and mystic bodies. Together, they forge a symbolic redemption in which Madre Castillo's fleshy feminine is transformed into a transcendent sign.

The inversion itself is not new, as Carolyn Walker Bynum shows in the symbolic transcendence of the feminine among religious women of the late Middle Ages. In her superb *Holy Feast and Holy Fast,* Bynum sees in the illness, fasting, and physical disciplines of late medieval religious women a heavily gendered symbolic practice. Comparing the lives of both men and women, she finds that the female body takes on in its suffering much more often than the male body those qualities of Christ's passion that speak visually and verbally of holy and redemptive food. In times of widespread food shortages across Europe, Bynum states, "women moved to God not merely by abandoning their flawed physicality but also by becoming the suffering and feeding humanity of the body on the cross, the food on the altar" (1987, 5). While the Counter-Reformation *vidas* seem to incorporate some of the meanings of holy food and abstinence of the medieval representations as an historical textual residue, the contextual reference has shifted. It is not a famine that convent society in Spanish America faces but rather the tensions between the laxity of convent rule and reformed ideals, the necessary involvement in worldly affairs by the nuns of a society in economic crisis, and the post-Tridentine sharpening of the exclusion of women from the worldly realm into a removed and contemplative containment. Madre Castillo's bivalent body, the Mary Magdalene who incarnates both the sin and its redemption, offers its human sacrifice for the salvation of her world.

THE MARTYR

Martyrdom and the redemptive suffering discussed above are intimately related. Reflecting on the characteristics of the early virgin martyrs, though, sheds light on some different aspects of Madre Castillo's use of archetypes in portraying her own subjectivity. The personification of martyrdom in Madre Castillo's *Vida* derives from both Job and the virgin martyrs of early Christendom. Early Christian virgins were punished for their refusal to worship pagan gods and for their rejection of pagan marriages proposed by their families. Their torture, dismemberment, and death was often executed at the hands of family members or would-be spouses. The tales draw out the gory spectacle of the torture (Cazelles 1991).

Stories of female martyrdom arose during the first four centuries of Christendom, but the prominence of these virgin martyrs as objects of cult worship continued long afterwards. With four exceptions, the female saints in the second book of Rivadeneira's *Flos sanctorum* are all martyrs. The Spanish world renewed the importance of the martyr with the forays of missionaries into heretical and heathen lands in the fourteenth through sixteenth centuries, but the protagonists were necessarily males. To women fell the lot of a symbolic martyrdom suffered at the hands of the enemy within. Describing María Gertrudis Theresa de Santa Inés, a Dominican compatriot of Madre Castillo, Calvo de la Riba says that she suffers at the hands of the Devil "afflictions, torments, and *martyrdom,* with which she vanquished, and destroyed all hell" (1752, 133, emphasis mine).[10] While the martyrs of the Spanish wars and the holy missions provided the context to which monastic martyrs responded, their martyrdom looked to the spectacle of the early virgins as well as the living torment of the innocent Job for its form. It is this symbolic martyrdom that Madre Castillo projects onto her own tribulation, which she structures around the key elements of *faith, spectacle,* and *will,* common in the deaths of the early virgin saints.

Faith motivates martyrdom. In the stories of early virgin martyrs, torture and death tested the Christian's faith and proved through her unwavering will her ultimate identification with Christ. Madre Castillo's self-inflicted mortification, her illnesses, the Devil's torment, and those of her community allow her to reenact the triumph of the faithful virginity of the early martyrs. Her faith is repeatedly tested and she often fails, but she returns to God over and over again, and at the end of the *Vida* her faith is still strong.

Spectacle takes center stage in the reports by onlookers of instances of monastic martyrdom. Giving testimony about the life of the Carmelite Madre Francisca María, Feliciana de San Diego relates what had been the deceased nun's public practice of mortification during Lent: "Sometimes she would go around carrying a cross on her back with a rope around her throat, her face covered with stinging nettles, her head covered with ash. At other times, she commanded another nun to pull her around at the end of a rope that she placed around her neck, dragging her on the ground like a beast" (Conventos, AHNB, vol. 66: 74).[11] Calvo de la Riba writes that Sor María Gertrudis's diabolical enemies "gave her the most cruel blows, pulled her from her hard bed, dragged her over the ground, kept her for many hours spinning like a mill wheel, and threw her with great force against the ground. They gave her strong blows to the hips and head, so violent that it broke the bricks" (1752, 110).[12] All these punishments were witnessed by onlookers who could not comprehend what they saw.

Spectacle functions differently in Madre Castillo's text, in which she does not claim to place her own self-infliction of bodily punishment under the public gaze. She alludes to spectacle in the observation by others of her radical religiosity and in their constant accusations of her affected piety. Where her spiritual and psychic suffering does submit to a public arena is in the screamed accusations by other nuns and the admonishments from the vicar and the abbess at convent chapter meetings. In her characteristic ambivalence, both poles of the opposition between her alleged hypocrisy and her implicit martyrdom focus the public eye. Finally, by writing her bleeding flesh into her text she is presenting her body to the eyes of her confessors and to whoever else might read her words.

Stating repeatedly that her attackers are virtuous people and that her own evil deserves punishment, Madre Castillo doubles her narrative back to redeem herself in visions like the one referred to in chapter 6, above, which she receives shortly after her mother's entrance into the convent. "I found myself one night descending through a narrow street full of stones, which, due to their unevenness, gave me great difficulty, because I was barefoot and on my shoulders I carried a boy about twelve years old; he carried his arms extended in the air, placed as if on a cross. . . . I saw that those nuns, whom I have mentioned, laughed at my journey, and I said with admiration: Lord give me strength! Why would they laugh at this? Do they not see that Our Lord Jesus Christ carried the cross for us?" (*SV*, chap. 16, 52).[13] Sor Francisca's participation in the crucifixion—that ultimate of martyrdoms—is met with the ridicule of her sister nuns. In rejecting her sacrifice, they persecute her for acting on her faith, for walking with Christ. Christ's enemy is to be found within, in the tepidity and hypocrisy of those who pledge their lives to follow him. A strong accusation, Madre Castillo's symbolic suggestion that her sister nuns embody the enemy is mitigated but not erased by the parallel assertions that it is the Devil, acting within them by God's permission, who martyrs her.

Finally, the martyr archetype emphasizes Madre Castillo's own agency, her own will. Weinstein and Bell remark that, "[t]his motif of human agency, in which the Christian decides upon a spiritual course and follows it to an ultimate conclusion despite all worldly considerations, is the essence of the martyr's story. In marked contrast to popular notions of the saint as a miracle-working vessel of supernatural power, the martyr is a hero honored as a supreme example of how men and women by the exercise of their own will can further God's work" (1982, 160). Here the importance of Madre Castillo's insistence on entering Santa Clara against warnings of its convulsive and worldly society comes into play, together with her persistence despite attempts to move her. She has chosen this atmosphere above the peacefulness of her home and the purportedly harmonious Carmelite community as a sacrifice, and, while entering the realm of confusion, her faith survives to the end of the narrative. She has exercised her will to choose martyrdom for her God.

A QUESTION OF AGENCY

The archetypes of hermit, mystic, redemptive fleshy sinner, and martyr provide a deep structure for Madre Castillo's autobiographical subject, and yet a full affirmation of any of these holy archetypes would throw her once again into the sin of pride. Pride (*soberbia*) is the first of the capital sins—those sins that engender others. Pride begets presumption, ambition, boasting, the despising of others, and the will to cause disputes and discord (Arbiol 1724, bk. 3, chap. 4). By positing pride and humility as the primary axis of sin and virtue with which the (female monastic) self must be concerned, Church ideologues seek to contain (female) individuation. Official discourse locates the principal damage perpetrated by the sin of pride in its division of the community, masking the threat the Church itself feels to its authority from the assertion of female individuality by saying that it is the women themselves who are hurt. I am not endorsing divisiveness in female community here but rather pointing out that the type of harmony required by the Church demanded unquestioning submission and thus repression of individual thought and creativity.

The threat felt by a male hierarchy from the self-confidence that might bolster female autonomy is also displaced, in discourse, onto the individual's soul, which risks burning in hell for its sin of pride. In accordance with this ideology, Madre Castillo must balance her expressive self with humble denunciation in the *Vida*. Even in her triumphal conclusion, she harbors the fear that her soul could be an evil vessel whose pride turns to poison all of the mercies that God pours into it (*SV,* chap. 55, 210). Each holy archetype with which she elevates her self must be undermined. Thus, the body of the repentant sinner never fully proclaims its own innocence, even as it assumes a redemptive martyrdom. The desire for an eremitic life is never fulfilled. The mystic must fear diabolical influence to the end of the *Vida*. As Foucault might note, though, the very attempt to suppress individuation produces a discourse that highlights it. The discourse of individuation permeates the *Vida* as its author experiments with the possibilities of subjecthood and tries to suppress it, painting herself into and out of the lives of saints. Therein she plays a complex game of reflections, perspectives, and interpretive levels: the saints provide her a mirror in which to see the perfection she strives for, and she reflects their perfection back in imitation; the sins of her world are mirrored in her own female weakness of the flesh, while she mirrors their evil in her innocent martyrdom. In the *Vida* these textual strategies interweave and superimpose themselves on one another to form a tense and oscillating whole.

Where in this reading can Madre Castillo's agency be located? Framing my study with a postmodern critical discourse that sees subjects as constructed rather than autonomous, I have sought agency in the slippage between prevalent discourses on the feminine and its relationship to authority, in the mismatch between the discourses and the material practices in which Madre Castillo is engaged, in the differences between present and historical ideologies of the feminine, and most importantly, in the contradictions that emerge from her particular juxtaposition of these discourses and practices in her *Vida*. I have read her agency in the resistance her text posits to a unified and submissive feminine self and in the strategic combination of orthodoxy and self-assertion that succeeded, albeit with a delay of almost a century, in preserving her memory in the minds of a wide readership. These textual strategies are evident in the decentered, fragmented, or multivalent subject of her *Vida* that critiques the impossible combination of roles and discourses that she is called to assume.

The magnitude and constancy of the conflict Sor Francisca experiences in the convent, the depths of despair she conveys, and the level of self-condemnation Madre Castillo expresses set her *Vida* apart from others, tantalizing and frustrating me with their enigma. I have argued that these elements of conflict, doubt, and self-judgment are brought into the genre by its circumstances of production, but why in Madre Castillo's *Vida* are they so much more acute than in the writings of her peers? Surely part of the explanation lies in the strength of her will and intellect. As Kathleen A. Myers observes in her introduction to the spiritual autobiography of María de San José, "[l]ife was often difficult for women who were strong-willed and who wished to assert their own choices, even when these followed the roles prescribed by society," and this difficulty led to the structuring of *vidas* through the conflict between ideal and real, the individual and authority (1993b, 19). But, of course, other writers were equally strong willed.

Myers offers an observation of difference between the voices of Madre Castillo and María de San José that helps to explain the depth of pain in the former's writing. Myers sees Madre Castillo's voice as expressing less individuality than that of María de San José. She sees Madre Castillo as a "model" nun who "could attempt to erase her 'yo' by portraying herself in her *Vida* as object acted upon by supernatural and human forces, and . . . in so doing, created a more powerful religious role for herself. In her autobiography, the nun from Tunja becomes the embodiment of Church teachings on the virtue of denying individual will" (1993b, 51). Perhaps the depth of her pain expresses, in proportion, the difficulty she experiences as an intelligent and strong-willed woman who conforms to orthodoxy by matching repeated affirmations of self with repeated self-punishment for her rebelliousness.

I see other hypotheses for explaining the piercing tone of the narrative, none satisfactory in itself. If, as Myers suggests, Madre Castillo's *Vida* earns her a "more powerful religious role," she writes it while she is still struggling against a battery of abbesses and vicars; thus her tone might express the insecurity she feels during her ascent. Perhaps her *Vida* portrays interpersonal conflicts concerning economic power and social status that were heightened by the scarce resources of an economy in crisis. Jodi Bilinkoff notes that, after Saint Teresa's death, radical expressions of spirituality like that of María Vela y Cueto fell under heightened suspicion (1989, 189–92), clearly one aspect in Madre Castillo's situation, though such suspicions would affect any *vida* written at the time. Bilinkoff goes on to suggest that the ruling class resisted what it perceived as class-inappropriate behavior on the part of María Vela; Madre Castillo probably represented the same conflict. Perhaps the explanation given by several *tunjanos* also plays a role: that Madre Castillo stood out intellectually to such an extent among her monastic colleagues that they assailed her out of their own incomprehension. Perhaps, rather, in a twist of this theory, her adversaries saw the powerful potential of her intellect and talent among the influential Jesuit priests and were uncomfortable with its implications. Finally, the depth of conflict that structures the *Vida* may be embedded within the coincidence of a number of particularly strong personalities, including that of Madre Castillo herself. Although the audacity of Juana Inés de la Cruz's writing may have led to her silence no matter who surrounded her, the fanaticism of Archbishop Aguiar y Seijas, the rigor of her confessor Núñez, and the conflict between the archbishop and Fernández de Santa Cruz, bishop of Puebla, certainly marked the battle over her "Carta atenagórica" and the risk of her "Respuesta a Sor Filotea," which led to her renunciation of books and pen. The severity of the turmoil and the constancy of the intrigue that appear in the *Vida* make this narrative one of the more compelling of its genre. Its attraction can also prove painful for the twentieth-century feminist, who finds herself celebrating the heights of self-expression of a great woman who wins the freedom of her word by elevating herself in both patriarchal and female traditions and who counteracts every elevation with an equally severe punishment.

· VIII ·

THE *AFECTOS ESPIRITUALES*
MYSTICISM OF THE INCARNATE WORD

> The gentle speech
> Of the lover I adore
> Drips milk and honey
> Amidst roses and irises.
> His mellifluous word
> Transpires like dew
> And with it blossoms
> The once withered heart.
> —MADRE CASTILLO, *Afecto 46* [1]

IF MADRE CASTILLO's *Vida* has intrigued some and troubled others with its knotty and critical view of convent life, her *Afectos espirituales* have won praise in literary historiography. While her prose is sometimes criticized as confused, repetitive, and marred by the errors of a hurried pen, it is also extolled for the beauty of its biblical language and for the spiritual elevation of its sentiments.[2] It is the *Afectos* that have won Madre Castillo the affectionate and reverential stature as "Colombia's mystic." Achury Valenzuela distinguishes between the *Afectos* and the *Vida* by calling the first the narration of her spiritual life and the second a narration of the "facts of her real life" (1968, cxxxiii). Madre Castillo wrote what she called her *papeles* (papers) at the behest of her confessors, as she did the *Vida*. These 251 leaves, filled with Madre Castillo's small handwriting, do explore her spiritual life and her mystic experiences in journal-like pieces, but they also accomplish much more.[3]

The manuscript is composed of a number of separately folded sections and individual pages on which Madre Castillo wrote pieces ranging in length from a single paragraph to more than ten pages. She submitted these texts to her confessors as she wrote them, probably each time that she filled a notebook or section. From her confessors she sought approval and correction. A number of their responses are interspersed among the pages of the manuscript, sometimes written on the same paper as an *afecto,* sometimes separately. The messages include comments on the doctrinal content of the pieces, but mostly they praise and encourage Madre Castillo in her writing and spiritual life. Only a few of the *afectos* carry specific dates, ranging from 1694 to 1728, and those that have been dated follow an approximately chronological order.[4] The dates appear to be penned by Madre Castillo, though differences in ink indicate that they were not written at the same time as the texts themselves. Midway through the manuscript, in a hand that seems to be Madre Castillo's, are the words, "Up to this point the year [17]16, now it is [17]24," which effectively divide the manuscript in two.[5] This interlude of eight years, during which Madre Castillo governed the convent for one term and finished writing her *Vida*, but apparently wrote few *afectos*, might explain some changes in the narrative voice between earlier and later texts.[6]

The texts of Madre Castillo's *papeles* were altered in several ways in publication. Editors modernized spelling and punctuation. A number of scholars accomplished the arduous labor of identifying the biblical texts that the author does not as she quotes or paraphrases them.[7] In the first edition (1843), in which about half of the pieces were published, Castillo y Alarcón divided the text into numbered *Sentimientos espirituales,* printing subtitles for each piece as supplied by prior readers (Achury Valenzuela 1968, cxcix). In 1942 the manuscript was published as the *Afectos espirituales,* and the editor reworked the divisions, attempting to respect the integrity of the pieces as Madre Castillo wrote them (cci). The author herself, however, did not number the pieces, and so their beginnings and endings are not always clear. The most recent edition, produced by Achury Valenzuela (1968), maintains the 1942 divisions.

The *Afectos* belong to another autobiographical genre common among religious women writers of the times, one different in significant ways from the *vida espiritual.* Saint Teresa of Avila's less-known *Exclamaciones o meditaciones del alma a sv Dios* (Exclamations of the soul to God) falls within this category.[8] In this text, Teresa of Avila expresses loving "complaints" to God about the pain of exile—the metaphor with which mystics describe this earthly life so far from God. She praises and petitions God, explores her weak nature, instructs her soul, and even applies biblical stories to her spiritual path, though she uses few direct quotes.

Madre Castillo's Spanish American contemporaries also engaged in this type of writing. Jerónima Nava y Saavedra opens her journalistic exploration of mystic experiences by expressing her desire to communicate these events to her confessor. They are extraordinary and undoubtedly supernatural, and she is concerned to submit them so that he might find and correct any errors they might contain (Nava 1994, 55). Her writing is autobiographical, linking her spirituality to her life in the world; but unlike the *vida,* this genre of the spiritual journal does not require her to judge or justify herself and her life history. The effect is to free Nava of a few of the chains of gender ideology that bind the *vida* subject to a more constant pain, martyrdom, and degradation than her writing exhibits. Nava also does not subordinate her discourse to a sense of chronological development nor treat her external life in much depth. The similar writings of María Magdalena Lorravaquio, attached to the manuscript of her very brief *Vida* and Daily Schedule, open with an invocation rather than a description of the task. An editor's note on the first page of the manuscript refers to them as "the particular favors that she continually received from Our Lord Jesus Christ" and indicates that they were written, along with her *Vida,* at the command of her confessors (1r).[9]

Both Nava and Lorravaquio share many concerns with Madre Castillo and many aspects of a common language. The primary substance of their autobiographical writing is the state of the soul and its relationship to God or Christ, the divine beloved. Like Madre Castillo, Nava and Lorravaquio both relate imaginary visions and they struggle with allegory to express the ineffable presence of God in their souls.[10] Angela Robledo, who has edited the Nava manuscript, emphasizes the importance of its discourse of love as an expression of Nava's desire for God's presence (Nava 1994, 17–22). Nava also shares with Madre Castillo a desire to teach but recognizes her exclusion from this possibility: "And the yearning to instruct and to love other souls that I feel is so great that my sex exasperates me because it keeps me from doing something for him [Christ] who did so much for me" (71).[11] Nevertheless, her text does contain teachings. One might read the embodiment of doctrine in the lessons that both Nava and Lorravaquio receive mystically as a private discourse on the education of their own souls. But Nava's voice takes up a prophetic or apostolic role when she condemns the sins of colonial society. She voices her criticism of the laxity of religious observance within her own Poor Clare convent and receives divine affirmation that, as abbess, she will reform its religious life. Lorravaquio withdraws even more radically from the external world, which she mentions only in her prayerful intercession on behalf of others. Her writings are filled with loving visions that draw on contemporary iconography—the baby Jesus, crystalline fountains, fields of lilies, a bleeding sheep—to comfort and teach her soul after it has been carried "out into the desert." Once there, she often experiences an exquisite and wordless union with God. While both Nava and Lorravaquio rest their pens after brief communications of the mystic lessons they have received, Madre Castillo develops these concerns into more lengthy treatises.

Like other women before her, Madre Castillo conceives of herself in the *Afectos* as God's amanuensis. The mystic knowledge she receives speaks of God, Christ, and Mary and of their relationship with mortal creatures. Especially prominent is the fundamental mystic concept of Christ's relationship of lover-husband to the seeker's soul. The *Afectos* also treat spiritual life and the responsibilities of the spiritual seeker to God, to her mortal companions, and to the moral purity of her own soul.[12] Madre Castillo elaborates doctrinal

lessons, instructing the soul to exercise virtues and follow God's commandments, and glossing the liturgical prayers through which the Church teaches
its flock. Finally, she decries the corruption of humanity and the laxity of
religious life in her world, but in more general terms than in the *Vida*.

Though my language intentionally frames Madre Castillo as teacher, she
proclaims herself to be merely a conduit of the knowledge she communicates,
and, as such, she explores the supernatural experience by which she receives
the knowledge. She writes of visions and of moments of union of her soul with
God, decrying the inadequacy of language to communicate them. She cries
out the desires of her soul, which suffers life in this world as an exile from
God. She turns the texts into soliloquies to her divine beloved as she laments
her sinfulness that impedes her journey, petitions God to teach and protect
her, and offers up her will to him. At times, she is filled with the consolation
and joy of his loving responses to her pleas, and she praises his greatness and
mercy. Although Madre Castillo occasionally feminizes God and Christ in her
description of his-their qualities, both are clearly male in their roles as husband
and father.

This mixing of autobiographical mysticism with doctrinal knowledge, common in the spiritual journals of Madre Castillo and her foremothers and
sisters, responds to the exclusion of writing women from the male halls of
universities and seminaries and from the genres in which male clerics most
often expressed theological knowledge. Nun writers had to invent other methods and forms when they felt compelled to exercise and express their intellects
and to explore their knowledge of God and of the relationship between human
beings and the Divine. As Arenal and Schlau observe, using a reference to
Saint Teresa's allegory for instructing seekers in the path of mental prayer
toward God, some religious women became "avid students in the *castillo
interior*" (1989a, 217). Arenal and Schlau note that "many pages have been
devoted to the study of mysticism and sexuality, but few to mysticism and
intellectuality" (226). Responding to their challenge, I address Madre Castillo's
mysticism as an encounter with knowledge.

Treatises that guided contemplative practice established a clear opposition
between mystic experience (appropriate for women) and the exercise of the
intellect (male territory). Miguel Godínez, for instance, differentiates mystic
theology from scholastic theology in that the first treats a "lovable truth" and
the second a "knowable truth" (1682, introduction).[13] The distinction depends
on the attribution to the soul by scholastic psychology of three powers or
faculties: will (*voluntad*), intellect (*entendimiento*), and memory (*memoria*). It
is the will's domain to love and to be moved to various emotions, while it is
the intellect that assumes discursive activity—that is, a "way to proceed in
treating some point and subject, with diverse intentions and various concepts"
(Covarrubias 1979, s.v. *discurso*),[14] and a way to reason through such means as

conversation or writing (Cuervo 1954, s.v. *discurrir*). The great Spanish mystics of the sixteenth century, Saint Teresa and Saint John of the Cross, share the fundamental belief that at the highest moment of mystic experience, the intellect with its discursive power is incapacitated while the will remains active and entirely absorbed in loving God. In this way, the mystics themselves classify the experience of mystic truth in opposition to the exercise of the intellect.

The divine knowledge that Madre Castillo transcribes takes a highly discursive form in the *Afectos,* though this does not imply an assertion on her part of intellectual activity. Madre Castillo does not explicitly affirm that in receiving the knowledge, her intellect is incapacitated, but her few descriptions of the mystic moment itself find harmony with those of Saint Teresa and Saint John of the Cross. Her primary experience of God's presence, however, occurs in an encounter with God's word. It is this word that releases the discursivity of the Scriptures into her explanations of the knowledge she receives. In her texts of mystic encounter, Madre Castillo fuses feminine mystic knowledge with masculine scriptural commentary. Sacred Scriptures center her texts; they provide her language, they fill her voice, and, most importantly, they are the space of her primary encounter with God. The central role that Scriptures play in the *Afectos* differentiates her writing markedly from that of both the Spanish mystics and her Spanish American sisters.

Achury Valenzuela addresses Madre Castillo's use of the Bible, providing historical background on the censorship of vernacular translations—most appeared on the indexes of books prohibited by the Inquisition—as well as on their availability in the Americas despite prohibitions (1968, cxix). Regarding the apparent transgression entailed in a woman's utilization of the Scriptures, however, he states only that Madre Castillo's confessors must have found serious reason to give their approval to such delicate material. The task of the present chapter is to explore Madre Castillo's mysticism and, within it, the significance of her translation and interpretation of biblical texts. The doctrinal content of the *Afectos* conforms to the ascetic ideology of the Counter-Reformation and does not challenge gender prescriptions; her recounting of experiences of mental prayer with their scriptural base does. Her mystic encounter with the Scriptures, its ritual setting, and the form in which she writes do not fit comfortably into standard genres and gender codes. While maintaining orthodoxy in the explicit message of her texts, Madre Castillo engages in a subtle sabotage of dominant male discourse by creating a feminine hermeneutic authority.

Madre Castillo carves out a space for her engagement in hermeneutic practice—and by this I mean the way she reads, interprets, and applies the Bible to her own life—by founding this engagement on the sanctioned feminine activities of mystic prayer, taking Holy Communion, and carrying out the ritual of the Divine Office. These monastic activities, in turn, shape the knowledge in her texts and the narrative structures through which the knowledge is communicated. I begin my explanation of Madre Castillo's hermeneutic practice by examining how she bridges the gap between her feminine self—bound to the body by contemporary discourse—and the intellectual character of scriptural commentary in her encounter with the "word made flesh." Next I explore the setting of this encounter, which most frequently occurs during the ritual of the Divine Office and the Mass and almost always involves the *Breviarium Romanum* (Roman Breviary), the Scripture-laden text of the Divine Office. I show that the *Afectos* take on a highly oral and frequently dramatic narrative of multiple voices and subjectivities, suggestive of the ritual itself. After exploring this ritual encounter, I look at the articulation of a method for this scriptural mysticism that begins to emerge in the *Afectos*. I study a single *Afecto* to show how Madre Castillo transforms the Scriptures into a guide for the soul's spiritual journey to its center in God. Next I relate Madre Castillo's mysticism to that of her sixteenth-century Spanish forerunners, showing how their treatises inform her encounter with God and discussing where the mysticism of the *Afectos* differs. After looking at how her mystic predecessors provide the raw materials for her method, I discuss another mode of authorization, that of the gendering of knowledge in the wisdom of Mary and the feminization of God. Finally, I analyze the continuities and changes in Madre Castillo's voice and subjectivity from the *Vida* to the *Afectos* to show her development of a teaching authority that will take on an even greater profile in the *Cuaderno de Enciso*. Through a complicated set of strategies, perhaps intentional, perhaps less consciously borrowed from the discursive practices that she is offered, Madre Castillo finds the means to inhabit the no-woman's land of scriptural hermeneutics.

THE WORD MADE FLESH

Opening her first text with the simple invocation of "J. M. J.," for Jesús, María, and José, Madre Castillo does not provide a title that might frame this collection as material for publication. The term *afectos,* chosen as the title of the 1942 edition, comes from the mystic tradition into which she inscribes her spiritual experiences: "Considering the different affects or effects that the soul feels in its relations with the divine majesty, I understood: sometimes the Lord manifests himself to the soul like a sweet, peaceable and loving spouse; and then, the soul feels only love and a desire for his pleasure; other times, he appears as a great Lord and king; and thus, the soul is occupied not only with love but also with fear, reverence and admiration" (*AE, Afecto* 29, 85).[15] The noun *afecto* has several secular meanings that relate to friendship, love, emotion, and passion, but it also plays a central role within the language of mysticism in referring to the soul's capacity to be penetrated and moved by God to pleasurable or painful sentiments (Viller et al. 1937, s.v. *affections*). Mystic writers associated the *afecto* with the movement of the soul's faculty of the will rather than with the intellect (Real Academia Española 1972, s.v. *afecto*). The title *Afectos,* then, speaks of "lovable" truth rather than "knowable" truth and cloaks the intellectual activity that Madre Castillo's writings engage.

Madre Castillo does not use the word *mística* to name her experiences, but they were understood as such by her spiritual directors. Protesting in a letter that he finds himself very inexpert in matters of mystic theology, one spiritual adviser classifies the various states of prayer that Madre Castillo has described to him. He recognizes one state as the contemplative mode: "that is the highest form of prayer to which God raises his spouses, the souls. . . . because of a great excess of love, the faculties are suspended and absorbed, not even yearning for heaven during this delight" (*AE* 545–46).[16] There are very few descriptions of this highest point of contemplation in the *Afectos*. One example is when the narrator recounts that "the soul found herself in an ineffable joy, in which it seemed that she was alone, apart from all creation, and alone with her God, not having even herself " (*Afecto* 13, 42).[17] Such affirmations are generally brief and lead quickly into a discourse of biblical knowledge. The words that immediately follow the above description are: "and she understood," which is one of the narrator's customary signals that she is shifting from the mystic moment to an interpretation of the knowledge gained therein. Other common markers of this shift include "I knew" and "as if he said"; the hypothetical "as if " refers to the incommensurability between divine locutions and human speech.[18] They are, rather, "the soft, sweet and delightful words that the soul receives, in the hidden place of her God and her center" (*Afecto* 99, 225).[19] The narrator laments the impossibility of translating them into her own language but attempts to do so anyway, using allegory and the language of the Scriptures.

One of Madre Castillo's allegorical descriptions of mystic locutions—an *endecha*—resonates with the imagery and amorous encounter of the "Cántico espiritual" of Saint John of the Cross, which begins:

> Where have You hidden Yourself,
> And abandoned me in my groaning, O my Beloved?
> You have fled like the hart,
> Having wounded me.
> I ran after You, crying; but You were gone.
>
> (1995)[20]

A fundamental difference between the two poems lies in Madre Castillo's focus on the word:

> The gentle speech
> Of the lover I adore
> Drips milk and honey
> Amidst roses and irises.
>   His mellifluous word
> Transpires like dew
> And with it blossoms
> The once withered heart.
>   So softly its delicate
> Whistling enters in,
> That my heart wonders
> Whether the sound is its own.
>   So surely it persuades,
> That like burning fire
> It melts mountains and cliffs
> As if they were wax.
>   So strong, so sonorous
> Is his divine breath
> It revives the dead,
> And the sleeping it wakes.
>   So sweet and so soft
> It is felt by my ear
> That it gladdens my bones
> In their most hidden place.
>   (*AE, Afecto* 46, 124–25) [21]

Like the "Cántico espiritual" and the Song of Songs on which it is based, this *endecha* describes an amorous encounter in a rustic setting between the poet and her divine beloved. Unlike the lover of the "Cántico," who passes briefly through an encounter with wisdom—"There He gave me His breasts, / There He taught me the science full of sweetness" (John of the Cross 1995, v. 27) [22] —and moves on to the metaphor of physical embrace, the poet of *Afecto* 46 experiences repeatedly in her heart and bones a flowering and happiness infused by her lover's word. Elsewhere, Madre Castillo associates this word with knowledge in the voice of God: "I also felt in the intimacy of my soul the essence of the Lord's voice, strong, powerful and majestic; the voice of the Lord on the waters. . . . This voice, then, of the Lord, preparing the deer, reveals what is dark, illuminates what is hidden. . . . This voice of the Lord provides light to understand the mysteries that the faith teaches" (*AE, Afecto* 155, 346–47). [23]

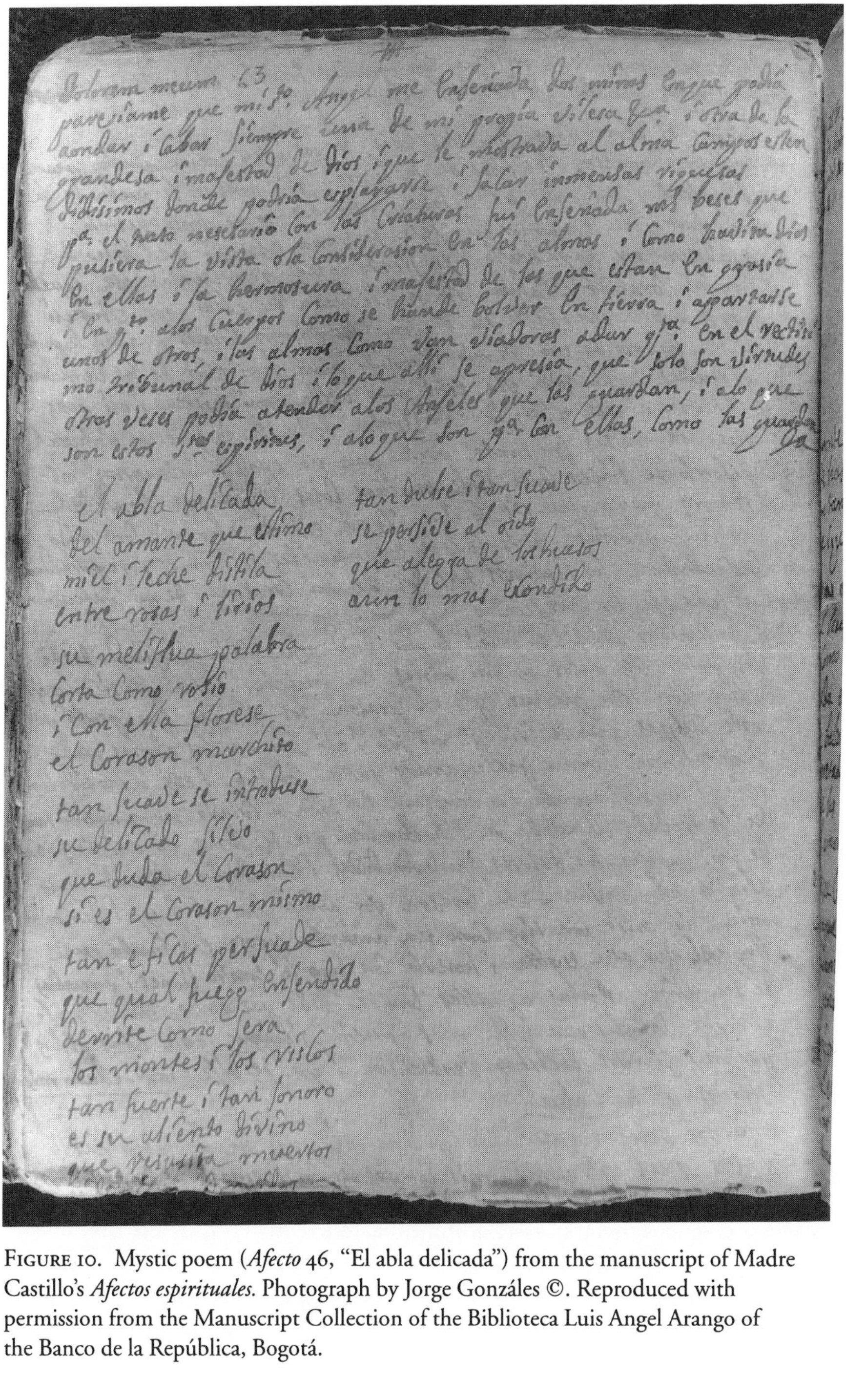

El abla delicada
del amante que estimo
miel i leche distila
entre rosas i lirios
su melíflua palabra
corta como rosio
i con ella florese
el corason marchito
tan suave se introduse
su delicado silvo
que buela el corason
si es el corason mismo
tan efícas persuade
que qual fuego ensendido
derrite como sera
los montes i los riscos
tan fuerte i tan sonoro
es su aliento divino
que resusita muertos

tan dulce i tan suave
se percibe al oido
que alegra de los huesos
aun lo mas escondido

FIGURE 10. Mystic poem (*Afecto* 46, "El abla delicada") from the manuscript of Madre Castillo's *Afectos espirituales.* Photograph by Jorge Gonzáles ©. Reproduced with permission from the Manuscript Collection of the Biblioteca Luis Angel Arango of the Banco de la República, Bogotá.

In the *endecha,* Madre Castillo explores the materiality of this word: it drips milk and honey, burns, melts, and whistles in an utterly sensory encounter with the soul. So incarnate is this word that Madre Castillo's metaphors imbue it with the power to alter material forms, and even to resuscitate the dead. The word and its material dimensions reappear at various moments in the *Afectos.* "[T]hat knowledge seems like a word, or a hidden speech, not like what is articulated or formed with the voice, but like dew, or like the drops that drip on the ground, that awaken [the soul's] thirst to know and love a goodness" (*Afecto* 19, 58).[24] "As if undone by joy, love and happiness, [the soul] knows the voice of her beloved, sweeter to her ears, softer to her palate and throat than honey. And this word seems not only to reach the ears of the soul, but gives sustenance, undoes her like fire to wax, penetrates her as light to fire" (*Afecto* 10 [B], 36).[25] Madre Castillo searches for metaphors of substance that awaken all of the senses and, with them, holy desire.

Paul Zumthor points out the material qualities of the voice when he theorizes its difference from the written word; it has tone, timbre, volume, and register (1990, 5). "More than a look or an expression, voice is sexual; it embodies rather than conveys an erotic message" (7). Zumthor's insights underline the sharing of materiality that is involved in the exchange of voices, and in the possibility of taking into one's own mouth the words of another. For Madre Castillo, this desire-filled interiorization of the divine word as milk and honey resonates with a eucharistic quality; Christ is the living Word of God, he is the Word made flesh. The divine and material word moves the soul to the affect of burning desire and penetrates it with the light of God's wisdom in divine union with her beloved.

Madre Castillo claims passivity in the encounter. She receives the word rather than thinks it; it moves her as an external force: "I understood that in all I have written, the soul can be perceived as an instrument of very thin flutes; because the air or breath of the one who plays it is like what is heard in the instrument, thus anything of God in these writings, is only that which his majesty sends by his spirit, through an instrument of cane, which is without virtue for anything, etc." (*AE, Afecto* 36, 101).[26] The soul, sounded by the breath of God, makes music back to God for him to hear; a mutuality is established between the two who are one in mystic union, yet the soul is entirely passive.

Music provides metaphors to communicate the material effects that mystic knowledge has on the soul: in *Afecto* 193, God is an instrumental ensemble whose trumpets awaken humanity from guilt and tepidness, whose bugle excites triumph, and whose zither calms and rests the senses and faculties of the body and soul (*AE* 486). Borrowed from the musical life of the convent, these metaphors project onto the supernatural experience some of the quality of ritual in which music is embedded. In the stirring music of high feast days, Madre Castillo finds an effective metaphor to convey the powerful emotion of the mystic encounter.

KNOWLEDGE IN THE RITUAL OF THE PSALMS

Liturgical ritual not only offers a metaphor for Madre Castillo's mystic experience, it also provides her a space of mystic encounter within her monastic obligation. While the *afectos* are set variously during spiritual exercises, moments of solitary mental prayer, or sleep, the most frequent scene is that of either the Divine Office (prayed by the nuns) or the Mass, officiated by the priest. Several references are made to the supernatural apprehension of wisdom during the reading of the Breviary, which is composed of hymns and scriptural texts in Latin, primarily Psalms, to be prayed aloud by the nuns. Often the mystic moment follows the sensory encounter with Christ in Holy Communion. The words "having taken communion, I understood this" appear throughout the text.[27]

Madre Castillo inscribed thirty-one verses of the "Cántico espiritual" into the first pages of her *Breviarium Romanum.* In the poem, Saint John of the Cross refashions the loving dialogue of the Song of Songs as an allegory of the mystic desire to ascend into union with God. Madre Castillo's encounter with the word also turns frequently into colloquy, or loving conversation between her soul and its beloved, as her exploration of the metaphor of the fluted instrument suggests. In one of the last *afectos* of the manuscript she writes such a dialogue, steeped in the allegorical tradition of the "Cántico" but crafted from metaphors she has evoked in various prior pieces:

Colloquy of a soul with Our Lord, as she was asleep, and, in her view, in intimate union with his divine Majesty through love:
My bride is to me like an instrument of very thin flutes, that sound softly to my ears.
You are to me, most loving God, like the consonance and harmony of all the musical instruments. . . .
My bride is to me like a moaning dove, who finds rest in my breast alone.
You are to me, most loving Lord, like a heart that burns amidst the entrails of my soul, radiating and penetrating all of her powers and faculties, giving her life, vigor and breath, warmth and happiness. . . .
My bride is to me like a little brook waiting in solitude for the weary traveler.
You are to me, my God, like an immense ocean-sea of mercies, joys, gifts and treasures, into which the waters enter, returning to their center to find rest. (*AE, Afecto* 193, 485–86)[28]

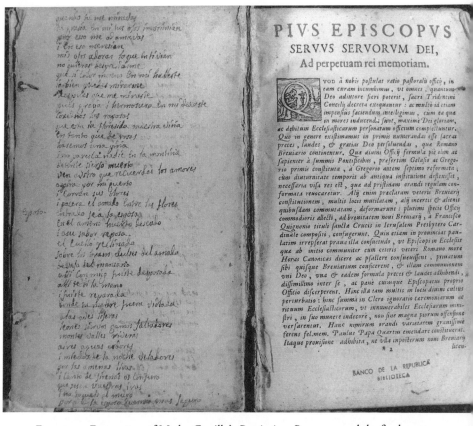

FIGURE 11. Front pages of Madre Castillo's *Breviarium Romanum* and the final verses that she has copied from Saint John of the Cross's "Cántico espiritual." Photograph by Jorge Gonzáles ©. Reproduced with permission from the Manuscript Collection of the Biblioteca Luis Angel Arango of the Banco de la República, Bogotá.

If in this colloquy, as in the *endecha,* Madre Castillo writes in the tradition of the sixteenth-century mystics, using metaphor and allegory to describe the indescribable, most of her reports of her encounter with the Divine diverge from the sixteenth-century mold. Their difference lies primarily in their focus on the Scriptures. Though the "Cántico espiritual" borrows from biblical allegory, Saint John of the Cross's explication of the poem distances the mystic experience that it describes from any act of reading that would include meditation on the Scriptures. Thus the Bible offers him the power of allegory to express an ineffable experience and gives authority to the expression, but does not itself enter into the encounter with the Divine. By inscribing the "Cántico espiritual" into her Breviary, Madre Castillo invokes Saint John of the Cross's use of the Scriptures to authorize her own. However, in joining his poem to her liturgical practice, wherein she finds mystic union, she also differentiates her mysticism from his. While Saint John's explication of his poem emphasizes the highest contemplative moment of a wordless union with God, the encounters that fill Madre Castillo's texts and move her will express not only a mystic encounter with God but also an intimate relationship with ritual and its scriptural liturgy. Unlike the dialogue of *Afecto* 193, most of Madre Castillo's texts fill the soliloquy and dialogue with scriptural words. These words function not only to create an allegory of mystic union but also to convey the substance of the knowledge received and the feelings exchanged. The scriptural words fill her voice and those of God and Christ in their mystic conversation. They also convey her interpretation of the word made flesh, the knowledge she receives from God.

In their scriptural dialogue, the *afectos* become the theater of the mystic experience in its consummate orality. *Afecto* 64 demonstrates this orality, built on the shifting of voices and of subject positions. In this piece, Madre Castillo communicates a lesson about the offense felt by God when humans sin. She begins, as she often does, with an autobiographical setting. She has become very disconsolate and confused after having experienced the scorn of others and having realized that her constant passions keep her from ever achieving any virtuous behavior (*AE* 152–53). This discouraging self-knowledge evokes the mystic encounter with the Scriptures through which the narrator will gain knowledge, which she applies in turn to her disheartened and sinful self, bringing it consoling instruction. Her voice becomes confessional as it continues to explore her vile nature at length; but in doing so, it also becomes exemplary: "I confess in his divine presence, that I never did a good work." [29] The narrator lights the way to the righteous path of humility by demonstrating self-knowledge and confession.

Her voice takes on greater exemplary value when she brings the word of God to bear on her condemnation. Not only is she vile but her resentment of the observations that others make of her sins flies in the face of God's teachings. Her reference to the Scriptures is explicit when she recognizes that she has not allowed their teachings to move her to an appreciation of the scorn but rather has always sought praise. She cites Isaiah 3:12, where God calls on his people to understand that those who say they are blessed only deceive them (*AE* 153). Transforming Isaiah's prophetic diatribe against the people of Israel into a condemnation of her personal spiritual sickness, the narrative voice has taken a new subject position, shifting from confessing sinner to interpreter of the Scriptures.

In the next shift, the Scriptures fuse seamlessly with the narrator's voice as she continues her self-condemnation, first speaking to an unnamed addressee —her confessor, herself, perhaps a wider audience—then shifting without warning to address God. "I know well when one sees so many benefits from God, and on my part, ingratitude and sins, that my evil is even greater than the sin of those unfortunate cities, which, fertile and abounding with benefits from heaven, saw so many abominations grow in them, and deserved the fire that came down from the sky to consume them [Lam 4:6 and 4:11]; but I do not want, my God, to make greater my evil with desperation, rather I will say: 'greater is your mercy, and better for me than life, and above life,' etc. [Ps 63:3]" (*AE* 153–54).[30]

Having switched from an autobiographical expression of distress to exemplary confession, to interpretation of the Scriptures, to voicing Scriptures with her own tongue in a lamentation to God, the narrator now gives over the "I" to God. First, however, she retreats from the soliloquy and alerts her reader that what is coming is a knowledge of God's word that has been impressed on her soul. While she does not explain the nature of divine locutions or *hablas* in every *afecto,* the words "I understood," "I knew," or "as if he said" always alert her reader to a transition into mystic communication: "And arriving here, I understood those words: 'hunt or catch the little foxes that destroy the vineyard' [Song 2:15], as if he were saying: I do not want you to destroy the vineyard of your soul by your dejection, but to take hold of and remove the defects that damage it, not to disintegrate in the sight of so much evil, but to recognize how much you need my help and favor to remove it" (*AE* 154).[31]

The divine communication continues, but now the narrative voice speaks about God rather than as God: "So many times they open their mouths to him, those who are like tigers, and bears and lions [Ps 22:13]; and so many times, even his spouses' souls, place within the temple of their heart, next to this sacred arc, the vain and accursed idol [1 Sm 5:2], clamoring with the people of their vain desires, affections and cares: *not this one, but Barrabas!* [Lk 23:18]" (*AE* 155).[32] The voice continues to carry divine knowledge to the soul, citing, interpreting, and applying God's word in the Scriptures to the personal experience of the mystic, but it is not now the voice of God speaking. Perhaps Madre Castillo intends no confusion, and this new interpretive voice is to be read unquestioningly as that of the autobiographical narrator, but the identity is not consistently obvious in the text. Often this interpreting voice addresses its own soul (*alma mía*), but only on a few occasions can the utterance be clearly identified with the autobiographical narrator.[33] As the autobiographical voice moves to scriptural commentary, its originally sinful confessing character is transformed into prophetic authority. In some *afectos,* especially later ones, autobiographical comments fall away and with them the presence of the sinful or tormented soul. There is no identification of the narrator, and so its voice can only be associated with the historical Madre Castillo or with God. As the voice often speaks about God, rather than as God, this leaves Madre Castillo and, more importantly, the Scriptures behind the authority of the text.

Afecto 64 does not exhaust the rich mobility of voice in Madre Castillo's writing; and on the other hand, some *afectos* do not display as much variety as 64 does. A number of important voices are missing from 64. In this *afecto* the narrator does not address the soul as *alma mía,* for instance, or engage in loving colloquy with the beloved Christ. In other *afectos* Christ responds to the narrator or the soul in the voice and role of husband. In some, scriptural quotes appear in Latin, set apart from the narrative voice. The use of Latin gives a more interpretive quality to the voice in the passage. Finally, in later *afectos,* an even more explicitly exegetical voice emerges when the narrator's primary focus shifts toward the dilucidation of a psalm or prayer in its own right.

The overall effect of the mobility of the voice and of the orality of the texts resonates, perhaps, more with the Divine Office or the Mass itself than with the mystic allegory of the "Cántico espiritual." In the ritual of the Mass, voices emerge from different spaces—the presbytery, the upper choir, the nave—and from the mouths of different people: the priest, the congregants, the nuns. These voices express the varied subjectivities of sinful or faithful creatures, divine beings, prophets, and saints; they utter supplication, confession, interpretation, instruction, exhortation, and praise. In a sense, the *afectos,* in their multiplicity of voices and the variety and character of the speech acts they engage, allow Madre Castillo to perform her own mass.

The project of interpreting the texts of the Mass is made explicit in three of the last *afectos*—*Afecto* 185, in which Madre Castillo comments on the *Avemaría; Afecto* 186, the Apostle's Creed; and *Afecto* 187, the antiphonal "Herodes Tractus"—and in a piece that appears in the *Cuaderno de Enciso,* published in Achury Valenzuela's 1968 edition of the *Obras completas* as the second of four "Afectos inéditos," in which she explicates the Lord's Prayer (*AE* 514). The narrator explains in glossing the *Avemaría* that she does so in obedience to her confessor (454). Her confessor has authorized an act through which she makes the celebration of the liturgy a more meaningful event. In the *Cuaderno de Enciso,* the same imperative comes from God. He instructs her to humble herself in the words of the Divine Office, which she understands to mean interpreting the liturgical prayers in terms that bring her to experience her own nothingness (518). In fact, one of the principal accomplishments of the *Afectos,* particularly in the latter half, seems to be the translation and personal application of the liturgy and especially of the extensive Latin texts of the Scriptures read or sung by the choir. In this way, the act of worship, which was celebrated in the language of the male ecclesiastical elite, becomes a space of meaning and participation for her, as her voice, and those of her sisters, carry much of the ritual.

The words understood by Madre Castillo's soul come to her through God's revelation of his sacred text by opening her mind to the language of the Mass: "I gave you intelligence of a language not studied, and more: I opened its meaning to you to understand its mysteries and deepest words, pronounced by my life-giving spirit" (*AE, Afecto* 98, 224).[34] Three times in the *Vida* Madre Castillo refers to this infused understanding of Latin, which began during her early days in the convent while she joined other nuns in the choir to sing the Psalms (*SV,* chap. 8, 23, 26; chap. 52, 197). Her knowledge of Latin is not gratuitous but responds to specific afflictions and needs of her soul, illuminating the Psalms in order to bring light to the significance of her suffering and thus to console her.

If the *Afectos* are read as a paradigm for convent practice, that is, if Madre Castillo conceived of her writings as instructional materials for other nuns, the result could have been a wider democratization of the performance of the Mass and the praying of the Divine Office. The practice implicit in the *Afectos* would serve to combat the tedium of a ritual that consumed much of the nuns' day. Canonical visitors to Santa Clara sometimes criticized the lack of respect for God evident in the nuns' attitudes toward their liturgical obligation; a more meaningful encounter with the Breviary might serve as a tool for reform. For those less gifted than Madre Castillo, unable to decipher the ritual language themselves, perhaps Madre Castillo provided instruction. Several factors considered in previous chapters support the hypothesis that the *afectos,* or a teaching based on them, reached a convent audience. Madre Castillo was assigned five times to the post of mistress of novices, where she would have been responsible for the young nuns' spiritual education. She had read Saint Teresa and was thus aware that in monastic tradition nuns did write instructional materials. In her probable familiarity with exemplary biographies, she also would have seen the transformation of private spiritual explorations like those of her *Afectos* into public instructional examples by the biographer-priests. But these are only hypotheses. Where there is stronger evidence for an instructional intention is in the structuring of the works themselves, whose examination I continue below.

Opening the Doors of the Hermeneutic Halls

How, in the early 1700s, was a nun in the Nuevo Reino de Granada allowed and even encouraged to interpret biblical texts, and what role did the character of her biblical hermeneutic play in that permission? In the sixteenth century, Saint Teresa repeatedly claimed her own ignorance of the Bible and avoided its commentary, though she did make one very telling and pertinent exception, which I examine below. A few short decades before Madre Castillo embarked on her literary journey, Juana Inés de la Cruz had also spoken to the enormity of such daring: "my not having written much on sacred subjects is not from disinclination or lack of application, but from an excess of the awe and reverence due those Sacred Letters, for the understanding of which I acknowledge myself so ill-equipped and which I am so unworthy to treat. . . . [H]ow should I dare to take this into my unworthy hands, when my sex, age, and especially my way of life all oppose it?" (1988, 208–9).[35] Sor Juana reminds her addressee, the Bishop of Puebla in feminine guise, that even young priests are discouraged from taking on the difficulties of interpreting the Song of Songs. Yet Madre Castillo's *Afectos* spring to life around the word of God—the biblical word. Achury Valenzuela has counted in the *Afectos* two thousand quotes and paraphrases of the Scriptures (1968, cliii).

Madre Castillo drops hints at various moments in the *Afectos* about how she comprehends her interpretive relationship to the Scriptures, a relationship that she will articulate in the form of a mystic method in the *Cuaderno de Enciso.* The Scriptures, she affirms, provide the soul with both instruction and consolation. In *Afecto* 143, the narrator queries her soul: "Do you not know that all things that are written, are written for the doctrine and light of the soul; so that with the consolation of the Scriptures she might ground, reinforce and strengthen herself in patience, and in it and them have hope? Do you not know that when the prophets speak of the person of Christ and recount his great tribulations, the soul is also to be understood therein, full of tribulation, desolate and afflicted, and that this was the example that was shown to your eyes, and the way, the truth and the life that guides life and nation?" (*AE* 317).[36] In *Afecto* 138 she calls the singing of the Psalms a consolation to the lonely bride of Christ, who suffers exile in her existence in this world (308–9). These affirmations give the Scriptures the function of providing a guidebook and spiritual comfort for the soul on its journey toward God. While she asserts the confessor's importance in directing the soul in both the *Afectos* and the *Cuaderno,* Madre Castillo exercises a measure of autonomy in taking a dangerous book off the shelf and giving it the functions of a spiritual director, only turning to her male confessor after her experience with the book has done its work.

It is in the *Cuaderno de Enciso* that Madre Castillo crystallizes her extensive learning process in the *Afectos* into an allegorical explanation of her mystical-liturgical method. It is helpful to look at the key opening paragraph of the *Cuaderno* before examining Madre Castillo's style of commentary in the *Afectos* in more detail:

> She understood that there was a field not comprehended by any intellect, composed of all of the sentiments, lights and knowledge that Our Lord wants us to find in the Psalms and the rest, etc., in which the soul, feeling divine love, and seeing that by the affects that she finds in her heart, can call God beloved, asks him to go out together with her into this field, where her heart is swollen until it runs with the feet of a deer down the road of his commandments; and, as if in competition with her, flowers appear with

excessive beauty and fragrance. The various sentiments that she finds there, the desires that flower there, the mysteries of her beloved's life, his mercies, all of his attributes (according to the capacity that he gives the soul) move her to desire to leave herself and her conditions and affections, the noise of the creatures, of her attachments etc., of desiring them, fearing them, delighting in them or being saddened by what is theirs, of wanting to please or displease, and as if with repugnance of everything that is not God—she calls him to go out together to the field of his truths, leaving the confusion and lie that is everything that is not God. (*AE* 513) [37]

The text invites the soul to call on God, her beloved, to go out with her into a field of "sentiments, lights and knowledge," terms associated with the mercies received from God during mystic union. The narrator is instructing those who desire mystic union of their soul with God to seek him in their encounter with the Scriptures, particularly in the Psalms. She is describing that amorous and mystic encounter with the word of God that she has already allegorized in the *endecha*. This opening text of the *Cuaderno* affirms that the seeker's encounter with the Scriptures is not intellectual in character but mystic, involving and moving the will to action. The encounter will draw her to God and his law, to a life of the spirit, and away from involvement with other human beings. It will allow her to divest herself of herself and submit to God's will.

It is not coincidental that in this introduction to her mystic encounter with the Scriptures Madre Castillo names specifically the Psalms, the book of the Bible that she cites most frequently. An obvious explanation of this preference lies in the fact that the Psalms make up the vast majority of texts prayed aloud by the nuns from the Breviary in the Divine Office. The Breviary distributes the texts in such a way that the nuns complete the cycle of the Psalms every week while carrying out their liturgical obligations. Other factors draw Madre Castillo to these texts or, rather, draw these songs into her mystic locutions: the contemporary interpretation of the "Psalms of David" as mystic soliloquies, the tradition of reading in the Old Testament a prefiguring of Christ, and the character of many of the Psalms as individual complaints and petitions that speak to Madre Castillo's own experiences of persecution. A reading of *Afecto* 123 brings out the affinities between the Psalms, Madre Castillo's mysticism, and her lived experience, and it shows how her hermeneutic responds to both contemporary interpretive methods and the demands of a mystic (nonintellectual) encounter with the word.

The *afecto* begins with the statement of a personal spiritual problem, framed in autobiographical terms. The remainder of the piece is taken up with a recounting of what the narrator "understood" in God's mystic response to her troubled soul. The knowledge contained in these interpretations of God's locutions brings the Psalms to bear on the problem, and concludes with a brief argument of why the experience of David is pertinent to a relationship be-tween the seeker (the narrator, the mystic, the narrator's addressee) and Christ. The divine message is intended to resolve the problem and to comfort the soul. The voice and the rhetorical strategies of the text infuse the autobio-graphical experience of mysticism with the character of a sermon or spiritual instruction.

THE AUTOBIOGRAPHICAL SETTING (*AE* 273)

The narrator begins by stating that she will tell what she remembers of knowledge that she received while feeling despondent after considering the lowliness of mortal creatures in light of the greatness of God. While she is praying the Psalms, she comes upon the verse, "Voce mea Dominum clamavi" (Ps 3:4): "I cry aloud to the Lord, and he answers me from his holy mountain [NEB]." [38] The Psalm consoles her as, in it, she understands that despite her lowliness God listens to her and responds to her prayers.

THE MYSTIC SETTING (*AE* 273–74)

The narrator recounts that despite the consolation she returned to her distress, tormented by temptations and darkness in her soul. At the moment that she received Holy Communion, she was also given a divine locution. She begins to relate the message of the locution with an allegory that instructs the soul to seek consolation in God rather than among her human peers: just as the bird would not find rest if she left her rightful airy abode for the dark caves of the earth, neither can the soul find rest in the earthly regions of human affections, but must leave this dark region, flying to God on the wings of love, truth, and resignation. The locution instructs her to exercise virtues, specifically humility and the suppression of her will, that will allow her to detach herself from her companions and to enter into mental prayer—that winged flight to God.

THE EXAMPLE OF DAVID IN THE PSALMS (*AE* 274–76)

Beginning with this allegory and continuing to the end of the *afecto,* the narrative voice abandons the autobiographical mode. It becomes that un-named interpreting voice that gives instruction to the soul. In the following three pages, the very words of the Psalms take over the narrator's voice in translations and paraphrases from Latin into Spanish.[39] Through these words, the narrator tells the soul that she should not despair because her father David before her experienced what she is suffering, and yet he never faltered from seeking his highest purpose.

The narrative voice becomes a space where phrases from more than a dozen different Psalms converge and are sorted into kindred groupings to describe the psalmist's persecution, to assure divine protection, to exclaim praise, and to exhort the seeker to learn from this example. The free association of the Psalms can be seen from the outset: "Do not think less of yourself or fear that you are lost because you feel such varied affects and tribulations, as your father David said thus: *that his virtue was dry like the tile, and that his bones had dried like the hay; that his virtue and light had abandoned him, lamp of his eyes; that he was like the wounded who arrived at the grave; that he was as if reduced to the dust of death*" (emphasis mine).[40] The first quote comes from Psalm 21:16 of the *Breviarium Romanum: aruit tamquam testa virtus mea, & lingua mea adhesit faucibus meis: & in puluerem mortis deduxisti me* (My virtue is dry as a potsherd, and my tongue adheres to my gullet. I am laid low in the dust of death). In the middle of this verse, the narrator has inserted a modified fragment from Psalm 102:4: *percussus est sum vt faenum* (I am beaten like grass). The metaphor of the grave elaborates on the dust of death. The references to light and lamp are picked up, later, in quotations from Psalm 119:105 when the voice turns to consolation. The narrator freely associates from among the verses attributed to David those that she finds most apt to interpret the locution and to respond to the beleaguered soul. She uses the language of ascetic life and mystic theology when she steps back to comment on the psalmist's suffering—that he is near death, despised, mistreated, persecuted, and ridiculed, a stranger to his own family and filled with fear: "And all of these *temptations* and *inner* and *exterior trials* did not take away the fact that he was a man in accordance with God's heart, because in all he had recourse to the Lord" (emphasis mine).[41] Madre Castillo inserts the language of mysticism into her rereading of the Scriptures when she relates the consoling promise to David: "Do not fear, then, the fears of the night [Ps 91:5], as my words *to the ears of your soul* will be light for your paths" (Ps 119:105, emphasis mine).[42]

CHRIST AS MEDIATOR (*AE 276*)

Finally, the narrative voice makes a summation of the examples brought forth from the Psalms and relates them to the story of Christ, speaking at first directly to and then about the soul: "See, then, that everything the Psalms say about David. . . . They say about the person of Christ, your spouse . . . and if the union that is made in the Holy Sacrament of the body and blood of Christ is as real and true with the soul, his bride, why should she not share the conditions of her Lord and husband, and follow his steps, if she be a faithful spouse? . . . He is the son of David according to the flesh, and she must desire to be the daughter of his spirit. He said, 'learn from me, for I am gentle and humble-hearted' [Mt 11:29]; and David had said, 'O Lord, remember David, in all of his gentleness' [Ps 132:1]."[43] In a quick hermeneutical move, the lessons from David's suffering and his faith in his protector, God, have been likened to Christ's Passion, and through this link have been brought as both example and consolation to the seeker—very specifically, to that writing nun who is suffering inner turmoil and the scathing criticism of her peers. Her suffering—the antagonism of the convent in which her every fault is brought before her pained soul by her adversaries—offers her the blessed opportunity to share in the Passion of her beloved Christ.

The narrative voice now reaches back in the Christian master narrative to the story of origins. She urges the seeker to accept this union with Christ in suffering by recalling that, in the beginning, God exhorted husband and wife to be two in one (Gn 2: 24). If the flesh-bound union of Adam and Eve that came of Eve's creation from Adam's side called them to be two as one, then the spiritual marriage of the soul to Christ demands much more. If the soul enters Christ's heart and, in turn, takes him into her heart through Holy Communion, then she must desire greatly to be like her husband, and that likeness demands that she accept the pain that is the emulation of his Passion.

The language of the Breviary accentuates the identification of David with Christ by putting in the psalmist's mouth the characterization that Christ gives of himself. Christ says that he is, in Madre Castillo's translation, *manso* (meek); David cries out to God to remember him in his *mansedumbre* (meekness). In the Breviary, the word David uses is *mansuetudinis* (gentleness), while the *Vulgate* names rather David's *adflictionis* or suffering. Theologians understood Christ's affirmation that he had come to fulfill the Scriptures as a call to read all of the Old Testament through Christological eyes. The narrator states this guiding interpretive principle in a reference to the book of "Revelation" when she says that the Lamb (Christ) was killed so that the seals on the Book might be broken (*AE, Afecto* 115, 259). If David prefigures the suffering of Christ, he also prefigures that of Christ's beloved, the mystic's soul. He expresses her suffering in the absence of her beloved, her sense of worthlessness, and her desire for the consolation of God. Both interpretive principles—David as proto-Christ and David as mystic psalmist—were current during Madre Castillo's lifetime.[44]

A FEMININE HERMENEUTIC

If the content of Madre Castillo's scriptural interpretation offered no surprises to her world, the hermeneutic authority that she exercised as a woman should have. This text and many others in the *Afectos* not only interpret the Scriptures and apply them to spiritual experience but do so in a form that incorporates the rhetoric of theological oratory, another priestly prerogative. In *Afecto* 123, the "sermon" begins with a human experience of suffering. It brings scriptural interpretation to bear in explaining the situation and exhorts the listener or reader to action, seeking to move her emotions and will through the use of an accessible and allegorical language.[45] This sermon, though, is veiled within the mystic moment and is authorized by the voice of God.

A note to Madre Castillo from one of her confessors confirms his view that her biblical discourse originates in a passive mystic moment and provides an explanation for why her hermeneutic activity slipped by the gendered lock on the doors to theological practice. After her exposition of Psalms 1 and 38 (39 in the Latin Vulgate and Breviary) in *Afectos* 164 and 165, the manuscript carries the following note: "My mother: what I understand from this gloss, as much from the first Psalm as from XXXIX, is a doctrine very much in conformity with the mystic locution of the celestial spirit, some places crying out to others, in the true intelligence of the Holy Fathers. This I say, according to theological knowledge of the inscription, although I find myself very distant from the affectionate [knowledge] of which our Redeemer spoke when he said: *confiteor tibi Pater, quia abscondisti haec a sapientibus, et revelasti ea parvulis* [Mt 11:25—I acknowledge you, Father, who hid this from the wise and revealed it to the children]. . . . So, for the instruction and confounding of cold disputes, the Lord is served when what he reveals in secret, you give to the pen" (*AE* 376, n. 1).[46] Her spiritual advisor has judged her interpretation sound. He recognizes it as not of her own intellect but as a locution from God. He encourages her role as amanuensis for such celestial communications by citing Jesus's own favoring of those who were marginalized from power when, as quoted in Matthew, he states that what God hid from the wise he revealed to the lowly. This passage had often been used to support mystic women writers before Madre Castillo. Finally, her correspondent has suggested the unique value of such mystic knowledge that is unobtainable through the "cold disputes" of scholastic theology.

As a twentieth-century feminist scholar, I seek behind Madre Castillo's communication of mystic locutions an active exercise of scholarship. In a desire to break those historical silences about women, I offer here an image of Madre Castillo at her desk, Breviary in one hand, pen in the other, *Vulgate* before her, her mind deeply engaged in discursive—intellectual—activity. It is this desire that has brought me to impose the label of "hermeneutic" on her mystic encounter. Another nonmystic interpretation would also allow admiration for her great intellect. A photographic or near perfect aural memory may have aided Madre Castillo to draw on her daily reading of the Psalms to bring together the tremendous associations and recombinations that she writes into the *Afectos*. Nevertheless, the exact nature of her historical experience of writing, whether contemplative, intellectual, or an interweaving of the two, remains hidden behind the text. But whether she herself understood the locutions to be entirely of God or the result of her reading and active thought, their representation as divine locutions was key in permitting her to continue to write and to engage in her scriptural encounters.

MADRE CASTILLO AND SIXTEENTH-CENTURY MYSTICISM

While her understanding of mystic theology comes from her reading of sixteenth-century mystics and the currency of their treatises in her milieu, Madre Castillo does not simply imitate these writers or limit the interpretation of her experiences by their texts. Her mysticism both imitates and diverges from that of her primary models—the great Carmelite mystics Saint Teresa and Saint John of the Cross, the founder of the Jesuit order, Saint Ignatius of Loyola, and the Jesuit theologian Father Luis de la Puente. The four Spanish theologians represent two divergent currents of spiritual practice: the Carmelites, a contemplative mode that seeks as its highest expression a wordless union with God, and the Jesuits, a meditative practice in which Scripture informs the process of seeking to submit one's will to God. While Saint Teresa's canonization, in 1622, gave final authorization for a powerful visionary and reformist model that would influence the lives and writings of the nuns of many orders, the Jesuits were simultaneously becoming an effective force in guiding spiritual life in the Americas, wielding the meditative practices of Saint Ignatius of Loyola's *Ejercicios espirituales* as a primary tool of propagation.[47] Madre Castillo synthesizes aspects of each spiritual model and immerses her synthesis in liturgical practice, creating her own feminine mystic encounter with the Scriptures.

If Madre Castillo does not name Saint Teresa's *Libro de la vida,* in which the Carmelite explains mental prayer, it is very likely that she either read it or knew of its contents. Achury Valenzuela defends propositions that Madre Castillo read both the *Libro de la vida* and the *Camino de perfección,* in which there is a brief description of *quietud* or the union of the soul with God.[48] In keeping with her "rhetoric of femininity" and her embracing of a wordless union, Saint Teresa eschews both the role of the Scriptures and of the intellect in her explanation of the process of contemplation or mental prayer. For her, mystic contemplation is a nonintellectual mode: its high point involves a paralysis of the intellect while the faculty of the will is entirely absorbed in the act of loving, and all activity is taken over by God.[49]

Passive mystic loving does include receiving divine locutions, and Saint Teresa's explanation of these locutions or *hablas* in *Las moradas del castillo interior* (*The interior castle*) shows sixteenth-century roots of Madre Castillo's word made flesh. In the sixth "mansion" Saint Teresa discusses locutions, which can come from deep within the soul, from the superior part of the soul, or can even be heard by the ears of the body (1970, chap. 3, 436). Though the *hablas* are received in the stage of prayer just prior to the soul's entry into that highest and innermost seventh mansion of union with God, they are also very dangerous; both the Devil and the creature's own imagination can produce words that appear to be divine communications. It is thus necessary for Saint Teresa to instruct the seeker in how to discern the origin of the locutions. The signs that she gives also characterize Madre Castillo's affirmations concerning her experience of God's word: the *hablas* have great power of persuasion, bringing immediate calm to a turbulent soul, remaining a long time, and conveying absolute certitude. They are different from human words, as "in a genuine locution one single word may contain a world of meaning such as the understanding alone could never put rapidly into human language" (1949 2: *Interior Castle*, sixth mansion, chap. 3, 284).[50] Moreover, the words are often accompanied by an even greater understanding that is not contained in them.

Saint John of the Cross also explores the material force of divine locutions in their impact on the soul. Madre Castillo's frequent use of such ideas as the dark night of the soul indicates that she was steeped in the mystic tradition of Saint John and perhaps read more of his works than just the "Cántico espiritual."[51] One type of supernatural apprehension of knowledge (which, Saint John affirms in his *Subida del Monte Carmelo* [Ascent of Mount Carmel], is given to a passive soul rather than to a discoursing intellect) is the *palabra sustancial* (substantial locution) (1980, 347; bk. 2, chaps. 28, 31). It imprints itself directly onto the soul and moves it to the experience of an affect. Madre Castillo draws from the concept of *palabras sustanciales* when she speaks of how her bones are moved to happiness by her beloved's voice, of how her soul is melted like wax by fire, and of how the voice that sounds the flute of her soul is felt as a movement in the heart even more than it is as a sound on the lips (*AE, Afecto* 46, 125; *Afecto* 10 [B], 36; *Afecto* 36, 101). As my discussion of the "Cántico" suggests, however, Saint John does not associate this mystic word with the biblical word, though he uses the Scriptures to explain mystic theology.[52]

Saint Teresa does not create an absolute separation of her mysticism from the Scriptures, but the few times that she does engage with the Scriptures, she dwells on the problematic nature of her actions. Her explanation of the divine source of her knowledge of the Song of Songs in *Conceptos del amor de Dios escritos por la beata Madre Teresa de Jesús sobre algunas palabras de los "Cantares", de Salomón (Conceptions of the Love of God.* Written by the Blessed Mother Teresa of Jesus upon Certain Words of the Songs of Solomon) finds agreement in Madre Castillo's explanation of her knowledge of the Scriptures. Saint Teresa's defense of the act of interpretation, however, expresses risks in a way that Madre Castillo's *Afectos* do not. Like most of Saint Teresa's writings, *Conceptos del amor de Dios* is addressed to her spiritual daughters. Saint Teresa believes they might find comfort and delight in some things that God has given her to understand about the Song of Songs, and that women are not to be excluded from enjoying the riches of the Lord. They should not, however, "argue about them and expound them, thinking that we can do so successfully without having first submitted our opinions to learned men. So, as the Lord well knows, I do not suppose I shall be successful in writing about this" (1949, 2: chap. 1, 362).[53] Understanding the Scriptures is so unfitting for women, she says repeatedly, that her daughters should not tire themselves in trying to comprehend what they find themselves incapable of in what they have read or heard in a sermon. Alison Weber's analysis of Saint Teresa's rhetoric invites us to suspect the explicit message of the text, especially when the mystic seems to wink at her daughters in writing, "it is something not meant for women—and many such things are not meant for men either" (Teresa de Jesús 1949, 2: chap. 1, 359).[54]

The fear is well placed. One of Teresa of Avila's confessors apparently ordered the manuscript destroyed, though she made sure that copies survived (1949, 2: 353–55). After her death, her ally Padre Gracián published the first edition of the *Conceptos del amor de Dios* from a surviving manuscript. The work was reprinted many times in the early seventeenth century, and, apart from the suppression of annotations between 1623 and 1630, it circulated freely (356). Despite the affirmation of the doctrinal soundness that publication assured, Gracián shows his awareness of potential criticism of the work by referring to the " 'Lutheran heresy' which encouraged 'women and idiots to read and expound the Divine writings' " (355), and by implication, he distances Saint Teresa's work from such erroneous practice.

Saint Teresa's own understanding of the Song of Songs is a gift from God. "For several years past, the Lord has been giving me such great joy in the hearing or reading of some of the texts from the *Songs* of Solomon that, although I have not clearly understood the meaning of the Latin in the vernacular, they have caused me greater recollection and moved my soul more than the highly devotional books which I can understand" (2: prologue, 356).[55] As Madre Castillo does in only a few of her later *Afectos,* Saint Teresa proceeds to comment on the Scriptures by removing her personal experience of their understanding from her text and leaving only the interpretation. She does not reenact the process of reception as Madre Castillo does in developing the encounter itself as an acceptable model for feminine interpretation of the text.

It is in bringing the Carmelite mysticism together with an Ignatian practice of meditation that Madre Castillo finds authorization for her mystic encounter with the biblical word, and perhaps some of its inspiration as well. The *Spiritual Exercises of St. Ignatius* do not mention the term *mystical theology* or discuss the desire of uniting of the soul with God, but rather seek the will of God through meditation on doctrinal and scriptural materials. Madre Castillo, too, talks about seeking God's knowledge in the Scriptures in order to follow his commandments (*AE* 513). The exercises aim to free the soul of inordinate attachments, as Madre Castillo states in her consonant project, to make it tire of everything that is not God. The textual base of Madre Castillo's experiences resonates with the method of the Ignatian exercises that she often performs under the guidance of Jesuit confessors. All three faculties of the soul play active roles in the *Spiritual Exercises*. The first week centers upon an examination of the practitioner's conscience through meditations on sin and the punishment of the damned. The following weeks focus the faculties on the Kingdom of Christ, the Passion, and the mysteries of Christ's life, providing references to the Gospel stories and, in the fourth week, specific citations of scriptural passages. Saint Ignatius suggests that, beginning in the second week, the practitioner read the Gospels, the lives of the saints, and the *Imitation of Christ* in order to nourish the meditative effort. Doctrinal texts enter the process as the practicant is encouraged to chant the Lord's Prayer rhythmically as one method of meditation. The individual is also instructed to have "colloquies" with the Virgin, Christ, and God the Father. All of this is to be accomplished under the close guidance of a spiritual director, perhaps especially because of the encounter with the Scriptures, whose translation into Spanish was in large part prohibited by the Inquisition.[56]

Writing half a century later, the Jesuit Father Luis de la Puente (1554–1624) finds himself in a Spain that has codified an orthodox model for mystic practice, molded by the writings of the Carmelite mystics. Father de la Puente's *Sentimientos y avisos espirituales,* written between 1579 and 1609 but published only posthumously, illustrate his blending of a search for mystic union, a discernment of God's will to order his soul, and a personal application of the Scriptures consonant with the instructions of the Ignatian exercises. The *Sentimientos* were given to Madre Castillo by one of her confessors so that she might find pleasure in reading them (*AE* 32, n. 1). Both de la Puente and Madre Castillo embark on an inner exploration that they develop into a generalization of knowledge about the relationship between the soul and God, though de la Puente's expositions are much shorter than those of Madre Castillo. Both take the dictum of the Ignatian exercises to reflect on the Scriptures and move this reflection into a relationship with mysticism. But where Madre Castillo's text blends autobiography with instruction, bringing instructional rhetoric into the text very quietly, de la Puente's *Sentimientos* reveal a clear organization around doctrinal elements. Where the narrative voice of the *Afectos* moves almost seamlessly between subject positions and speakers, de la Puente's use of the Bible is clearly and consistently set off by his use of Latin. Madre Castillo enacts the mystic moment, and biblical prose fill both her voice and God's. De la Puente remains outside of the encounter, explaining it and recounting the light he has received about a biblical passage but not attempting to reenact the experience of the locution itself. As a priest he has no need to veil his engagement with the sacred text.

In borrowing from divergent spiritual traditions of the sixteenth century to create a biblical mysticism, what is at stake for Madre Castillo is the elaboration of a specifically feminine hermeneutic authority. She needs a model in which knowledge may be discursively expressed, yet a baldly discursive engagement of her intellect with the Scriptures would seem suspiciously like male theology. Saint Teresa avoids the Scriptures or touches them with great delicacy, but she serves Madre Castillo as an authorized model of feminine mysticism and of an encounter with a divinely spoken word. The mysticism of Saint John of the Cross bolsters her understanding of the material aspects of such a word while giving her a poem that she uses to bridge the gap between mystic encounter and liturgical ritual. Saint Ignatius provides her with a meditative practice that encourages her to engage the Bible, and Father Luis de la Puente offers an example of an instructional discourse that results from such engagement. Madre Castillo reads selectively and combines elements of these practices within an orthodox practice of liturgical prayer. She does so in such a way that the discourse she produces will be identified as mystic but will permit her to create the feminine hermeneutic she desires. Reading this mystic from the Nuevo Reino de Granada against her Spanish forebears places the daring nature of her feminine hermeneutic in relief.

THE GENDERING OF FIGURES OF AUTHORITY

In addition to framing her interpretation of the Scriptures within ritual and mysticism, Madre Castillo also justifies feminine engagement with knowledge through her gendering of God, Christ, and Mary. If she belittles femaleness by giving herself the epithets of "blind little woman," "poor little despised and vile female," and "poor discarded woman" (*Afecto* 147, 325; *Afecto* 187, 477; *Afecto* 110, 249),[57] she also brings a stronger woman into the pages of the *Afectos*. In so doing, she writes within an extensive tradition of convent literature, though she develops her feminine models of knowledge and authority to a lesser extent than some of her most prominent feminist predecessors. I use the term *feminist* cautiously, recognizing the anachronism of applying it to sixteenth- and seventeenth-century women. With the term, I refer to the ways in which women such as Saint Teresa of Avila, María de Jesús de Agreda, María Anna Agueda de San Ignacio, and Juana Inés de la Cruz broke down the images that limited women's self-concept and the walls that contained women's lived experience, writing into their texts models of feminine authority and agency.

Arenal and Schlau note that nuns' writings in general "give a more egalitarian view of the world," at least in terms of gender equality (1989a, 216). These critics mention in particular the appearance of Mary as a figure of wisdom (220). When the *Afectos* show Mary as a source of knowledge, the images borrowed from a literary tradition center on the virgin's milk; it is through this milk that Mary bestows her teachings (*Afecto* 19, 55; *Afecto* 132, 297; *Afecto* 134, 301; *Afecto* 136, 304). Madre Castillo brings out an active female agency in Mary as she transfers to her the words of praise that are directed in Psalm 103 to the God of Creation: "Oh that my soul would find you [Christ], and find you in my mother's breasts, so that my soul would be fed by her mercies, and in her protection I would have my refuge; in her doctrine and example, my nourishment and security!, as the breasts of her teaching are like towers of defense [Song 8:10]. Oh, my Mother, and mother of life, your breasts are like *the wine that comforts and gladdens the heart of man* [Ps 104:15]" (*Afecto* 19, 56, emphasis mine).[58]

An explicitly strong female subjectivity appears in a few places in the *Afectos*, replacing the self-proclaimed worthlessness most common to the seeker's declarations. Mary is the model for the "strong woman and spouse" as she exhibits strength in her suffering on Calvary (*Afecto* 74, 174). The narrator remembers another strong biblical woman, unnamed, who gathered linen and wool and worked them with her hands; she remarks at how much the linen must be beaten to become white enough to receive the colors of divine love (*Afecto* 157, 351). This woman models the strength and activity necessary for the seeker to purify herself to receive God. The narrator instructs the soul that she needs this strength in order to share the crucifixion with Christ. She must face suffering with virility (*varonilmente*), like a woman born of man, like a woman who has "come out of the side of man" (*Afecto* 189, 481). Could this last reference be to a redemption of the daughters of Eve?

Madre Castillo's mortal women are occasionally strong, and her celestial women are always strong, active, and wise. Her God and Christ, in turn, sometimes take on the feminine characteristics of gentleness and vulnerability. The "mother of wisdom," whose doctrinal milk the narrator desires in *Afecto* 172, also nurses her son as he takes on the vulnerable and dependent image of the baby, showing the way for humanity by becoming the recipient himself. Christ is likened even more to his brides, when his naked and "virginal body" (*cuerpo virginal*) submits to the humiliation of the whip (*Afecto* 118, 263). God, the father, shows a feminine side when he is like a mother teaching a child to walk (*Afecto* 182, 437). His wisdom is called the "sweetest milk of his doctrine" (*Afecto* 172, 396). Following after the picture of Mary as she nurses her children with wisdom, this image of a motherly God builds a strong resemblance between his actions and Mary's and, by similitude, imbues the feminine with greater authority. Crossing the boundaries of gendered representation, feminizing God and Christ, and attributing to Mary and to other women the qualities of strength and wisdom associated with masculinity and with God, Madre Castillo diminishes the distance between authority and woman. She blurs the patriarchal association of power and knowledge with maleness, which is based on the creation of man—and not woman—in the likeness of God. In this way, she authorizes her own acquisition and transmission of the knowledge that her texts embody.

Voice and Subjectivity: Between the *Vida* and the *Cuaderno*

The *Afectos*, with their greater confidence, optimism, and freedom of voice, pose a clear contrast to the *Vida*, but how is this difference achieved? Autobiographical incidents like those in the *Vida* enter the *Afectos*, and, conversely, frequent visions and even transcriptions of a few *afectos* can be found in the *Vida*, yet the two texts diverge widely in both content and tone. The contrast between the overridingly negative tone of the *Vida* and the eminently affirming, generally somber, but sometimes joyful tone of the *Afectos* can be explained in great measure by the changes in both voice and subjectivity between the two texts.[59] When the *Cuaderno de Enciso* is added to the comparison, the voice and subjectivity of the *Afectos* can be seen as in a state of transition between the other two. By noting this intermediate character, I do not intend to diminish the full development and value of the *Afectos* in their own right.

The submissive, pained, and fearful "I" of the *Vida* has not entirely disappeared from the *Afectos*. Many of the pieces are introduced by a statement that the soul "understood" or received a mystic lesson when feeling confusion or tribulation. A passage from *Afecto* 82, in the first half, might have been taken straight out of the *Vida:* "My God, what more disproportionate and deformed thing can a vile little woman wish, repugnant as a rotten dunghill, full of vice and quick to anger, so many times fallen in such great sins, than to admire herself or that others admire her?" (*AE, Afecto* 82, 193).[60] As in the *Vida*, the narrator of the *Afectos* occasionally expresses anxiety about her writings and asks her confessor whether he thinks she should burn them, stating that writing is torment and she fears she is writing only nonsense and madnesses (116, n. 1). Yet these expressions of pain and self-degradation are considerably less present than in the *Vida*, and these autobiographical comments appear less frequently in the second half of the manuscript than in the first, suggesting a growth in confidence in her writing role.

The authorial voice in the *Afectos* exhibits greater autonomy than in the *Vida*. Madre Castillo's confessors, while present, take on the roles of judge or commentator much less than in the *Vida*. The number of times in which the confessors are addressed as readers or mentioned is proportionately much lower. References to the confessor also decrease between earlier and later *afectos.* While the focus on exterior life and social relations in the *Vida* brings with it a constant involvement of the confessors, above and beyond their roles as addressees and instigators of the writing, the relative absence of exterior life in the *Afectos* diminishes their overall presence and their directive and censorial force.

The freedom of the narrative voice in the *Afectos* depends on the change in the object of narration. A discussion of spiritual virtues and experiences in their own right, and the word of God itself, replace the complete absorption with Sor Francisca and her life that structures the *Vida.* As the object of narration changes, so too does the relationship between narrator and story. The narrator no longer has to maintain the constantly confessional and self-humiliating tone of the *Vida* because she is not called by the journal task to judge her life. In the *Afectos* the shift in the object of the narration allows her to become a teacher. A rhetorical move by which she separates herself from her own soul facilitates her new role. She becomes her soul's shepherd, instructing it in accordance with the knowledge she receives in the divine locutions. "I knew [mystically] that each soul is both sheep and shepherd of her affects, that if she ceased to watch over them, they would depart from God, and would carry the soul to the lion's mouth. I remembered what Our Lord said 'if you love me, feed my sheep'(John 21:17)" (*AE, Afecto* 7, 17).[61] As the voice becomes a conduit of mystic knowledge as well as the point of both interpretation and instruction to her own soul, the negative characterization of the autobiographical seeking soul becomes more distant from the narrating voice, thus giving this voice more confidence. The fact that it is sometimes God who speaks in the text also infuses the writing with a tone of confidence lacking in the *Vida.* The narrator occasionally accentuates the homiletic quality of the rhetoric by shifting from addressing a singular *tú* (the seeker or soul) to a plural *vosotros* (all of God's flock), taking on a homiletic tone. The examples she uses move occasionally to statements on humanity as a whole.

Finally, the divine origin of the biblical word that fills the *Afectos,* and her resultant status as "useless cane," provide the necessary authority for her (pen) to discourse so confidently on the written word of God. Madre Castillo's "I," as the place where knowledge is received and from which it is transmitted, while present throughout, becomes progressively less intrusive. Her inner self as the locus of experience is more common in earlier pieces, where the scene is set within autobiographical references such as: "I felt a great tribulation and confusion, with temptations and persecutions, both inner and external, leading me to lend an ear to mortal creatures" (*AE, Afecto* 52, 133).[62] As the narrator's "I" becomes less intrusive, the autobiographical tone dissipates and the focus turns more toward the content of the lessons.

The relationship of the narrator to the Scriptures exhibits an increasing authority from earlier to later texts. In the early *afectos* the Scriptures blend seamlessly with the narrator's voice, providing the emotion and metaphors that express the spiritual experience. In the later *afectos* the narrative voice more frequently makes explicit her role as interpreter of the Scriptures. In *Afecto* 184, for example, no autobiographical reference identifies the narrator with Madre Castillo, and there is no exclamation of "I understood" to mark a transition to a divine voice. When such phrases appear as, "[t]hen look; in almost all of the Psalms of David," expressing the narrator's role in biblical commentary, would these explicit references and interpretations not give the narrator—associated with the historical writer—more authority in the eyes of the reader?

Widely divergent in tone and content—one filled with negativity, the other uplifting, one dwelling on the miseries of a convent life, the other on the path away from the world and to God—the *Vida* and the *Afectos* embody two faces of the same whole. In a sense, their specific differences point to a sole author, a sole female religious author writing during the Counter-Reformation. If there are deep disparities in tone, content, voice, and subjectivity, the doctrinal substance of the two works is the same. The *Afectos* provide the theology that underlies and explains Sor Francisca's extreme behavior and emotions in the *Vida*. *Afecto* 103 explicitly links the mystic knowledge acquired to Sor Francisca's battles in the *Vida:*

> I knew [that is, I received the knowledge in a mystic locution] that with God's creatures, who inhabit this house of the Lord of the universe, and more so with his brides in the house of religion, I should behave myself and regard myself as a poor little one, vile and naked, whom a great lord, took into his house, purely out of mercy, so that she should live in the company of his children and servants; 1st She [the poor little one] would assist, obliging and diligent, in doing what was commanded of her and in pleasing, as she was able to, the children and servants of her Lord. 2nd She would not meddle in affairs nor desire to flatter others or to be noted by them. 3rd She would content herself with whatever they said to her, without complaining of oversights or disdain. 4th She would look upon all with esteem; only herself would she find contemptible. 5th She would do with care what was commanded of her. 6th She would suffer injuries without giving occasion for them, because everything occurs in the sight of her Lord. (*AE, Afecto* 103, 232)[63]

If the lessons of the *Afectos* are lived in the *Vida* with very few consolations, the *Afectos* themselves become the space of Madre Castillo's consolation and mystic reward. In the *Afectos,* she escapes the strife of the *Vida,* finds divine assurance for her salvation, and takes on the estimable position of teacher.

Such daring is permitted because the lack of the *Vida* imperative frees her from constant self-judgment. The relative absence of external life, and thus of the society of the Convento de Santa Clara, frees her voice from the fear of hubris, the subjectivity of the disgruntled critic. Despite monastic detractors, Madre Castillo's careful development of female authority in the *Afectos* over more than thirty-five years of her life in the convent found crucial support in her confessors' approval. Negotiating a treacherous terrain, Madre Castillo made possible her creative control over the engagement of her intellect in daily liturgical duties, and perhaps even shared this freedom with her sister nuns. In the Counter-Reformation atmosphere of colonial religious society, Madre Castillo molded her limited freedom by em*body*ing her mind and by veiling it in the double habits of mysticism and monasticism.

THE *CUADERNO DE ENCISO*
A THEOLOGY OF HUMILIATION AND
ITS MYSTIC REWARDS

Just as he who is in the sepulchre is surrounded by nothing but the tomb to his right, to his left, above and below him, and the earth of the grave seems to swallow, eat and devour the interred, becoming one with him and converting him into itself, removing the flesh from his bones and turning even them into dust, just like the worldly dead, so you must pray, ask and desire to be united, completely changed and traversed in Jesus's heart, in the glorious sepulchre of his love, and in the most ample field of his blood that is the sepulchre of the wanderers and of those who have no place on earth to rest or lay their heads.
                                        —Madre Castillo, *Cuaderno de Enciso*[1]

INTO the blank pages of an accounting book, known now as the *Cuaderno de Enciso* because it was given to Madre Castillo by her brother-in-law, Don José de Enciso y Cárdenas, Madre Castillo copied five poems, several devotional texts, a number of revised *Afectos,* and a few original pieces (Achury Valenzuela 1968, cxcvi). The author of three of the poems has been identified as Juana Inés de la Cruz, and two are of unknown authorship, possibly compositions by Madre Castillo; one is dedicated to Mary, another to acts of penitence and contrition.[2] The next thirty-five pages comprise a meditation on the Passion and various treatises, including one on the sin of *murmuración* and one on mystic contemplation. Achury Valenzuela argues that the very different literary style of these texts, and the scholarly arsenal on which they draw—absent in Madre Castillo's known writings—prove that they are not original work (Castillo 1968, 2: 496).

Of greatest interest in the *Cuaderno* are the final forty-eight pages—54r–93r, including missing leaves—into which Madre Castillo has recopied thirty-three of her *Afectos,* reediting and reordering them and adding to them four pieces unique to this manuscript.[3] I have examined the handwriting of these pages carefully. It matches that of the *Vida* and the *Afectos;* and though the hand is not entirely uniform, its variations conform to those natural in the handwriting of a single person. Read as a unit, these forty-eight pages effectively provide a guidebook for the soul's spiritual journey, one built on the theology of humility and humiliation that buttresses one face of the *Vida*'s autobiographical subject. For the sake of clarity, I will henceforth refer to these pages of the *Cuaderno* as "the guidebook." I am also aware that this title is an imposition based on a hypothesis that I seek to substantiate and that there is the possibility that the title misreads Madre Castillo's intentions.

The degree to which Madre Castillo intended the guidebook to be read publicly is unclear. Scholarship has traditionally asserted the privacy of her writing in all of her works, but this text has not been studied as a unit until now. The structure of the piece and the types of changes that Madre Castillo has made to the texts from their form in the *Afectos* manuscript give credence to a hypothesis of public intent. Certainly, her five years as mistress of novices and her nine years as abbess placed her in positions from which she guided other nuns in their spiritual lives. In these roles, she could well have developed a text whose content undergirded her instruction. At the very least, the guidebook shows the evolution of her own theological understanding from explorations of separate themes to the elaboration of a coherent treatise on the soul's path to God.

The manuscript does not carry the more self-conscious marks of public intent of the lengthy theological works of her Mexican contemporary, María Anna Agueda de San Ignacio. Sor María Anna Agueda herself uses the word *tratado* (treatise) to refer to the first two sections of her *Marabillas del divino amor, selladas con el sello de la verdad* (Marvels of divine love, sealed with the seal of truth), which Jennifer Lee Eich calls "an intellectualization and theological exegesis of Sor María Anna Agueda's devotion to the Virgin Mary" (1992, 60–61). In this description, Eich points out that although the treatise reveals a prescriptive mold given by its sacred and scholarly sources and by Sor María Anna Agueda's demonstrated command of Latin, it constitutes a "textualization of personal beliefs and experiences—an intimate spiritual exegesis camouflaged as theological text" (57). The work's publication only two years after the author's death speaks of the high regard that her writing commanded during her lifetime (56).

Though without the self-consciousness and length of Sor María Anna Agueda's treatises, and having possibly lacked clerical encouragement for its publication, Madre Castillo's work shares with that of her Mexican contemporary the character of an "intellectualization" and "theological exegesis" of a personal experience of devotion. The text's narrator, an unidentified female "I," alternately instructs her own soul and an unnamed "you" in the proper path to God. She draws sometimes on her own experience but more frequently on that of an unnamed soul—*una alma*—the same soul that is the text's frequent addressee. She also maintains the relationship between knowledge and the Scriptures that she developed in the *Afectos*. The sense that the narrator is instructing the addressee/reader along a spiritual path is clearly developed in the first ten segments of the guidebook (what I will call "part one") through the particular sequencing of the situations and challenges that the soul faces. Madre Castillo gives these ten segments subtitles that offer the treatise a sense of completeness. A clear break between parts one and two of the guidebook is achieved by a stylistic change from a double- to a single-column text and by the abandonment of explanatory headings. The break may indicate the end of the project in Madre Castillo's mind; part two differs from part one in that it offers various personal narrations that explore, in no apparent order, the themes treated in the first section. This second section may constitute an autonomous reworking of several of her favorite *Afectos,* but it can also be read as a further development of themes from part one and thus as composing a single text together with parts one and three. The third and last part of the guidebook resumes the treatiselike character evident in part one, both in its organization and use of headings. This final section examines the two central themes of Madre Castillo's theology introduced in part one: humility and mystic union.

My purpose in this chapter is to examine both the content of the guidebook and those aspects of the manuscript's form that give it a simultaneously pedagogical, theological, and personal character. I begin with a brief treatment of content and form by demonstrating how the tight organization of part one, together with Madre Castillo's revisions of the original pieces, gives the guidebook a more public and instructional character than the *Afectos.* Second, I examine the narrative voice as that of a teacher, looking at the language and speech acts that bring into the guidebook a rhetoric of theological oratory—in other words, of the sermon. Third, I explore the message of the text and the effect of its Counter-Reformation force. I close this chapter by studying the mystic moment as Madre Castillo portrays it in these pages, in which joy is ever infused with and defined by suffering.

A Treatise for the Soul

Madre Castillo opens part one of the guidebook by proposing that God wants the soul to find a field of affections, light, and knowledge of himself in the Psalms and other Scriptures (*CE* 54v). Beginning with this field, metaphors of landscape weave a thread of unity through the next nine segments. The subtitles describe a soul who departs into the field of truths, occupies herself with the field of life, examines the harms and benefits of temporality, and ascends the mountain of myrrh.[4] She (the soul) finds the source of the living waters in a field of humiliation and comes to rest in the glorious sepulchre that is the wound in Christ's side. She learns that tribulation is God's greatest gift and consolation to mortal creatures. She ascends the mountain of eternal life in the Lord's Prayer and, finally, finds in her confessor an earthly guide for her journey toward eternal life.[5] The biblical imagery of a natural geography provides Madre Castillo with a coherent source of metaphors that she uses to explain the soul's journey throughout the guidebook.

The themes of these ten segments follow a logical sequence. The opening piece invites the soul to a new beginning, out into the field of spiritual knowledge to follow the path of God's commandments. The picture of the soul as a deer, running with God over fragrant fields and called to climb the mountain of God, resonates with the imagery of the Song of Songs, which was used by many mystics to express that ineffable mystic union with God. But while mystic union is treated in part one, and developed at greater length in part three, Madre Castillo pays little attention to the process of mental prayer as Saint Teresa teaches it in the *Libro de la vida*. Saint Teresa deals with some of the same aspects that are central to Madre Castillo's treatise on spiritual life, such as the soul's difficulties, its necessary purgation, and the attitude and actions of the seeker in her social relationships; but the Carmelite's primary focus is elsewhere. The heart of her teaching is to examine the process of mental prayer itself, to explore the psychospiritual experience during four successive stages in which the seeker becomes ever more passive as God takes over and gathers her into joyous union. Madre Castillo concentrates most of her attention on the suffering that purifies the soul, the seeker's imperative to a humbling knowledge of self-worthlessness, and her submission to God's will. Her treatment of mystic union occupies a small portion of her treatise, and she explores it as if it were all of one character rather than a long process of differentiated moments.

After inviting the soul through the Psalms and Scriptures toward God's law and love, the narrating voice anticipates the entire journey that the soul faces as she "departs into the field of truths." The path moves the soul from her desire for God to the experience of fear as she realizes her helplessness. Once she has embarked, she suffers the scorn of others for her new behavior, and this scorn leads her to seek an intimate knowledge of herself. Self-examination reveals that she is vile and worthless. The resulting plunge in her emotions turns to hope, which leads her to discern God's presence with her. Here she feels immense awe at the abysmal distance between herself and God, between his forgiving love and her evil. Experience of this chasm and the consoling knowledge that God wishes to be its bridge overwhelms the soul with the desire to find joy in suffering for God's sake, and her voice bursts forth in praise.

Having outlined the entire journey, Madre Castillo turns to its key moments and concerns. In the third segment, the narrative voice instructs the soul in her spousal responsibilities to God's family, meaning that the seeker must serve as intercessor and pray for the souls of others. Fourth, she takes up the great maxim of the Counter-Reformation, that this world and everything in it will pass. She adds a personal twist to the message, finding in the ephemeral nature of the temporal world the comforting knowledge that she need not concern herself with the opinions of God's creatures but only with God himself. This message, which also pervades the *Vida*, does not give the soul license to disobey her superiors but rather encourages her to find in the punishments they mete out the joys of a brief experience of suffering that will lead to eternal life. In the fifth segment of part one, the attacks leveled at the seeker continue to define the soul's ascent up the mountain of bitter myrrh in imitation of Christ's Passion. God's willingness to be humiliated in the vulnerable humanity of the crucified Christ provides the sixth lesson, which links the soul to God to the extent that she too allows herself to be humbled and humiliated. This field of humiliation provides the most important key to God's living waters, meaning that it is the seeker's death to herself that brings her to life in God. Thus, in the seventh moment, the soul becomes divested of herself, having submitted her will to God, and she experiences a glorious and mystic death cradled in the womb-like wound of Christ's side. In her eighth lesson, she realizes that to suffer is to receive God's greatest gift to humanity: God's love is greatest not when he gives of himself to an undeserving and worthless being but rather when he longs for a gift from that same lump of vile humanity. Since to suffer the absence of God is the greatest gift she, a worthless being, can offer, it follows that God's acceptance of her suffering reveals his greatest love. The final two lessons of part one instruct the soul in how to maintain humility once it is achieved. The narrating voice models a meditative exercise on the Lord's Prayer that explores the application of the prayer to the soul through the lens of her nothingness. Finally, the soul is instructed to find comfort and an intermediary to God in her spiritual guide or confessor, treating him as her matchmaker and as a type of John the Baptist who prepares the way of the Lord in the desert of her soul.

In addition to reorganizing her *papeles* in order to create a coherent guide, Madre Castillo rewrites the pieces themselves in two important ways. Firstly, she removes from the original *afectos* all of the autobiographical content that might identify her as their author or her life experience as that of the narrator. In many though not all cases, she also changes the identity of the soul whose experiences and knowledge fill the pieces, from the personal "I" or "my soul" frequently used in the *Afectos* to a distanced "she" or "a soul." Secondly, Madre Castillo responds in at least one documented case to the comments of a confessor and clarifies the doctrinal content of an *afecto* before transferring it into the guidebook.

The amount of editing that any piece undergoes between the *Afectos* and the *Cuaderno* depends primarily on the degree to which the original *afecto* interweaves visionary or mystic knowledge with specific references to the circumstances under which Sor Francisca acquired it. For instance, in transcribing *Afecto* 86 into the section of the guidebook entitled, "Of the occupation of the soul in the field of life," Madre Castillo suppresses the following personal references: "Today I understood"; "And it is thus that, many times, and almost always, [the holy souls of purgatory] were represented to me, and it seemed to me that I saw some in dreams with these similarities to the ill"; and "Wishing then to pray for my parents and siblings, I understood this" (*AE* 198–99).[6]

Madre Castillo omits almost a third of the original text of *Afecto* 9, most of which includes similar personal references, when she transposes it into the *Cuaderno* as "Of the ascent of the soul to the mountain of myrrh" (*CE* 57r–v). In addition to the omission of personal references, some changes clarify the content of the text. The effect of the majority of Madre Castillo's editing is to give an impersonal or general character to the narrator's voice and to the identity of the soul, who serves as both the conduit of God's knowledge and the narrator's explicit addressee. By erasing her specific identity from the text, Madre Castillo gives prominence to the divine source of the knowledge she imparts, thus imbuing the narrative with greater authority. Even when the narrator brings attention to herself through her use of the personal pronoun *I*, this unidentified and disembodied voice carries with it the authority of the Divine, to which it serves only as conduit. When it is the unnamed soul/ protagonist who takes up the *I* to speak of herself or to God, the seeker/ addressee is presented with an instructional model of behavior. She witnesses the unnamed soul respond to the knowledge conveyed by the narrator. In the move from the *Afectos* to the *Cuaderno,* Madre Castillo deflects the reader's attention away from the interaction between her inner state, her external experiences in the convent, and the lessons she is given by God, and onto the content of those lessons and the sense that every soul must pass through this journey.

Identifying the extent of the doctrinal revisions Madre Castillo undertook in response to her confessors' concerns would demand a detailed comparison and the knowledge of a church scholar, but one example pointed out by Achury Valenzuela is suggestive of her attitude toward revisions. Finding only a fragment of *Afecto* 10, and on its reverse an unsigned note identified by a third hand as from "her confessor," Achury Valenzuela matched the fragment with the end of a completed text in the *Cuaderno:* "Of the departure of the soul to the field of truths" (Castillo 1968, 2: 32, n. 1). The noteworthy changes in the *Cuaderno* version are two and respond to the confessor, who asks the meaning of the original words "[b]ecause it was already beginning to dawn," saying that he wishes to know if this is to note the time at which you had the sentiment and spoke the words of the Psalm, 'Rise up Psalter and cythar,' or whether they perchance have some other meaning. The other [question] is that in the final lines of the sentiment you say that Our Lord, 'with his divinity shelters, and with his humanity pardons,' and it is necessary to explain this last further, because although it is true that the humanity of Jesus Christ Our Lord was that which, with his passion and death, won us pardon, it is properly God who pardons us. . . . It could also have another meaning, understanding for humanity, his mercy. (32)[7]

In the *Cuaderno,* Madre Castillo changes the first sentence to make an apparently syntactical clarification, stating: "And in that silence and solitude, with tenderness and joy of the soul she tells her beloved in the Sacrament, 'rise up my Psalter and Cythar, rise up in the morning, as your light is now dawning on your soul' " (35).[8] In the final sentence, she clarifies the more delicate doctrinal question of who it is who pardons the sinner, stating that "the soul found a strong place of refuge in the God and Lord of virtues, who, *as God, pardons* and, *'made human, shows his kindness more'* " (38).[9] Would Madre Castillo have reorganized her *Afectos* into a coherent guidebook to instruct the soul, removed obvious autobiographical markers, and revised style and content to clarify any doctrinal muddiness for the value that the exercise held for her own soul? Perhaps. But the nature of the changes as well as Madre Castillo's use of other pedagogical strategies make plausible the hypothesis that in the *Afectos,* and even more so in the *Cuaderno,* she developed within herself a sense of teaching authority, albeit as a human conduit of divine knowledge, and that she hoped, or perhaps even ensured, that her teaching would reach a wider readership.

Personal Prose and a Rhetoric of Theological Oratory

Various rhetorical strategies imbue the guidebook's narrative voice with a pedagogical quality that intertwines the instruction by a teacher to the spiritual seeker, the language of the mystic, and elements of theological oratory. A first strategy that accomplishes this mixing of discourses emerges from Madre Castillo's use of voice and dialogue. A second finds expression in the highly figurative language of the guidebook (brought in from the *Afectos*)—its use of metaphor, allegory, and parable, which mediate between the Divine and the human. A third strategy involves Madre Castillo's recourse to a rhetoric of persuasion.

As I discussed in chapter 8, the voice of the *Afectos* is both shifting and multiple. That is, the first-person point of enunciation and the second-person addressee slide from one referent to another in a text that revolves around soliloquy and dialogue. The messages of the guidebook are also communicated between an "I" and a "you," whose referents move between earthly and divine figures. The voice of the "I" is often spoken by the soul who seeks God and on her path encounters fears and joys, knowledge of the Divine and of herself, God's presence and his painful absence. Often the "I" is the teacher, or primary narrator, who interprets the seeking soul to the reader ("you"), at times distancing herself by speaking of *una alma* (a soul) whom she observes, at others expressing a close relationship with the seeking soul by claiming it as her own (*alma mía*) and thus bringing the experience under discussion into her own subjectivity. Sometimes the teaching voice breaks the confines of the I/you relationship to speak more freely of all mankind *(el hombre),* acquiring greater authority of tone through the wider scope of the lesson's object. At times, God or Christ takes up the "I" in a dialogue with the seeking soul, and the text enacts the mystic experience. In all cases, the "I" becomes a space of mediation between the inaccessible spiritual form of God's knowledge and the earthly reader as the "I" receives mystic knowledge—often through the Scriptures—and forges with it her instruction to the "you" of the text. The addressee of the text, its "you," is occupied alternately by the generic soul, by the teacher's own soul, and occasionally by God, whom the teacher praises and the seeker petitions. Sometimes the teaching voice, at one with humanity, exhorts a plural "you" into relationship with God, as in "Sing to the Lord all the earth. Sing his mercy and justice" (*CE* 55v).[10] The third person in the text, that *una alma* or *el alma,* serves the purposes of the teaching voice as both an example and a conduit of divine knowledge, as the teacher describes the soul's experience along the spiritual journey. Sometimes the third-person marker is occupied by all of mankind—*el hombre*—and then the teaching voice gathers herself up into a prophetic stance, decrying human weakness.

The communicational scheme in contemporary texts of spiritual instruction is generally simpler than that of Madre Castillo. In his sermons Juan de Avila addresses his listeners as *vosotros* (you, plural) and at times as *tú* (singular). He speaks from a first-person "I," a knowing subject who instructs his flock. At times he also addresses himself to God in praise ([1596] 1970). Fray Luis de Granada preaches without using a personal "I" or "you" but does join his own subjectivity to that of his listeners in exhorting an "us" into right relationship with God (1962). Madre Castillo cannot separate her teaching voice from that of the seeking soul, perhaps because of her discomfort with a voice that is both female and uniformly authoritative and that, as such, challenges the male exclusivity of the apostolic privilege. Perhaps her assumption of authority is complicated with a sense that her anonymity cannot be guaranteed even after her editing. Perhaps the entanglement of autobiographical and teaching voices expresses the interconnectedness of these roles in her monastic experience. Certainly, the text creates a paradigm different from that of its male counterparts with its interweaving of teacher's and learner's voices.

Madre Castillo writes in metaphors, allegories, and parables, finding in the Scriptures sources for the language and illustrations of her teaching voice in the guidebook. This voice reaches so deeply into the figurative language of the Bible that the prose loses its anchor in everyday reality. Madre Castillo's use of figurative language reveals her belief in its power to mediate between the Divine and the human. Though she does not specifically discuss her use of such language, she does address God's use of images to teach the soul. If the experience of mystic union defies the human capacity of verbal expression, many spiritual mysteries lie beyond even human comprehension. Therefore, God uses the likenesses of corporeal things or earthly images to raise the lowly human understanding toward those spiritual things that it does not understand and in this way moves mortals to love and desire the incomprehensible (*CE* 78r). Her ultimate justification of the importance of imaginary visions lies in Christ himself.[11] God, she writes, "did not come to the world as an ineffable light" (78v).[12] God's voice intervenes in her text, asking whether his word made flesh and bread is not a stronger proof of his love than such an ineffable mystery. Christ as corporeal mediator between God's spiritual mystery and human limitations justifies for Madre Castillo the acquisition of divine knowledge through the "imaginary" vision—which always risked human and diabolic interference in its meaning, in contrast to the ineffable and wordless but safe knowledge of God gained in mystic union.

Madre Castillo's argument parallels the mediatory function of Christ as word that underlies Erasmus of Rotterdam's interest in rhetoric and especially in the power of metaphor and allegory in the moral transformation of an audience (Hoffman 1994, 11). "[W]e see Erasmus' hermeneutic as governed by the idea of language as mediation. Language, especially God's speech in Scripture, draws the reader into the truth through the process of interpretation. And it is the peculiar drawing power of allegory (the middle between the historical/literal and the spiritual/mystical sense of Scripture) that performs this metaphorical function. Here the divine word intercedes between heaven and earth as it translates the reader from the flesh into the spirit" (6). The mediatory power of figurative language in the Scriptures is founded upon Christ, who is the word made flesh, both fully human and fully divine. In this double nature, he becomes a third term that bridges the dualism of the spirit and the flesh: he becomes the "supreme mediator" (11). Erasmus promotes the use of parable, metaphor, and allegory as teaching methods that accommodate a difficult message to the capacity of the student and, by moving and delighting the emotions, impress the meaning more deeply onto the listener (1993b, 259–266).

Allegory is perhaps Madre Castillo's favorite rhetorical strategy. A paraphrase of the Song of Songs, which explains to a troubled soul the variety of affects that move her when she experiences the presence of God, is the most extensive allegorical narrative of the guidebook:

> That whole colloquy between the spouse and her beloved in that song of love, do you not see how it is woven out of awe-inspiring variety. Now she keeps watch and seeks her beloved. Now she sleeps and is sought by her beloved. Now she suffers, faints and feels her soul melt like wax at the voice of her master. Now she finds him and, determined, promises not to leave him again until the blessed time. Now she hides from him and finds herself like the night in its shadows. Now she asks after him. Now she makes signs to him. Now she is beside herself with love, and she requests the sacred kiss. Now she wishes to run behind her beloved. Now she loves him and sees in him the beauty of the lily of the valley. Now she wishes to follow him like the little goat and deer of the fields. Now she attends to the adornments that her spouse has given her. Now she occupies herself entirely in loving and pondering the perfections of her beloved. Now she sees the cedars and cypresses of which her house is made. Now she invites him to the country-side to see the vineyards and to live in the villages. And do you not see how she, without understanding it, finds herself sometimes troubled by the ar-mies of Aminadabad, because her beloved tests her in various ways, mixing myrrh with fragrances and perchance giving her to taste of the honeycomb. And don't you see how, sheltered in her breast, he might show himself at times a handful of myrrh and at others, squeezing his spouse in the working of his fingers, and tightening them, his hands distill the chosen myrrh. Do you not see her, her protection wounded, despoiled of her vestments? And other times, do you not see how they pronounce her blessed, seeing her rest on her beloved, etc. But in all of this there is nothing more than that love and pain. I am his and he is mine. My beloved is mine. I am his. (*CE* 92v–93r) [13]

Madre Castillo provides little interpretation for the allegory, though little was needed to evoke the ineffable and loving union of the soul with God, as the mystic interpretation was well known through such texts as the "Cántico espiritual" of Saint John of the Cross. Madre Castillo's introduction to the allegorical paraphrase is brief: "Having some doubt regarding the various accidents that she felt within herself with different affects and effects, [the soul] understood this" (92v).[14] She expects the reader to understand that the moments of distance and pain between the biblical lovers represent the spiri-tual turmoil of the soul who feel's God's absence, that the beloved distilling his lover's myrrh in the pressure of his fingers speaks metaphorically of the soul's pain when tested by God, and that the lover resting on her beloved signifies a joyous union between the soul and the Divine. All of these meanings are thoroughly supported by the teachings of the preceding pages of the guide-book. Madre Castillo's concluding interpretation of the lesson is equally brief: "So, look at the way the heavens and the earth are equalized here, God with his creature, the Most High with the dust, the Creator with the making of his hands! And look to what you will give in exchange for this goodness. Look at the firmness of your promise: that you left, etc.!" (93r).[15] Madre Castillo gives the usual interpretation of the Song of Songs as the highest expression of desire and intimacy with the Divine, but she adds to it an admonition. Reminding the soul of the abysmal gap that God overcomes to bring her, undeserving, into his love, she exhorts the soul to respond to God's promise with all that she can offer: to leave all else behind and dedicate herself solely to God. Even in this interpretation, Madre Castillo's language remains without a foot on the firm ground of daily life, perhaps because the message itself, like that of all of the guidebook, demands the nun's removal from that worldly life.

Madre Castillo does not actually complete her written admonition to the soul, employing instead the elliptic "etc." where the original piece in *Afecto* 107 reads: "Notice the firmness of the promise: you who left all things and followed me will receive twice one hundred and will possess eternal life" (*AE* 241; cf. Mt 19:27–29).[16] Does Madre Castillo's frequent use of the device "etc." indicate that her writing is purely a private exercise? Knowing what the "etc." replaces, she does not have to write it out in full solely for her own benefit. Does the elliptic "etc." reveal the guidebook as a script for teaching, in which case she could also supply the needed text? The abbreviation was used by some preachers in the written version of their sermons to indicate a partially cited biblical text (see Vázquez 1943, 22). Does Madre Castillo assume that her reader will know the verse too? The assumption is not unreasonable for either a confessor or another nun who prays from the Breviary several times a day, every day of the year.

The lessons of the guidebook do not always depend on such extensive allegories. Many times the allegories are brief or are reduced to metaphor. The second segment of the guidebook strings together a series of short allegorical images with even briefer metaphors to represent an overview of the soul's journey toward God. The soul is a small animal when she sets out in the rain on the overwhelming and lonely journey. She must become the lowly worm and the despised owl in order to be transformed into the resurrected Phoenix. She is called to live on the rooftop as the solitary bird who shakes off the dirt of the earth, and as the dove who cries out faithfully to her only mate (*CE* 54r–v).

Sometimes Madre Castillo brings nonbiblical stories to the service of her teaching, emulating the use of parables that is central to that of Christ. To illustrate the importance of humility, for example, she tells of a daughter who serves her powerful father and takes no notice of her own humble dress, seeing only his needs and desires:

And her father might well draw her to him: because he is keeping her beautiful clothing, jewels and adornments for the day of her wedding. But if, in the meantime, he wishes to give her some of them, and if she is a faithful daughter, she will take them only for the pleasure and fancy of her father, who is served by having his children rich and honorable. What would happen, then, if this daughter became so enamored with her adornments that she placed her pleasure in them and in herself and was thus less attentive to any occupation of her father's pleasure and service, and no longer employed herself in the lowly and humble labors of his house? Would she not be exposed to horrifying errors, and, hearing her dress praised, would she not seek lovers of her beauty? . . . And would the Lord not throw her from the heights and grandeurs of his love, hurling to the earth the one who once was a pedestal to his feet? . . . So, my soul, you must look only to your Father's pleasure in order to free yourself of such horrible evils. Be as he would have you, happy because you see that you love and desire him alone. Value his gifts as given by your beloved Father from whose hand everything must be received with great love and gratitude, both his light and his darkness [Ps 139:12]. (79r) [17]

Madre Castillo weaves into the parable scriptural references that indicate a practice of exegesis behind its construction. To my knowledge, the tale is not itself biblical, though its form and language resonate with elements of the parables Jesus used in his teaching.

The final pedagogical tool that I have identified in the guidebook is an exercise of meditation modeled on the spiritual exercises of Saint Ignatius. In the ninth segment of part one of the guidebook, Madre Castillo relates that the unnamed "she"—that seeking soul—while suffering great tribulations, has learned that she should "apply the consideration of humbling herself in all things, and in particular in all of the words of the Divine Office, and beginning with the Lord's Prayer she understood thusly" (60r).[18] What follows is a phrase-by-phrase gloss of the Lord's Prayer, in which each element evokes in the soul's first-person voice an emotional experience of humbling self-knowledge, a recognition of God's great magnanimity, and a petition for God's saving grace. The enactment of the exercise by the anonymous soul provides a model for any reader to do the same.

HUMILIATION AS THE PATH TO RESURRECTION

What is the message conveyed by this teaching voice? Madre Castillo finds inspiration and authority in the great female (and frequently subversive) intellectuals and mystics who have gone before her. She works out a space for herself within male apostolic privilege by exploring and experimenting with a literary form that is cloaked in a mystic practice sanctioned for women. If she stretches and cracks the limitations on the feminine in her methods, the explicit content of the message she develops with this freedom is highly orthodox. Her teachings seek to persuade the will into self-control in a strategy consonant with the aim of the Counter-Reformation.[19] Madre Castillo points the soul toward God on a rocky path of humiliation that ends in the surrender of the will. Her narrator uses both the word *humildad,* which can be translated as "humility" and the word *humillación* or "humiliation" at different times in her discourse, but it is the self-degrading experience of humiliation that plays the strongest redemptive role in the text. The narrator of the *Afectos* brings out the relationship between the two when she asks herself how she can desire humility (*humildad*) without humiliation (*humillación*) (*AE, Afecto* 62, 150).

If pride is the root of all sins and leads the soul to hell, then humility, in Madre Castillo's words, "is like a very precious stone of strange beauty that enclosed in itself all the beauty of the other virtues, and thus it is composed of various and attractive colors that do not confuse themselves with each other nor hinder its beauty" (*CE* 85r).[20] The central place of humility in the doctrine for the soul that Madre Castillo explores finds expression in her dedication of sixteen of the twenty-one pages of part three to its elaboration. Having introduced humility and its importance to salvation in part one, and having developed the concept in greater depth through seven large pages of small script in part three, the narrative voice expresses the endlessness of her task and the difficulty of writing about it: "Although up to here she had written some of what Our Lord gave her to understand about knowledge of the self, she felt like one who experiences a sharp pain and struggles to describe it, and after having said a great deal remains with the pain as intact as at the beginning, or like he who runs all day in a circle and at the end finds that he has not advanced at all on his path" (88v).[21]

Renewing her attempt to bring the soul/addressee not only to a comprehension of humility but to its practice, Madre Castillo inserts another Ignatian-style exercise into the text. The Ignatian *Spiritual Exercises* provided a method for the seeker to discover God's will for his or her actions, occupying all three faculties of the soul—memory, understanding, and will—with a specific text of biblical or doctrinal provenance. The seeker was to allow the eyes of the soul to focus on the images evoked by the text and to ask God for joy, pain, shame, or suffering according to the subject matter. The desired result was that the seeker's affections would be moved through the use of the will, so that he or she would become disposed to submit his or her own will to that of God. In like manner, Madre Castillo provides in her text a series of considerations on humility designed to move the soul to a humble attitude. The seeker should begin by considering the immeasurable attributes of God and contrasting them with the nothingness of her self (*CE* 90r). She is to reflect on the vices that invade her when God is distant in the metaphoric image of a body covered in cysts, an image that resonates with that of her own body in the *Vida* (90r–v). A further consideration shows the seeker the miseries that surround her body and soul in her exile from God: her ignorance, the disorder of her life, her inconstancy, her temptations, and the afflictions she suffers at the hands of others. "What or who is man but ignorance and deceit?" the narrator asks, raising the experience of her addressee to the level of a general human ailment.[22] Man, she continues, is a being who laughs at that which should motivate lament, cries when God sends reason for joy, desires what he should fear, fears what he should desire, and, in general, ignores his destiny (90v–91r). His only hope is in God, the wise doctor and strong captain. "Why," she asks her soul, "is it necessary to desire anything better than humiliation and poverty?"[23]

Madre Castillo seeks to persuade the addressee to accept and even relish humility by suggesting two motivations: the temporary nature of her sojourn on earth and the redemptive quality of the virtues. The first motivating force is that of consolation in the Counter-Reformation tenet that "all this will pass"; suffering is only temporary. Here Madre Castillo plays with the richness of symbolic imagery in evoking two rivers, one to be rejected and one to be desired. Echoing the medieval poet Jorge Manrique, whose river of life flows to its death in the sea, Madre Castillo warns her addressee not to embrace the current of the river of human things—this great Babylon—but to hold fast in faith, enduring the pain of humility, so that she might "drink of the eternal joy of that river that gladdens the city of God" (*CE* 56r–v).[24] She is speaking of the *desengaño*, the belief that the apparent "truths" of this life are but a deceit, and that Truth and life eternal await us only after death and only in God. Humiliation in the brief life of this world will be rewarded with eternal joy in the next.

Humiliation comes at the hands of those mortals who torment the seeker for her spiritual practices, but the source of her suffering is, ultimately, God's testing of her soul. In the guidebook, Madre Castillo's references to real earthly tormentors are brief and cryptic: "those who mortify and afflict [the soul]" and "the gift is not to seek from the creatures anything but thorns" (*CE* 57r).[25] Yet she brings these references to the sorts of accusations that she faced in the convent into the guidebook at a point when the soul's journey is just under-way, thus framing them as a result of that departure into a spiritual practice. Such a subtext of real everyday persecution would be clear to a contemporary reader, steeped in a society that both suspects and admires radical religiosity.

God's testing brings the soul to recognize her helplessness against her own weakness. Having lifted the metaphoric cross to follow her beloved, the soul ascends the mountain of bitter myrrh, is inundated by tribulations, and sees only her own poverty: "under the blows of tribulations her *memory* finds itself immobilized so that it cannot remember anything that might alleviate or encourage her; rather as one who hangs from a nail that pierces her; everything that occurs is pain. Equal and even greater suffering she finds in her *understanding*, whose discourses, penetrating her, leave her incapable of any operation from which could come light or relief, the *will* with such tedium, tepidity, coldness and repugnance. There is the shout of the people and the insult of her enemies: . . . You encouraged others so that they would not fall, but now you have fallen. So come down from the cross, leave this life [of mental prayer]" (*CE* 57r, emphasis mine).[26] Madre Castillo uses the scholastic psychology of the faculties of the soul to show the paralysis of the helpless seeker when faced with any kind of challenge. There is nothing to fear, and yet the soul experiences these tests in confusion and bitterness. The price of humility is the humiliation of meeting one's nothingness face to face, but its rewards are great. God lifts up the helpless soul and clothes her in his virtues; after all, his tests are but proof of his love. "No sane man swept another's house or cleaned the clothing that he was going to throw on the dung heap"(57r).[27] God crucifies the soul of his beloved in preparation for their union.

The humiliation of the soul to the point of helplessness brings her into experiential knowledge of the doctrine of Christ's redemptive crucifixion. God is the source of the living water, and the soul drinks of this living water by learning the example God gave when he submitted to the ultimate humility of dying in human form, helpless by choice, at the hands of others. The soul understands God's humility and its instructive power within her: "[a]llowing your beauty and majesty to be obscured, you gave light to my soul: and when you multiplied your light in the tempest of pains and the astonishment of nature, denying refreshment to your thirst; the fountains of waters appeared in the doctrine and example of your abandon, humility and poverty" (*CE* 58v).[28] By allowing herself to be humiliated by others, and by suffering the psychological pain of God's spiritual tests, the seeker lives in her own flesh and spirit the lesson of God's sacrificial love. Thus, too, she becomes the despised worm and dies to her self-love, only to be raised from the ashes as the Phoenix, symbol of resurrection and of the eternal life of love (54r). The seeker allows God to bring her to him in the afterlife, but also in a mystic embrace that shows her from here, in this world, a glimpse of that later glory.

Madre Castillo's treatment of humility/humiliation describes the absolute impossibility of a human being's achievement of good. The seeker's adoption of such an understanding of humility leads to isolation: first, the radical practice of self-humiliation elicits criticism from her peers; second, any desire for consolation, and especially for affirmation from her peers, is born of pride and thus counteracts the ideal of humility. Human relationships are to be shunned for the true love of God.

This negative vision of the social is not shared by Madre Castillo's sixteenth-century predecessors, who set in motion the great explosion of nuns' writings on inner spirituality. Fray Luis de Granada and his contemporary Saint Teresa posit the spiritual progress of the human soul through a recognition of self-worthlessness toward union with God, but their discussion of the soul's capacity to exercise virtues sounds a more optimistic note. These Catholic intellectuals promote humility but do not dwell endlessly on humiliation. Both sixteenth-century authors write into their guidance of inner spirituality the encouragement of loving community. Fray Luis de Granada holds forth the love of mother for child as a model to the Christian and projects this image onto the need for Church unity: "Thus if the parts of a body, although they have diverse tasks and forms among themselves, love each other very much because they are all given life by the same rational soul, how much greater reason it must be for the faithful to love each other, as all are given life by this divine Spirit, which, being more noble, is so much more powerful to create unity in the things wherein it exists" ([1556] 1929, bk. 2, chap. 11, 217).[29] He also demonstrates his optimism in human nature when he dedicates a chapter of the *Guía de pecadores* to the exercise of virtues with respect to one's neighbor, expressing confidence that the seeker can be successful (bk. 2, chap. 11). Saint Teresa's message to the Discalced Carmelites envisions both the strife of imperfect human relations and the possibility of affirming community. She warns her convent readership in the *Moradas* against the antagonism that arises when one person takes up the road of contemplative practice and those around her do not. These others distance themselves from her, criticize her, say that she is deceived by the devil and that she is deceiving her confessors, and yet Saint Teresa also demonstrates a firm confidence in the creation of harmonious community when she dedicates an entire chapter of the *Camino de perfección* (chap. 6) to the loving relationships that nuns should have with every one of their sisters. Her spiritual daughters reward her confidence, acting out her legacy of female community in their leadership and literary celebrations (see Arenal and Schlau 1989b).

If Saint Teresa exercised a freedom that she denied her followers in her insistence on rigid enclosure, she encouraged and instructed them to create strong autonomous female communities within the walls, and she provided as she could the economic independence from aristocratic foundations that had stifled their full development of an inner life and a democratic society. Madre Castillo's vision of the spiritual recognizes divisions in female community and deepens them, encouraging each nun to draw inside herself and to avoid emotional contact with others as much as possible. Her understanding of purification through torment at the hands of other human beings sets up a holy suspicion that seems to destroy the possibility of autonomous female community, facilitating through separation even greater male control over the institution. The portrayal of her alliances with confessors against the persecution of the abbesses, as read in the *Vida,* supports such a view.

On the other hand, the *Vida* hints at hidden possibilities of community. Sor Francisca does find consolation in the company of the novices during her second term as mistress of novices (*SV,* chap. 27, 101–2), and she speaks of trying to use with them a pedagogy of example, help, encouragement, and consolation rather than one of harsh rule. Her election as abbess by at least a simple majority in 1718, and by overwhelming majorities in 1729 and 1738, shows the power and influence that she wields in the convent. While her success may result from her exercise of authority and from the social status of her family, it may also be an indication that her leadership is affirmed by the positive interpersonal relationships of a supportive community. If these relationships do exist, they are masked in the *Afectos* and guidebook and are vilified as the cause of scandal in the *Vida.* Does Madre Castillo see harmonious female community as impossible or undesirable, or do the omissions in her written portraits diverge from her experience as they bow to that powerfully limiting Counter-Reformation ideology of death to the world? Her texts themselves are evidence of the destructive force that Counter-Reformation ideology could wield against female community when taken to its logical extreme. Madre Castillo superseded the limitations of her own prescriptions, "enjoying" power in this world while denouncing it in her texts. Her doctrine of humility, as elaborated in the guidebook, left a legacy that might have inspired other nuns to a painful joy of mystic escape and to an intelligent and vivid portrayal of their spiritual journey, but it could also have facilitated the control of the Counter-Reformation over its subjects through persuasion— unless, of course, her readers followed her example rather than her message.

A MYSTIC SEPULCHRE

In a tiny notebook, which to date has been published only in a limited facsimile edition, Madre Castillo composed or copied a poem whose images resonate with Saint Teresa's famous transverberation (Castillo 1994). Saint Teresa's passage in her *Libro de la vida* is noted by twentieth-century critics for its eroticism: "In his [the angel's] hands I saw a long golden spear and at the end of the iron tip I seemed to see a point of fire. With this he seemed to pierce my heart several times so that it penetrated to my entrails. When he drew it out, I thought he was drawing them out with it and he left me completely afire with a great love for God" (Teresa de Jesús 1949, 1: chap. 29, 192).[30] Sweet suffering is the paradoxical hallmark of the mystic experience, and yet while Saint Teresa emphasizes the ineffable sweetness and desire stirred by the spiritual pain, Madre Castillo draws primarily the images of death

and injury that accompany the crowning moment of the soul's humility/
humiliation. In the mystic allegory of Madre Castillo's small notebook, the
poetic voice calls on her beloved to wound her more and more with the sweet
rigor of the spear that gives her life and manifests his great love for her. This
poem crystallizes the essence of the mystic experience as it is explored in the
Cuaderno de Enciso. In part one of Madre Castillo's guidebook, she discusses
this moment of union in a section she calls "Of the Glorious Sepulchre,"
anchoring her explanation in the image of the crucifixion (*CE* 58r–v). The
soul awakes, embracing the crucifix, and the teacher describes her desire to fill
the wounds on Christ's hands and feet with acts of contrition, humility, love,
and faith. After partaking of the Sacrament, the soul receives Christ's invitation to bury herself in the fifth wound—the hole in Christ's side that was
opened by the soldier's spear. The burial constitutes a symbolic death to
the world, a withdrawal from any emotional investment in interpersonal
relationships, an acceptance of her inability to act on her own in any positive
way, and an ultimate submission of her will and her life to God. In this
submission, she glimpses and desires that glorious mystic death that can
momentarily overcome her exile from God: "I want my soul, my body and
heart, my strength, my health and time, all the operations of my senses and
faculties to be spent, burned and consumed in the fire of divine love, in loving
and suffering. And in this most glorious sepulchre I wish to remain forever"
(*CE* 58v).[31]

Almost at the end of the guidebook Madre Castillo breaks with the negativity in the uplifting images of the Song of Songs (see page 208, above). This
final exploration of mystic union, still mixed with fear and pain, crowns the
guidebook with a more joyful tone than is found anywhere before this point.
The brief closing section that follows uplifts the seeker in a rare affirmation,
stating that it is the intention behind the labors of the soul and not their
greatness that gives them value in the eyes of God. The guidebook closes with
the soul's optimistic call to her divine beloved: "Come living love. Raise,
conserve and keep for yourself the fruits of my heart and soul. Come loving,
soft, sweet, gentle good" (*CE* 93v).[32] This placement of the delightful side of
sweet suffering at the close of the text suggests that humiliating suffering will
endure throughout this life and must center the soul's attention but that a
joyous release rewards the pain.

I have called this chapter "A Theology of Humiliation and Its Mystic
Rewards." In doing so, I do not claim that Madre Castillo's guidebook for the
soul was considered "theology" at the time; it does not launch a broad inquiry
into the nature of God's existence and that of humanity. It does, however,
engage certain theological functions and forms. Madre Castillo explores in
depth the nature of the relationship between God and humanity. She builds

this exploration not only on personal experience but also on a deep familiarity with the Scriptures, engaging in a hermeneutics that interprets and applies the Scriptures to the individual's experience of mental prayer in her search for union with God. She does not use the logical argumentation and dialectics of scholastic theology that Juana Inés de la Cruz dared to engage in her "Carta atenagórica" but rather a language capable of persuading the will by moving the emotions. Her choice of rhetoric conforms to the exclusion of women from training in the writings of the Church fathers and medieval theologians, literature and training that is fundamental to scholastic disputation.

In its greater simplicity, her language coincides with the conception of theology promoted by Erasmus: "The foremost goal of theologians is to interpret the divine Scriptures with wisdom, to speak seriously and effectively of faith and piety, not to reason about trifling questions, but to drive out tears, and to inflame the hearts to heavenly things" (1993b, 193). "Theology has to do with life," he said, "rather than with the syllogistic arguments of the scholastics, who quibble over contentious questions by means of dialectics and Aristotelian philosophy" (297–304, paraphrased in Hoffman 1994, 38). By evoking Erasmus, I do not suggest direct influence for no evidence exists that Madre Castillo had access to his writings, but the democratizing effect of the Dutch scholar's attitude toward theology and biblical translation did resonate in Spain. Like-minded scholars of Alcalá de Henares helped to open doors to women's participation in intellectual and leadership activities in the Church, doors that the Counter-Reformation anxiously closed as completely as it could. Where Madre Castillo did encounter a rhetoric of theological oratory that spoke simply about the Scriptures in an attempt to move the listener was in her exposure to the preaching of her day. This theological rhetoric was available in the pulpit of her convent's church, as in the writings of those Spanish theologians who wrote for popular audiences: Fray Luis de Granada, Francisco de Osuna, Saint Teresa, Saint John of the Cross.[33]

Like Erasmus, Madre Castillo holds as the core of her theological narrative the Scriptures and their interpretation, but the scholar from Rotterdam would not have found Madre Castillo's exegesis sound. Erasmus believed that a theologian must face the Scriptures with moral and spiritual purity, meditating on the Bible day and night in order to arrive at a satisfactory interpretation (Hoffman 1994, 92). Such were the ideals and practice that built the foundations for Madre Castillo's exegesis. But Erasmus was also the great biblical humanist, and his theologian was to be instructed in Greek, Hebrew, and Latin in order to reach meanings as close to the original as possible. Madre Castillo knew only Spanish and Latin, which limited her to the already interpretive text of the *Vulgate*. The theologian was to bring to the study of the highly figurative biblical language the precepts of rhetoric, grammar, and poetry. Madre Castillo was self-taught in these areas and did not have the advantage of the great humanistic library of a Juana Inés de la Cruz. Finally, Erasmus promoted the guidance of the early Church Fathers in reading the Scriptures. Madre Castillo admits no access to these interpretive volumes. The guiding light of her exegesis is a Counter-Reformation ideology of humility, her spiritual experience of torment and joy, and her day-to-day struggle with pride, power, and an antagonistic milieu.

Though the basis of her hermeneutical efforts may not have passed a strict theological test, her homiletic rhetoric had a better chance. The genera of oratorical rhetoric important to sixteenth- and seventeenth-century preachers were those of *suasorium* and *encomiasticum*. The first "consists of teaching, persuading, exhorting, consoling, counseling, and admonishing," while the second "concerns doxology and thanksgiving" (Erasmus 1993a, 268–274, paraphrased by Hoffman 1994, 47). The speaker-addressee relationship of *suasorium* implies the quality of teacher in the narrative voice and that of seeker in the listener or reader. In the relationship of *encomiasticum,* the preacher-teacher shifts into the position of child of God in order to direct praise and thanksgiving to his or her creator.

Teaching, persuading, exhorting, consoling, counseling, admonishing, and giving praise and thanks are all speech acts in which Madre Castillo and her narrative voices engage. As a conduit of mystic knowledge from God to humanity, she teaches, providing explanations in the accessibility of figurative language and persuading by means of its compelling force. She consoles her own soul, as well as that unnamed seeking soul, by explaining their pain and suffering as a path toward God. She frequently admonishes her addressee to action because her loving God will also punish severely those who choose to ignore him, and because the distance an idle soul creates between herself and God is itself severe punishment. Madre Castillo's narrator praises and thanks God for his inexplicable mercy as she adopts the voice of both the seeking and suffering soul and the humble teacher.

In short, Madre Castillo takes up in the guidebook of the *Cuaderno* the theological concerns of God's relationship to his creatures and his creatures' corresponding obligations. She develops a coherent treatise to instruct spiritual seekers on the various aspects comprehended by the path to God and to his law, and she shines before her audience the beauty of mystic surrender as the reward for this struggle with humiliation. All of these things she does not by arguing the scholastic ins and outs of divine and mortal existence but by employing a rhetoric that will move the soul's emotions sufficiently to bring the seeker to moral action. Madre Castillo endeavors to affect the will of her audience in the drama of the seeker's soliloquies, in vivid imagery drawn from the Bible and from the awe-inspiring figures of Baroque visual art, and in the passionate rhetoric of theological oratory. If a public intent behind the guidebook cannot be definitively proven, then its message, its organization, and the narrative and rhetorical strategies with which Madre Castillo molds the texts demand at least the serious consideration of such a purpose. These aspects of the book offer the strong possibility that the historical writer identified herself with public authority through its teaching voice. The text invites us to consider that Madre Castillo may have shared her writings with a monastic audience, giving *pláticas espirituales* (spiritual instruction) as mistress of novices and as abbess, with her *papeles* in hand. Like Saint Teresa's self-deprecating female voice that builds solidarity with her monastic daughters, Madre Castillo's narrator in the *Cuaderno* invites the identification and solidarity of a female audience with her through its melding and intermixing of the subjectivities of teacher and seeker.

The cost of this public textual authority in the *Cuaderno* itself is the loss of personal identity. In order to cleanse the text of suspect female authority, Madre Castillo must maintain the suggestion, albeit less insistent than in the *Afectos,* that she is merely a conduit of divine knowledge. She must purge the text of any hint of dangerous hubris by distancing her historical identity from the messages she gives. To do this she erases her autobiography from the narrator's voice. The guidebook's narrator is female, and she is also a mystic, but she is not explicitly Madre Castillo. If its message of humility is confining and patriarchal, and if the cost to Madre Castillo of a public audience is erasure of the personal, the guidebook does empower its audience to run the paths of God's commandments in the flowering fields of encounter with the Holy Scriptures. The hermeneutic it offers opens the door of a male realm to its audience of religious women.

CONCLUSIONS

Who was Francisca Josefa de la Concepción de Castillo? Was she the humiliated and worthless Francisca of the *Vida,* always under attack, fully deserving of scorn, or was she the woman from the influential family of colonial bureaucrats and landholders who struggled and won power against feisty abbesses by using the patriarchal system—her family, her Jesuit alliances—to garner her worldly prize? Was she the pious reformer or the disobedient and sinful nun? Was she the mystic of the *Afectos,* whose sweet pain of union—more painful than sweet, more desired than fulfilled—comforted her soul after it was bruised at the hands of mortal creatures, the Devil, and her own weaknesses? Was she the proud and gifted intellectual, straining under the limitations of the Counter-Reformation ideology of gender, the woman who criticized the impossibly contradictory subjectivities she was called to occupy? Did she intend to show readers the damage wrought by an ideology that called on her to beat herself down whenever she expressed the very strength and creativity that, in times past, had been rewarded in powerful churchwomen? Was she the woman who insured her posterity by imbuing her feminine flesh with a symbolic power of redemption, setting her suffering body within the image of a sinful Church and world? Did she subvert Counter-Reformation restrictions, brilliantly carving a cranny in which to study the Scriptures and even to teach about them, by receiving the word in flesh and dressing hermeneutic activity in female monastic garb? Or did she stumble into this empowerment when desire drew her to the Bible and the only paths open to her were mysticism and ritual? If I have argued some of these possibilities more than others, I submit that, at one time or another, Madre Castillo probably felt the call or exercised all or most of these versions of her selfhood.

Madre Castillo's intellectual freedom, limited as it was, depended on her own gifted intelligence and determination, the support of her confessors, and her ability to see the expressive possibilities offered by the various feminine writing genres of her day. In the *Vida,* she is able to explore her lived experience as a woman in a colonial convent, yet the autobiographical demands of the genre encourage a pained and conflicted voice. In her spiritual journal— her *Afectos*—she finds what is possibly the most liberating format of the three texts, a place in which she can explore the joys of mystic union and create and recreate a highly sensual encounter with the Divine and with knowledge. If she begins to displace her autobiographical self in these texts as her voice takes on a feminized hermeneutic authority, she maintains a relationship between her free flights and her historical subjectivity. The message of the *Cuaderno* is the most orthodox of the three texts: that the path to mystic reward is filled with the sharp rocks of humiliation. It is a message that confines women and separates them from each other within the monastic community, reinforcing patriarchal control. In experiencing her greatest authority and her most confident and public voice, Madre Castillo sacrifices a portrayal of her experience as a historical woman. If her voice carries authority, here it is as vessel rather than as herself.

In all three works, Madre Castillo weaves texts of great narrative interest as she reworks the scripts and discourses given her by male clergy and female foremothers, conforming in great measure to their restrictions but stretching the space of expression in ways that leave all of her texts profoundly marked by gender. They are feminine texts—not because she is in touch with some universal womanhood but because, as a woman living in Tunja at the turn of the eighteenth century, she works with the materials, the possibilities, and the limitations at hand. Given materials similar to those of her great Mexican contemporaries, Madre Castillo crafts very different texts. Juana Inés de la Cruz broke boldly out of those genres offered to religious women and launched a literary career in which she produced not only devotional materials but also poetry of love and satire as well as her great poetic exploration of knowledge, *El sueño.* She honed religious theater from classic and pagan roots and penned a brazenly theological critique and a secular defense of women's intellectual development. María Anna Agueda de San Ignacio chose the feminine genre as mystic amanuensis, though, daringly, she left unmentioned this subjectivity as conduit in some of her writings. She dedicated her greatest works to a rereading of Mary, in the tradition of the Spanish María de Jesús de Agreda, and presented an active model of feminine intellectuality. Madre Castillo exercises more caution than her contemporaries, presents a message more amenable to patriarchal ideology, and expresses more graphically the pain she experiences in her intellectual pursuits. The patriarchy of her discourses also has its chinks. These spaces allow her to produce prose of pleasure and pain, to respond to a deeply creative urge by taking on the beauty of imagery and allegory and working and reworking it into a voice expressive of at least some aspects of her lived experience. These holes in the containment field allow her to find satisfaction—comfort she calls it—in a feminized intellectual encounter with a dangerous text and to speak about its relevance to her experience, if in a voice that is not entirely free. She writes in her *papeles* a message of submission, and yet she lives in those papers an experience of subtle subversion. Just as she has read rebellious women in the imperfectly purged annals of female history, she too leaves a legacy in which can be seen the cautious and tortured resistance of a strong-willed woman.

NOTES

Chapter 1: Interested Readings

1. [Padre mío], hoy día de la Natividad de Nuestra Señora, empiezo en su nombre a hacer lo que vuestra paternidad me manda y a pensar y considerar delante del Señor todos los años de mi vida en amargura de mi alma, pues todos los hallo gastados mal, y así me aterro de hacer memoria de ellos.

The first two words in the 1968 edition read "Por ser," an incorrect transcription of the "p.m." of the manuscript.

2. Among literary historians, Hernández Sánchez-Barba (1978) and Sainz de Medrano (1976) do not mention Madre Castillo. Iñigo Madrigal's volume on the colonial period names her twice (1982). Bellini gives her two sentences, while Goic (1988) and Gómez Gil (1968) dedicate brief paragraphs, noting the resemblance of her writings to those of Saint Teresa and Saint John of the Cross (Goic) and calling her "the mystic par excellence of Spanish America" (Gómez Gil, 127). Madre Castillo fares best in Anderson-Imbert's value-laden critique of her style and reverent appreciation of her spirituality (1969). Aside from Juana Inés de la Cruz, the only other colonial women authors to be (briefly) mentioned in these histories are Amarilis and Clarinda.

3. Sidonie Smith (1987) also posits the importance of considering women writers as readers. I return to the ideas of both of these critics in chapter 2.

4. I discuss agency and the subject in more depth in chapter 2, where I work with the ideas of Paul Smith (1988) and Sidonie Smith (1987).

5. The known original manuscripts include the *Afectos espirituales* (MS 71); *Su vida* (MS 72); the *Cuaderno de Enciso* (MS 73), into which Madre Castillo transcribed texts by other authors as well as reworkings of selected *Afectos;* a devotional book in which meditations and liturgical material have been copied by Madre Castillo and others (MS 76); and her *Cuaderno de cuentas* (MS 74), the accounting book kept during two of Madre Castillo's three terms as abbess. All are housed in the Biblioteca Luis Angel Arango in Bogotá. A sixth manuscript was published in 1994 in facsimile edition by Colcultura. It is a twelve-page notebook, owned by the family, that contains three poems and a description of the attributes and special charges of seven angels. The originality of the poems and texts in this notebook is yet to be determined, as Madre Castillo frequently copied the writings of other authors for devotional purposes. However, at least one of the poems, "De la salud la fuente," is attributed to Madre Castillo in the *Obras completas,* where it appears with minor changes (Castillo 1968, 2:

509). The family also owns an *emblema* or religious emblematic drawing attributed to Madre Castillo, which was displayed in the Museo de Santa Clara's 1994 exhibit in Bogotá, "Afectos y cilicios, la clarisa Josefa de Castillo 1671–1742."

6. Breve noticia de la patria y padres.

7. The earliest reference to Madre Castillo that I have found is in Vergara y Vergara ([1867] 1958, 201–2).

8. [E]l más eminente de nuestros autores coloniales.

9. [E]l escritor de que se trata fue mujer.

10. Achury Valenzuela published an early critical edition of a number of the *Afectos espirituales* (1962), ten articles that appear to be the basis for the book-length introduction to the 1968 edition of the *Obras completas,* and a more recent descriptive article on the *Cuaderno de Enciso* (1982).

11. Vergara y Vergara calls Madre Castillo an *escritor sagrado* (sacred writer) ([1867] 1958, 201), and Marcelino Menéndez y Pelayo calls her an imitator of Saint Teresa ([1911] 1948, 426–31); but the defense of Madre Castillo as a mystic writer seems first to have been expounded in the 1890 speeches cited above.

12. Several of these poets read at the "Séptimo Encuentro de Poetas Colombianas" in Roldanillo, Colombia, July 4–7, 1991.

13. Fewer than one-quarter of these studies were published outside of Colombia. Claudio G. Antoni's dissertation, "A comparative examination of style in the works of Madre Castillo" (1979) differs somewhat from other works and merits special notice. His discussion sees the long-touted influence of Saint Teresa as content-based and minor. Instead, he carries out a comparative analysis of the styles of Madre Castillo, Saint Catherine of Siena, and Saint Mary Magdalene of Pazzis based on the linguistic methods of analysis of Michael Riffaterre (1971) and Nils Enkvist (1973).

14. Morales Borrero and María Antonia del Niño Dios, whose biography I discuss below, write from within feminine religious communities. I propose that many feminist scholars today see ourselves as working in shared political and cultural efforts and thus forming a feeling of community, albeit diffuse.

CHAPTER 2: THE GENRE OF THE *VIDA ESPIRITUAL*

1. Poco cultivado fue en España durante los siglos pasados el género autobiográfico, ya que no podemos incluir en éste las numerosas vidas espirituales que nuestras religiosas escribieron, donde los hechos externos quedan relegados al olvido o mencionados ligeramente; rara excepción entre ellas es la de Santa Teresa, en cuyo privilegiado espíritu se unieron la contemplación y la acción.

2. Como se ha repetido tantas veces, no es una autobiografía en sentido estricto, ni la historia ajena de una vida, pues prescinde de cualesquiera elementos temporales y espaciales. No hay fechas ni nombres, salvo muy raras excepciones. Falta la individualización de los personajes principales, a los que se alude genéricamente y con apelativos despersonalizadores. En su apariencia formal es, antes que nada, un tratado didáctico con base en la práctica de la oración mental.

3. A note on terminology: The short title *Vida* (Life) was frequently attached to the manuscripts themselves, but it was also used for a great many other autobiographical

forms including soldier's lives, lives of nobles, and the fictional lives of the picaresque. In fact, the word and its equivalents in other languages represent a myriad of different fictional, autobiographical, and biographical forms. For the purposes of this book, then, I mention three *vida* genres: the texts of the autobiographical genre that I propose to describe, and for which I will use the terms *vida* or *vida espiritual* (spiritual life); priestly biographies, to which I will refer as biographical or exemplary *vidas;* and the tradition of saints' lives, which I will name as such.

4. See, for example, the works of Bella Brodzki and Celeste Schenck (1988), Estelle C. Jelinek (1980; 1986), Felicity A. Nussbaum (1989), Sidonie Smith (1987), and Domna C. Stanton (1984) on women's autobiography in general, and for a treatment of bibliography on the Hispanic world, see chapter 3.

5. James D. Fernández also discusses the role played by Spain's religious, legal, and bureacratic institutions in the production of early modern autobiographical writing (1992, 11).

6. In addition to the scholarship of Nussbaum (1989) and S. Smith (1987), I work with critical theory on autobiography and on the subject as discussed by Anthony J. Cascardi (1992), Michel Foucault (1978), Hans Ulrich Gumbrecht (forthcoming), Georges Gusdorf (1980), and Paul Smith (1988).

7. It is interesting to note the similarity between the community described by Gusdorf and the convent community, in which time is marked by ecclesiastical cycles and members take on a limited number of traditional names, which are used over and over through the history of the community: María de San José, Clara de Santa Inés, Francisca Josefa de la Concepción.

8. For a thorough study of the religious movements of early sixteenth-century Spain, including a recognition of the significant participation of women during this time, see Bataillon (1950), Ortega Costa (1989), and Bilinkoff (1989).

9. Such ideological closure was not complete, as George Mariscal (1991) demonstrates in his study of the "contradictory subjects" of both Cervantes and Quevedo.

10. [C]onoceráse al hereje no por la fe sino por la *libertad de conciencia* que predica y *por hazerse singular* siembra ziçania en lugar de trigo. [Emphasis mine.]

The term *cizaña* names a type of grass and is also translated as "dissension." This statement is quoted in Mariscal (1991, 92).

11. Antonio Gómez-Moriana discusses Kristeva's use of Bakhtin's expression *dialogical space* (1988, 46). I use the term *discourse* in a broad sense to denote language in action, both spoken and written interaction in verbal form as well as the construction of meaning through nonverbal sign systems. In relation to the *vida espiritual,* these discourses involve practices of meaning-making that surround such concepts as the feminine, piety, authority, and monasticism and that develop, change, and coexist in contradiction with other historical and sometimes suppressed discourses. As Diane Macdonell points out, such discourses are often identified with institutions that develop and deploy them (1986, 2), in this case, the Church, the Inquisition, and feminine monasticism. Discourses often mark the position of the speaker within a social web of power in which these institutions operate.

One example of a nonverbal discourse pertinent to this dicussion would be the visual organization of a church. A central altar displays the ornate monstrance that holds the host or body of Christ, behind which stands, in sumptuous splendor, a reredo of saints. A mysteriously invisible choir of nuns chants awe-inspiring Latin psalms from behind an ornate wooden grille, and the priest alone mediates between the great Mystery, the awesome mysteriousness of the atmosphere, and the lay congregation. This organization of signs communicates strong messages to all of the parties regarding the meanings of their religion and the hierarchies of power and importance of each individual involved.

12. The discussion is of *Roland Barthes par lui-même* (Barthes 1975b, 51–58).

13. Greenspan applies this term to medieval women's spiritual autobiography, positing that "[w]omen's 'autohagiography' demands examination as a popular sub-genre of medieval religious literature, with conventions, narrative strategies, and purposes distinct from those employed by autobiography" (1991, 157). Myers describes the Mexican María de San José as aspiring to inscribe the first volume of her *vida* into hagiographic literature (1993b, 7). Arenal and Schlau refer to the remarkably self-aggrandizing *vida* of the eighteenth-century Mexican Madre María Marcela as autohagiography (1989b, 362). They also clarify in the introduction to their book that the incorporation into *vidas* of "prescribed structures, order, meanings, themes, and formulas," including the "hagiographical and biblical rhetoric of the Church," does not extinguish originality. "[W]hen they are removed from a rigid framework, the Lives, poems, plays, and letters written by the Sisters reveal patterns that contradict their stated intentions and express, instead, the authors' individuality" (2). Margo Glantz engages in an extensive discussion of Sor Juana Inés de la Cruz's "Respuesta" in terms of its relationship to hagiography (1995).

14. For a discussion of the structuring of María de San José's autobiographical narrative through categories of religious experience, see Myers's introduction to *Word from New Spain* (1993b, 20 ff.).

15. See chapter 1, n. 1, above for the original Spanish text.

16. [A]viendo escrito *toda la istoria de mi vida*, desde mi niñés asta que salí para esta fundasión desta siudá de Oaxaca. . . . Señor i Dios Mío, no es de las menores misericordias la que aora me haséis i me avé(s)is echo en admitir ésta mi confesión, dando *quenta de toda mi vida*. [Emphasis mine.]

17. En el nombre de la Santíssima Trinidad . . . en cuyo nombre, y por cuyo amor obedesco a este mandato . . . *manifestando el discurso* y distribución del tiempo *de mi vida*. [Emphasis mine.]

18. Mandaronle sus confesores fuesse escribiendo *su vida*, y *los particulares regalos que de continuo recevía* de Nuestro Señor Jesuchristo. [Emphasis mine.]

19. Algunas de las mercedes que hizo Dios a Doña María Vela cuya vida es la que queda escrita, mandado del Padre Salzedo . . . que . . . mandó que *cada día le diese cuenta por escrito de lo que hacía y pasaba por su alma*, que es lo que sigue. [Emphasis mine.]

20. [El Padre Francisco de Herrera] mandóme *muchas veces que escribiera y le mostrara los sentimientos* que Nuestro Señor me daba. [Emphasis mine.]

21. [L]e ordené *me diese por escrito quenta de los sentimientos interiores* de su espíritu. [Emphasis mine.]

22. Revolveré, Señor, en mi memoria delante de ti todos los años de mi vida.

23. "I, the worst of all," is how Juana Inés de la Cruz signed, toward the end of her life, a document kept in the archives of the Convento de San Jerónimo. In it she asks her sisters' forgiveness and requests that they commend her to God upon her death. The epithet evokes her ultimate submission, in which she renounced her library and her intellectual activities shortly before her untimely death. See discussion by Octavio Paz (1982, pt. 6, chap. 5).

24. The words she uses in Spanish are: *bestia* (María de Jesús 1947, 218), *espadachín* (219), *rea de toda culpa* (220), *vil* (220), *caballo* (221), *la más infame que hay* (224), *animal* (225), and *perversa criatura* (237).

25. Sidonie Smith is drawing on the work of Michael Sprinker (1980, 325).

26. [L]a lectura generalizada de la Sagrada Escritura es fuente inagotable de herejías.

27. El Apóstol San Pablo, vaso de escogimiento, dando forma a la Iglesia de los de Corintho dice: «Las mujeres callen en la iglesia, que no les es permitido hablar, sino ser sujetas conforme al mandamiento de la ley divina, y si quieren saber algo, pregúntenlo en casa a sus maridos». En otra parte, el mismo Apóstol escribe a Timoteo, su discípulo, en esta forma: «. . . Por tanto, como la mujer sea naturalmente animal enfermo, y su juicio no esté de todas partes seguro, y pueda ser muy ligeramente engañado, según mostró nuestra madre Eva, que por muy poco se dejó embobecer y persuadir del demonio: por todos estos repectos y por otros algunos que se callan, no es bien que ella enseñe».

28. [S]ino para un solo oficio simple y doméstico, así les limitó el entender, y por consiguiente, les tasó las palabras y las razones.

29. The *Amigas* were women who taught young girls in their own homes. It was from the instruction of an *Amiga* that Juana Inés de la Cruz learned to read (Juana Inés de la Cruz 1957, 4: 445).

30. Especialmente a las mugeres, no se les ha de permitir, que se hagan Doctoras Mysticas, sino enseñarlas, que aprendan a callar, y dexarse governar, con obediencia prompta, humilde, y silenciosa en el camino de la perfección.

31. Las mujeres por la condición de su sexo, son en estas materias generalmente más fáciles de ser engañadas; y más acomodadas para engañar, y consiguientemente, que sus revelaciones y visiones traen de ay una sospecha especial, que se necesita con particularidad excluir, haziendo de ellas más exacto examen.

32. Myers writes, for example, about the establishment by Madre María de San José of the androgenous nature of her body through chastity and self-mortification (1992, 41).

33. Examples where men are called authors can be found in the official approvals that introduce the texts of Godínez (1682) and Ossorio de las Peñas (1649).

34. La razón escrita que alegamos para fundar algún propósito, y la firmíssima es la que se trae de la Sagrada Escritura, de los Concilios, de las tradiciones de los santos doctores, y en su proporción de los demás que han escrito y escriven.

35. [E]l que escrive; algunas vezes sinifica autor de algunas obras escritas, y otras el copiador, que llamamos escritor de libros.

36. [L]a delgada pluma del muy *Reverendo Padre* Alonso de Andrade, de la misma Compañía de Iesus . . . con tantas, y tan eruditos libros se ha merecido los aplausos, que dignamente le da el mundo.

37. [E]spira sabiduría, exhala genio y ingenio, y destella valentías del arte y el estudio, porque, agotando esmeros al artificio, tropos a la retórica y conceptos a toda la erudición sacra y natural, sólo dexa que hacer a la admiración.

38. [R]ecogida de los escritos de los santos, padres y doctores católicos, con humano estudio, no como imaginada en los retiros de la contemplación con sólo devoto afecto, sino como recibida por revelación divina en estos últimos tiempos, siendo una muger iliterata el sugeto, a quien se comunicó, y el instrumento de escribirla.

39. [Q]ue ya se han de callar por oficio las mugeres en la Iglesia Santa y oír a los maestros.

40. [M]e parecía, que a la hora de la muerte no he de tener otra cosa que más me atormente, y cause pena, que estos escritos (Muriel 1982, 397).

41. Aquí oí una voz . . . que era de su Majestad . . . y me dijo estas razones: Mira que yo te asisto y no te falto; escríbelo, que todo es de mí, y nada de ti y si no, mira si por ti sola hubieras podido dar un solo paso y hecho lo que has hecho.

42. See epigraph, chapter 3.

43. [A]lgunos sentimientos que han pasado por mi alma.

44. [V]ía que de los dedos de mi mano derecha distilaba una riqueza, como perlas preciosas y resplandecientes, y como oro; mas era de un modo que corría y se liquidaba, como el bálsamo, sin perder su resplandor. . . . y entendí: que en lo que en los papeles está escrito, no es nacido de mí, ni del espíritu malo, sino de Dios, y de su luz, que por sus incomprensibles juicios me lo ha hecho escrebir.

45. No sé si acertaré a decir. Estas cosas y otras semejantes escribo, padre mío, porque me lo manda vuestra paternidad, y por darle más claramente cuenta de todo, no porque yo esté firme en otra cosa, más de en lo que nos enseña nuestra santa fe, ni tenga más determinación que estar al juicio y orden de mis confesores y prelados, que he conocido siempre ser el camino seguro.

46. También me trajo a la memoria todos los pasos y caminos de mi vida, no como aquí pueden ir escritos, sino como Dios lo pudo manifestar al alma, sin riesgo de temores ni dudas, sin olvidos de la memoria, ni confusiones del entendimiento. . . . Pero mejor los explicarán algunas palabras que entendí entonces, o digo que escrebí (no porque fueran palabras expresas, sino una luz que se imprimía en el alma, y la convencía, habiendo recebido a Nuestro Señor Sacramentado).

47. La primera si son regladas por el conocimiento de razones doctas, y Maestros experimentados en espíritu. *La segunda por el efecto que hazen en el alma del que recibe este fervor.* La tercera, por la Materia que contienen y su verdad. La quarta, si conforman con las Escrituras Sagradas, o se oponen a ellas. *La quinta por parte de la persona si es de vida aprobada, y virtud conocida.* [Emphasis mine.]

48. [Y]o lo digo lo que ha pasado por mí, como me lo mandan, y si no fuere bien, romperálo a quien lo envío—que sabrá mejor entender lo que va mal que yo (Teresa de Jesús 1915, chap. 10, par. 7).

49. The feminine authority of Mary in Sor María Anna Agueda's treatises is central to Jennifer Lee Eich's discussion of this author (1992).

50. Aquí me enseñó el Señor el grandísimo bien que es pasar trabajos y persecuciones por El; porque fue tanto el acrecentamiento que vi en mi alma de amor de Dios y otras muchas cosas, que yo me espantaba; y esto me hace no poder dejar de desear trabajos. . . . Entonces me comenzaron más grandes los ímpetus de amor de Dios que tengo dicho, y mayores arrobamientos, aunque yo callaba y no decía a nadie estas ganancias (Teresa de Jesús 1970, chap. 33, 199–200).

51. [U]na plática nacida de embidia, que procura manchar y obscurecer la vida y virtud agena.

52. [L]a lengua maldiciente y murmuradora es pinzel del demonio y semejante a la vívora.

53. [S]i conoció a la Madre Teresa de Jesús, y si conoció a sus padres, y dónde era natural, y quiénes fueron sus padrinos, y dónde se bautizó, and

si sabe que la Madre Teresa de Jesús fuese mujer de grande espíritu y de mucha oración y que por medio de ella tuvo gran trato con Dios Nuestro Señor.

54. My search included Serrano y Sanz (1905), Randolph Pope (1974), WorldCat, and the Sutro Collection of the California State Library.

55. The *Sentimientos* were first published in a biography by a Father Cachupín in 1652, and later separately in 1671 by Father Tirso González. The *Meditaciones* were published in 1605 (Puente [1671] 1958, 295, 298).

56. IV. Ejercicio para tener confusión y contrición de los pecados. . . . *Primero punto:* estriba en la consideración de la Inmensidad y Sabiduría infinita de Dios, con su pureza suma. Imaginando que Dios Nuestro Señor es una sustancia de inmensa grandeza.

Y imaginarme a mí, como un gusanillo o arador, dentro desta Divina Inmensidad, tan llena de ojos, y que dentro della, y a vista suya, hice todos los pecados pasados, y hago los presente, provocándole con ellos a enojo, asco y vómito.

57. This biographical information is taken from Charles E. P. Simmons's study of the Jesuit controversy (1966) and from the article on Palafox y Mendoza in the *Enciclopedia Universal Ilustrada Europeo-Americana* (Espasa-Calpe 1920, 41: 72–74).

58. [E]ste pobre gusano, tierra, polvo, nada, postrado con todo su corazon, potencias, facultades, y sentidos.

59. Llora este pecador.

60. Le ha ido creciendo de suerte el amor, que algunas veces, si no brotáran por los ojos los afectos interiores, le parece que rebentaría el pecho; y hasta que salen las lágrimas, y con esto desahoga el corazon, padece el alma mucho en aquellos interiores movimientos.

61. [P]orque habiéndolo consultado con sus Confesores, lo juzgaron por útil, y conveniente; pues no se había de publicar viviendo este pobre pecador, ni después, sino ignorándose el nombre, y ocultando quanto se pudiere la noticia del sugeto.

62. Del diario, y exercicios en que se ocupa las veinte y quatro horas del día quando no visita.

63. [A]monestado y persuadido que escribiesse este tratado presente. Estando, pues,

bien descuidado de esto, me fue mandado lo escribiesse en este presente año de 1706.

64. [Q]ualquiera, que después de mi muerte leyere esto, y en qualquier tiempo.

65. ADONAI Ad majorem nominis tui gloriam, Domine Rex Saeculorum, qui sedens super thronum tuae magnitudinis, & Dominans in aeternum, abyssum, & cor hominis investigasti: atque universa conspicis, & cuncta nosti. Tu scis, quia non propter me, sed propter te, istud ago, & scribo pro tuo amore, & honore, ac pro honore Virginis Mariae, per voluntatem tuam; & ad hoc necnon compusus sum, haud sine contradictiones per legem repugnantem: sed dixi, nunc coepi.

CHAPTER 3:
RELIGIOUS WOMEN'S WRITING IN SPAIN AND SPANISH AMERICA

1. Ordenó, que por la misma mano de la atormentada María, se escribieran los avisos para su dirección: siendo éste el mayor tormento de su gravíssimo martyrio; porque le parecía, que fingía todo lo que escrivía, persuadida a que por tan vil instrumento, e indigna mano, no havía de hablar el Señor.

2. For recent studies of medieval women writers, see Petroff (1986), Bynum (1987), and Holloway, Wright, and Bechtold (1990).

3. For discussions of López de Córdoba, see Pope (1974), Ayerbe-Chaux (1977), Deyermond (1983), and Kaminsky and Johnson (1984).

4. Bilinkoff comments on the relationship of Doña María Vela's asceticism to medieval practice (1989, 186–87).

5. Muriel notes the book's widespread readership (1982, 315). The Biblioteca Nacional in Bogotá, Colombia, owns a 1681 edition inscribed with the name of the seventeenth-century Colombian historian Juan Flórez de Ocáriz.

6. Other early Spanish women authors include the Augustinian Valentina Pinelo, who wrote a biography of Saint Anne (1601) (Arenal and Schlau 1989a), the Poor Clare María de la Antigua (1566–1617), whose life and writings influenced later nuns, especially her *Desengaño de religiosos* (1678?), and Petronila de San José, who wrote a biography of Cecilia del Nacimiento (n.d.) (Arenal and Schlau 1989a).

As the present work goes to press, another study has been added to the published scholarship on Spanish nuns: Sherry M. Velasco's 1996 book on another Isabel de Jesús (1611–1682).

7. Arenal and Schlau treat the Lorravaquio manuscript (1989b, 346–49, 374–78). They also present a Mexican *vida* not discussed in Muriel, that of the Capuchine Madre María Marcela (1759–18—) who lived in Querétaro (1989b, 360–63, 405–10). Muriel discusses many other writers and types of writing, including the theologian María Anna Agueda de San Ignacio and her theological treatise (1982).

8. See Kathleen Ann Ross's treatment of the *Parayso occidental* by Sigüenza y Góngora as a text into which erupt the feminine voices of the Conceptionist nuns of the convent of Jesús María in Mexico (1985), and Manuel Ramos Medina's history of the Discalced Carmelite convent of San José, founded in Mexico in 1616 (1990). One of the founders of the Discalced Carmelite Order in Mexico City was Mariana de la Encarnación (1571–1657), whose recounting of the foundation can be found in manuscript form in the library of the University of Texas at Austin (1823). See also Arenal

and Schlau (1989b, 343–46, 363–74). Muriel writes about Indian nuns in *Las indias caciques de Corpus Christi* (1963), and Arenal and Schlau discuss Madre Teodora de San Agustín and other anonymous Indian writers (1989b, 355–59, 396–405).

9. The past few years have brought a virtual explosion in feminist scholarship on Sor Juana Inés de la Cruz, especially during the tercentenary of her death in 1995. I do not attempt to offer even a representative sample of this bibliography, though I do list in my works cited a very few of the recent critical volumes that include feminist scholarship. See Merrim (1991), Poot and Urrutia (1993), Coloquio Internacional Juana Inés de la Cruz (1995), Sabat de Rivers (1995a, 1995b), and Glantz (1996).

10. Selections from the remainder of the *vida* are forthcoming in a collaboration between Myers and Amanda Powell, in *A Wild Country out in the Garden* (Bloomington: Indiana University Press).

11. The biographies in question are written by Pedro Pablo de Villamor (Madrid, 1723), cited in Germán María del Perpetuo Socorro and Martínez Delgado (1947) and Pedro Calvo de la Riba (1752), respectively.

12. Representative works by the writers named in this chapter are listed in the bibliography of Spanish and Spanish American Religious Women Writers at the end of this book.

CHAPTER 4: FEMALE MONASTICISM: A LIFE UNBECOMING?

1. Hallé que el convento a toda prisa se iba acabando: por lo que tocaba a sus rentas, empeñado en muchas cantidades; el archivo, sin ningún papel; ni de dónde poder tomar noticia de nada, porque todo corría por el síndico y él decía que no tenía nada, y que si se había de comprar una carga de leña, había de ser empeñando la capa o la espada. Había pleitos muchos y muy penosos, y todo tan confuso, y a mi parecer tan sin camino, que yo no sabía más que clamar a Nuestro Señor y a la Madre de la vida y de la misericordia, María Santísima. Yo me hallaba del todo ignorante, ni aun el estilo de hablar con los seglares sabía.

2. See chapter 2, n. 11, for an explanation of my use of the term *discourse*. By *practices* I mean patterns of human interaction that are historically constructed and institutionally related.

3. See also Elizabeth Alvilda Petroff, *Medieval Women's Visionary Literature* (1986).

4. The preference for Mary Magdalene was codified in the *Ancren Riwle,* a thirteenth-century English rule written for settlements of women recluses (Eckenstein 1896, 313). Although in the New Testament Martha's sister Mary and Mary Magdalene are two different women, the medieval hagiography of Mary Magdalene conflates the two.

5. Nina M. Scott (1994) examines Sor Juana's feminine genealogy and the significance of many of these individual women to her argument.

6. "The Royal Convent of Saint Clare of this city of Tunja" is how the convent is named in the numerous documents that record its everyday business.

7. The great importance of letter writing between the Discalced Carmelite founders can be seen in Arenal and Schlau's treatment of Saint Teresa's spiritual daughters (1989b, 19–117, especially 23–30).

8. The founding mothers of the Convento de la Concepción in Santa Fe as well as San Juan Bautista and Santa Clara in Mérida (Venezuela) came from the Poor Clare convent in Tunja (Lavrín 1986, 172). The Discalced Carmelite convent in Santa Fe was founded by a laywoman but received two nuns from the Conceptionist convent in Santa Fe as advisers (Germán María del Perpetuo Socorro and Martínez Delgado 1947, 154). Josefina Muriel (1946) outlines the expansion of female orders in New Spain, specifying which convents were begun by already-existing communities.

9. [G]uardar las Reglas y Ordenaciones, que han hecho los Señores Arzobispos de Santafé, quitándolas unas, y poniendo otras temporales entre las perpetuas, con que se ha causado confusión.

10. His changes concern primarily the requirements for entrance into different convent ranks and the number of votes allowed to nuns of the same family (Germán María del Perpetuo Socorro and Martínez Delgado 1947, 159–62).

11. Compare chap. 3 of the *Regla primera* (Merinero 1748, 9–10) and chap. 11 of the *Regla segunda* (39–40).

12. [M]uy cristiana, muy importante y necesaria a la ciudad de Tunja y comarcanas, por haber mucho número de doncellas de padres pobres y sin dote para se poder casar.

13. Colmenares discusses this crisis (1982, 244).

14. See Colmenares for a discussion of the elite's redoubled effort in eighteenth-century Nuevo Reino de Granada to defend itself against the suspicion of racial mixing (1982, 294).

15. The canonical hours are Matins, Lauds, Prime, Tierce, Sext, Nones, Vespers, and Compline (Merinero 1748, 35; *Regla segunda,* chap. 6, 35).

16. *Villanescas* are a type of popular song. *Chanzonetas* are ballads sung on festive occasions, including Christmas.

17. The choir library was more extensive in 1583, though the type of books it contained is very similar. Authors for the most part are not listed in the inventory, so I have supplied them where possible. Sometimes descriptions are given instead of titles. The list includes two books of the works of the hours of the Order of Saint Augustine, the epistles of Saint Jerome, a book titled *La verdad,* two editions of the *Flos santorum* (saints' lives), Luis de Granada's *Guía de pecadores* and *Libro de la meditación y oración,* the *Libro memorial de la vida cristiana,* Antonio de Guevara's *Monte Calvario,* Rodrigo Fernández de Santaela's *Vocabulario eclesiástico,* Juan Gerson's *Imitatio Christi,* a book on spiritual life, a book on purifying the conscience, *Flor de virtudes,* a manual for confessors by Navarro, *Repertorio de* [*clabel?*], a book on the mysteries of the rosary, Felipe de Meneses's *Luz del alma cristiana, Doctrina cristiana,* a religious calendar, two Breviaries, the *Diccionario de los privilegios y reglas de Señoras de Santa Clara,* five tomes of Francisco de Osuna's *Abecedario espiritual,* a book of Latin hours, Rodrigo Sánchez de Arévalo's *Espejo de la vida humana,* and books by "the Carthusian" on the Christian life (*LC,* 6v–7r).

18. The Nieremberg book, found in the present-day convent library, is a 1643 edition that carries an inscription in what María Antonia del Niño Dios identifies as Madre Castillo's handwriting and, in another hand, the legend "Este libro es del uso de Francisca de la Concepción" (This book is used by Francisca de la Concepción).

María Antonia del Niño Dios has also found, in the present library, a book on the holy angels by Andrés de Pozo (Madrid 1708), which she believes influenced Madre Castillo's thought. The convent owns a 1675 edition of Saint Ignatius of Loyola's *Ejercicios espirituales,* which contains twelve vivid illustrations of hell, like those that influenced Francisca's childhood visions (see chapter 6, pages 132–33 of this book) (María Antonia del Niño Dios 1993, 26, n. 12).

19. [P]or ningún caso se vistan las religiosas, para representar, aun entre ellas mismas, hábito de hombre, o de mujer secular, que es cosa muy grave, muy agena, e indigna de religiosa, y peligrosa.

20. Information from the *Libro de capítulo* (*LC*) and *Elecciones de abadesas* (*EA*) shows the presence of the following girls, who entered the convent at the ages indicated. In many cases, I have identified the complete religious name of the girl/nun by use of the *Libro de visita.* María de Santiago, under age twelve (*EA*, 10-1-1621 [folios are unnumbered and arranged by the date on which the habit was conferred]; *LC*, 93v); Agustina del Sacramento, seven (*LC*, 8-30-1632, 107v [dates in the *Libro de capítulo* refer to the date of profession]); Juana de la Cruz, seven (*EA*, 7-26-1628; *LC*, 10-2-1637, 111v); Luisa de San Miguel, six (*EA*, 7-26-1628; *LC*, 1-6-1640, 112v), Inés, eight (*EA*, 9-8-1629); Lauriana del Sacramento, six or seven (*EA*, 6-24-1630; *LC*, 9-17-1641, 114r); Francisca de los Santos, three (*EA*, 11-30-1634; *LC*, 6-13-1636, 136r); María de San Bernardo, seven (*EA*, 2-27-1635; *LC*, 9-18-1642, 115v); Ursula de los Angeles, seven (*EA*, 4-21-1635; *LC*, 2-13-1646, 116v); Leonor de San Francisco, seven (*EA*, 5-6-1640; *LC*, 1-22-1652, 118r); Micaela de San Francisco (*donada mestiza*), as a girl (*EA*, 5-13-1640); María de San Gabriel, five (*EA*, 3-29-1644; *LC*, 2-2-1655, 119r); María del Niño Jesús, raised in the convent (*EA*, 3-9-1650; *LC*, 6-1-1653, 118v); María Teresa de la Encarnación, nine (*EA*, 6-23-1663; *LC*, 8-12-1663, 127v); Josefa de la Concepción, raised in the convent (*EA*, 1-9-1664; 5-25-1664, 140r).

21. Such schools did exist in the female convents of the Franciscan order and were governed by a separate rule, which is contained in the *Constituciones generales* (Merinero 1748, 177–82).

22. Originally, twenty-four places were reserved for black-veiled nuns paying dowries of a thousand pesos. Any additional nuns would have to pay a double dowry of two thousand pesos (Paniagua Pérez 1993, 299–314). In 1620, Archbishop Fernando Arias de Ugarte, concerned about the financial difficulties faced by the convent, calculated that the community could sustain fifty-one black-veiled nuns bringing a dowry of one thousand pesos each (*LV* 22v). Any additional nuns would have to provide a dowry of fifteen hundred pesos. He also instructed the convent to limit the community to twenty white-veiled nuns and *donadas*. Several entries in *Elecciones de abadesas* indicate that two thousand pesos were again required by the end of the seventeenth century.

23. All of the white-veiled nuns for whom dowry amounts are recorded in the volume titled *Elecciones de abadesas* brought three hundred pesos to the convent. The *Constituciones generales* of the female Franciscan orders use the term *donada* as a synonym for *lega*, or lay nun (Merinero 1748, chap. 12, 143); but in the *Libro de visita* from Santa Clara, *lega* and *donada* are listed as separate categories.

24. In 1669, five nuns are listed as *monjas legas de coro* in the *Libro de visita* (131v). In his 1664 visit, Archbishop Juan de Arguinao specified that no lay nun be given a white veil for the choir without a dowry of five hundred pesos (127v).

25. At least one *donada* is identified as a *mestiza* (*EA*, 5-13-1640). Concerning the existence of black slaves as domestic servants in the Tunja region, see Rueda (1989, 11). Madre Castillo herself mentions a *mulata* in the convent (*SV* 109).

26. The Pamplona *Ordenaciones* specify that no *mestizas* or free mulattas may take the black veil unless they represent an important addition to the convent. In such cases, all of the voting nuns as well as the archbishop would have to agree to accept the postulant (Magdalena de Jesús 1722, chap. 1). The founder of the Carmelite convent in Santa Fe tried to exclude any but Spanish women of pure lineage from the ranks of the choir nuns, while the lay nuns could be Spanish, quadroons (of one-quarter African blood), or *mestizas* as long as they were virtuous (Germán María del Perpetuo Socorro 1947, 146 §2 and 147 §3). In approving the constitutions, though, Juan de Bonilla Navarro affirmed with his apostolic authority that any woman could take the veil, even if she were a quadroon, as long as she was virtuous (160 §2). Kathryn Burns has chronicled a fascinating story of race and rank in the convent of Santa Clara in Cuzco during the mid-sixteenth century. In its early years, the convent served as an institution in which the *mestiza* daughters of wealthy Spanish men could be educated in Spanish culture. In 1565, town cabildo members protested the distinction that the nuns were enforcing between Spaniards and *mestizas*. The cabildo had found that the encomenderos' *mestiza* daughters were being discriminated against by being made to wear the white veil, worn also by novices and *donadas*, but not by professed Spanish nuns. Despite the protest, the separation of the community into unequal racial groupings persisted (Burns 1995).

27. See, for example, the periodic reporting required by the syndic in the presence of the *difinitorio* and vicar (*LV* 145v).

28. The titles for these offices, as given in the register of nuns recorded during canonical visits are, respectively: *difinidoras, maestra de novicias, vicaria del coro, sacristanas, porteras, escuchas* (*del locutorio*), *graderas, enfermeras, secretaria, tornera, acompañadora para los que entran en el convento, provisora,* and *obreras*. The duties pertaining to these offices are described in detail in the *Constituciones generales* (Merinero 1748, chap. 10, 127–41) and the Pamplona rule, which lists in addition the offices of *coristas* or choir leaders, *depositarias* to care for the valuables, *refitoleras* to oversee the common meals, *hortelanas* who worked in the vegetable garden, *comisarias para el cuidado de las estancias* who oversaw the farm production, and the *celadora* or monitor, whose charges included watching over the common dormitories (Magdalena de Jesús 1722, chap. 2, par. 13).

29. Proceedings are recorded for nineteen visits in the 1600s and four in the early 1700s.

30. Conflicts arose when a servant would take a new mistress without the permission of the first. In three visits, this behavior was expressly prohibited (*LV* 81v, 134v, 155r).

31. The book of *Elecciones de abadesas* records, for example, that Josefa de la Concepción was accepted as a white-veiled choir nun with a dowry of three hundred

rather than five hundred pesos because of her piety and the need they had for her in the choir (5-7-1664). Two daughters of Francisco de Vargas were accepted as black-veiled nuns having presented only half of the two thousand peso dowry each, as the archbishop judged sufficient the causes represented to him for the petition (8-7-1678). The daughter of Augustín de Escobar Tamayo and Teresa de Rivera was admitted with a fifteen hundred peso dowry due to the financial difficulties of both city and convent and because of the low number of nuns in the convent (10-23-1706).

32. Que, biniendo a este nuestro convento diciendo que querían visitarnos, y rrespondiendo nosotras que la visita se había de hacer por la rrexa del comulgatorio o en el locutorio, rreplicaron que no avía de ser sino dentro de la clausura. Y porque les defendimos la entrada, binieron de mano armada y arreb(a)entaron las puertas y cerroxos y al fin entraron con grande alboroto diciéndonos palabras feas y quitándome a mí la dicha abadessa el belo y puniendo las manos con palabras muy afrentosas.

33. The allowance of personal accumulation by friars may be one explanation for the greater wealth of the female convent, where dowries were invested for the needs of the entire community (Pino Alvarez 1989, 52).

34. One form of the *censo* authorized the purchase of an annuity and another, the charge of an annuity in exchange for property (Montaner y Simón 1888, 1139–40).

35. Such documents drawn up in the years 1681–1742 can be found in the Archivo Regional de Boyacá in Tunja (AHT) (1681, vol. 161: 274; 1691, vol. 126: 471–72) and (Notaría 1, 1720, vol. 177: 273–80; Notaría 2, 1727, vol. 179: 135–36).

CHAPTER 5: MADRE CASTILLO IN THE INSTITUTION: AN ASCENSION TO POWER

1. Madre Castillo names the day of Saint Bruno as her birthday (*SV* 4), while María Antonia del Niño Dios gives it as the date of her baptism (1993, 18), though she does not identify her source. She attributes to oral tradition within the Convento de Santa Clara the report that Francisca Josefa de Castillo was born in Tunja.

2. Her mother bore the same family name as three of Tunja's *alcaldes ordinarios* (elected magistrates) of the midcentury: Martín Niño y Rojas (1641, 1647), Juan de Guevara Niño y Rojas (1649), and Francisco de Ayala Niño y Rojas (1655); see Rojas (1962, 630–31).

3. Achury Valenzuela makes the connection to Catalina de Sanabria (1968, xxxi). María Antonia del Niño Dios cites Florez de Ocáriz to substantiate the relationship to the founder (1993, 36).

4. María Antonia del Niño Dios identifies this aunt as Ana Francisca de la Trini-dad, daughter of Captain Francisco Niño and Doña Francisca de Rojas. She professed on January 15, 1642, and died before her niece entered the convent (1993, 26, n. 11). She does not appear on the rolls of the 1678 visit, eleven years before her niece's entrance (*LV* 150r).

5. See "Informaciones de la vida, virtudes, [   ] de la Madre Francisca María del Niño Jesús" (Conventos, AHNB, vol. 66: 1–353). María Antonia del Niño Dios identifies the Carmelite as the daughter of Fernando León de Caicedo, Knight of the Order of Santiago and Doña Francisca Florián Maldonado, which would make her

Francisca Caicedo y Maldonado (1993, 119). The names given by Restrepo and Rivas and by Márquez are slightly different; see n. 6, following.

6. According to Restrepo and Rivas, Madre Castillo's brother, Captain Pedro Antonio del Castillo, married Doña Josepha de Caicedo y Salabarrieta. Doña Josepha was the daughter of Don Fernando de Caicedo y Floriano (Restrepo and Rivas 1928, 173–76), who was Francisca María del Niño Jesús's brother (159–60), making her also a "Caicedo y Floriano." The Carmelite abbess was the daughter of Don Fernando Leonel de Caicedo y Mayorga (158). In the "Interrogatorio" designed by Bernardo Márquez to ascertain Madre Francisca María's sanctity after her death, she is identified as Doña Francisca Beltrán de Caicedo, daughter of Don Fernando Beltrán de Caicedo and Doña Francisca Florián Maldonado (Márquez 1709, question 2). This confusion in the recording of names between various documentary sources is mirrored in the frequent inconsistency of the times, seen in the parents' names given in the records of the taking of the habit and the profession of the nuns of the Convento Real de Santa Clara (*LC; EA*).

7. [T]odas unánimes y conformes, la recibieron con mucho gusto, atentas a la virtud y ejemplar vida, con que será muy útil e importante Religiosa.

The letter is cited in the later dowry guarantee of Francisca Josefa de la Concepción (María Antonia del Niño Dios 1993, 42–43). Sor Francisca's taking of the habit is recorded on August 12, 1692, in the *Libro de capítulo* (131v).

8. [S]ecretos del convento donde están expresadas castigos sentencias que se han executado en diferentes ocasiones.

9. En quatro de setiembre de mil y seiscientos y noventa y quatro años yso profesion de monja de velo negro Fransisca Josepha de la Consepción, hija lijítima de Don Fransisco Bentura del Castillo y de Doña María de Gebara con lisensia del Yll*ustrísi*mo y R*everendísi*mo Señor M*aest*ro Don Frai Ygnacio Arsobispo deste Nuebo Reino. Abiendo presedido las dilijensias nesesarias que manda el Sacro Consilio de Tre*n*to. Profesó en manos de la Madre Vicaria Antonia de los Angeles con lisensia de su Yll*ustrísi*ma por estar enferma la M*adr*e Abb*ades*a Paula de S*an* Ygnacio. En presensia de la comunidad, con asistensia de N*uest*ro P*adr*e Vicario el D*oct*or Don Joseph Ossorio Nieto de Pax y porque conste la firmaron = D*oct*or Don Joseph Osorio Nieto de Paz, Antonia de los Angeles, vicaria, María del Niño Jesús, secretaria, Fran*cis*ca Josepha de la Consepción.

10. The earliest date inscribed on the *Afectos* manuscript is 1694, although Madre Castillo's nephew and first editor says that she began writing in 1690 (Castillo 1843, vi).

11. See chapter 8, p. 168, below.

12. María Antonia del Niño Dios quotes the *difinitorio* letter indicating Sor Francisca's reception on the basis of a dowry of 1,500 pesos (1993, 42). The *Libro de capítulo* records several dowries of a thousand pesos, and at least one of fifteen hundred, but none of two thousand. The records, however, are incomplete, detailing dowry amounts for only a portion of the aspirants. Similar dowries of the time are recorded in the Archivo Regional de Boyacá (Notaría 1, 1718, vol. 176: 261–65; 1720, vol. 177: 159; 1723, vol. 178: 117–34; 1740, vol. 183: 17–18; Notaría 2, 1729, vol. 179: 135–36).

13. Neither the *Vida,* María Antonia del Niño Dios (1993), nor documents studied from the Archivo Regional de Boyacá explain the provenance of the money and jewels.

14. *Castellanos* and *patacones* had roughly the same value as the peso. In Madre Castillo's *Libro de cuentas* the terms *peso* and *patacón* are used interchangeably and are both worth eight *reales.* The precious materials contained in the monstrance are enumerated differently in Gustavo Mateus's *Tunja: El arte de los siglos XVI–XVII–XVIII* (1989), fig. 251: 750 large and many small emeralds, 37 diamonds, 2 rubies, 42 amethysts, 6 topazes, and 700 pearls.

15. [U]na rosa de treinta y siete diamantes, uno más grande que los otros . . . otras dos rositas de esmeraldas . . . constaba la una de catorce piedras y la otra de diez y nueve, que por todas, hacen treinta y tres esmeraldas.

16. If she managed personal wealth after entering the convent, Sor Francisca was by no means alone. In 1704, María de los Angeles and Catalina de Santa Rosa petitioned the *alcalde ordinario* to intervene against Tomás de Vargas, who had taken partial possession of their lands and dwelling (AHT, ARB, 1703–4, vol. 137: 458–59). In 1719, Micaela del Sacramento requested permission to sell a black slave to provide for her food and clothing needs (Notaría 2, ARB, 1719, vol. 169: 149–50). In 1729, Madre Francisca Josefa de la Concepción claimed the interest owed to an individual nun on a *censo* (AHT, ARB, 1729, vol. 156: 336). In 1735, Felipa de la Encarnación loaned out 100 *pesos* for which she was to receive interest (Notaría 1, ARB, 1735, vol. 181: 412). In 1739, Josefa de Jesús requested permission from the provisor and vicar general to grant juridical power for obtaining payment of a pension (Notaría 2, ARB, 1739, vol. 183: 115). In 1740, Antonia de San José received permission to sell a slave (Notaría 2, ARB, 1740, vol. 180: 275).

17. [G]uardar muy fielmente el secreto de las cosas, que le dicen, que escriba, o sabe por cartas. Asiste en capítulos, y demás partes, y negocios, de que se ha de dar fe.

18. [E]l Oficio se cante, y el divino culto, y rezo todo con mucha devoción; haciendo se diga con la debida pausa, comenzando todas juntas, y acabando a un mesmo tiempo, para que haya uniformidad, y consonancia, teniendo gran cuidado, en que las religiosas, ayuden al coro, en lo cantado, y rezado, y cuando alguna se descuidare, adviértalo con caridad.

19. [Quiere] volver por el crédito que [le han] quitado y nombrarle otra vez maestra de novicias.

Madre Castillo does not name the abbesses, but they can be identified by comparing the events narrated against archival records of the dates abbesses served.

20. I have found no numbers for total choir nuns in 1718, but in 1720 there were twenty-four, only sixteen of whom had the six years of profession required to vote in an election for abbess, as stipulated in the Franciscan *Constituciones generales* (Merinero 1748, chap. 9, 121). However, the election of 1669 indicates that all fifty of the professed choir nuns voted, even though three had professed within the past six years (*LV* 138). The probable ex-novices in question were Antonia del Sacramento, Micaela de Jesús, and Teresa de San Francisco from Sor Francisca's term as their mistress in 1702, and Mariana de San Bartolomé, Mariana de San José, Felipa de la Encarnación, and María de la Trinidad from her term in 1707. Dates for novices are found in the

Libro de capítulo, Elecciones de abadesas, and the 1707 visit recorded in the *Libro de visita* (172r). The registry of nuns in 1720 is found in an agreement of nuns to sell certain houses dated November 26, 1720 (Notaría 1, ARB, vol. 177: fols. 273r–280r).

21. The council included Lugarda de Santa María, abbess; Antonia del Sacramento, vicaress, who had been under Sor Francisca's care as mistress of novices from January 20, 1702, until her profession on August 12, 1702; the *difinidoras* Micaela de Jesús, who spent the same period as novice as her sister Antonia del Sacramento; María de la Trinidad, who was a novice during the March 1707 visit of Don José Osorio Nieto de Paz, and therefore was likely to have been under Sor Francisca's direction when she became mistress of novices again on July 20, 1707; Felipa de la Encarnación, probably the Felipa Fernández who took the habit as novice on February 6, 1707, and was likely still there for at least six months of Sor Francisca's direction; and Ana de Santa María. Sor Francisca was, by now, Madre Francisca and served with Felipa de San Ignacio on the council as *madre del consejo.* Josefa de San Andrés was secretary. The members of the council in 1727 are identified in the Archivo Regional de Boyacá (Notaría 2, vol. 179: 135r–136v). The years that these nuns spent in the novitiate are compiled from the dates of their taking of the habit, their profession, and from lists of professed nuns that appear in the *Libro de capítulo, Libro de visita,* and *Elecciones de abadesas.*

22. In 1706 Mariana de Escobar was also excused five hundred pesos from the two thousand–peso dowry, "due to the arrears in the wealth of this city, and the income of this convent and of the low number of nuns therein" (por lo atrasado de los caudales desta ciudad y rentas deste combento y ser corto el número de religiosas que en él ay) (*EA,* October 23, 1706). The convent housed only nineteen black-veiled or choir nuns at this historical low point in its size (*LV* 171v–172r).

23. [E]stando sin herencia o legítima alguna de sus padres, en suma pobreza, por favorecer sus deseos piadosos, el gobernador Don José de Enciso y Cárdenas su tío, ofrece dar mil pesos para su dote. Y estando la susodicha Doña Mariana, dotada del cielo de una de las mejores voces que se han oído en esta ciudad y habiendo hecho examen de ella delante de nuestro Padre Vicario, y hallando ser muy necesaria para el culto divino en el Coro, que con la falta de las hijas de Don José Paredes Calderón, habiendo muerto la una, y dejado el hábito la otra, se halla destituído de voces.

Spelling modernized by María Antonia del Niño Dios. This appears to be a separate tome from the *Elecciones de Abadesas. . . Legajo 1°,* which I have consulted.

24. [D]ecían que me quería alzar con el convento y quitarme las llaves de él, que lo traía revuelto y abanderizado; y que mi *jarcia* (que así llamaban a mis parientes) de día y de noche lo destruía.

25. María Antonia del Niño Dios quotes the "Acta de petición para la Toma de Hábito" from the *Legajo Especial, Libro de elecciones Profesiones y tomas de hábito del Real Convento* in which Antonia Castillo's convent childhood is mentioned (1993, 321).

26. Almost all of Madre Castillo's confessors were Jesuits. Diego Solano (1622–85) baptized Francisca Josefa and encouraged her as a young girl to enter the convent (Achury Valenzuela 1968, lxiii). Pedro Calderón was her godfather for her confirmation in 1685 and continued to guide her spiritually in the convent (lxvii). Pedro García

was one of her childhood confessors (lxx). Matías de Tapia, who said mass occasionally at the rural home of the Castillo family, supported her decision to enter the convent when she was faced by the opposition of her family (lxxi, 10). Francisco de Herrera served as Sor Francisca's first spiritual director in the convent during his charge as the convent's confessor (lxxii), and he was the first confessor to instruct her to write down her mystic experiences (*SV,* chap. 10, 29). Juan de Tobar was Sor Francisca's confessor between 1696 and 1702, while rector of the Jesuit school in Tunja (lxxv). Juan Martínez Rubio succeeded Tobar as Sor Francisca's confessor until sometime around 1709 (lxxvii–lxxxiv). Another Jesuit confessor mentioned by Madre Castillo, who followed Martínez Rubio, was Juan Manuel Romero (lxxxv), attending her until 1717 or 1720 (xc). He was replaced by Diego de Tapia, who directed the Jesuit school in Tunja until 1724 (xc and xcv). Madre Castillo does not mention Diego de Moya by name in her *Vida,* but his letter to her niece, Madre Francisca del Niño Jesús, on November 28, 1746, indicates that he was her confessor during the last few years of her life (xcvi). During the latter part of her life, Madre Castillo seems not to have had a fixed confessor, but Achury Valenzuela proposes that her confessors may have included the Franciscans Fray Felipe Arguindegui and Fray Luis de Herrera, and the Jesuit Tomás Casabona (xcvii).

27. "[M]i muy estimada Señora," "mi Madre Francisca," "Vuestra Reverencia," and "nunca la he olvidado y estoy con mil deseos de verla."

The letters written to Madre Castillo from her confessors are found in the *Obras completas* (Castillo 1968, 2: 535–50).

28. [M]uy afecta y reconocida a la Compañía.

29. A number of documents signed by Montalvo de Tobar in this capacity can be found in the Archivo Regional de Boyacá (Notaría 1, ARB, 1720–22, vol. 177: 159–489).

30. See also a document concerning the dispute between the convent and the Colegio de la Compañía over the haciendas in Gámeza (María Antonia del Niño Dios 1993, 227, n. 1).

31. By comparing the 1720 roster (Notaría 1, ARB, vol. 177: 273–80) with those of 1707 (*LV* 171v–172r) and 1691 (AHT, ARB, vol. 126: 471–72) and with the records of habits and professions in the *Libro de capítulo,* I have ascertained that, of the twenty-two black-veiled nuns in 1720, six had professed before Sor Francisca, and fifteen later, at least seven of whom, including her niece Francisca del Niño Jesús, were novices under her guidance.

32. Several of such receipts are presented as documentation in support of a larger case concerning a property held on *censo* in the Archivo Histórico de Tunja (1698, vol. 133: 258).

33. La Madre Francisca de la Concepsión, en la causa que sigo sobre la restitusión que tengo pedido se haga a mi convento de las quadras que tiene sobre la fuente grande de esta ciudad, las que embarasa Francisco Lópes sin título justo para ello, digo que aunque por mi parte se le avisó la reveldía por no aver respondido ni dicho cosa alguna al traslado que de mi pedimento se le dio, y sin embargo no ha respondido por lo qual le aviso segunda reveldía para que Vuestra merced se sirva como lo suplico de averla por avisada y mandar hacer como tengo pedido en mi primer escrito por ser conforme a justicia, ella mediante.

A V*uestra* m*erce*d pido, y suplico provea, y mande como llevo pedido, con justicia, costas, y en lo necesario etc.

Fran*cis*ca Jos*e*pha de la Consep*ció*n Abb*ades*a [September 24, 1738]

34. See the epigraph to chapter 4.

35. [A] favor de su primo Pedro Diego del Castillo y Guevara que debía su abuelo a los herederos de Cathalina de Guevara, nuestra abuela.

36. Más, en 23 de febrero de 1742 años se hizo el entierro de la Madre Francisca de la Concepción, y en las misas que se dijeron de cuerpo presente, novenario, cera, achuelas y misas y vigilias, del día de las honras, se gastaron cincuenta y siete pesos.

Spelling and punctuation modernized by María Antonia del Niño Dios.

CHAPTER 6: *SU VIDA:* SPIRITUAL TRIALS AND WORLDLY TROUBLES

1. Although it is customary to refer to the soul as "it," the soul of Madre Castillo's visions frequently takes the clearly feminine character of bride or daughter. See also chapter 8, n. 12.

2. [P]ues muchas veces han dicho a voces: que desde que este demonio entró en este convento, no se puede sufrir; que soy revoltosa, cizañera, fingidora; que no sé quien es Dios; que hasta los güesos de los muertos desentierro con la lengua; me hacía y he hecho esta cuenta: aunque por la misericordia de Dios no me remuerde la conciencia, mas qué sé yo si me engaña el amor propio, teniendo tanto, más fácil y más creíble es que yo me engañe, que no tantas que veo cómo sirven a Dios, etc.

. . . Por mucho tiempo, y no sé si diga lo más ordinario, en llegando el cuerpo a tomar el sueño, quédase el alma en oración con más encendidos afectos que pudiera dispierta, y con grande paz. . . . En particular, una noche, que me parecía verlo desnudo y arrodillado sobre la cruz, y que una nubecita muy leve le iba enlazando y subiendo por el cuerpo, y mi alma, deshaciéndose en afectos de su Señor, entendía que ella era aquella nubecita, y me parece que he entendido que el mostrar Nuestro Señor estas cosas en sueños, es la causa de estar continuamente con tantas turbaciones y temores.

3. [M]e pareció andar sobre un entresuelo hecho de ladrillos, puestos punta con punta, como en el aire, y con gran peligro, y mirando abajo vía un río de fuego, negro y horrible, y que entre él andaban tantas serpientes, sapos y culebras, como caras y brazos de hombres que se vían sumidos en aquel pozo o río.

4. See chapter 2, page 50, above.

5. The book by Molina must be *Exercicios espirituales de las excelencias, provecho, y necessidades de la oración mental, reducidos a doctrina y meditaciones sacadas de los santos padres y doctores de la Iglesia* (Spiritual exercises on the excellences, benefits, and necessities of mental prayer, reduced to doctrine and meditations taken from the holy fathers and doctors of the Church), written by Antonio de Molina (1560?–1619).

6. [C]omo quien se arranca las entrañas . . . con la repugnancia que si viniera al suplicio.

7. See the epigraphs to chapter 2 and their subsequent discussion.

8. Pobrecilla, combatida por la tempestad, sin ninguna consolación, no temas, no morirás. . . . Más son por ti que contra ti. El dragón soberbio arrastró la tercera parte

de las estrellas; y el poder de mi brazo omnipotente triunfará de él como una paja, pobre, flaca y débil. . . . ¡Ea!, alienta tu corazón, pobrecilla mujer, anégate en el mar de las misericordias mías. Mira que vendrá la aurora y se acabará la lucha y batalla, y se dará fin a las tinieblas, en entrando la aurora María, fuerte, suave, apacible y misericordiosa.

9. Veo todo el tiempo pasado de mi vida tan lleno de culpas y tan descaminado, que ojos me faltarán para llorar en esta región, tan lejos de vivir como verdadera hija de mi Padre Dios.

10. Saint Teresa addresses particular friendships in *Camino de perfección* (1970, chap. 6).

11. The daggers (†) indicate nuns who died in office, and mark the year of their death.

12. See the epigraph to chapter 4, page 73.

13. No queráis temer a los que pueden matar el cuerpo. . . . [Mt 10:28]. No temáis las palabras de los hombres.

14. [C]omo un río o pedazo de mar, y a las religiosas que andaban por encima de él, como mosquitos o gusanitos sobre el agua; y que luego algunas, en particular la madre abadesa, dando unas pequeñas vueltas, se hundían en aquella agua y desaparecían; yo me quedé espantada, y entendí moriría breve la prelada.

15. In addition to granting indulgences to those who gave alms for the Crusade—a cause no longer in existence—the bull granted indulgences for those who gave donations for church building, repairs, and pious works, or who offered special prayers for the Crusade. The indulgence absolved the faithful of specific sins or of not fulfilling certain difficult vows. It could also permit the faithful to eat meat during most of Lent and many other fast days (Herbermann et al., 1908, 543). Perhaps Madre Castillo is pointing out the laxity of the former abbess in not fasting, or in violations of the vow of poverty, for either of which she was apparently unable to receive absolution through the the Bull of the Crusade.

16.   Vén, alma peregrina,
       en alas del amor;
       cierva herida, al descanso
       del pecho de tu Dios.

          Llega ya a las corrientes,
       que gloria y vida son,
       de aquel río de deleites
       de la ciudad de Dios.

CHAPTER 7: *SU VIDA:* HOLY ARCHETYPES

1. The choir library in the Convento Real de Santa Clara did hold two editions of the *Flos sanctorum* in the late 1500s (see chapter 4, n. 17). Though I have found no records of the convent library during Madre Castillo's lifetime, it would be surprising if she did not have some access to this standard source of saints' lives.

2. I have been unable to consult the first volume of Rivadeneira, which covers the months from January to June.

3. Algunas veces hacía procesiones de imágenes o remedaba las profesiones y hábitos de las monjas, no porque tuviera inclinación a tomar ese estado; pues *sólo me inclinaba a vivir como los ermitaños en los desiertos y cuevas del campo.* [Emphasis mine.]

4. The authors from whom Madre Castillo obtained her theoretical knowledge of mystic and meditative practice include Ignatius of Loyola, Osuna, John of the Cross, Teresa of Jesus, Antonio de Molina, and Luis de la Puente, all mentioned in the *Vida* or the *Afectos espirituales*.

5. Assí mismo certifico, haver oído en dicho convento la continuación de sus raptos, y arrobamientos continuados por todos los días, y por muchas horas, de donde se manifestaba el grado de unión tan eminente a que llegó, y algunas vezes duraban estos raptos dos, y más días, como supe haver acontecido tres días antes de la Purificación de Nuestra Señora, en que estuvo casi tres días fuera de sí, juzgando las religiosas ser alguna enfermedad, llamaron médico, y haviendo entrado el siervo de Dios el *Padre* Martín Niño de la Compañía de Jesús, reconoció ser rapto, y arrobamiento; y consolando a sus hijas, mandó que le diessen una sustancia, y poniéndolo por execución, repetía la sierva de Dios: *Dexadme, que estoy con mi querido.*

6. La devoción de algunos, acaso afinada de la curiosidad, hizo tan fuertes instancias a las fundadoras, para que les permitiesen ver aquella maravilla, que las rindieron, a que estando la Sierva de Dios arrobada después de haber comulgado, como solía, abriessen la comulgatoria, para que le viessen por ella. Hazíase así las Religiosas le quitaban el velo, que tenía sobre el Rostro para que viessen su extraordinaria hermosura, y los Seglares hazían la experiencia de moverla con un soplo desde afuera.

7. Sólo me acuerdo que en empezando a caer el sol, me hallaba como el perrito que busca a su amo por toda la casa y no lo halla; así me parecía que sentía mi alma por su Dios y se iban aniquilando para ella todas las cosas.

8. Nunca la bieron alterada ni descompuesta ni desir palabra injuriosa ni de murmurasión ni contra aquellas que condenavan su frequensia en comulgar.

9. Andaba toda la ciudad haciendo penitencia, restituciones, confesiones, etc; pues estando yo una tarde en un güertecito, y viendo una imagen de Nuestro Señor Crucificado, sentía un desmayo, como que todos los güesos me los desencajaban, y mi alma me parecía se iba deshaciendo, entendiendo el gran tormento que causó a Nuestro Señor cuando lo clavaron, el desencajarse los güesos de su lugares, y que fue una de las penas y dolores que más lo atormentaron; así por el intensísimo dolor que sintió en el cuerpo, como por lo que significaba: que es la división y desunión de las personas espirituales, y más de los que son como los güesos en que se sustenta toda la armonía del cuerpo, esto es, los predicadores y prelados.

10. [P]enas, tormentos, y *martyrios,* con que venció, y abatió al infierno todo. [Emphasis mine.]

11. Unas vezes yva cargada con una cruz a cuestas con soga a la gargantta, tapado el rostro, con picantes orttigas, ensenizada la cavesa, ottras vezes mandava a ottra religiossa que la llevasse de diestro de una soga que se ponía al cuello arrastrándose por el suelo como bestia.

12. [D]ábanle cruelíssimos golpes, sacábanla de su duro lecho, arrastrábanla por la tierra, teníanla por muchas horas, gyrando como una rueda de molino, y despidién-

dola con grande fuerza contra la tierra, le daban fuertes golpes en las caderas, y cabeza tan violentos, que quebraba los ladrillos.

13. Hallábame una noche bajando por una calle estrecha y llena de piedras, que por su desigualdad me daban mucho trabajo, porque yo llevaba los pies descalzos y sobre mis hombros un muchacho como de doce años; él llevaba los brazos extendidos al aire y puestos en cruz. . . . Yo miraba que aquellas religiosas que he dicho, se reían de mi camino, y decía con admiración: ¡Válgame Dios! ¿Por qué se reirán de esto? ¿No verán que Nuestro Señor Jesucristo llevó por nosotros la cruz?

CHAPTER 8: THE *AFECTOS ESPIRITUALES:*
MYSTICISM OF THE INCARNATE WORD

1. See n. 21, below.

2. Gómez Restrepo considers Madre Castillo to be the only writer in the Nuevo Reino de Granada with sufficient merit to figure in literary histories of Castillian letters (1953, 50). He judges the *Afectos* superior to the *Vida*, referring to the richness of their phrasing, their brilliant generalizations, and their biblical flavor (97). Anderson-Imbert finds Madre Castillo to be "the woman who, after Sor Juana, reached the highest poetic expression in this [the seventeenth] century," and, while she is "disorderly, digressive, without doctrinal rigor," he continues, "the metaphors shine out from her pages" (1969, 129). It is Camacho Guizado who calls her style repetitive and confusing (1978, 38) and Achury Valenzuela who points out her grammatical errors (1968, cxxiii).

3. The original manuscript of the *Afectos espirituales* is preserved in the Biblioteca Luis Angel Arango in Bogotá, bound together with twelve letters—ten addressed to Madre Castillo from her confessors, one written by her, and one addressed to her niece by Padre Diego de Moya, who performed her funeral sermon.

4. According to Achury Valenzuela, it was Don Antonio María de Castillo y Alarcón who had the various manuscripts bound after receiving them from the convent in 1813 (1968, cxcv–cxcvi).

5. Hasta *a*quí el año de 16, aora es el de 24 (Castillo ms. 71, fol. 125; *AE* 245, n. a).

6. The break between 1716 and 1724 is not absolute. Fol. 65v and perhaps as many as the next ten folios of the manuscript are out of order and correspond to 1717 (*AE, Afectos* 49–61, 128–49). The date 1717 is written on fol. 65v (*AE* 128), and the incident related corresponds to an event in the *Vida* that can be dated to 1717.

7. These include primarily Dr. Miguel Tobar y Serrate and the R. P. Eduardo Acosta. The corresponding labor in the *Vida* was done by the R. P. Belarmino Toral. See Achury Valenzuela 1982, 58.

8. The full title, as given to these 1569 writings by Fray Luis de León, is *Exclamaciones o meditaciones del alma a sv Dios escritas por la Madre Teresa de Jesús, en differentes días, conforme al espíritu que le comunicaua nuestro señor después de auer comulgado, año de mil y quinientos y sesenta y nueve* (Teresa de Jesús 1970, 515).

9. Mandáronle sus confessores fuesse escribiendo su vida, y los particulares regalos que de continuo recevía de Nuestro Señor Jesuchristo.

10. In *Las Moradas,* Saint Teresa distinguishes the *visión imaginaria* (imaginary vision) from the *visión intelectual* (intellectual vision). The first involves a type of image, though not one seen by the eyes of the body, and for that reason it is more vulnerable to interference by the Devil (1970, *morada* 6, chap. 9, 460–61). The second and higher form of vision that is given by God involves no perceivable images (1970, *morada* 6, chap. 8).

11. Y la ansia de ynstruir y amor que tengo a las almas es tanta que me ynpasienta mi sexo porque me ympide el que yo haga algo por quien tanto hizo por mí.

12. My use of the term *seeker* is an imposition onto Madre Castillo's texts that I have found necessary in order to resolve a syntactical problem presented by her often-unnamed addressee and the often-unnamed soul, or object, of her lessons. I believe that the term respects the spirit of her prose as the wisdom it contains teaches both herself and this unnamed addressee how to seek God. In characterizing the seeker as feminine, I wish to avoid the awkward repetitiveness of the phrase "he or she" throughout this chapter, and I believe that Madre Castillo's primary intent was to address her own personal situation and, probably, that of her sister nuns as the consummate "brides of Christ." Madre Castillo often alternates between referring to an unnamed person and to the person's soul. When she speaks of a person, I will say *seeker;* when she speaks of the soul, I will use the word *soul.* Madre Castillo refers to the soul as "she," as I will too. Her choice of pronoun comes from the feminine gender of the Spanish noun *alma,* but it also reflects a practice of talking about herself in the third person, and it allows an association of the unnamed soul with what I believe is her ideal addressee: the young nun.

13. *Verdad amable* versus *verdad conocible.*

14. [M]odo de proceder en tratar algún punto y materia, por diversos propósitos y varios conceptos.

15. Pensando los diferentes afectos o efectos que el alma siente en el trato con la divina majestad, entendí: unas veces se manifiesta el Señor al alma como esposo dulce, apacible y amante; y así, todo lo que siente es amor y deseo de su agrado; otras, se muestra como Señor grande y rey grande; y así, junto con el amor, la ocupa aún más el temor, reverencia y admiración.

16. [Q]ue es el supremo a que Dios levanta a sus esposas, las almas. . . . por el grande exceso de amor, quedan las potencias tan suspensas y absortas, que ni el cielo se apetece durante este gozo.

17. [S]e hallaba el alma en una inefable dicha, que es parecerle estaba sola de todo lo criado, y sola con su Dios, sin tenerse a sí misma.

18. Entendí, conocí, como si dijera.

19. Las palabras suaves, dulces y regaladas que el alma recibe, en lo escondido de su Dios y su centro.

20. ¿Adónde te escondiste, / Amado, y me dejaste con gemido? / Como el ciervo huiste / habiéndome herido; / salí tras ti clamando, y eras ido. (1980, 82)

21. El habla delicada / Del amante que estimo, / Miel y leche destila / Entre rosas y lirios. // Su melíflua palabra / Corta como rocío, / Y con ella florece / El corazón marchito. // Tan suave se introduce / Su delicado silbo, / Que duda el corazón, / Si es el corazón mismo. // Tan eficaz persuade, / Que cual fuego encendido / Derrite como

cera / Los montes y los riscos. // Tan fuerte y tan sonoro / Es su aliento divino, / Que resucita muertos, / Y despierta dormidos. // Tan dulce y tan suave / Se percibe al oído, / Que alegra de los huesos / Aun lo más escondido.

22. Allí me dio su pecho / allí me enseñó ciencia muy sabrosa (Juan de la Cruz 1980, 88).

23. También sentí en lo íntimo de mi alma ser aquella voz del Señor fuerte, poderosa y majestuosa; la voz del Señor sobre las aguas. . . . Esta voz, pues, del Señor, preparando los ciervos, revela lo oscuro, aclara lo escondido. . . . Esta voz del Señor da claridad para entender los misterios que la fe enseña.

24. [P]arece que aquel conocimiento es como una palabra, o una habla escondida, no como la que se articula o forma con la voz, mas como el rocío, o como las gotas que destilan en la tierra, que despiertan su sed de conocer y amar un bien.

25. [C]omo deshecha de gozo, de amor y de alegría, [el alma] conoce la voz de su amado, más dulce a sus oídos, más suave a su paladar y garganta que la miel. Y esta palabra, parece que no sólo llega a los oídos del alma, sino que la sirve de sustento y la deshace como el fuego a la cera, la penetra como la luz al fuego.

26. Entendí que el comparar el alma a un instrumento de flautas muy delgadas, se entendía por todo lo que llevo escrito; porque como el aire o aliento del que toca, es el que se oye en aquel instrumento, así lo que aquí hubiere de Dios, solo es lo que su majestad envía de su espíritu, por un instrumento de caña, sin virtud para nada, etc.

27. Habiendo comulgado, entendí esto.

28. Coloquio de una alma con Nuestro Senor, estando dormida, y, a su parecer, en el sueño unida íntimamente con su divina Majestad por amor:

Mi esposa es para mí como un instrumento de flautas muy delgadas, que suavemente suenan a mis oídos.

Tú eres para mí, amantísimo Dios, como la consonancia y armonía de todos los intrumentos músicos. . . .

Mi esposa es para mí como una paloma gemidora, que sólo halla descanso en mi pecho.

Tú eres para mí, amantísimo Señor, como un corazón que se abrasa en medio de las entrañas de mi alma, difundiéndose y penetrándose por todas sus potencias y facultades, dándole vida, vigor y aliento, calor y alegría. . . .

Mi esposa es para mí como un arroyuelo en la soledad para el caminante fatigado.

Tú eres para mí, Dios mío, como un inmenso mar-océano de gracias, de dichas, de dones y tesoros, donde, entrando las aguas, vuelven a su centro y hallan su descanso.

29. [Y]o lo confieso en su divina presencia, que jamás hice obra buena.

30. Bien conozco que a vista de tantos beneficios de Dios, y ingratitudes y culpas mías, está hecha mayor mi maldad, que el pecado de aquellas infelices ciudades, que fértiles y abundantes de beneficios del cielo, crecieron tanto en ellas las abominaciones, que merecieron que bajara fuego del cielo a consumirlas [Lam 4:6]; mas no quiero, Dios mío, hacer mayor mi maldad con la desesperación, antes diré: «mayor es tu misericordia, y mejor para mí que la vida, y sobre la vida», etc. [Ps 63:3].

Unless otherwise noted, all biblical references are to the numbering system used in English translations of the Bible. The Latin *Vulgate* or the *Breviarium Romanum,* which Madre Castillo used, differs slightly in the Psalms and Isaiah.

31. Y llegando aquí entendí aquellas palabras: «cazad, o coged las pequeñuelas zorras que demuelen la viña» [Song 2:15], como si dijera: no quiero que demuelas la viña de tu alma con el descaecimiento, mas que cojas y quites los defectos que la dañan; no que descaezcas a vista de tanto mal, sino que conozcas cuánto necesitas de mi ayuda y favor para quitarlo.

32. Cuántas veces abren sobre él su boca, los que son como tigres, y osos y leones [Ps 22:13]; y cuántas, aún las almas de sus esposas, ponen en el templo de su corazón, junto a esta arca sagrada, el ídolo vano y maldito [1 Sm 5:2], clamando con el pueblo de sus vanos deseos, amores y cuidados: *¡no a éste, sino a Barrabás!* [Lk 23:18].

33. The voice that addresses "my soul" is explicitly linked to autobiographical statements in *Afectos* 7 (*AE* 19), 59 (144), 74 (173), 82 (193), and others.

34. Yo te di inteligencia de una lengua no estudiada, y más: te abrí el sentido para entender las misteriosas y profundísimas palabras suyas, pronunciadas de mi espíritu vivífico.

35. [E]l no haber escrito mucho de asuntos sagrados no ha sido desafición, ni de aplicación la falta, sino sobra de temor y reverencia debida a aquellas Sagradas Letras, para cuya inteligencia yo me conozco tan incapaz y para cuyo manejo soy tan indigna. . . . Pues ¿cómo me atreviera yo a tomarlo en mis indignas manos, repugnándolo el sexo, la edad y sobre todo las costumbres? (1957, 4: 443, ll. 131–36, 151–54).

36. ¿No sabes que todas las cosas que están escritas, son escritas para la doctrina y luz del alma; para que con la consolación de las escrituras se funde, afiance y afirme en la paciencia, y en ella, y en ellas tenga esperanza? ¿No sabes que hablando los Profetas en persona de Cristo y contando sus grandes tribulaciones, se entiende también del alma atribulada, desolada y afligida, y que éste fue el ejemplar que se mostró a tus ojos, y el camino, verdad y vida que guía a la vida y a la patria?

37. De todos los sentimientos, luces y conocimientos que en los salmos y demás etc., quiere Nuestro Señor que halle el alma, entendía componerse un campo no comprehendido de ningún entendimiento, en donde el alma, en sintiendo el amor divino y viendo que, según los afectos que halla en su corazón, puede decirle a Dios, amado, le pide que salgan a este campo a donde es dilatado su corazón para correr con pies de ciervo el camino de sus mandamientos, y allí como a porfía aparecen las flores con aventajada hermosura y fragancia. Los varios sentimientos que allí halla, los deseos que allí florecen, los misterios de la vida del amado, sus misericordias, sus atributos todos (conforme la capacidad que da al alma), la hacen desear salir de sí misma, y de sus condiciones y afectos, del ruido de las criaturas, de sus quereres, etc., de desearlas, tenerlas, alegrarse o entristecerse de sus cosas, de querer agradar o desagradar; y como con hastío de todo lo que no es Dios, lo llama para que salgan al campo de sus verdades, dejando la confusión y mentira, que es todo lo que no es Dios.

38. *Voce mea Dominum clamavi.* Mi voz clamó al Señor y me oyó de su Santo Monte [Ps 3:4].

39. The Psalms quoted or paraphrased are numbers 6, 18, 22, 24, 31, 32, 57, 61, 69, 73, 91, 102, 119, and 120, though not in this order.

40. No te desprecies ni des por perdida por sentir en ti tan varios afectos y tribulaciones, pues tu padre David decía de sí: *que estaba seca su virtud como la teja, y*

que se habían secado como el heno sus güesos; que lo había desamparado su virtud y la luz, lumbre de sus ojos; que estaba como el llagado que ya llegó al sepulcro; que estaba como reducido al polvo de muerte. [Emphasis mine.]

41. Y todas estas *tentaciones y pruebas interiores y exteriores* no le quitaron el ser hombre a medida del corazón de Dios, porque en todo tenía recurso al Señor. [Emphasis mine.]

42. No temas, pues, los temores nocturnos [Ps 91:5], que mis palabras *a los oídos de tu alma* serán luz de tus caminos [Ps 119:105]. [Emphasis mine.]

43. Pues mira todo lo que dicen los salmos de David. . . . Hablan en persona de Cristo, esposo tuyo, . . . y si la unión que se hace en el Santísimo Sacramento del cuerpo y sangre de Cristo es tan real y verdadera con el alma, esposa suya, ¿cómo no ha de participar de las condiciones de su Señor y esposo, y seguir sus pasos, si fueres fiel esposa? . . . El es hijo de David según la carne, y ella ha de desear ser hija de su espíritu. El dijo, «aprended de mí que soy manso y humilde de corazón» [Mt 11:29]; y David había dicho, «acuérdate Señor de David y de todas sus mansedumbres» [Ps 132:1].

44. Fray Luis de León's *De los nombres de Cristo* ([1587] 1914–38) digs deeply into the Old Testament in search of names with which to characterize Christ. When Saint John of the Cross explains the purification of the soul in his *Noche oscura,* he sees examples of mysticism not only in the experiences of David but also in those of Jeremiah and even Moses.

45. I discuss Madre Castillo's use of the rhetoric of theological oratory further in chapter 9.

46. Madre mía: lo que entiendo de esta glosa, así del primero Psalmo como del XXXIX, es una doctrina muy conforme a la mística locución del celestial espíritu, voceándose unos lugares a otros, en la inteligencia genuina de los Santos Padres. Esto digo, según el conocimiento teológico de la letra, aunque muy lejos me hallo del afectuoso, de quien hablaba nuestro Redentor cuando decía: *confiteor tibi Pater, quia abscondisti haec a sapientibus, et revelasti ea parvulis* [Mt 11:25]. . . . Pues para enseñanza y confusión de frías disputas, será el Señor servido que lo que revela en secreto, le dé a la pluma.

47. In the Nuevo Reino de Granada, the Jesuits did not limit their concern with spiritual exercises to their own members. The Father General, Padre Tirso González, writes in a letter to the Provincial Padre Juan Martínez Rubio, who would later become Madre Castillo's confessor, that both secular and ecclesiastical persons should be encouraged to practice spiritual exercises (Cartas PP. Generales; Archivo de la Provincia de Toledo [Madrid]; Rome, February 7, 1699 [132: 67], quoted in Pacheco 1989, 3: 392).

48. Achury Valenzuela defends the first premise through a comparison of more than thirty quotes from the two autobiographies (1968, clxxix–clxxxiv). When Madre Castillo writes in the *Vida* that she has read "a book on particular friendships," she is referring to chap. 15 of Saint Teresa's *Camino de perfección* (Castillo 1968, 1: 53, n. 1).

49. For a description of this mystic paralysis, see the *Libro de la vida* (Teresa de Jesús 1970, chap. 18, 121).

50. [C]on una se comprende mucho, lo que nuestro entendimiento no podría componer tan de presto (Teresa de Jesús 1970, *Las moradas, morada* 6, chap. 3, 441).

51. A text on "The spiritual matrimony of the soul with God" that Madre Castillo has copied into the *Cuaderno de Enciso* (fols. 33–36) provides a good example of the form in which such indirect access to the mystic doctrines of the sixteenth century was possible. This piece parallels the ten degrees of the ladder of love as they are developed in the *Noche oscura* of Saint John of the Cross.

52. Jean Vilnet lists a total of 924 biblical citations in San Juan's four prose works (1949, 35).

53. [D]isputarlas y enseñarlas, pareciéndoles aciertan, sin que lo muestren a letrados, eso sí. Así que ni yo pienso acertar en lo que escriba (Teresa de Jesús 1970, chap. 1, 490).

54. [N]o es para mujeres, ni aun para hombres muchas cosas (ibid., 488).

55. Habiéndome a mí el Señor, de algunos años acá, dado un regalo grande cada vez que oigo o leo algunas palabras de los *Cantares* de Salomón, en tanto extremo, que sin entender la claridad del latín en romance, me recogía más y movía mi alma que los libros muy devotos que entiendo (ibid., prólogo, 487).

56. For details on the various indexes of prohibited books and their effects on biblical translations, see Bataillon (1950, 2: 144–48).

57. Mujercilla ciega, pobrecilla despreciada y vil, pobre y desechada mujer.

58. ¡Que ya te hallara mi alma [a Cristo], y te hallara en los pechos de mi madre, para que de sus misericordias fuera mi alma alimentada, para que en su protección tuviera mi refugio; en su doctrina y ejemplo, mi alimento y seguridad!, pues los pechos de mi enseñanza son como torres de defensa [Song 8:10]. ¡Oh, Madre mía, y madre de la vida, tus pechos son como *el vino que conforta y alegra el corazón del hombre* [Ps 104:15]. [Emphasis mine.]

59. In using the term *voice,* I am referring here to the relationship between the narrator and the content of the narration as it is expressed in the narrator's use of language.

60. ¿Pues qué cosa, Dios mío, más desproporcionada y disforme que una mujercilla vil, asquerosa como un muladar podrido, viciosa y fácil para la ira, tantas veces caída en tan grandes culpas, pueda o quiera estimarse, o que la estimen?

61. [C]onocí que cada alma es juntamente oveja y pastor de sus afectos, que dejando de velar sobre ellos saldrían de Dios, y llevarían al alma a la boca del león. Acordéme de lo que dijo Nuestro Señor, «si me amas, apacienta mis ovejas» [Jn 21:17].

62. Sentí una grande tribulación y confusión, con tentaciones y persecuciones, interiores y exteriores, de dar oídos a las criaturas.

63. Conocí que con las criaturas de Dios, que habitan esta casa del Señor del universo, y más con sus esposas en la casa de la religión, debía portarme y estimarme como una pobrecita, vil y desnuda, a quien un gran señor, por pura piedad, entró a su casa, a que morase en la compañía de sus hijos y siervos; 1º Atendería solícita y diligente a hacer lo que le mandaban y a dar gusto, en lo que alcanzaba, a los hijos y siervos de su Señor. 2º No se entrometería en los negocios ni querría adular ni sobresalir. 3º Se contentaría con cualquiera cosa que le dieran, sin quejarse de olvidos o desprecios. 4º Miraría a todos con estimación; solo a sí misma hallaría despreciable. 5º

Haría con cuidado lo que se le mandaba. 6º Sufriría las injurias sin dar ocasión a ellas, pues todo pasa a vista de su Señor.

CHAPTER 9: THE *CUADERNO DE ENCISO:* A THEOLOGY OF HUMILIATION AND ITS MYSTIC REWARDS

1. Así como el que está en la sepoltura a la diestra i a la siniestra, en lo superior e inferior, no le llega otra cosa que el sepulcro, i la tierra de la sepultura parese que traga, come i debora al sepultado, uniéndolo i combirtiendo en sí, descarnando i desnudando los huesos i aun asta ellos volviéndolos en polvo, como los muertos del siglo, así has de rogar, pedir i desear ser unida toda mudada i traspasada en el corasón de Jesús en el glorioso sepulcro de su amor, i campo estendidísimo de su sangre que es sepulcro de los peregrinos i de aquellos que no tienen en la tierra lugar de descanso ni donde reclinar la cabesa.

2. Achury Valenzuela cites the work of Alfonso Méndez Plancarte (*Abside*, July 1942) in identifying the poems of Sor Juana, which include fragments from the *Divino Narciso* and from Letras XVIII and XIX (Castillo 1968, 2: 493–94).

3. The *Afectos* that have been revised in the *Cuaderno* are numbered 10, 86, 87, 9, 1, 116, 117, 10b, 39, 40, 41, 42, 98, 99, 73, 74, 75, 100, 114, 118, 119, 115, 80, 81, 82, 158, 159, 160, 161, 162, 163, 105, 106, 107, and 108 in the 1968 edition. See Achury Valenzuela (1982, 73–76).

4. See chapter 8, n. 12 above, regarding my designation of the soul as female.

5. The respective subtitles of these sections are: "De la salida del alma al campo de las verdades" (Of the departure of the soul into the field of truths); "De la ocupación del alma en el campo de la vida" (Of the occupation of the soul in the field of life); "Del daño o provecho del tiempo" (Of the harm and benefits of temporality); "De la subida del Alma al monte de la mirra" (Of the soul's ascent up the mountain of myrrh); "De cómo las fuentes de las aguas se allan en el campo de la humillasión" (Of how the sources of the living waters are found in the field of humiliation); "Del sepulchro glorioso" (Of the glorious sepulchre); "Consolasión del ánima en la tribulasión" (Of the consolation of the soul in tribulation); "Monte de la vida eterna en el Padre Nuestro" (Mountain of eternal life in the Lord's Prayer); and "Guía para la vida eterna" (Guide for eternal life).

6. Este día entendí. . . . Y es así que muchas veces, y casi siempre, se me representaron, y me parece vide algunas entre sueños con estas semejanzas de enfermas. . . . Queriendo yo entonces pedir por mis padres y hermanos, entendí esto.

7. «Porque empezaba ya a amanecer»; y deseo saber, si esto es advertir el tiempo en que tuvo el sentimiento y dijo las palabras del salmo, «Levántate Salterio y cítara» o si acaso tiene otro sentido. La otra es que en los últimos renglones del sentimiento dice que Nuestro Señor, «con su divinidad ampara, y con su humanidad perdona» y esto último es menester explicarlo más, porque aunque es verdad que la humanidad de Jesucristo Nuestro Señor fue la que con su pasión y muerte nos mereció el perdón, pero propiamente quien perdona es Dios. . . . También pueden tener otro sentido, entendiendo por humanidad, la misericorida y piedad.

8. Y en aquel silencio y soledad, con ternuras y gozo del alma le dice a su amado en

el sacramento, «levántate salterio y cítara mía, levántate en la mañana, pues amanece ya tu luz al alma.»

9. [H]alló el alma lugar de firme refugio en el Dios y Señor de las virtudes, que *como Dios perdona y,* «humanado muestra más su benignidad.»

10. Cantad al Señor toda la tierra. Cantad misericordia i juisio.

11. For a definition of imaginary visions, see chapter 8, n. 10 above.

12. No vino al mundo como lus inefable.

13. [T]odo aquel coloquio entre la esposa i su querido esposo en aquel cantar de amor no ves cómo está texido de admirable variedad. Ia bela i busca a su amado. Ia duerme i es buscada de su querido. Ia padese desmaios i siente derretirse su alma como sera a la vos de su dueño. Ia le alla i animosa promete no dejarle más asta la bienaventuransa. Ia se le esconde i se alla como la noche en sus sombras. Ya pregunta por él ia da sus señas. Ia el amor la saca de sí, i pide el sagrado ósculo. Ia quiere correr tras su querido. Ia le ama i considera como al hermosío lirio de los valles. Ia le quiere seguir como al cabritillo i al siervo de los campos. Ia atiende a los adornos que le a dado su esposo. Ia se ocupa toda en amar i ponderar las perfecsiones de su querido. Ya be los sedros i sipreses de que es echa su casa. Ya lo comvida al campo i a ver la viñas i a morar en las villas. ¿Y no ves cómo sin entenderlo ella, se alla a veses conturbada en sí misma por los exérsitos de Aminadabad, porque con ella se porta su querido ejersitándola en barias cosas, mesclándole la mirra con aromas i dándole tal ves a gustar el panal con la miel? ¿I no ves cómo abrigado en sus pechos tal ves se muestra m(o)anojito de mirra i otras veses hase que exersitándose su esposa en el travajo sus dedos apretando el uso distilen mirra escojida [a] sus manos? ¿No la ves erida de las guardas despojada de sus vestiduras? I otras veses, ¿no ves cómo la predican por bienaventurada viéndola estrivar en su querido etc.? Mas en todo esto no ai más que aquel amor y (amor i) dolor. Io soi suia i él es mío; mi amado para mí io para él.

14. Teniendo duda por los barios asidentes que sentía en sí con diferentes afectos i efectos entendió esto.

15. Pues, ¡mira este igualarse el cielo con el suelo, Dios con la criatura, el Altísimo con el polvo, el Criador con la echura de sus manos! I mira qué darás por este bien. Mira la firmesa de aquella promesa; vosotros que dejaste, etc.

16. Advierte la firmeza de aquella promesa: vosotros, que dejasteis todas las cosas y me seguisteis, recibiréis cien doblado, y poseeréis la vida eterna.

17. I bien puede su p*adre* traerla a sí: porque las galas, joias i aderesos se los gua*rd*a para el día de las bodas. Mas si en tanto que llegan quiere darle algunas, ella si es hija fiel, las toma sólo por el gusto i plaser de su p*adre*, que se sirve de tener sus hijos ricos i onrrados. ¿Qué fuera pues, si esta hija tanto se enamorara de los adornos que pusiera el gusto en ellos i en sí misma i ia no estubiera tan atenta a qualquiera ocupasión del gusto i servisio de su p*adre* ni se empleara en las obras vajas i humildes de su casa? ¿No estava espuesta a orrorosos ierros i que, oiendo alavansas de su aliño, buscara amadores de su hermosura? . . . ¡I que arrojara el Señor de lo exelso, i de las grandesas de su amor, i echara a la tierra a la que antes era estrado de sus pies? . . . Así que, alma mía, sólo deves mirar el gusto de tu P*adre* para librarte de males tan orrendos. Está como él quisiere tenerte, con gusto como veas que a El sólo amas i deseas. I sus dones estímalos

como dádivas de tu q*ueri*do P*adre* de cuia mano todo se a de resevir con amor i agradesim*iento* como su lus así sus tinieblas [Ps 139:12].

18. En medio de grandes tribulasiones que estava padesiendo entendió esto: que aplicara la considerasión a umillarse en todas las cosa*s* i en particular en todas las palabras del ofisio divino i empesando del P*adre* N*uestro* entendió así.

19. See the discussion of Anthony Cascardi's work, chapter 2, pp. 23–24, above.

20. [C]omo una piedra pres*iosí*sima de tan estraña hermosura que enserraba en sí toda la hermosura de las demás virtudes i así está compuesta de barios i agrasiados colores sin confundirse los unos con los otros ni estorbar su hermosura.

21. Aunque hasta aquí escribió algo de lo que N*uestro* Señor le dio a entender aserca del propio conosim*iento*, le paresía como uno que tien*e* un dolor agudo que travaja en querer esplicarlo, i al cabo de haver dicho mucho se queda con su dolor tan entero como al prinsipio, o como el que corriendo todo el día en sircuito al fin alla que no a andado nada de su camino.

22. Qué es el hombre, o quién es el h*ombre* sino ignoransia i engaño?

23. Para qué es nes*esario* alma mía quere(s)*r* cosas maiores que ni humillasión i pobresa?

24. [D]onde bebieras de los gosos eternos de aquel río que alegra la ciudad de Dios.

25. [L]os que la mortifican i aflijen. . . . Finesa es no buscar de las criaturas sino las espinas.

26. [A] golpes de tribulasiones queda clavada su *mem[ori]a* para no acordarse de cosa que la alivie ni aliente; antes como quien pende de un clavo que la traspasa; quanto a ella ocurre es dolor. Igual i aun mayor pena alla en su *entendim[ien]to* cuios discursos, penetrándola, la dejan como inmóvil para toda operasión de adonde le pueda venir lus o alivio. La *voluntad* con tal tedio, tibiesa, frialdad i repugnansia; allí es la grita del pueblo i los valdones de sus enemigos. . . . A otros alentaste para que no descaesieran: pero tú ya descaesiste; por tanto vaja de la crus dexa ia esta vida. [Emphasis mine.]

27. [N]ingún hombre cuerdo barrió la casa agena ni limpió la bestidura que avía de arrojar al muladar.

28. Con dejar obscurecer tu hermosura, i magestad: diste lus a mi alma: i quando multiplicaste tu lus en tempestad de penas y asombro de la naturalesa, caresiéndote del refrijerio a tu sed: aparesieron las fuentes de las aguas, en la doctrina i ex*em*plo de tu desamparo, humildad y pobresa.

29. Pues si los miembros de un cuerpo, aunque tengan diversos oficios y figuras entre sí, se aman tanto por ser todos animados con una misma ánima racional, ¿cuánto mayor razón será que se amen los fieles entre sí, pues todos son animados con este Espíritu divino, que cuanto es más noble, tanto es más poderoso para causar unidad en las cosas donde está?

30. Veíale en las manos un dardo de oro largo, y al fin del hierro me parecía tener un poco de fuego. Este me parecía meter por el corazón algunas veces, y que me llegaba a las entrañas. Al sacarle, me parecía las llevaba consigo, y me dejaba toda abrasada en amor grande de Dios (Teresa de Jesús 1970, chap. 29, 177).

31. Quiero que mi alma, mi cuerpo i corasón, mis fuerzas, mi salud, y tiempo,

todas las operasiones de mis sentidos i potensias, se gasten, se ardan i se consuman en el fuego del divino amor, en am(m)ar i padeser. I en este gloriosísimo sepulcro quiero quedar para sienpre.

32. Ben amor vivífico. Cría, conserva i guarda para ti los frutos del corasón i alma. Ben amoroso bien, suave, dulse, apasible.

33. For a discussion of the convent library, see chapter 4, p. 87, and chapter 4, n. 17, above.

WORKS CITED

Archival Sources

Actas de elecciones de abadesas y de peticiones para las tomas de hábito y profesiones del Real Convento. Legajo especial. Colonial Archive. Convento de Santa Clara, Tunja. Quoted in María Antonia del Niño Dios, *Flor de santidad* (Tunja: Contraloría General de Boyacá, Academia Boyacense de Historia, 1993), 112.

Archivo Histórico de Tunja. Vols. 126–75 (1691–1741). Archivo Regional de Boyacá, Tunja.

Audiencia de Santa Fe. Archivo General de Indias. Quoted in Ulises Rojas, *Corregidores y justicias mayores de Tunja y su provincia desde la fundación de la ciudad hasta 1816* (Tunja: Academia Boyacense de Historia, 1962), 408, 457.

"Capellanías de los Rojas." 1696. Archivo Colonial de la Parroquia Mayor de Santiago de Tunja. Quoted in María Antonia del Niño Dios, *Flor de santidad* (Tunja: Contraloría General de Boyacá, Academia Boyacense de Historia, 1993), 73.

Breviarivm Romanvm. [1682?] Antwerp: n.p. Used by Madre Castillo. MS 75. Manuscritos. Biblioteca Luis Angel Arango, Bogotá.

Cartas PP Generales. Archivo de la Provincia de Toledo [Madrid]. Rome, February 7, 1699 (132:67). Quoted in Juan Manuel Pacheco, *Los jesuitas en Colombia,* vol. 3 (Bogotá: Oficina de Publicaciones Javeriana, 1989), 3:392.

Conventos. Colonial Collection. Vols. 14, 19, 40, 66, 68. Archivo Histórico Nacional de Bogotá.

Cuaderno de cuentas. Archivo Colonial. Convento Real de Santa Clara, Tunja. Quoted in María Antonia del Niño Dios, *Flor de santidad* (Tunja: Contraloría General de Boyacá, Academia Boyacense de Historia, 1993), 250, n. 1.

Devocionario. In the possession of Madre Castillo. MS 76. Manuscritos. Biblioteca Luis Angel Arango, Bogotá. Only portions of this *Devocionario* were copied from other sources in Madre Castillo's handwriting.

Elecciones de abadesas, tomas de hábito y otros documentos importantes, desde el año de 1584 hasta el de 1687 . . . Legajo 1. Archivo Colonial. Convento Real de Santa Clara, Tunja.

Legajo especial, elecciones de abadesas, profesiones y tomas de hábito, desde el año de 1690, hasta el de mil setecientos cuarenta y dos (1742). Archivo Colonial. Convento Real de Santa Clara, Tunja. Quoted in María Antonia del Niño Dios, *Flor de santidad* (Tunja: Contraloría General de Boyacá, Academia Boyacense de Historia, 1993).

Libro de capítulo y de las rentas quel monasterio de S[eñor]a Sancta Clara la R[ea]l tiene y posesiones y scripturas. [Title on spine: *Rentas y profesiones y hábitos años 1584 a 1884.*] Archivo Colonial. Convento Real de Santa Clara, Tunja.

Libro de cuentas de las abadesas Francisca de la Trinidad (1695–98) y Catalina de San Bernardo (1698–1704). Archivo Colonial. Convento Real de Santa Clara, Tunja. Quoted in María Antonia del Niño Dios, *Flor de santidad* (Tunja: Contraloría General de Boyacá, Academia Boyacense de Historia, 1993), 73.

Libro de cuentas de la abadesa Josefa Gertrudis de San Andrés (1741–44). Archivo Colonial. Convento Real de Santa Clara, Tunja. Quoted in María Antonia del Niño Dios, *Flor de santidad* (Tunja: Contraloría General de Boyacá, Academia Boyacense de Historia, 1993), 470.

Libro de visita del convento de monjas de Sancta Clara la Real de la ciudad de Tunja y donde se asientan los bienes y cosas de sacristía e yglesia del que comiença desde . . . junio de mil y seis y veinte años. [Title on spine: *Visitas canónicas años 1620 a 1822.*] Archivo Colonial. Convento Real de Santa Clara. Tunja.

Lobo Guerrero, Bartolomé. 1606. *Constituciones synodales, celebradas en la ciudad de Sancta Fe del Nuevo Reyno de Granada por el señor doctor don Bartolomé Lobo Guerrero, arçobispo del dicho nuevo Reyno, acabadas de promulgar a dos de septiembre de mil y seis cientos y seis años.* MS. Biblioteca, Colegio de San Bartolomé, Bogotá.

Márquez, Bernardo. 1709. "Interrogatorio de preguntas a cuyo tenor se han de examinar los testigos que declararen en la Información de la Madre Francisca María del Niño Jesús." Archivo Histórico Nacional de Bogotá. Conventos. Vol. 66, 25–30.

Notaría 1. Vols. 176–83 (1718–1740). Archivo Regional de Boyacá, Tunja.

Notaría 2. Vols. 169–84 (1719–41). Archivo Regional de Boyacá, Tunja.

SPANISH AND SPANISH AMERICAN RELIGIOUS WOMEN WRITERS

Agreda, María de Jesús de. 1670. *Mystica ciudad de Dios. . . . Historia divina, y vida de la Virgen Madre de Dios.* 3 vols. Madrid: Bernardo de Villa-Diego.

———. 1681. *Mystica ciudad de Dios.* 3 vols. Lisbon: Emprenta de Antonio Craesbeeck de Mello.

———. 1970. *Mística ciudad de Dios: Vida de la Virgen María.* Madrid: Pareso.

———. 1978. *The Mystical City of God: The Popular Abridgement.* Trans. Fiscar Marison and George John Blatter. Rockford, Ill.: TAN Books and Publishers.

———. 1994. Face of the Earth and Map of the Spheres, Report to Father Manero, and The Crucible of Trials. In Clark Colahan, *The Visions of Sor María de Agreda: Writing, Knowledge and Power.* Tucson and London: University of Arizona Press.

Ana de San Bartolomé. 1981–85. *Obras completas de la Beata Ana de San Bartolomé.* Ed. Julián Urkiza. 2 vols. Rome: Edizioni Teresianum.

Antonia Lucía del Espíritu Santo. 1793. Report of a prophetic vision. In *Relación del origen y fundación del monasterio del Señor San Joaquín de Religiosas Nazarenas.* . . . Compiladora Sor Josefa de la Providencia. Lima: Imprenta Real de los Niños Expósitos.

Castillo, Francisca Josefa de la Concepción de. [1694] 1942. Record of profession. *Repertorio boyacense* 15, no. 127: 771.

———. [1713–24?] *Su vida.* MS 72. Manuscritos. Biblioteca Luis Angel Arango, Bogotá.

———. [1690–1728?] *Afectos espirituales.* MS 71. Manuscritos. Biblioteca Luis Angel Arango, Bogotá.

———. [1694?–1728] *Cuaderno de Enciso.* MS 73. Manuscritos. Biblioteca Luis Angel Arango, Bogotá.

———. 1718, 1732. *Cuaderno de cuentas del Real Convento de Santa Clara.* MS 74. Manuscritos. Biblioteca Luis Angel Arango, Bogotá.

———. 1817. *Vida de la venerable Madre Francisca Josefa de la Concepción . . . escrita por ella misma.* Philadelphia: T. H. Palmer.

———. 1843. *Sentimientos espirituales de la venerable Madre Francisca Josefa de la Concepción de Castillo.* Santafé de Bogotá: Bruno Espinosa de los Monteros.

———. 1942. *Afectos espirituales.* Bogotá: Editorial A.B.C.

———. 1968. *Obras completas de la Madre Francisca Josefa de la Concepción de Castillo.* 2 vols. Ed. Darío Achury Valenzuela. Bogotá: Banco de la República.

———. 1985. *Madre Castillo's Afectos Espirituales:* Translation and Commentary by Kathleen Jeanette Jarvis. Master's thesis, University of Texas at Austin.

———. 1994. Untitled facsimile reproduction of a twelve-page devotional notebook. Santa Fe de Bogotá: Colcultura.

Constanza de Castilla. [1454–74?] Collection of prayers, devotional treatises, and liturgical offices. MS 7495. Biblioteca Nacional, Madrid.

Isabel de Jesús, Venerable Madre. 1675. *Vida de la Venerable Madre Isabel de Jesús, recoleta augustina en el convento de San Juan Bautista de la villa de Arenas. Dictada por ella misma y añadido lo que faltó de su dichosa muerte.* Madrid: Viuda de Francisco Nieto. Excerpts published in Arenal and Schlau 1989b. See Other Works Cited, below.

Isabel de la Madre de Dios. 1989. *Manifestaciones.* In Eugenio Ayape Moriones, *Historia de dos monjas místicas del siglo XVII* (Madrid: Ediciones Avgvstinvs).

Josefa de la Providencia, Sor, comp. 1793. *Relación del origen y fundación del monasterio del señor San Joaquín de Religiosas Nazarenas . . . contenida en algunos apuntes de la vida y virtudes de la venerable Madre Antonia Lucía del Espíritu Santo. . . .* Lima: Imprenta Real de los Niños Expósitos. Excerpts published in Arenal and Schlau 1989b. See Other Works Cited, below.

Juana de la Cruz, Madre. 1990. *El libro del conorte.* Escorial MS J-II-18 and Archivio Segreto Vaticano, Congregazione Riti, MS 3074, Scripta Proc. ord. Selections published in Ronald Surtz, *The Guitar of God: Gender, Power, and Authority in the Visionary World of Mother Juana de la Cruz (1481–1534)* (Philadelphia: University of Pennsylvania Press).

Juana Inés de la Cruz, Sor. 1957. *Obras completas.* 4 vols. Ed. Alfonso Méndez Plancarte (1–3) and Alberto G. Salcedo (4). Mexico City: Fondo de Cultura Económica.

———. 1988. *A Sor Juana Anthology.* Trans. Alan S. Trueblood. Cambridge, Mass., and London: Harvard University Press.

————. 1994. *La respuesta/The Answer.* Including a selection of poems. Critical edition and translation by Electa Arenal and Amanda Powell. New York: Feminist Press at the City University of New York.

López de Córdoba, Leonor. 1883. *Relación que deja escrita para sus descendientes Leonor de Córdoba.* Vol. 81 of CODIN. Madrid: Miguel Ginesta.

————. 1984. Translation of the *Relación* in To Restore Honor and Fortune: The Autobiography of Leonor López de Córdoba, by Amy Katz Kaminsky and Elaine Dorough Johnson. In *The Female Autograph,* ed. Domna C. Stanton (New York: New York Literary Forum).

Lorravaquio Muñoz, Madre María Magdalena. *Libro en que se contiene la vida de la Madre María Magdalena, monja profesa del Convento del Señor San Jerónimo de la ciudad de México.* MS 1244. Nettie Lee Benson Collection, University of Texas at Austin. Excerpts published in Arenal and Schlau 1989b. See Other Works Cited, below.

Magdalena de Jesús. 1722. *Ordenaciones y reglas para el Convento de Nuestra Madre Santa Clara de la ciudad de Pamplona.* Madrid: Francisco del Hierro.

Mancanedo y Maldonado, Mariana de San Joseph, Madre. 1645. *Vida de la venerable M[adre] Mariana de S[an] Joseph, fundadora de la Recolección de las Monjas Augustinas, priora de Real Conuento de la Encarnacion.* Madrid: Imprenta Real.

Marcela de San Félix. 1988. *Literatura conventual femenina: Sor Marcela de San Félix, hija de Lope de Vega. Obra completa.* Ed. Electa Arenal and Georgina Sabat de Rivers. Barcelona: Producciones y promociones universitarias.

María Anna Agueda de San Ignacio. 1758. *Marabillas del divino amor, selladas con el sello de la verdad. . . .* Mexico City: Imprenta de la Bibliotheca Mexicana. Excerpts published in Arenal and Schlau 1989b. See Other Works Cited, below.

María de Jesús, Sor. 1947. Escritos de la hermana María de Jesús. In *Historia del Monasterio de Carmelitas Descalzas de San José de Bogotá,* by Germán María del Perpetuo Socorro and Luis Martínez Delgado. Bogotá: Editorial Cromos.

María de la Antigua. [1678?] *Desengaño de religiosos y de almas que tratan de virtud.* Also published as *Vida ejemplar, admirables virtudes y muerte prodigiosa de . . . María de la Antigua.* Madrid: Sebastián de San Agustín, 1677.

María de San José. 1978. *Instrucción de novicias.* Ed. Juan Luis Astigárraga. Rome: Instituto Histórico Teresiano.

————. 1979. *Escritos espirituales.* Ed. Simeón de la Sagrada Familia. Rome: Postulación General.

María de San José, Madre. 1993. *Word from New Spain: The Spiritual Autobiography of Madre María de San José (1656–1719).* Ed. Kathleen A. Myers. Liverpool: Liverpool University Press.

————. Forthcoming. *A Wild Country out in the Garden.* Ed. Kathleen A. Myers. Trans. Amanda Powell. Bloomington: Indiana University Press.

María de Santo Domingo. 1948. *«Libro de la oración» de Sor María de Santo Domingo.* Ed. José Manuel Blecua. Madrid: Hauser y Menet.

————. 1990. *The Book of Prayer of Sor María de Santo Domingo: A Study and Translation.* Ed. Mary E. Giles. Albany: State University of New York Press.

María Manuela de Santa Ana. [1700s]. *Vida* and *Esquelas originales de correspondencia espiritual y poesías místicas.* Archive of the Convento de Santa Rosa, Lima, Peru.

María Marcela, Madre. 1844. *Vida de la Madre María Marcela, religiosa capuchina del Convento de Querétaro.* Biblioteca Nacional, México. Excerpts published in Arenal and Schlau 1989b. See Other Works Cited, below.

Mariana de la Encarnación. 1823. *Relación de la fundación del convento antiguo de Santa Teresa (1571–1657).* MS G 79. Perry-Castañeda Library, University of Texas, Austin. Excerpts published in Arenal and Schlau 1989b. See Other Works Cited, below.

Mariana de San Joseph, Madre. 1627. *Ejercicios espirituales y repartimiento de todas las horas.* Madrid, n.p.

———. 1634. *Devocionario de oraciones y exercicios para almas devotas.* Madrid, n.p.

———. Forthcoming. *Obras completas.* Ed. Teodoro Calvo de la Madrid. Madrid: Colección de Espirituales Españoles de la Fundación Universitaria Española.

Nava i Saavedra, Madre Jerónima del Espíritu Santo. 1994. *Autobiografía de una monja venerable: Jerónima Nava y Saavedra (1669–1727).* Ed. Angela Inés Robledo. Cali: Universidad del Valle (Colombia).

Padilla, Elvira de. 1947. Constitutions for the Discalced Carmelite convent in Santa Fe, Nuevo Reino de Granada. Published in *Historia del Monasterio de Carmelitas Descalzas de San José de Bogotá y noticias breves de las Hijas del Carmelo en Bogotá,* by Germán María del Perpetuo Socorro and Luis Martínez Delgado. Bogotá: Editorial Cromos.

Petronila de San José. *Breve relación de la vida y virtudes de nuestra beata Madre Cecilia del Nacimiento Religiosa Descalza Carmelita en el convento de las de Valladolid.* MS 95. Convento de la Concepción (Discalced Carmelite), Valladolid (Spain). Cited in Arenal and Schlau 1989b. See Other Works Cited, below.

Pinelo, Valentina. 1601. *Libro de alabanzas y excelencias de la gloriosa Santa Anna, compuesto por Doña Valentina Pinelo, monja profesa en el Monasterio de San Leandro de Sevilla, de la Orden de San Agustín.* Seville: Clemente Hidalgo.

Sebastiana de las Vírgenes (1671–1737). *Vida de la madre . . . monja concepcionista en el monasterio de S. José de Gracia de México: Sus memorias y notas de su confesor el S[eñor] D[octor] D[on] Bartolomé de Ita.* MS ACSJ. Catedral Metropolitana, Mexico City.

Sobrino Morillas, Cecilia del Nacimiento (1570–1646). *De la Madre María de San Alberto, mi hermana.* MS 93. Convento de la Concepción, Valladolid (Spain). Excerpts published in Arenal and Schlau 1989b. See Other Works Cited, below.

———. 1971. *Obras completas.* Ed. José M. Cerón. Madrid: Espiritualidad.

Sobrino Morillas, Sor María de San Alberto. *Favores recibidos de Nuestro Señor.* MS 88. *Fiestecica del Nacimiento.* MS 100. *Todo lo que está aquí es poesía de Nuestra Madre Santa Teresa hecha y escrita por la Madre María de San Alberto.* MS 94. Convento de la Concepción (Discalced Carmelite), Valladolid (Spain). Excerpts published in Arenal and Schlau 1989b. See Other Works Cited, below.

Suárez, Sor Úrsula. 1984. *Relación autobiográfica.* Ed. Mario Ferreccio Podestá. Santiago: Academia Chilena de la Historia (Chile).

Teodora de San Agustín, Madre (1700s). Letters. Archivo Franciscano, Mexico City. Excerpts published in Arenal and Schlau 1989b. See Other Works Cited, below.

Teresa de Cartagena, Sor. 1967. *Arboleda de los enfermos: Admiraçión operum Dey.* Ed. Lewis Joseph Hutton. *Boletín de la Real Academia Española,* supp. 16. Madrid: Real Academia Española.

Teresa de Jesús, Santa. 1915. *Obras de Santa Teresa de Jesús.* 9 vols. Ed. P[adre] Silverio de Santa Teresa. Burgos: Tipografía El Monte Carmelo (Spain).

———. 1949. *The Complete Works of Saint Teresa of Jesus.* 3 vols. Trans. and ed. E. Allison Peers from the critical edition of P[adre] Silverio de Santa Teresa. New York: Sheed and Ward.

———. 1970. *Obras completas.* Ed. Luis Santullano. Madrid: Aguilar.

Teresa of Avila, Saint. See Teresa de Jesús, Santa.

Vela y Cueto, Doña María. 1960. *The Third Mystic of Avila: The Self-Revelation of María Vela, a Sixteenth Century Spanish Nun.* Trans. Frances Parkinson Keyes. New York: Farrar, Straus and Cudahy.

———. 1961. *Autobiografia y Libro de las mercedes.* Edited with an introduction by Olegario González Hernández. Barcelona: Juan Flors.

OTHER WORKS CITED

Abelard and Heloise. 1977. *The Story of His Misfortunes and The Personal Letters.* Trans. Betty Radice. London: Folio Society.

Achury Valenzuela, Darío. 1962. *Análisis crítico de los afectos espirituales de Sor Francisca Josefa de la Concepción de Castillo.* Bogotá: Ministerio de Educación Nacional.

———. 1968. Introducción. *Obras completas de la Madre Francisca Josefa de la Concepción de Castillo.* Vol. 1. Bogotá: Banco de la República.

———. 1982. Un manuscrito de la madre Castillo: El llamado Cuaderno de Enciso. *Boletín cultural y bibliográfico* 19, no. 1: 47–86.

Ancelet-Hustache, Jeanne. 1929. *Les Clarisses.* Abbeville, Somme: F. Paillart.

Anderson-Imbert, Enrique. 1969. *Spanish-American Literature: A History.* Trans. John V. Falconieri. Detroit: Wayne State University Press.

Andrade, Alonso de. 1651. *Vida del venerable padre Bernardino Realino, de la Compañía de Jesús.* Madrid: María de Quiñones.

Antoni, Claudio G. 1979. A Comparative Examination of Style in the Works of Madre Castillo. Ph.D. diss., City University of New York.

Anunciación, El Rmo. Padre Fr. Juan de la. 1698. *La inocencia vindicada: Respuesta a un papel anonymo contra la* Vida interior *del ilustrissimo señor Don Juan de Palafox y Mendoza.* Madrid: Manuel Ruiz Murga.

Arbiol y Diez, Antonio. 1714. *La familia regulada.* Barcelona: Joseph Texidó.

———. 1716. *Sor Jacinta de Atondo, religiosa de nuestra seráfica madre Santa Clara.* N.p.: Herederos de Manuel Román.

———. 1724. *Desengaños mysticos a las almas detenidas, o engañadas en el camino de la perfección.* 5th–7th eds. Madrid: Thomas Rodríguez.

Arenal, Electa. 1983. The Convent as Catalyst for Autonomy: Two Hispanic Nuns of the Seventeenth Century. In *Women in Hispanic Literature: Icons and Fallen Idols*, ed. Beth Miller. Berkeley and Los Angeles: University of California Press.

Arenal, Electa, and Stacey Schlau. 1989a. "Leyendo yo y escribiendo ella": The Convent as Intellectual Community. *Journal of Hispanic Philology* 13, no. 3 (Spring): 214–29.

———. 1989b. *Untold Sisters: Hispanic Nuns in Their Works*. Translations by Amanda Powell. Albuquerque: University of New Mexico Press.

———. 1990. Stratagems of the Strong, Stratagems of the Weak: Autobiographical Prose of the Seventeenth-Century Hispanic Convent. *Tulsa Studies in Women's Literature* 9, no. 1 (March): 25–42.

Armacanqui Ticpacti, Elia. 1993. Sor María Manuela de Santa Ana: A Peruvian Window on the World. *Monographic Review/Revista Monográfica* (Odessa, Texas) 9: 125–39.

Avila, Beato Juan de. [1596] 1970. La carne de Cristo, manjar del alma. In *Obras completas*, vol. 2. Madrid: Biblioteca de Autores Cristianos.

Ayape Moriones, Eugenio. 1989. *Historia de dos monjas místicas del siglo XVII*. Madrid: Ediciones Avgvstinvs.

Ayerbe-Chaux, Reinaldo. 1977. Las *Memorias* de doña Leonor López de Córdoba. *Journal of Hispanic Philology* 2: 11–33.

Barthes, Roland. 1975a. The Death of the Author. In *Image, Music, Text*, ed. Stephan Heath. New York: Hill and Wang.

———. 1975b. *Roland Barthes par lui-même*. Paris: Seuil.

Bataillon, Marcel. 1950. *Erasmo y España: Estudios sobre la historia espiritual del siglo xvi*. Trans. Antonio Alatorre. 2 vols. Mexico City: Fondo de Cultura Económica.

Bell, Susan Groag, and Marilyn Yalom, eds. 1990. *Revealing Lives: Autobiography, Biography and Gender*. Albany: State University of New York Press.

Bellini, Giuseppe. 1985. *Historia de la literatura hispanoamericana*. Madrid: Castalia.

Bilinkoff, Jodi. 1989. *The Avila of Saint Teresa: Religious Reform in a Sixteenth-Century City*. Ithaca and London: Cornell University Press.

———. 1993. Confessors, Penitents, and the Construction of Identities in Early Modern Avila. In *Culture and Identity in Early Modern Europe (1500–1800)*, ed. Barbara B. Diefendorf and Carla Hesse. Ann Arbor: University of Michigan Press.

Brodzki, Bella, and Celeste Schenck, eds. 1988. *Life/Lines: Theorizing Women's Autobiography*. Ithaca and London: Cornell University Press.

Browne, George Forrest. 1919. *The Importance of Women in Anglo-Saxon Times*. London: Society for Promoting Christian Knowledge. Quoted in Equality of Souls, Inequality of Sexes: Woman in Medieval Theology, by Eleanor Commo McLaughlin, in *Religion* and *Sexism: Images of Woman in the Jewish and Christian Traditions*, ed. Rosemary Radford Ruether (New York: Simon and Schuster, 1974), 237.

Burns, Kathryn. 1995. Cloistered Mestizas and the Construction of Sixteenth-Century Cuzco. Paper presented at the Conference of the Latin American Studies Association, Washington, D.C., September 28–30.

Butler, Alban. [1756–59] 1985. *Lives of the Saints*. Ed. Michael Walsh. San Francisco: Harper and Row.

Bynum, Carolyn Walker. 1987. *Holy Feast and Holy Fast: The Religious Significance of Food to Medieval Women*. Berkeley: University of California Press.

Calvo de la Riba, Pedro. 1752. *Historia de la singular vida, y admirables virtudes de la venerable Madre Sor María Gertrudis Theresa de Santa Inés*. Madrid: Imprenta de Phelipe Millan.

Camacho Guizado, Eduardo. 1978. *Sobre literatura colombiana e hispanoamericana*. Bogotá: Instituto Colombiano de Cultura.

Carrasquilla, Rafael María. 1935. *Oraciones*. Colombia: Editorial Minerva.

Cascardi, Anthony J. 1992. Afterword. The Subject of Control. In *Culture and Control in Counter-Reformation Spain*, ed. Anne J. Cruz and Mary Elizabeth Perry. Minneapolis and Oxford: University of Minnesota Press.

Castillo y Bolívar, Joseph. 1733. *Ramillete sagrado compuesto de flores, que cultivó en heroicas virtudes la venerable sierva de Dios Feliciana de San Ignacio Mariaca*. Lima: Imprenta de la Calle de Palacio.

Cazelles, Brigitte. 1991. *The Lady as Saint: A Collection of French Hagiographic Romances of the Thirteenth Century*. Philadelphia: University of Pennsylvania Press.

Certeau, Michel de. 1982. *La Fable mystique: XVIe–XVIIe siècle*. Paris: Gallimard.

Cervantes, Fernando. 1994. *The Devil in the New World: The Impact of Diabolism in New Spain*. New Haven and London: Yale University Press.

Chicharro, Dámaso. 1979. Introduction to *Libro de la vida* by Teresa de Jesús. Madrid: Ediciones Cátedra.

Colahan, Clark. 1994. *The Visions of Sor María de Agreda: Writing, Knowledge and Power*. Tucson and London: University of Arizona Press.

Colmenares, Germán. 1970. *La provincia de Tunja en el Nuevo Reino de Granada: Ensayo de historia social, 1539–1800*. Bogotá: Universidad de los Andes.

———. 1982. La economía y la sociedad coloniales, 1550–1800. In *Manual de historia de Colombia*, vol. 1. 2d ed. Bogotá: Procultura.

Coloquio Internacional Sor Juana Inés de la Cruz y el Pensamiento Novohispano (1995: Universidad Autónoma de México). *Memoria del Coloquio Internacional Sor Juana Inés de la Cruz y el Pensamiento Novohispano, 1995*. Toluca, Estado de México: Instituto Mexiquense de Cultura, 1995.

Corominas, Joan. 1954. *Diccionario crítico etimológico de la lengua castellana*. Bern: Editorial Francke.

Covarrubias Horozco, Sebastián de. [1611] 1979. *Tesoro de la lengua castellana o española*. Madrid: Ediciones Turner.

Cuervo, J. R. 1954. *Diccionario de construcción y régimen de la lengua castellana*. Bogotá: Caro y Cuervo.

Daça, Antonio. 1614. *Historia, vida, y milagros, éxtasis y revelaciones de la bienaventurada Virgen Sor Iuana de la Cruz*. Madrid: Luis Sánchez.

De Man, Paul. 1984. *The Rhetoric of Romanticism*. New Haven: Yale University Press.

Deuterocanonical Books of the Bible, The. The Apocrypha. Web Chapel by Steve Woods. World Wide Web. Available from http://web2.airmail.het/webchap/apoc. Access date: March 1996.

De Vances, Marcos. 1699. *Reglas, constituciones, ordenaciones de las religiosas de Santa*

Clara: De la ciudad de Santa Feê de Bogotá: En el Nuebo Reyno de Granada: De las Indias de el Peru. Rome: Lucas Antonio Chracas.

Deyermond, Alan. 1978. *La edad media.* Vol. 1 of *Historia de la literatura española.* 4th ed. Barcelona and Caracas: Editorial Ariel.

————. 1983. Spain's First Women Writers. In *Women in Hispanic Literature: Icons and Fallen Idols,* ed. Beth Miller. Berkeley and Los Angeles: University of California Press.

Donahue, Darcy. 1989. Writing Lives: Nuns and Confessors as Auto/Biographers in Early Modern Spain. *Journal of Hispanic Philology* 13, no. 3 (Spring): 230–39.

Eckenstein, Lina. 1896. *Woman under Monasticism.* Cambridge: Cambridge University Press.

Eich, Jennifer Lee. 1992. The Mystic Tradition and Mexico: Sor María Anna Agueda de San Ignacio. Ph.D. diss., University of California, Los Angeles.

Enkvist, Nils. 1973. *Linguistic Stylistics.* The Hague: Mouton.

Erasmus of Rotterdam, Desiderius. 1993a. *Ecclesiastes Sive de Ratione Concionandi.* In *Desiderius Erasmus Roterodamus: Ausgewählte Werke,* ed. Hajo Holborn and Annemarie Holborn, Munich. Paraphrased in Manfred Hoffman, *Rhetoric and Theology: The Hermeneutic of Erasmus* (Toronto: University of Toronto Press, 1994), 47.

————. 1993b. *Ratio Verae Theologiae.* In *Desiderius Erasmus Roterodamus: Ausgewählte Werke,* ed. Hajo Holborn and Annemarie Holborn, Munich. Quoted in Manfred Hoffman, *Rhetoric and Theology: The Hermeneutic of Erasmus* (Toronto: University of Toronto Press, 1994), 18–22, 35, 38.

Espasa-Calpe. 1920. "Palafox y Mendoza, Juan de." *Enciclopedia Universal Ilustrada Europeo-Americana.* Vol. 41. Madrid: Espasa-Calpe.

Fernández, James D. 1992. *Apology to Apostrophe: Autobiography and the Rhetoric of Self-Representation in Spain.* Durham, N.C.: Duke University Press.

Fleishman, Avrom. 1983. *Figures of Autobiography: The Language of Self-Writing in Victorian and Modern England.* Berkeley and Los Angeles: University of California Press. Quoted in Sidonie Smith, *A Poetics of Women's Autobiography: Marginality and the Fictions of Self-Representation* (Bloomington and Indianapolis: Indiana University Press), 47.

Foucault, Michel. 1977. What is an Author? In *Language, Counter-Memory, Practice: Selected Essays and Interviews.* Trans. Donald F. Bouchad. Ithaca: Cornell University Press.

————. 1978. *The History of Sexuality.* Vol. 1: *An Introduction.* Trans. Robert Hurley. New York: Pantheon Books.

Franco, Jean. 1989. Writers in Spite of Themselves: The Mystical Nuns of Seventeenth-Century Mexico. In *Plotting Women: Gender and Representation in Mexico.* New York: Columbia University Press.

Germán María del Perpetuo Socorro and Luis Martínez Delgado. 1947. *Historia del Monasterio de Carmelitas Descalzas de San José de Bogotá y noticias breves de las Hijas del Carmelo en Bogotá.* Bogotá: Editorial Cromos.

Giles, Mary E. 1990. *The Book of Prayer of Sor María of Santo Domingo: A Study and Translation.* Albany: State University of New York Press.

Glantz, Margo. *Sor Juana Inés de la Cruz: ¿Hagiografía o autobiografía?* Mexico City: Grijalbo, Universidad Nacional Autónoma de México, 1995.

———. *Sor Juana Inés de la Cruz: Saberes y placeres.* Toluca, Estado de México: Instituto Mexiquense de Cultura, 1996.

Godínez, Miguel. 1682. *Práctica de la theología mystica.* Sevilla: Lic D. Juan de Salazar y Bolea.

Goic, Cedomil, ed. 1988. *Historia y crítica de la literatura hispanoamericana.* Vol. 1. Barcelona: Editorial Crítica, Grupo Editorial Grijalbo.

Gómez Gil, Orlando. 1968. *Historia crítica de la literatura hispanoamericana.* New York: Holt, Rinehart and Winston.

Gómez-Moriana, Antonio. 1984. Autobiografía y discurso ritual. *Co-textes* (Montpellier) 8 (December): 81–103.

———. 1988. Narration and Argumentation in Autobiographical Discourse. In *Autobiography in Early Modern Spain,* ed. Nicholas Spadaccini and Jenaro Talens. Minneapolis: Prisma Institute, 1988.

Gómez Restrepo, Antonio. 1953. *Historia de la literatura colombiana.* Vol. 2. 3d ed. Bogotá: Editorial Cosmos.

González, Tirso. 1699. Letter. Archivo de la Provincia de Toledo [Madrid]; Cartas PP. Generales (132: 67). Quoted in Juan Manuel, Pacheco, *Los jesuitas en Colombia,* vol. 3 (Bogotá: Oficina de Publicaciones de la Universidad Javeriana, 1989).

Granada, Luis de. [1570] 1925. *Memorial de la vida cristiana.* Madrid: Hernando. Quoted in Kathleen A. Myers, *Word from New Spain: The Spiritual Autobiography of Madre María de San José (1656–1719)* (Liverpool: Liverpool University Press, 1993).

———. [1556] 1929. *Guía de pecadores.* Ed. Matías Martínez Burgos. Madrid: Ediciones de «La Lectura».

———. 1962. Sermón de las caídas públicas. In *Historia de Sor María de la visitación y sermón de las caídas públicas.* Ed. Juan Flors. Barcelona: Imprenta Clarasó.

Greenspan, Kate. 1991. The Autohagiographical Tradition in Medieval Women's Devotional Writing. *a/b: Auto/Biography Studies* 6, no. 2 (Fall): 157–68.

Groot, José Manuel. [1889] 1953. *Historia eclesiástica y civil de Nueva Granada.* 2d ed. Vols. 1–2. Bogotá: Editorial A.B.C.

Gumbrecht, Hans Ulrich. 1997. Sign Conceptions in European Everyday Culture between Renaissance and Early Nineteenth Century. In *Semiotik: Ein Handbuch zu den zeichentheoretischen Grundlagen vom Natur und Kultur.* Ed. R. Posner, K. Robering and T. A. Sebeok. Walter de Gruyter: Berlin.

Gusdorf, Georges. 1980. Conditions and Limits of Autobiography. In *Autobiography: Essays Theoretical and Critical.* Ed. James Olney. Princeton: Princeton University Press.

Helyot. 1714. *Histoire des ordres monastiques.* Quoted in Lina Eckenstein, *Woman under Monasticism* (Cambridge: Cambridge University Press, 1896), 191.

Herbermann, Charles G. et al. 1908. "Crusade, Bull of the." *The Catholic Encyclopedia.* Vol. 4. New York: Robert Appleton Co.

Hernández Sánchez-Barba, Mario. 1978. *Historia y literatura en Hispano-América, 1492–1820.* Madrid: Fundación Juan March.

Hildegard von Bingen. 1954. *Wisse die Wege: Scivias.* Trans. and ed. Maura Böckeler. Salzburg: Otto Müller Verlag.

Hoffman, Manfred. 1994. *Rhetoric and Theology: The Hermeneutic of Erasmus.* Toronto: University of Toronto Press.

Holloway, Julia Bolton, Constance S. Wright, and Joan Bechtold, eds. 1990. *Equally in God's Image: Women in the Middle Ages.* New York: P. Lang.

Ignatius of Loyola. 1958. *The Spiritual Journal of St. Ignatius of Loyola: February, 1544–45.* Trans. William J. Young. Woodstock, Md.: Woodstock College Press.

———. 1964. *The Spiritual Exercises of St. Ignatius.* Trans. Anthony Mottola. Garden City, N.Y.: Image Books.

———. 1985. *A Pilgrim's Journey: The Autobiography of Ignatius of Loyola.* Trans. Joseph N. Tylenda. Wilmington, Del.: Michael Glazier.

Imirizaldu, Jesús. 1977. *Monjas y beatas embaucadoras.* Madrid: Editor Nacional.

Iñigo Madrigal, Luis, ed. 1982. *Historia de la literatura hispanoamericana.* Vol. 1. Madrid: Cátedra.

Jaramillo, María Mercedes, Angela Inés Robledo, and Flor María Rodríguez-Arenas. 1991. *¿Y LAS MUJERES? Ensayos sobre literatura colombiana.* Medellín: OTRAPARTE, Editorial de la Universidad de Antioquia (Colombia).

Jay, Paul. 1984. *Being in the Text: Self-Presentation from Wordsworth to Barthes.* Ithaca, N.Y.: Cornell University Press.

Jelinek, Estelle C., ed. 1980. *Women's Autobiography: Essays in Criticism.* Bloomington: Indiana University Press.

———. 1986. *The Tradition of Women's Autobiography: From Antiquity to the Present.* Boston: Twayne Publishers.

John of the Cross, Saint. See Juan de la Cruz.

Johnson, Penelope D. 1991. *Equal in Monastic Profession: Religious Women in Medieval France.* Chicago: University of Chicago Press.

Joseph de San Benito. 1746. *Vida interior y cartas, que escribió a diferentes personas Fray Joseph de San Benito, religioso lego en el monasterio de Nuestra Señora de Montserrat del Principado de Cataluña.* Madrid: Antonio Marín.

Juan, Jorge, and Juan de Ulloa. [1749] 1918. *Noticias secretas de América.* Vol. 2. Madrid: Editorial América.

Juan de la Cruz [John of the Cross, Saint]. [1909] 1995. *A Spiritual Canticle of the Soul and the Bridegroom Christ.* Trans. David Lewis. Intro. Benedict Zimmerman. Electronic edition with modernization of English by Harry Plantinga. World Wide Web. Available from http://ccel.wheaton.edu/john-of-the-cross/canticle/canticle.html. Access date: March 1996.

———. 1980. *Obras completas.* Madrid: Editorial de Espiritualidad.

Kaminsky, Amy Katz, and Elaine Dorough Johnson. 1984. To Restore Honor and Fortune: The Autobiography of Leonor López de Córdoba. In *The Female Autograph.* Ed. Domna C. Stanton. New York: New York Literary Forum.

Lavrín, Asunción. 1963. Religious Life of Mexican Women in the XVIII Century. Ph.D. diss., Harvard University.

———. 1972. Values and Meaning of Monastic Life for Nuns of Colonial Mexico. *Catholic Historical Review* 58: 367–87.

———. 1978. *Latin American Women: Historical Perspectives.* Westport, Conn.: Greenwood Press.

———. 1983a. Unlike Sor Juana? The Model Nun in the Religious Literature of Colonial Mexico. *University of Dayton Review* 16, no. 3: 75–92.

———. 1983b. Women and Religion in Spanish America. In *Women and Religion in America,* ed. Rosemary Radford Ruether and Rosemary Skinner Keller. Vol. 2 of *The Colonial and Revolutionary Periods.* San Francisco: Harper and Row.

———. 1986. Female Religious. In *Cities and Society in Colonial Latin America,* ed. Louisa Schell Hoberman and Susan Migden Socolow. Albuquerque: University of New Mexico Press.

León, Luis de. [1583] 1987. *La perfecta casada.* Madrid: Taurus Ediciones.

———. [1587] 1914–38. *De los nombres de Cristo.* Vols. 28, 33, 41. Clásicos castellanos. Ed. Federico de Onís. Madrid: Ediciones «La Lectura».

Macdonell, Diane. 1986. *Theories of Discourse: An Introduction.* Oxford: Basil Blackwell.

María Antonia del Niño Dios, Sor. 1993. *Flor de santidad: La Madre Castillo.* Tunja: Contraloría General de Boyacá, Academia Boyacense de Historia.

Mariscal, George. 1991. *Contradictory Subjects: Quevedo, Cervantes, and Seventeenth-Century Spanish Culture.* Ithaca and London: Cornell University Press.

Marroquín, José Manuel. 1929. *Discursos académicos y otros escritos sobre filología y corrección del lenguaje.* Bogotá: Editorial Santafé.

Mateus Cortes, Gustavo. *Tunja: El arte de los siglos XVI–XVII–XVIII.* Bogotá: Litografía Arco, 1989.

May, Georges. 1979. *L'Autobiographie.* Paris: Presses Universitaires de France.

McLaughlin, Eleanor Commo. 1974. Equality of Souls, Inequality of Sexes: Woman in Medieval Theology. In *Religion and Sexism: Images of Woman in the Jewish and Christian Traditions,* ed. Rosemary Radford Ruether. New York: Simon and Schuster.

Menéndez y Pelayo, Marcelino. [1911] 1948. *Historia de la poesía hispano-americana.* Vol. 1. Santander (Colombia): Aldus.

Merinero, Fr. Juan, ed. 1748. *Constituciones generales para todas las monjas, y religiosas, sujetas a la obediencia de la orden de nuestro Padre S[a]n Francisco. . . . [con] aprobación del Capítulo General, celebrado en Roma a 11 de Junio de 1639.* Madrid: Imprenta de la Causa de la V. Madre María de Jesús de Agreda.

Merrim, Stephanie, ed. 1987. *Narciso desdoblado:* Narcissistic Stratagems in *El divino narciso* and the *Respuesta a Sor Filotea de la Cruz. Bulletin of Hispanic Studies* 64. no. 2 (April): 111–17.

———. 1991. *Feminist Perspectives on Sor Juana Inés de la Cruz.* Detroit: Wayne State University Press.

Montaner y Simón. 1888. *Diccionario enciclopédico hispano-americano de literatura, ciencia y artes.* Barcelona: Montaner y Simón.

Morales Borrero, María Teresa. 1968. *La Madre Castillo: Su espiritualidad y su estilo.* Bogotá: Instituto Caro y Cuervo.

Muriel, Josefina. 1946. *Conventos de monjas en la Nueva España.* Mexico City: Editorial Santiago.

————. 1963. *Las indias caciques de Corpus Christi*. Mexico City: Instituto de Historia, Universidad Autónoma Nacional de México.

————. 1982. *Cultura femenina novohispana*. Mexico City: Universidad Nacional Autónoma de México.

Myers, Kathleen A. 1992. The Addressee Determines the Discourse. *Bulletin of Hispanic Studies* 69, no. 1 (January): 39–47.

————. 1993a. "Miraba las cosas que decía": Convent Writing, Picaresque Tales, and the *Relación autobiográfica* by Ursula Suárez (1666–1749). *Romance Quarterly* 40, no. 3 (Summer): 156–72.

————. 1993b. Introduction to *Word from New Spain: The Spiritual Autobiography of Madre María de San José (1656–1719)*. Liverpool: Liverpool University Press.

New English Bible. 1970. Translated under the supervision of the Joint Committee on the New Translation of the Bible. New York: Cambridge University Press.

Nieto, José C. 1979. *Mystic, Rebel, Saint: A Study of St. John of the Cross*. Geneva: Librairie Droz.

Nussbaum, Felicity. 1989. *The Autobiographical Subject: Gender and Ideology in Eighteenth-Century England*. Baltimore and London: Johns Hopkins University Press.

Obregón, Luis Bernardino de. 1724. *Vida y virtudes del siervo de Dios Bernardino de Obregón*. Madrid: Bernardo Peralta, Imprenta de Música.

Olney, James. 1980. Autobiography and the Humanities. Proposal submitted to the National Endowment for the Humanities, June 1, 1980. Quoted in Sidonie Smith, *A Poetics of Women's Autobiography: Marginality and the Fictions of Self-Representation* (Bloomington and Indianapolis: Indiana University Press, 1987), 3.

Ortega Costa, Milagros. 1989. Spanish Women in the Reformation. In *Women in Reformation and Counter-Reformation Europe: Public and Private Worlds*, ed. Sherrin Marshall. Bloomington and Indianapolis: Indiana University Press.

Ossorio de las Peñas, Antonio. 1649. *Sermones de las maravillas de Dios en sus santos*. Madrid: Domingo García y Morrás.

Osuna, Francisco de. [1527] 1981. *The Third Spiritual Alphabet*. Trans. Mary E. Giles. New York: Paulist Press.

Oviedo, Juan Antonio de. 1752. *Vida admirable, apostólicos ministerios y heroicas virtudes del venerable Padre Joseph Vidal, professo de la Compañía de Jesús en la provincia de Nueva España*. Mexico City: Imprenta del Real y Más Antiguo Colegio de San Ildefonso.

Pacheco, Juan Manuel. 1971. *La evangelización del Nuevo Reino: Siglo XVI*. Part 1. Vol. 13 of *Historia extensa de Colombia*. Bogotá: Academia Colombiana de Historia, Ediciones Lerner.

————. 1989. *Los jesuitas en Colombia*. Vol. 3. Bogotá: Oficina de Publicaciones de la Universidad Javeriana.

Palafox y Mendoza, Juan de. 1772. *Vida interior, o confesiones del ilustrísimo, excelentísimo, y v[enerable] siervo de Dios don Juan de Palafox y Mendoza, . . .* Madrid: Imprenta de Josef Doblado.

Paniagua Pérez, Jesús. 1993. El monacato femenino en la audiencia de Santa Fe (siglos XVI y XVII). In *I [primer] congreso internacional del monacato femenino en*

España, Portugal y América, 1492–1992. Vol. 1. Ed. Jesús Paniagua Pérez and María Isabel Viforcos Marinas. León: Universidad de León.

Paz, Octavio. 1982. *Sor Juana Inés de la Cruz, o, Las trampas de la fe*. Mexico City: Fondo de Cultura Económica.

Petroff, Elizabeth Alvilda, ed. 1986. *Medieval Women's Visionary Literature*. New York and Oxford: Oxford University Press.

Pino Alvarez, Gladys Marina. 1989. Mecanismos para la acumulación de riqueza en los conventos de Santa Clara y San Agustín, Tunja, siglo XVIII. Master's thesis, Universidad Pedagógica y Tecnológica de Colombia, Tunja.

Poot, Sara, and Elena Urrutia, eds. 1993. *Y diversa de mí misma entre vuestras plumas ando*. Mexico City: Colegio de México.

Pope, Randolph. 1974. *La autobiografía española hasta Torres Villarroel*. Bern: Herbert Lang.

Puente, Luis de la. [1671] 1958. *Obras escogidas*. Vol. III. Biblioteca de Autores Españoles. Ed. Camilo María Abad. Madrid: Ediciones Atlás.

Ramos Medina, Manuel. 1990. *Imagen de santidad en un mundo profano: Historia de una fundación*. Mexico City: Universidad Iberoamericana.

Real Academia Española. 1972. *Diccionario histórico de la lengua española*. Madrid: Real Academia Española.

Restrepo Saenz, José María, and Raimundo Rivas. 1928. *Genealogías de Santa Fe de Bogotá*. Vol. 1. Bogotá: Librería Colombiana.

Reyna, María del Carmen. 1990. *El convento de San Jerónimo: Vida conventual y finanzas*. Mexico City: Instituto Nacional de Antropología e Historia.

Riffaterre, Michael. 1971. *Essais de stylistique*. Paris: Flammarion.

Rivadeneira, Pedro de. 1601. *Flos sanctorum, o Libro de las vidas de los santos*. Vol. 2. Madrid: Luis Sánchez.

Robertson, Elizabeth. 1990. An Anchorhold of Her Own: Female Anchoritic Literature in Thirteenth-Century England. In *Equally in God's Image: Women in the Middle Ages*, ed. Julia Bolton Holloway, Constance S. Wright, and Joan Bechtold. New York: Peter Lang.

Robledo, Angela Inés. 1989. Disociaciones múltiples y juegos narcisistas en *Afectos* y *Su vida* de la Madre Castillo. *Correo de los Andes* (Bogotá) 57 (May): 34–50.

———. 1991. La pluralidad discursiva como mecanismo de afirmación personal en *Su vida* de Francisca Josefa de Castillo. In *¿Y LAS MUJERES? Ensayos sobre literatura colombiana*, ed. María Mercedes Jaramillo, Angela Inés Robledo, and Flor María Rodríguez-Arenas. Medellín: OTRAPARTE, Editorial de la Universidad de Antioquia (Colombia).

Rojas, Ulises. 1962. *Corregidores y justicias mayores de Tunja y su provincia desde la fundación de la ciudad hasta 1816*. Tunja: Academia Boyacense de Historia.

Ross, Kathleen Ann. 1985. Carlos de Sigüenza y Góngora's "Parayso Occidental": Baroque Narrative in a Colonial Convent. Ph.D. diss., Yale University.

Rueda Méndez, David. 1989. *Introducción a la Historia de la esclavitud negra en la provincia de Tunja—Siglo XVIII*. Nuevas Lecturas de Historia. Ser. 6. Tunja: Publicaciones del Magister en Historia, Universidad Pedagógica y Tecnológica de Colombia.

Ruether, Rosemary Radford. 1974. Misogynism and Virginal Feminism in the Fathers of the Church. In *Religion* and *Sexism: Images of Woman in the Jewish and Christian Tradition*. New York: Simon and Schuster.

Sabat de Rivers, Georgina, guest editor. 1995a. *Sor Juana Inés de la Cruz and Her Worlds*. Special issue of *Colonial Latin American Review* 4, no. 2.

———, ed. 1995b. *Sor Juana Inés de la Cruz and Her Worlds*. New York: City College of New York, Department of Romance Languages.

Sainz de Medrano, Luis. 1976. *Historia de la literatura hispanoamericana*. Madrid: Guadiana.

Scott, Nina M. 1994. "La gran turba de las que merecieron nombres": Sor Juana's Foremothers in "La Respuesta a Sor Filotea." In *Coded Encounters: Writing, Gender and Ethnicity in Colonial Latin America*, ed. Francisco Javier Cevallos-Candau, Jeffrey A. Cole, Nina M. Scott, and Nicomedes Suárez-Araúz. Amherst: University of Massachusetts Press.

Serrano y Sanz, Manuel. [1903] 1975. *Apuntes para una biblioteca de escritoras españolas*. Madrid: Atlas.

———. 1905. *Memorias y autobiografías*. Madrid: Librería Editorial de Bailly/Bailliere e Hijos.

Simmons, Charles E. P. 1966. Palafox and His Critics: Reappraising a Controversy. *Hispanic American Historical Review* 46: 394–406.

Smith, Paul. 1988. *Discerning the Subject*. Minneapolis: University of Minnesota Press.

Smith, Sidonie. 1987. *A Poetics of Women's Autobiography: Marginality and the Fictions of Self-Representation*. Bloomington and Indianapolis: Indiana University Press.

Soeiro, Susan A. 1974. A Baroque Nunnery: The Economic and Social Role of a Colonial Convent: Santa Clara do Destêrro, Salvador, Bahia, 1677–1800. Ph.D. diss., New York University.

Solano, Diego. *Vida illustre en esclarezidos exemplos de virtud de la modestíssima, penitente virgen doña Antonia de Cabañas*. MS 3. Libros Raros y Curiosos. Biblioteca Nacional de Bogotá.

Sprinker, Michael. 1980. Fictions of the Self: The End of Autobiography. In *Autobiography: Essays Theoretical and Critical*, ed. James Olney. Princeton: Princeton University Press.

Stanton, Domna C., ed. 1984. *The Female Autograph*. New York: New York Literary Forum.

Surtz, Ronald E. 1990. *The Guitar of God: Gender, Power, and Authority in the Visionary World of Mother Juana de la Cruz (1481–1534)*. Philadelphia: University of Pennsylvania Press.

———. 1995. *Writing Women in Late Medieval and Early Modern Spain: The Mothers of Saint Teresa of Avila*. Philadelphia: University of Pennsylvania Press.

Tambling, Jeremy. 1990. *Confession: Sexuality, Sin, the Subject*. Manchester and New York: Manchester University Press.

Valdés, Joseph Eugenio. 1765. *Vida admirable y penitente de la V. M. Sor Sebastiana Josepha de la SS. Trinidad*. Mexico City. Quoted in *The Devil in the New World* by Fernando Cervantes (New Haven and London: Yale University Press, 1994), 112.

Vañes, Carlos Alonso. 1990. *Doña Ana de Austria, abadesa del Real Monasterio de las Huelgas.* Madrid: Patrimonio Nacional.

Vázquez, Fray Dionisio. 1943. *Sermones.* Ed. P. Félix G. Olmedo. Madrid: Espasa-Calpe.

Velasco, Sherry M. 1996. *Demons, Nausea and Resistance in the Autobiography of Isabel de Jesús (1611–1682).* Albuquerque: University of New Mexico Press.

Vélez de Piedrahita, Rocío. 1988. La Madre Castillo. In *Manual de literatura colombiana.* Vol. 1. Bogotá: Procultura/Planeta.

Vergara y Vergara, José María. [1867] 1958. *Historia de la literatura en Nueva Granada desde la conquista hasta la independencia, 1538–1820.* Bogotá: Biblioteca de la Presidencia.

Viller, Marcel, F. Cavallera, J. de Guibert et al., eds. 1937. *Dictionnaire de spiritualité ascétique et mystique, dotrine et histoire.* Paris: Gabriel Beauchesne et ses fils.

Vilnet, Jean. *Bible et mystique chez Saint Jean de la Croix.* Brussels: Desclée de Brouwer, 1949. Quoted in José C. Nieto, *Mystic, Rebel, Saint: A Study of St. John of the Cross* (Geneva: Librairie Droz, 1979), 42.

Vives, Juan Luis. [1524] 1944. *Instrucción de la mujer cristiana.* 3d ed. Buenos Aires and Mexico City: Espasa-Calpe Argentina.

Warner, Marina. 1976. *Alone of All Her Sex: The Myth and Cult of the Virgin Mary.* New York: Alfred A. Knopf.

Weber, Alison. 1990. *Teresa of Avila and the Rhetoric of Femininity.* Princeton: Princeton University Press.

———. 1992. Saint Teresa, Demonologist. In *Culture and Control in Counter-Reformation Spain,* ed. Anne J. Cruz and Mary Elizabeth Perry. Minneapolis and Oxford: University of Minnesota Press.

Weinstein, Donald, and Rudolph M. Bell. 1982. *Saints and Society: The Two Worlds of Western Christendom, 1000–1700.* Chicago and London: University of Chicago Press.

Ximenes Samaniego, Joseph. 1670. Prologue to *Mystica ciudad de Dios,* by María de Jesús de Agreda. Vol. 3. Madrid: Bernardo de Villa-Diego.

———. 1688. *Relación de la vida de la Venerable Madre Sor María de Jesús.* In *Mystica ciudad de Dios,* by María de Jesús de Agreda. N.p.: n.p.

Zumthor, Paul. 1990. *Oral Poetry: An Introduction.* Trans. Kathryn Murphy-Judy. Minneapolis: University of Minnesota Press.

INDEX

abbess, office of, 90–92
abbesses, as managers, 98–99, 119
abbesses of the Convento Real de Santa
  Clara, Tunja
  Antonia de la Trinidad, 112, 142–43,
    145, 147
  Catalina de San Bernardo, 112, 142,
    145, 146
  Francisca de la Trinidad, 117, 142
  Francisca de San Joseph, 142, 145–46
  Isabel de Jesús María, 143, 144, 145,
    158
  Lugarda de Santa María, 118
  María de San Gabriel, 145
  Paula de la Trinidad, 105, 142–43
  Paula de San Ignacio, 98, 105, 142
Abelard, Peter, 75–76
Achury Valenzuela, Darío, 7–8, 115, 167,
    168, 189, 199, 243n. 2, 243n. 4,
    247n. 48, 249n. 2
  editor of MC's works, 9–10, 183,
    224n. 10
Adam, 28, 187
afecto, in language of mysticism, 172–73
Afectos espirituales (Castillo), 6, 105, 167–
    98
  editing of, in CE, 203–5, 249n. 3
  as instructional materials, 182
  manuscript of, 243n. 3
  mystical autobiography, 168
  praised as literature, 167
  publication of, 7, 105, 168
  title of, 172–73
  writing of, 43, 105, 167–68
agency
  in autobiographical writing, 3–4, 26,
    27–29

effect of loss of, on women, 25–26
  in nuns' writings, 193
  and subjecthood, 20–24; in SV, 163–
    66
  of Virgin Mary, in AE, 194
Agreda, María de Jesús de (Spain), 40,
    68, 79, 149, 193, 221
  Crucible of Trials, 68
  Face of the Earth and Map of the
    Sphere, 68
  Mystica ciudad de Dios, 40, 48, 68, 78
  mystic rapture/mystic death of, 155
Aguiar y Seijas, Francisco (archbishop of
    Mexico), 165
Alcalá de Henares, scholars of, 22, 30,
    217
Alcántara, Pedro de, 65
Aldhelm. See Ealdhelm
Alfonso VIII (king of Castile), 76
Alfredo del S.C. de Jesús, 52
allegory
  in AE, 173–74
  in CE, 207–9
alumbrados. See illuminists
Alvinogorta, Francisco de, 121
amanuensis of God
  MC as, in AE, 169, 188
  mystic as, 39–41, 169, 221
Amigas (teachers of girls), 36–37,
    227n. 29
Ana de San Bartolomé (Spain), 52, 67
Ana Josefa de la Trinidad (niece of MC),
    115
Andrade, Alonso de, 39
Angela of Foligno, 64
Antoni, Claudio G., 224n. 13
Antonia de Jesús (niece of MC), 115

Antonia de los Angeles (vicaress), 105
Antonia Lucía del Espíritu Santo (Peru),
    70
Anunciación, Juan de la, 57
anxiety of authorship, 20, 36–38, 42
Apostles' Creed, MC's commentary on,
    in *AE*, 181
Arbiol y Diez, Antonio, 152
    biographer of Jacinta de Atondo, 41
    misogynist view of women, 37–38
archetypes, holy, in *SV*, 149–66. *See also*
    hermit; martyr; mystic; suffering
Arenal, Electa, 63, 67, 69, 70, 150, 152,
    170, 193
    and autohagiography, 29, 226n. 13
    and feminist criticism of nuns'
    writings, 12–13
Arias de Ugarte, Fernando (archbishop),
    82, 96, 233n. 22
Armacanqui Ticpacti, Elia, 70
Arzo, Nicolás, 97
asceticism, 65, 83–84, 157, 171
    in Convento Real de Santa Clara,
    99–100
    in MC's childhood, 133–34
Augustine, Saint
    concept of women, 38
    Confessions of, as model for spiritual
    autobiography, 30
Augustinian Recollects, 67
authority
    from divine source, in *CE*, 204, 219,
    220
    feminine models of, 48–49, 193
    and gender, 35–41
    imparted by teaching voice, in *CE*,
    219
    in MC's biblical hermeneutic, in *AE*,
    171–72, 196–98
    of male and female writers, 39–40
    Saint Teresa of Avila's ambivalence
    toward, 66
    in women's writings, 40–41, 48–49
authorship, female. *See* nun writers;
    vidas espirituales; vida-writing
authorship, male, 36, 39–40, 54–59
autobiographical theory, 24–29
autobiographical writing. *See also vidas
    espirituales; vida*-writing
    definition of, 17–18

early modern history of, 21
    by men, 19, 54–59
    and mystic experiences, 168–69
    by religious women writers, 2, 17–20,
    28–54
    and subjecthood, 24–29
autobiographies, spiritual. *See vidas
    espirituales; vida*-writing
autohagiography, 29, 149, 226n. 13. *See
    also vida*-writing
autonomy, female, 5, 66
    in convents, 65
    in Counter-Reformation, 77–79
    in Middle Ages, 74–77
Ave María, commentary on, in *AE*, 181
Avila, Juan de, 65, 206
Avila, Spain, in 16th century, 65

banks, convents as, 98–99
Baroque art and imagery, 22, 24, 99
    in *CE*, 218
    in mystic visions, 35
beatification, 51–54
Bell, Rudoph M., 51, 132, 163
Bernard, Saint, 50
Bible. *See also* Psalms; Song of Songs
    in *AE*, 171, 177–89, 192
    in *CE*, 200, 202, 207, 216–17
    reading of, by women, 36, 75, 171
    sources available to MC, 9, 139, 217
    in spiritual exercises, 191–92
    in *SV*, 137–39
    vernacular translations of, 30, 36, 171,
    192
biblical references in MC's works
    Genesis, 187
    Isaiah, 179
    John, Gospel of, 196
    Lamentations, 180
    I Maccabees, 145
    Matthew, Gospel of, 138, 145, 187,
    188
    Psalms, 137, 180, 184–87, 188, 194,
    210, 246n. 39
    Revelations of St. John, 187
    Romans, 138
    I Samuel, 138
    Song of Songs, 137, 174, 180, 194,
    208, 216

Bilinkoff, Jodi, 46–47, 65–66, 68, 165
biographies
of nun writers, 18–19
relationship of, to *vidas espirituales*,
51–54
of religious women, 74, 154
body. *See* female body
Bonilla Navarro, Juan de (canon), 83,
234n. 26
Borja, Francisco de, 88
Breviarium Romanum. See Roman
Breviary
Bridget of Sweden, Saint, 64, 79
Bruno, Saint, 102, 135, 151
Bull of the Holy Crusade, 146, 241n. 15
Burgos, Nicolás de, 107
Burns, Kathryn, 234n. 26
Bynum, Carolyn Walker, 77, 160

Caicedo y Aguilar, Francisco José, 121
Caicedo y Salabarrieta, Josefa de
(sister-in-law of MC), 103, 114, 115
Calderón de la Barca, Pedro, 22
Calvo de la Riba, Pedro, 41–42, 162
Camacho de Guzmán, Lucas
(brother-in-law of MC), 103, 115
canonization. *See also* beatification
requirements for, 51–52
of Saint Teresa of Avila, 51
Carlos José (prince of Spain), 87
Carlos V (king of Spain), 22
Carmelite reformation, 65–67
Carmelites, Discalced, 66–67. *See also*
under Castillo, Francisca Josefa de
la Concepción de
Carrasquilla, Rafael María, 8–9
Cascardi, Anthony J., 23–24
Castillo, Francisca Josefa de la
Concepción de. *See also* titles of
individual works
as abbess, 105, 116, 118, 120 table, 122
accusations against, by other nuns, in
SV, 109, 137–38, 140–44, 147–48,
159, 162
and act of writing, 42
ascension to power by, 101–7, 124
authority, aversion to, 144–45
authority in writing of, 42–44, 220
birth and baptism of, 102

as business manager of convent, 118–
24
celestial endorsement of, 43
childhood of, in *SV,* 132–35
as choir mistress, 111
and confessors, 115–17, 137, 143, 238–
39n. 26
conflict in self-portrayal of, 73–74
conflict over family members, 113–15
conflict with abbesses, in *SV,* 141–46
conflict with nuns, 117–18, 141
and conflict with servants, in *SV,* 141
conversion of, in *SV,* 133
Cuaderno de cuentas (accounting
book), 122
death of, 7, 124–25
desire to burn her papers, 42–43
and the Devil, 1, 42–43, 44–46, 132,
134, 149
and Discalced Carmelites, 103–4,
146, 152
dowry of, 107, 236n. 12
education of, in *SV,* 133, 217–18
efforts to reform convent by, 146,
156
election as abbess, 112, 117–18, 122
emblema (religious drawing) by,
224n. 5
emulation of feminine authorities by,
49
entrance into convent, 103, 107, 134
expulsion from office of choir
mistress, 111–12
family members of, in convent, 113–
15
family of, 102–3, 121–22
and financial affairs of convent, 118–
22
holy family of, 149–50
illnesses of, 132–33, 157–61
and Jesuits, 116–17
and knowledge of Latin, 139, 182, 217
legal knowledge of, 119–21
literary criticism of, 6, 7–13
literary reputation of, 8, 10, 224n. 11,
243n. 2
manuscripts of, 223n. 5
as mistress of novices, 112, 117–18,
122, 215
as mother adviser, 122

Castillo, Francisca Josefa de la
Concepción de (continued)
and murmuración, 159
as musician, 86, 111
as mystic, 10, 155–56, see also under
mysticism
as novice, 104
and novices, 112, 117–18, 239n. 31
and other nuns, 11, 162–63
offices held by, 106 table, 111–12
poetry of, 223n. 5; in AE, 174; in CE,
199
political activity of, 79, 81, 101–3, 115,
116–18, 143–44
power seeking denied by, 144–45
profession of, as nun, 95, 104–5
property of, 107, 114
reading by, 87–88, 133–34, 192
as secretary, 111
Sentimientos espirituales, 7, 105, see
also Afectos espirituales
servants of, 107
and 16th-century mysticism, 189–93,
248n. 51
and spiritual exercises, 192
spiritual struggle of, 135–40
teaching role of, 170, 172, 196, 219
wealth of, 107–9
writings of, 105, 221
Castillo, Madre (MC). See Castillo,
Francisca Josefa de la Concepción
de
Castillo y Alarcón, Antonio María de
(Castillo descendant, referred to as
nephew of MC) and MC's writings,
7, 168, 243n. 4
Castillo y Bolívar, Joseph del, 39
Castillo y Caicedo, Juan Estevan de
(nephew of MC), 104
Castillo y Guevara, Catalina Ludgarda
(sister of MC), 102–3, 113, 115
Castillo y Guevara, Francisco (nephew
of MC), 104
Castillo y Guevara, Juana Angela (sister
of MC), 103, 113
Castillo y Guevara, Pedro Antonio de
(also Pedro Antonio Diego, and
Pedro Diego; family name Guevara
sometimes omitted; brother of
MC), 102, 113, 114, 115, 118, 122, 145

Castillo y Toledo, Francisco Ventura de
(father of MC), 102, 105
Catherine of Alexandria, Saint (also
known as Saint Catherine of
Egypt), 36, 78, 79
Catherine of Siena, Saint, 36, 64, 79,
149, 156
censos (mortgages or leases), 98, 235n. 34
Cervantes, Fernando, 45
Cervantes, Miguel de, 22, 225n. 9
Chicharro, Dámaso, 17–18, 29, 135
Chinchilla, Joseph de, 154
Christ
affirmation of mystic experience,
42
as baby Jesus in SV, 149
as celestial spouse, in SV, 149, 157,
159
and David, in AE, 185–87
and female body, 77
feminization of, in AE, 194
as lover-husband, in AE, 169
as mediator, in AE, 186–87
prefigured in Old Testament, 184
redemptive crucifixion of, in CE,
203, 213, 216
as the soul's divine beloved, 169
as Word of God, in AE, 176
church as nonverbal discourse, 225n. 11
Church. See also Counter-Reformation
calendar of, as narrative structure in
SV, 135
and control of knowledge, 22
and female subjectivity, 19
power of, 21, 24
and secularism, 21–22
threatened by reformist ideas, 30
Cisneros, Francisco Jiménez de,
Cardinal, 22, 30, 65
Cistercians, 68
Clara María de Jesús (niece of MC),
115
Clare of Assisi, Saint, 64, 77, 79, 109,
149. See also Poor Clares
founder of Poor Clares, 83
clergy, male. See also confessors
authorship of, 39–40
and convents, 76, 91–97
colloquy, in AE, 177
Colohan, Clark, 68

Colombia. *See* Nuevo Reino de Granada

comedias, as occasion for sin, 133, 157

community, female, 21, 214, 225n. 7

negative vision of, in *CE*, 213–15, 220

Conceptionists, 68

confession

in *AE*, 179–80

in Counter-Reformation, 23, 33

confessional narrative, in *vidas espirituales*, 30–31, 33–35

confessors. *See also under* Castillo, Francisca Josefa de la Concepción de

and nuns, 46–48, 116

role of, in *vida*-writing, 32–33, 41

Constanza de Castilla (Spain), 64

constitutions. *See under* convents, Spanish American

contemplation, 20–21, 170, 173, 179, 189. *See also* mental prayer

contemplative ideal, 78, 151

contemplative practice, in *AE*, 173

Convento de la Concepción, Santa Fe de Bogotá, 232n. 8

Convento de la Concepción, Tunja, 92, 103

Convento de la Encarnación, Avila, 50

Convento de Nuestra Madre Santa Clara, Pamplona (Nuevo Reino de Granada), 82–83, 87

Convento de San Agustín, Tunja, 98

Convento de San Juan Bautista, Mérida (Venezuela), 232n. 8

Convento de Santa Clara, Cartagena, 104

Convento de Santa Clara, Mérida (Venezuela), 232n. 8

Convent of Santa Clara do Destêrro, Brazil, 99

Convento Real de Santa Clara, Tunja

abbesses of, 124 table

canonical visitors to, 93–97

children in, 94

choir nuns (black-veiled, or *monjas de coro*) in, 88–90, 90 table, 233n. 22

Colonial Archives of, 11

conflict in, 94

council (*difinitorio*) of, 91, 238n. 21

council members (*difinidoras*) of, 91

Divine Office, praying of, by nuns in, 84, 89

dowries of nuns in, 85, 96, 233nn. 22, 23, 234n. 24, 234n. 31, 235n. 33, 238n. 22

economic crisis of, 118

education of novices in, 88

elections of abbesses in, 90–92, 237n. 20

enclosure of nuns in, 84, 96

finances of, 83, 96–99, 120–22

founding of, 83

and Franciscans, 97–98

girls in, 88, 233n. 20

governance of, 90–92

history of, 5

Latin taught to novices in, 36

laxity of convent rule in, 81, 83–85, 92–96, 159–60

lay nuns (*monjas legas*) in, 89, 234n. 24

lay women of the house (*legas de casa*) in, 89

library of, 87–88, 232n. 17, 232–33n. 18, 241n. 1

liturgical obligations of nuns in, 182

MC's manuscripts in, 1, 7

and male clergy, 93–97

male visitors to, 94–96

monstrance of, 107–9

mother advisers (*madres de consejo*) of, 91

musical instruments in, 85–86

number of women in, 89–90

and politics, 98–99

and poverty, 83

property of nuns in, 84, 237n. 16

racial diversity in, 89, 234n. 25

and rule, 84

servants (*sirvientas, donadas*) in, 84, 88, 89, 94–95, 96, 233n. 22, 234n. 30

social function of, 99

social structure of, 89

spiritual life of, 93–94

and syndics, 91, 96–97, 121

and vicars, 91, 92

white veiled nuns (*monjas de velo blanco*) in, 84, 89, 233nn. 22, 23

convents. *See also* convents, Spanish
American; individual names,
beginning with "Convent,"
"Convento," "Monasterio"
as centers of learning, 67
Counter-Reformation restrictions
on, 77
decline in artistic activities in, 77
decline in status of women in, 76
duties of nuns in, 85
in early Middle Ages, 74–76
economic support of, 65–66
egalitarian community in, 65, 77–78
enclosure in, 23, 49–50, 85, 96
male clergy's control of, 76
and political activity, 74, 76, 78
property held in common in, 77–78
Saint Teresa of Avila's reforms of, 77–
78
schools in, 233n. 21
social structures of, 65, 89
women's leadership in early Middle
Ages in, 75
women's scholarship in early Middle
Ages in, 75–76
convents, Spanish American. *See also*
Convento Real de Santa Clara,
Tunja
and the arts, 85–88
as banks, 98–99
constitutions of, 82–83, 113
constitutions of, written by women,
71, 82–83
"devotions" by male suitors, 93
and education, 88
enclosure in, 84, 92–93
endowments of, 77–78
family members in, 112–13
founders of, 82, 232n. 8
founding of, 82, 85
intellectual life in, 86–88
laxity in, 84–85, 92–96
and male clergy, 91–97
offices in, 91–92, 234n. 28
and politics, 92, 97–99
and race, 89–90, 234n. 26
reforms of, 92–93
social function of, 85
conversos (Christians of Jewish ancestry),
30

Copernican revolution, 21
Corominas, Joan, 39
Council of Trent, 77
Counter-Reformation. *See also* Church;
Inquisition
ascetic ideology of, 171
as context for MC's writings, 2
as destructive of female community,
215
and ideology of suffering, 203, 212
and misogyny, 34, 66
and mysticism, 152
and restrictions on convent life, 77–
78
rewriting of female saints' lives
during, 78
in Spain, 22
and subjectivity, 23–24
and *vida*-writing, 19, 38
and women, 3, 217
Covarrubias Horozco, Sebastián de, 22,
39, 50
Creole identity, in nuns' writings, 69
Cuaderno de Enciso (Castillo), 199–219,
220
Afectos espirituales revised in, 203–5
autobiographical references removed
from, 203–4, 219
confessors' roles in revisions of, 204–5
instructional character of, 200–201,
205, 219
narrative voices in, 206–7, 218–19
pedagogical tools in, 205–10
poetry in, 215–16
rhetorical strategies in, 205–10, 217–19
as spiritual guidebook, 199–200
structure of, 199–201
writing of, 6

David
and Christ, in *AE*, 185–87
as mystic, 247n. 44
De Man, Paul, 24
desengaño (disillusionment), 22, 211
Devil, the. *See also under* Castillo,
Francisca Josefa de la Concepción
de
essential to salvation, 45
racial representations of, 45–46, 69

in *SV,* 138, 163
as tool of Counter-Reformation, 44
in *vida*-writing, 42, 44–46
discourse
   definition of, 225n. 11
   and power, 6
Divine Office, 184. *See also under*
   Convento Real de Santa Clara
   in *AE,* 172, 177, 181
   in convents, 6, 37–38
doctrinal knowledge, in *AE,* 169–70, 181
doctrinal texts, in spiritual exercises, 192
Domínguez Urregolabeitia, Francisco, 8
Dominic, Saint, 155
Donahue, Darcy, 47
dowries, 85. *See also under* Convento
   Real de Santa Clara

Ealdhelm (also known as Aldhelm),
   75
Eckenstein, Lina, 74–75, 79
education
   in convents, 88
   of girls and women, 36–38
   of young men, 36
Eich, Jennifer Lee, 29, 69, 70, 200,
   229n. 49
Elisabeth of Hungary, Saint, 79
Elisabeth of Schönau, Saint, 75
Enciso y Cárdenas, José de
   (brother-in-law of MC), 103, 114,
   199
enclosure, of nuns, 23, 49–50, 76, 85, 96.
   See also under Convento Real de
   Santa Clara; convents
   effect on spiritual expression of, 156
   and Saint Teresa of Avila, 49–50
Enlightenment, 3, 26
Erasmians, 22, 30
Erasmus of Rotterdam, Desiderius, 207,
   217–18
eroticism
   in nuns' writings, 67, 215
   in writings of Saint Teresa of Avila,
   215
Eve
   expulsion from Paradise, 28
   union with Adam, in *AE,* 187
   women as daughters of, 3, 28, 38

faith
   and martyrdom, 161
   as motive for martyrdom, in *SV,* 161–
   62
Feliciana de San Diego, 162
Felipe II (king of Spain), 22
Felipe IV (king of Spain), 57, 102
female body
   in early Christian theology, 38–39
   as focus in mysticism, 77
   in nuns' writings, 38–40
   redemptive symbolism of, 156–61
   and symbolic linkage to Christ,
   77
feminine figures of authority, 28–29,
   48–49, 78, 193
feminist criticism
   of MC's writings, 6–7
   of nuns' writings, 12–13, 224n. 14
Fernández, James D., 30, 31, 225n. 5
Fernández de Santa Cruz, Manuel
   (bishop of Puebla, New Spain),
   165
figurative language, in *CE,* 201–2, 207–
   10, 217–18
Fleishman, Avrom, 29
Foucault, Michel, 4, 46, 116, 164
Francisca, Sor. *See* Castillo, Francisca
   Josefa de la Concepción de
Francisca del Niño Jesús (niece of MC),
   114–15, 147, 239n. 31
Francisca Josefa de la Concepción. *See*
   Castillo, Francisca Josefa de la
   Concepción de
Francisca María del Niño Jesús
   (Carmelite abbess), 70, 125, 162,
   236n. 6
   beatification process of, 53–54
   and MC, 103, 152
   mystical raptures of, 154
   public mortification of, 162
Francisca, Sor. *See* Castillo, Francisca
   Josefa de la Concepción de
Francis of Assisi, Saint, 77, 149
Franco, Jean, 155
Freud, Sigmund, 12

Garay, Juana de. *See* Juana de la
   Encarnación

gender
  in autobiographical writing, 27–29,
    55–59
  impact of, ignored by early
    commentaries on MC, 8–9
  in nuns' writings, 12
  and self-representation, 19
  gendering of authority figures, in *AE*,
    172, 193–95
Gertrude the Great, Saint, 64, 79
Giles, Mary E., 64
Glantz, Margo, 226n. 13
God. *See also under* soul
  as Author, 39, 43
  as divine beloved, in *AE*, 169–70,
    172
  feminization of, in *AE*, 170, 194
  humility of, 213
  life as exile from, 170
  as Lord and King, in *AE*, 172
  voice of, in *AE*, 174
Godínez, Miguel, 152, 154, 170
Gracián, Jerónimo, 191
Granada, Luis de, 33, 206, 214, 217
Greenspan, Kate, 29, 149, 150, 226n. 13
Groot, José Manuel, 92–93
Guevara, Catalina de, 121–22
Guevara, Diego de (maternal
    grandfather of MC), 102
Guevara Niño y Rojas, María de
    (mother of MC), 102, 105, 113
Gumbrecht, Hans Ulrich, 20
Gusdorf, Georges, 21–22, 25

hagiography, 30, 226n. 13. *See also*
    autohagiography
Hegel, Georg W. F., 26–27
Héloïse, 75–76
heresy, 19, 22, 31, 51, 155
  fear of, by MC, in *SV*, 136
hermeneutic, feminine
  in *AE*, 171–72, 182–89, 220
  in *CE*, 217
hermit, as archetype, in *SV*, 150–52
"Herodes Tractus," in *AE*, 181
Herrad of Hohenburg, 75
Herrera, Francisco de (confessor), 33,
    105, 131, 137–38, 143
Hildegard of Bingen, 28, 36, 63, 75

Holy Communion, in *AE*, 172, 177, 187
homiletic rhetoric (preaching, sermon)
  in *AE*, 187–88
  in *CE*, 217–18
Host, importance of, to Poor Clares, 109
Hours, canonical, 232n. 15
Hrotsvit of Gandersheim, 63, 75
humiliation. *See also* humility
  of the soul, in *CE*, 210–15, 216
  of MC, in *SV*, 142–43
humility, 31, 214. *See also* humiliation
  as narrative strategy in *CE*, 211–15,
    216
  as narrative strategy in *vidas
    espirituales*, 34–35

Ignacia de San José (niece of MC), 115
Ignatian spiritual exercises. *See* spiritual
    exercises
Ignatius of Loyola, Saint, 22, 54–56, 65,
    152, 210, 211
  as male *vida*-writer, 54–56
  as mystic model of MC, 189, 191–93
  Pilgrim's Journey, 54
  *Spiritual Exercises of St. Ignatius
    (Ejercicios espirituales)*, 152, 189, 191–
    92, 210, 211, 233n. 18
illness
  in confessional narratives, 35, 157
  spiritual interpretation of, by MC, in
    SV, 157–61
illuminists (*alumbrados*), 22, 30, 66
imagery
  biblical, in *CE*, 218
  of crucifixion, in *CE*, 216
  of Song of Songs in *CE*, 202, 216
  in *SV*, 139
  used by God to teach soul, in *CE*, 207
imitation of Christ, 68, 70
Inés del Santísimo Sacramento (Spain),
    67
Innocent III, Pope, 83
Innocent IV, Pope, 83
Innocent X, Pope, 57
Inquisition, 18, 152. *See also*
    Counter-Reformation
  censorship of vernacular translations
    of the Bible, 171, 192
  persecution of reformist groups, 31

indulgences, granted by Bull of the Holy
    Crusade, 241n. 15
intellect
    as faculty of the soul, 170
    and mysticism, 170–71
    women's, 28, 36–38, 67
interrogatorio, in beatification, 52–54
irony
    in Saint Teresa of Avila's Camino de
        perfección, 66
    in Saint Teresa of Avila's rhetoric of
        femininity, 35, 139
    in SV, 139
Isabel de Jesús (Spain), 34, 67
Isabel de la Madre de Dios (Spain), 67–
    68

Jacinta de Atondo (Spain), 41–42
jarchas, 64
Jay, Paul, 24
Jeremiah, as mystic, 247n. 44
Jesuits, 65, 189, 247n. 47
Jesus Christ. See Christ
Job, 161
John of the Cross, Saint, 137, 173, 177–
    79, 208, 217, 247n. 44, 248n. 51
    "Cántico espiritual," 173–74, 177,
        178–79, 208
    and mystic experience, 171
    as mystic model for MC, 189–90,
        193
    Noche oscura, 247n. 44, 248n. 51
    Subida del Monte Carmelo, 190
Johnson, Penelope D., 75
Josefa de la Providencia (Peru), 70
Joseph de San Benito
    as male vida-writer, 58–59
    Vida interior, 54
Juana de Jesús. See Macías de Figueroa,
    Juana
Juana de la Cruz (Spain), 40, 64
Juana de la Encarnación (cousin of
    MC), 122
Juana Inés de la Cruz (New Spain), 2,
    10, 152, 199, 227n. 29
    and the Bible, 183
    "Carta atenagórica," 165, 217
    defense of women's intellect, 69
    feminine figure of authority, 49, 193

feminist scholarship on, 69, 231n. 9
    library of, 218, 227n. 23
    literary career of, 220–21
    "Respuesta a Sor Filotea," 34, 49, 79,
        165, 226n. 13
    self-defense by, 38
    self-denigration in writings of, 34
    submission of, 165, 227n. 23
    "El sueño," 220
Juan de la Cruz, San. See John of the
    Cross, Saint
Julian of Norwich, 64

Kempe, Margery, 64
knowledge
    and the Bible, in CE, 200
    and power, 6, 12

Lacan, Jacques, 27, 28
Latin
    and MC, in SV, 139, 182
    nuns' knowledge of, 7, 36
Lavrín, Asunción, 12
laxity, in convents, 81, 83–85, 92–96, 169
Leander of Seville, 39
León, Luis de, 38, 243n. 8, 247n. 44
    misogynist view of women of, 37
literary tradition, feminine, 11
liturgical prayer, in AE, 170
Lobo Guerrero, Bartolomé
    (archbishop), 93
locutions, mystic or divine, 173, 189–90
    in AE, 174, 188
locutorio (convent parlor), 95
Lope de Vega. See Vega, Lope de
López, Francisco, 119–20
López de Córdoba, Leonor (Spain), 64
Lord's Prayer
    in CE, 210
    commentary on, in AE, 181
Lorravaquio Muñoz, María Magdalena
    (New Spain), 32, 69
    mystical interpretation of illness of,
        156–57
    spiritual journal of, 169
    Vida, 169
Luján, Micaela, 68
Lutheranism, 30, 191

Macdonnell, Diane, 225n. 11
Macías de Figueroa, Juana (founder of the Convento Real de Santa Clara), 103
Magdalena de Jesús (Nuevo Reino de Granada), 71, 82–83, 113
Magdalena de la Cruz (Spain), 18, 44
male authorship. *See* authorship, male
male clergy. *See* clergy, male
Manrique, Jorge, 212
Marcela de San Felíx (Spain), 68
Margarita de la Cruz (niece of MC), 103, 115
María Anna Agueda de San Ignacio (New Spain), 149, 193, 221, 229n. 49
Marabillas del divino amor, 200
theological treatises of, 49, 70, 200
María Antonia del Niño Dios, 95, 101–2, 103, 105, 112, 113, 114, 116, 117, 131, 224n. 14, 232–33n. 18
biographer of MC, 11–12
Flor de santidad, 11–12, 74
María de Jesús (Nuevo Reino de Granada), 33, 49, 70
María de Jesús Tomelín, 69
María del Niño Jesús, 105
María de San José (New Spain), 32, 41, 49, 69, 164
androgenous nature of, 227n. 32
radical religiosity of, 157
thematic structures in her *vida,* 135–36
María de San José (Spain), 67
María de Santo Domingo (Spain), 64
María Gertrudis del Sacramento (niece of MC), 115
María Gertrudis Theresa de Santa Inés (Nuevo Reino de Granada), 41, 63, 70, 88
martyrdom and mortification of, 161
María Magdalena de Pazzis. *See* Mary Magdalene of Pazzis, Saint
María Manuela de Santa Ana (Peru), 70
Mariana de San Joseph (niece of MC), 103, 113–14, 146
Mariana de San Joseph (Spain), 49, 67
Mariscal, George, 22, 225n. 9
Marroquín, José Manuel, 8–9
Martha (sister of Mary), 76

Martínez Rubio, Juan (confessor), 142, 143, 146
martyr as archetype, in *SV,* 150, 161–66
martyrdom
of early virgins, 161–62
in *SV,* 140, 159, 162
writing as, 41–42
Mary (sister of Martha). *See* Mary Magdalene
Mary, Virgin, 155
feminine authority of, 35, 40, 48, 70, 78, 169, 229n. 49
and MC, 149–50
in *Mystica ciudad de Dios,* 68
as strong woman, 194
wisdom of, 194
Mary Magdalene, Saint, 76, 78, 149–51, 231n. 4
Mary Magdalene of Pazzis, Saint, 49, 79, 149
as model for MC, 158–59
Mass, in *AE,* 172, 177, 181
May, Georges, 24–25
Mechthild of Magdeburg, 64
memory, as faculty of the soul, 24, 170
mental prayer, 66, 152, 189, 217. *See also* contemplation
and pride, in *SV,* 138
process of, in *CE,* 202
and Saint Teresa of Avila, 66, 189, 202
scriptural base of, in *AE,* 171
Mesa Cortés, Agustín José de (brother-in-law of MC), 102, 113
Mesa Cortés y Castillo, Mariana de. *See* Mariana de San Joseph
metaphors
in *AE,* 176–77
in *CE,* 201, 207
miracles
in *SV,* 155
required for canonization, 51
misogyny, 34, 37–38, 66
Molina, Antonio, 134
Monasterio de monjas de Señora Santa Clara, Cuzco, 234n. 26
Monasterio de San José (Discalced Carmelite), Santa Fe de Bogotá, 71, 82, 232n. 8, 234n. 26
attraction of, to MC, 103–4
Monasterio de Santa Clara, Tunja, 5

Monasterio de Santa Inés de Monte
    Policiano, Santa Fe de Bogotá, 42,
    88
monasticism. *See also* convents
    Anglo-Saxon, 74–76
    female, 5, 74–79
monstrance, of the Convento Real de
    Santa Clara, 107–9
Montalvo de Tobar, Pedro, 116–17
Morales Borrero, María Teresa, 10,
    224n. 14
mortification, 45, 56, 68, 162
    of MC, 133, 162
    of María Gertrudis Theresa de Santa
    Inés, 162
Moses, as mystic, 247n. 44
Moya, Diego de (confessor), 9, 125, 131
Muriel, Josefina, 12, 68–69
murmuración (gossip)
    in *CE* and *SV,* 133, 158–59
    in convents, 50
Myers, Kathleen A., 29, 63, 69, 71, 135,
    164, 165, 226n. 13, 227n. 32
mystic
    as archetype, in *SV,* 150, 152–56
    as spectacle, 155
mystic death, 155
mystic encounters
    in *SV,* 155–56
    signs of, in nuns' writings, 155
mysticism
    as access to authority for women, 40
    authentication of, in MC's writing,
    155–56
    in autobiographical writing, 168–69
    in confessional narratives, 35
    as encounter with God's word, in *AE,*
    170–71
    ineffable quality of, 44
    and intellect, 170–71
    and intellectual exercise, 77, 170
    and knowledge, in *AE,* 170
    and life as exile from God, 21, 168
    of MC, in *AE,* 171, 189–93
    as MC's method, in *CE,* 183
    physical signs of, 150, 154
    and psychoanalysis, 12
    of religious women during
    Counter-Reformation, 152
    of 16th-century Spain, 20–21, 189–93

mystic prayer, in *AE,* 172–73
mystic theology, 152, 154, 170, 189

narrative structures
    in *AE,* 195–97
    in *SV,* 129–31
    in *vidas espirituales,* 29–54, 135–36
Nava y Saavedra, Jerónima del Espíritu
    Santo (Nuevo Reino de Granada),
    70, 168–69
Nieremberg, Juan Eusebio, 87, 232–
    33n. 18
Niño, Martín, 154
Niño y Rojas, María (maternal
    grandmother of MC), 102
Nuevo Reino de Granada (colonial
    name for Colombia), 98, 121
Núñez de Miranda, Antonio, 165
nun writers, 2, 63–71, 75. *See also vidas
    espirituales; vida*-writing
    of Chile, 71
    Indian, 69, 231n. 8
    medieval European, 63–64, 75
    of New Spain (Mexico), 68–70
    of Nuevo Reino de Granada
    (Colombia), 70–71
    of Peru, 70
    recent scholarship on, 12–13, 63–71
    of Spain, 64–68
    of Spanish America, 2, 68–71, 230–
    31n. 8
    and subjecthood, 28–29
nuns. *See* Convento Real de Santa Clara;
    convents; nun writers
Nussbaum, Felicity, 3, 4, 26, 27–28

obedience
    as compelling MC's writing, 1, 42
    in convent life, 90
    as motivation for *vida*-writing, 41–
    44
    nuns' resistance to, 92
    as source of conflict in *SV,* 138–39
Olney, James, 24
orality
    in *AE,* 179–82
    in *CE,* 205–7, 218–19
Osa Guerbillano, Antonio de, 97

Osorio Nieto de Paz, José, 105
Osuna, Francisco de, 152, 158, 217

Padilla, Elvira de (Nuevo Reino de
    Granada), 71, 82–83, 113
Palacios Berruecos, Juana. *See* María de
    San José
Palafox y Mendoza, Juan de, 54
    as male *vida*-writer, 57–58
    Vida interior, 54
parables
    in *CE,* 209–10
    in *SV,* 137
Paredes Calderón, José, 114
passivity, of MC, in *AE,* 176
Paul, Saint, 28, 37, 66
persecution
    of Carmelite reformers, 67
    and subject, 26–27
    as theme in *AE,* 162, 184
    as theme in *CE,* 212
    as theme in *SV,* 134, 152, 156
    in *vida*-writing, 45–46, 57, 156, 157
Peter the Venerable, 75–76
picaresque. *See under* Suárez, Ursula
Pino Alvarez, Gladys Marina, 98, 118
Pizan, Christine de, 64
Poor Clares. *See also* Convento Real de
    Santa Clara
    constitutions of, 82–83
    duties of, 85, 108, 184
    laxity among, 169
    and poverty, 83
    rules of, 84, 90–91, 232n. 11
Pope, Randolph, 54
post-structuralism. *See under* self;
    subject
poverty, in monasticism, 83–84, 93. *See
    also under* Convento Real de Santa
    Clara; Poor Clares
power, and knowledge, 6, 12
prayer. *See* contemplation; Divine
    Office; liturgical prayer; mental
    prayer
preaching. *See* homiletic rhetoric
pride
    as capital sin, 163
    MC's, 139, 163–64
Protestantism, 19, 21–22, 77

Psalms, in *AE,* 184–87
psychoanalysis, in literary criticism of
    MC's writings, 12
Puente, Luis de la, 54
    as male autobiographical writer, 56–
    57
    as mystic model for MC, 189, 192–93

Quevedo, Francisco de, 22, 225n. 9

race
    in convents, 89–90, 234n. 26
    and fear of miscegenation, 85
    in nun writing, 12
radical religiosity
    of MC, 94, 116, 162
    suspicion of, by
        Counter-Reformation, 129
    in women, 48, 68, 156–57, 165
Ramos Medina, Manuel, 69
redemption
    of Christ crucified, in *CE,* 213, 216
    in confessional narrative, 35
    by humiliation, in *CE,* 211
    as theme in *SV,* 50, 139, 148, 164
reform
    of convent life in *SV,* 95, 146–48,
    156
    religious, 65–67
    by Saint Teresa of Avila, 65–76, 77
    of Spanish American convents, 92–
    93
resistance
    and agency, 26
    in nuns' writings, 26, 27
    in women's writings, 4
rhetoric of theological oratory. *See*
    homiletic rhetoric
ritual, as settings in *AE,* 177–82
Rivadeneira, Pedro de, 78, 150
Robledo, Angela Inés, 12, 169
Rodríguez de León, Pedro, 85–86
Roman Breviary, 85, 184
    in *AE,* 172, 177
    "Cantico espiritual" inscribed in
        MC's copy of, 177–78
Romero, Juan Manuel, 143
Rose of Lima, Saint, 79, 132

Ross, Kathleen Ann, 69, 230n. 8
rules, of Poor Clares, 84, 90–91, 232n. 11

saints. *See also* feminine figures of
    authority; names of individual
    saints
    and the Church, 31
    in writings of MC, 79
saints' lives, books of, 36, 37, 74, 78, 151,
    161, 192
    influence on MC, 3–4, 79, 132, 134,
        150, 164
    rewriting of, in
        Counter-Reformation, 78
Salguero, Francisco, 83
salvation, in confessional narratives, 35
Sanabria, Catalina de (ancestress of
    MC), 103
Sanz Lozano, Antonio (archbishop),
    92
scapegoat, in *SV*, 159
Schlau, Stacey, 12–13, 29, 63, 67, 69, 70,
    150, 152, 170, 194, 226n. 13
schools, in convents, 233n. 21
Scriptures. *See* Bible
Sebastiana de las Vírgenes (Villanueva
    Cervantes Espinosa de los
    Monteros) (New Spain), 69
Sebastiana Joseph de la Santísima
    Trinidad (New Spain), 45
secularism, and the Church, 21–22
seeker, unnamed addressee, in *AE*, 170,
    244n. 12
self
    affirmation of, in *vida*-writing, 31,
        34–35, 56–59
    autonomous, of Enlightenment, 3,
        26
    conflictive portrayal of, by MC, in
        AE, 179–80; —, in *SV*, 1, 73–74,
        102, 111, 129–48, 149–66, 220
    denigration of, in *vida*-writing, 31,
        33–34
    exploration of, by women, 23, 28
    judgment of, in *vida*-writing, 33
    post-structuralist concept of, 3, 26
sepulcher, imagery of, in *CE*, 216
Serrano y Sanz, Manuel, 2, 17–18, 29, 51,
    135

sin
    in confessional narratives, 35
    in MC's childhood, 133
    in self-representation, 33–35
slaves, 89, 113, 234n. 25
    in *SV*, 132
Smith, Paul, 4, 26–27
Smith, Sidonie, 4, 18, 25, 27
Sobrino Morillas, Cecilia del
    Nacimiento (Spain), 67
Sobrino Morillas, María de San Alberto
    (Spain), 67
Soeiro, Susan A., 85, 99
Solano, Diego, 102
solitude, desire for
    by MC, in *SV*, 134, 152
    by nuns, 151–52
Song of Songs, 67, 183
    in *AE*, 174
    as allegory of mystical union with
        God, 177, 202
    paraphrase of, in *CE*, 208
    in writings of Saint Teresa of Avila,
        191
Soto, Pedro de, 36
Sotomayor, Augustín del, 96–97
soul
    as addressee, in *CE*, 200
    faculties of, 170, 192, 211, 213
    and God, 152, 168–69, 189–91; —, in
        SV, 137–40, 154, 158, 183–87
    humiliation of, in *CE*, 212–13
    in mystic expression, 24
    purification of, 42, 45, 157; —, in *CE*,
        202, 214–15; —, in *SV*, 116, 139,
        141–43, 158
    spiritual journey of, in *CE*, 199–203,
        211–13
    in union with God or Christ, 21, 154,
        189; —, in *AE*, 170, 172–77, 184,
        187, 208–9, 216; —, in *CE*, 208–9,
        216; —, in *SV*, 1, 129, 137, 159,
        169
spectacle
    in martyrdom, 161–62
    in the mystic, 155
    in *SV*, 162–63
spiritual autobiographies. *See vidas
    espirituales; vida*-writing
spiritual directors. *See* confessors

spiritual exercises, 152, 191–92, 247n. 47
    in *CE*, 210, 211–12
    in Luis de la Puente's writings, 56–57
spiritual journals
    as autobiographical genre, 168
    and *vidas espirituales*, 32–33
spiritual journey, in *SV*, 135–36
Stanton, Domna C., 29
Suárez, Ursula (Chile), 71
    use of the picaresque by, 71
subject
    in autobiographical writing, 3, 24–29
    in beatification process, 52–53
    modern theories of, 20, 23–24, 26–27
    in post-structuralism, 3–4, 18, 26–27, 29
subjecthood
    and autobiography, 24–29
    in Counter-Reformation, 20, 22–24
    and human agency, 20–24
    male, 28
    and mysticism, 21
    and women, 26, 28–29
subjectivity
    in *AE*, 194–97
    (female) and the Church, 19
    in *SV*, 74, 129, 131, 144–45, 148, 161, 163
subversion, in women's writings, 19, 34–35, 210
suffering. *See also* soul, purification of
    as archetype, in *SV*, 150, 156–61
    gendered symbolism of, 160
    sweet, in mystic experience, 215–16
Surtz, Ronald E., 64
Su vida (Castillo), 129–66, 220
    publication of, 7, 70
    writing of, 1, 105–7, 131
syndics
    in Convento Real de Santa Clara, 91
    dependence on, by nuns, 96

Tambling, Jeremy, 19
Tapia, Diego de (confessor), 105, 116–17, 143
Tarazona, bishop of , 40
temptation, redefinition of, in *SV*, 137–38

Teresa de Ahumada. *See* Teresa of Avila, Saint
Teresa de Cartagena (Spain), 64
Teresa de Jesús (niece of Saint Teresa of Avila), 52
Teresa de Jesús, Santa. *See* Teresa of Avila, Saint
Teresa of Avila, Saint, 2, 10, 31, 33–35, 216–17, 219
    and autonomy for women, 66
    beatification of, 51–53
    and the Bible, 182, 189, 190–91
    Camino de perfección, 44, 66, 141, 189, 214
    canonization of, 51
    and Carmelite reform, 65–67, 77
    and community, 214
    Conceptos del amor de Dios, 190–91
    and confessors, 47–48
    and the Devil, 44–45
    eroticism in writings of, 215
    Exclamaciones o meditaciones del alma a su Dios, 168
    feminine authority and agency of, 193
    founder of Discalced Carmelite order, 66
    humility and self-affirmation of, 34–35
    influence of, 4, 28, 67, 79, 82, 152
    and Inquisition, 66
    and intellect, 189
    Interior Castle, *see Las moradas del castillo interior*
    Libro de las fundaciones, 45, 66, 79, 132, 148
    Libro de la vida (also *Libro*), 4, 20, 33–34, 44, 48, 49–50, 66, 148, 189, 215
    and locutions, 189–90
    in MC's texts, 79, 137, 148, 149
    as model for MC, 150, 151, 189, 190–91, 193
    Las moradas del castillo interior, 66, 189, 214
    and mystic experience, 171
    persecution of, 50, 156
    rhetorical strength of, 66
    sainthood of, 66
    transverberation of, 215
    and visions, 244n. 10

Teresa of Jesus, Mother. *See* Teresa of
  Avila, Saint
Thecla, Saint, 36, 78
theology
  in *CE,* 200–201, 217–19
  in María Anna Agueda de San
    Ignacio's writing, 70
Thomas Aquinas, Saint, 28, 38
Torquemada, Juan de, Cardinal, 40,
  47
Torres, Cristóbal de (archbishop), 96
Tovar, Juan de (confessor), 143
Tunja, Colombia, xvii

understanding, as faculty of the soul,
  24
universities, exclusion of women from,
  in Middle Ages, 63, 77, 170
Urban IV, Pope, 84
Urban VIII, Pope, 85
Urbina, Ignacio de (archbishop), 94,
  104–5, 146

Valdés, Juan Bautista de, 98, 102
Vega, Lope de, 22, 68
Vela y Cueto, María (Spain), 33, 68, 156,
  165
Vélez de Piedrahita, Rocío, 12
Verde y Castillo, José de la, 121, 122
vidas espirituales, 17–59. *See also* nun
    writers; *vida*-writing
  authority in, 40–41, 48–49
  as autobiographical writing, 4, 29–
    33
  and beatification process, 51–54
  and biographical traditions, 51–54
  and Catholic doctrine, 51
  as confessional narratives, 30–31, 33–
    35
  as control and self-expression, 23
  and Counter-Reformation ideology,
    20, 22–23
  as defense against heresy, 18, 31
  and Inquisitorial confessions, 18
  as literary genre, 224n. 3
  by male authors, 19, 54–59
  as martyrdom, 42
  narrative structures in, 29–54

and nun-confessor relationships, 18
obedience as motivation for writing,
  41–44
scripts and formulas used in, 13, 28,
  35
self-affirmation in, 34–35
self-denigration in, 33–34
as sources for biographies, 18, 40
and spiritual journals, 32
and subjecthood, 19
as threat and glory to the Church,
  19
vida-writing. *See also* nun writers; *vidas
    espirituales*
  as autobiographical writing, 29–33
  as autohagiography, 29
  confessors' roles in, 32–33, 40
  and Devil, 44–46
  as personal and public activity, 40–
    41
  by religious women, 31, 35–36, 38,
    40–41
virility, of virginity, 38–39
virtues. *See also* humility, poverty
  and canonization, 51
visions
  in *AE,* 170
  as affirmation of nuns' lives, 48
  authenticity of, 47
  in confessional narratives, 35
  narrative function of, in *SV,* 13, 136,
    146
  in *SV,* 129, 136, 139, 140, 144, 145, 146,
    147, 155, 156, 160, 162
Vives, Juan Luis, 36–37
voices, narrative.
  in *AE,* 179–82
  in *CE,* 205–7, 218–19
vows, of nuns, 77
  and canonical visits, 93
  of enclosure, 84, 96
  of Poor Clares, 84

Weber, Alison, 29, 34, 44, 66, 139,
  191
Weinstein, Donald, 51, 132, 163
will, 24, 44, 170
women. *See also* monasticism, female;
  nun writers

women (*continued*)
in Christian theology, 28
in Counter-Reformation ideology, 2–3, 28
as daughters of Eve, 3, 28, 38
education of, 36–38
roles of, limited in later Middle Ages, 63–64
Spanish, as writers, 64
and theological expression, 36, 38–40, 70, 170, 187–88, 193, 199–219
virility of, 38–39
as writers, 2
word, materiality of, in *AE,* 176
Word (of God), in *AE,* 171, 172–77, 183–84

world, nuns' removal from, 73, 83–84, 92–93
worldliness
of convent life, 49–50
and Saint Teresa of Avila, 49–50
in *SV,* 141–48
writing, act of. *See also* authorship, male; *vida*-writing
by men, 39–40, 54–59
by women, 1, 31, 35–36, 37–38, 40–44

Ximenes Samaniego, Joseph, 37, 40

Zumthor, Paul, 176